Learning to Think:
Disciplinary Perspectives

Learning to Think: Disciplinary Perspectives

Janet Donald

JOSSEY-BASS
A Wiley Company
San Francisco

Published by

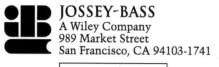

JOSSEY-BASS
A Wiley Company
989 Market Street
San Francisco, CA 94103-1741

www.josseybass.com

Jossey-Bass books and products are available through most bookstores. To contact Jossey-Bass directly, call (888) 378-2537, fax to (800) 605-2665, or visit our website at www.josseybass.com.

Substantial discounts on bulk quantities of Jossey-Bass books are available to corporations, professional associations, and other organizations. For details and discount information, contact the special sales department at Jossey-Bass.

We at Jossey-Bass strive to use the most environmentally sensitive paper stocks available to us. Our publications are printed on acid-free recycled stock whenever possible, and our paper always meets or exceeds minimum GPO and EPA requirements.

Library of Congress Cataloging-in-Publication Data
Donald, Janet Gail, 1940-
    Learning to think: Disciplinary Perspectives / Janet Gail Donald.— 1st ed.
      p. cm. — (The Jossey-Bass higher and adult education series)
    Includes bibliographical references (p.) and index.
    ISBN 0-7879-1032-5
    1. Learning, Psychology of. 2. Education, Higher. 3. Cognitive styles. 4. Knowledge, Theory of.
I. Title. II. Series.
LB1060 .D64 2002
370.15'23—dc21
                                                                      2001006384

FIRST EDITION
HB Printing   10 9 8 7 6 5 4 3 2

The Jossey-Bass

Higher and Adult Education Series

CONTENTS

PREFACE

L earning to think in a discipline is a demanding scholarly undertaking that is not often associated with the development of university students. Although the intellectual development of postsecondary students is gaining increased attention in the knowledge era, relating student development to the processes of inquiry in different disciplines is unexplored terrain. Philosophers and psychologists have defined inquiry in terms of cognition, mental models, comprehension, intelligence, insight, research, reason, and argument, but how one learns to think is not well understood. My main purpose in this book is to reach a deeper understanding of thinking processes by exploring the approaches to thinking taken in different disciplines and then considering how they could be applied to student intellectual development.

In each discipline, three questions guide the exploration. First, what kind of learning environment does the discipline provide? Second, according to the discipline, what knowledge and higher-order thinking processes are important for students to learn? Third, what are the optimal ways of cultivating these thinking processes? Encompassing all of the disciplines, a final question is, How can postsecondary institutions promote students' intellectual development in all disciplines?

Students arrive on campus with great expectations but little understanding of the challenges that lie ahead. For the most part, they have left a sheltered environment to come to a place where the responsibility for their learning and their well-being will be their own. To help students develop the thinking processes they need to meet these challenges, we need a framework for learning that takes into account the role of disciplines or domains of knowledge yet goes beyond the acquisition of knowledge to encompass ways of constructing and using it in the disciplines. This book is about how knowledge is structured and how professors and students perceive learning in their fields. It is about learning processes as they occur in courses and in disciplines but also about the epistemological foundations that guide and facilitate learning and the strategies for constructing and using knowledge.

To understand a field of study, students must learn its perspectives and processes. Intellectual development requires linking domain knowledge and processes of inquiry. There are obstacles to overcome, however. Three conditions work against the process of intellectual development in postsecondary programs of study. First, the burgeoning quantity of knowledge threatens to overload search and classification processes. Second, increased educational participation at the postsecondary level means a more heterogeneous student body, more students who are less well prepared or have less well-defined learning goals, and less time for instructors to give personalized attention to individual learners. Third, specialization and decentralization in response to increased amounts of knowledge are accompanied by risks of fragmentation and incoherence. Each condition has led to an increased emphasis on content to the detriment of development of thinking processes. In consequence, many students approach their studies in a superficial manner—memorizing without developing the knowledge structures or representations that will allow them to retrieve, relate, and use their knowledge at a later date. Their study strategies actually prevent them from learning—that is, changing and expanding their knowledge structures and thinking processes. One desired outcome of this book is to help reverse this trend and increase higher-order learning by showing how knowledge and thinking processes are associated in various fields of study.

Learning and instruction occur for the most part in the framework of a discipline or domain, yet we need approaches that combine knowledge from different domains to respond to the problems that confront society, from the global economy to global warming. For this to occur, however, we need to understand better how specific disciplines are organized. Although research has been done in certain fields to explicate the nature of the discipline and learning in it, we do not have readily available representations of how knowledge is structured and how experts think in a domain. The nature of knowledge in a domain is complex, and this complexity has led researchers at different times to proclaim the task of creating a disciplinary framework an impossible mission. One argument is that because fields are evolving and knowledge is continually being constructed, understanding is necessarily incomplete. Another argument is that knowledge is intrinsically amorphous or indefinable. Nevertheless, educators have no choice but to attempt to understand as much as possible about the frames of reference used in each area of study. The plan is then to explore the implications of disciplinary frameworks in a comparative format so that differences and commonalities between disciplines can be elucidated. This book analyzes those differences and commonalities in order to derive approaches to improve learning more generally.

The book is intended for faculty and administrators in universities and colleges, educational researchers, and anyone interested in postsecondary education. Faculty may gain insights into the representation and development of curricula, courses, and programs to improve teaching and learning processes. The variation across disciplines may prove piquant for faculty members attempting to explain to students how their discipline is situated and operates in comparison with others. Administrators, particularly of programs and departments, will find in the book suggestions for policy initiatives that are needed to create a supportive learning environment and for organizing teaching and learning. The general audience may gain insight into the complex world of postsecondary learning through the deconstruction of the maze of expectations. Professors of education may find a particular use for the comparisons of the disciplines in planning courses on teaching methods, as an aid in providing students with insights into how their discipline or field of study is constructed, and in refining their own conceptual framework in their field. Faculty developers and professors in other fields may find the education professors' insights into the instructional process not only enlightening but motivating.

Origin of the Book

This book is based on the results of over twenty-five years of research on learning in different disciplines, and on the higher education literature on thinking and intellectual development. The program of research began in 1976, when as a member of a center founded to improve teaching and learning on my campus I decided that I needed to understand more about the expectations for learning in different disciplines. I therefore asked professors in a wide variety of disciplines to work with me to determine how they structured knowledge in their courses. The research involved finding out not only what language or terminology the professors used but also the most appropriate methods for analyzing and representing knowledge and describing the learning task in their courses. Sixteen courses were selected from the sciences, social sciences, and humanities to provide a broad spectrum of disciplines. Over a three-year period, my research team and I worked with the professors teaching these courses to uncover the principal course concepts, why some courses prove difficult for students, and why the learning demands differ from course to course.

This research established ways of understanding how professors organize content in their courses, but we did not know how students responded to the content organization. We therefore did parallel studies over the next three years to determine how students in the same courses developed knowledge structures. At the beginning and end of each course, the students provided us with data on their understanding of the principal concepts uncovered in the previous series of studies. We then evaluated how well their knowledge of the concepts predicted success in the course in comparison with their general ability and previous experience. In each course a research assistant attended class and documented the use of the concepts in class. From these studies we began to have a sense of the extent to which knowledge structures in a course could explain the learning task, but we recognized that we needed a way to understand the processes of inquiry or thinking being modeled and promoted in these courses.

The question that arose was this: What thinking processes are required and learned in courses in specific disciplines? To answer this question we first investigated courses in various disciplines at McGill University, including several from the previous studies, to define the thinking processes professors intended students to develop in them. Then, at four other English-language research universities, parallel courses, pure and applied, were selected from the physical sciences (physics, engineering), the social sciences (psychology, education), and the humanities (English literature and language) to be studied for the knowledge structures, thinking processes, and attitudes expected and learned in them. Model or expert professors in these disciplines were interviewed at the University of Western Ontario in Canada (my alma mater, and hence an environment in which I could compare my own perspective as an undergraduate and graduate student with that of a professor), Cambridge University in the United Kingdom, Stanford University in the United States, and Monash University in Australia. These studies provided a foundation for understanding professors' expectations of what students in their courses and their disciplines would learn and what the disciplines required of experts in the field. In these studies, which took place from 1986 to 1991, we developed and tested a working model of thinking processes based on disciplinary approaches to inquiry but in a general format that could be used to guide the instructional process (Donald, 1992a).

To complement the professors' perspectives and to gain the perspective of students, in 1990 to 1991 classes were observed and groups of students from the courses of the model professors were interviewed to determine their views on what they were expected to learn in their programs. Although these studies were designed to trace the use of thinking processes in specific courses, they revealed another factor affecting performance in the courses. Student personal and social issues frequently competed with student learning. For example, a Cambridge student was adapting to the acerbic life of tutorials—biweekly discussions about eighteenth-century English literature—after actively participating in the anti-apartheid movement in South Africa. Stanford students pondered how they would live up to the social responsibilities that accompany a privileged childhood.

The recognition of students' personal life space and accompanying quandaries led to a series of in-depth studies of student learning and development in the same disciplines. These took the form, first—from 1991 to 1994—of ethnographic studies in which graduate student participant-observers with a background in these disciplines attended classes and tutorials, took examinations, and logged their experiences and those of other students in the courses. From 1994 to 1997, students' conceptions and experience of learning in selected courses in these disciplines were studied by questionnaire and interview, while at the same time their professors were interviewed to establish their conceptions of learning in these courses. In 1996, the study was expanded to include academic seminars instituted expressly to challenge students to think.

Aims of the Book

The studies provided a wealth of data and experiences that, taken together, describe how professors and students perceive the learning process in their fields. In this book, the aim is first to create a framework for understanding student intellectual development and for learning to think in different disciplines. Chapter One provides the framework. The attempt to establish what higher-order thinking processes we expect graduating students to have and the role of the disciplines in cultivating these thinking processes guides the discourse in Chapters Two to Eight. In each chapter I describe the context and principal methods of inquiry in the disciplines and their effects on learning and thinking, and also examine what this means for students and how we might therefore improve the instructional process. The attempt is to present the perspective of scholars in each discipline, doing justice to the discipline through thick description that allows readers to look through the lens of the discipline. A parallel intent is to analyze the learning context in order to arrive at optimal learning conditions.

The book begins at the most specific, fundamental, or microcosmic level of disciplinary discourse, and then proceeds to enlarge, expand, or diversify to the most macroscopic level. In Chapter Two the focus is on physics as the prototypical discipline, and on how students learn physics. In Chapter Three learning in an engineering program, where the paramount learning goal is to apply knowledge, is contrasted with learning physics. Chapter Four shows how learning occurs in knowledge-intensive disciplines, such as chemistry and the life sciences, and provides a comparison across the natural sciences.

The focus turns to the social sciences in the following three chapters. In Chapter Five, learning psychology, a social science with a spectrum of pure and applied areas, is examined, and then, in Chapters Six and Seven, two professionally oriented disciplines, law and education, are compared. In Chapter Eight, models of thinking in the humanities, with a focus on English literature, are explored. In each chapter, I begin with the disciplinary context, then describe student experience in a course. This is followed by professors' and students' perceptions of the learning task in the discipline. The nature of concepts and how students learn them and the development of thinking processes are then analyzed. Each chapter concludes with challenges for instruction that arise from the analysis of the field and a synopsis of the disciplinary perspective.

Each chapter was carefully reviewed by experts in the discipline. These experts, who frequently had taken part in the studies in their area, helped refine my understanding of their field. As in any intellectual endeavor, further refinement is probable, and I invite readers to participate in the process. In Chapter Nine, the aim is to examine how postsecondary institutions and their faculty can promote students' intellectual development in and across disciplines. To do this, I bring together the implications of the findings from the previous chapters for students, professors, administrators, instructional psychologists, and educators in general.

Acknowledgments

A great many people participated in the research projects that allowed this book to be written. Some were persuaded to involve themselves on a continuing basis, which meant invasion into their offices, texts, reference material, and course material, their classes, and their undergraduate and graduate students over a period of many years. The staff at the Centre for University Teaching and Learning contributed through the years. My colleagues at McGill University were especially helpful in testing the methods and theories I was using to investigate different aspects of the learning experience, and welcomed my research assistants and myself into their classes. They also did particular service in commenting on the draft chapters as I produced them over the past two years, as did my partner Chris Vroom. My hosts at Cambridge, Harvard, Monash, Stanford, and the University of Western Ontario helped in innumerable ways to smooth my path during my visits to interview professors and students. I have listed the participating professors according to discipline. The research assistants often participated in several projects, some while completing their graduate work and theses. I thank them all.

I want to acknowledge the assistance provided for the research by the Social Science and Humanities Research Council of Canada and the Quebec Funds for the training of researchers and aid to research teams. The research grants have spanned a period of over twenty-five years, and the program could not have progressed without this continuing support.

Participating physics professors: L. M. Brown, Les Dickie, Charles Gale, Dik Harris, Bill Lindstrom, Eric Mazur, Walter E. Meyerhof, Bob Moore, Ted Morris, Bill Rachinger, G. S. Rose, H. A. Schwettman, Fred Smith, P. Whippey, A. T. Winter.

Participating engineering professors: James L. Adams, Pierre Belanger, J. E. Carroll, G.S.P. Castle, Peter Le P. Darval, John Dealy, Robert H. Eustis, Maynard Fuller, Ralph Harris, R. Knystautas, Steve McFee, Tim Merritt, Frank Mucciardi, Tomas J. F. Pavlasek, R.F.D. Porter-Goff, P. A. Rosati, Paul Rossiter, Juan Vera.

Participating chemistry and biology professors: Lise Bentzen, Martin Druger, A. Eisenberg, Dave Harpp, Stuart Hill, Donald Kramer, Martin Lechowicz, Robert Marchessault.

Participating psychology professors: Ross Day, Peter Denny, Don Donderi, Philip N. Johnson-Laird, John Macnamara, Anthony Marley, Allan Paivio, Tom J. Triggs, Barbara Tversky, Lorraine K. Tyler, Philip G. Zimbardo.

Participating law professors: Richard Janda, Yves-Marie Morissette, Margaret Somerville.

Participating education professors: Mark Aulls, Bob Calfee, Eleanor Duckworth, George Geis, Paul Hirst, Michael Hoover, Jerry Mackay, Mary Maguire, Jack Martin, Phil Nagy, Richard Selleck, Lee Shulman, Howard Stutt, Gary Torbit, R. T. White, Joan Whitehead.

Participating English literature/humanities professors: Gillian Beer, Dorothy Bray, Michael Bristol, Natalie Cooke, Allan Gedalof, Paul Gaudet, David Halliburton, Chris Heppner, C. T. Probyn, Stephen J. Randall, Ron Rebholz, A. S. Spearing, W. B. Steele, Jenny Strauss, Helen Vendler, Gary Wihl, J. F. Woodruff.

People I would like to thank especially for their help and insights, and for small and large kindnesses: Dorothy Bray, Natalie Cooke, John Dealy, Don Donderi, Gale Erlandson, David Halliburton, Dik Harris, Paul Hirst, Pat Hutchings, Mary Maguire, Anthony Marley, Eric Mazur, Jerry Mackay, Bill McKeachie, Bob Moore, R.F.D. Porter-Goff, Lee Shulman, Margaret Somerville, Mary Deane Sorcinelli, Juan Vera, James Wilkinson, Laura Winer, Sheila Wright, Philip G. Zimbardo.

Research assistants: Sally E. Addison, Mary Alexander, Vanessa Anastasopoulos, Alan Bailin, Dianne Bateman, Mary Bates, Jennifer Barnett, Allison Bentley, Mobina Bhimani, Brent Blakely, Dianne Brady, Joetta Browns, Christie Buchanan,

Susan Craig, Janet David, Brian Denison, Christina DeSimone, Gordon Dionne, Anne Douglas, Paul Dubuc, Anne Dychtenburg, Seyma Faust, Mary Flaherty, Elda Figuera, Shona French, Kathy Frost, Eithne Giulfoyle, Rosemary Haddad, Suzanne Hamon, Bryn Holmes, Joyce Isbitsky, Barbara Kadanoff, Katherine Kallos, Jacqueline Kierulf, Donal McAnaney, Jane McConnell, Carol McKeogh, Elizabeth McMillan-Davey, Joanne Meade, Nancy Miller, Deborah Mizener, Diane Nener, Evelyn Reinstein, Elizabeth Rucker, Janet Scott Boeckh, Marion Shulman, Kathryn Smith Higuchi, Julianna Switaj, Allison Talacko, Janica Tessier, David Williams.

December 2001   Janet Donald
Montreal, Canada

THE AUTHOR

JANET DONALD is professor in the Department of Educational and Counseling Psychology at McGill University and the former director of the Centre for University Teaching and Learning. Her research activities have focused on postsecondary learning and teaching and have included evaluation and institutional research. Her recent research has been on the quality of postsecondary learning and teaching, particularly fostering higher-order learning. In her previous book *Improving the Environment for Learning: Academic Leaders Talk About What Works* (1997), Donald discussed benchmark practices for improving student learning from the perspective of postsecondary education experts. She has examined disciplinary differences in knowledge validation, the role of higher education centers in improving the academy, evaluation of undergraduate education, and the role of the pedagogue. Donald won the Distinguished Researcher Award from the Canadian Society for the Study of Higher Education in 1994, its Distinguished Member Award in 1998, and the McKeachie Career Award from the American Educational Research Association in 2000. She was elected a Fellow of the Royal Society of Canada in 2001.

Learning to Think:
Disciplinary Perspectives

CHAPTER ONE

LEARNING TO THINK:
A Cross-Disciplinary Perspective

Physics is all about the way you approach a question. You have to be analytical and not at all intuitive, to break it down into its parts, and not look at the question all at once.

PHYSICS STUDENT

There isn't always a right answer. Different theories can account for the same results with the same validity. How to think analytically is important—in other words, don't believe everything you read, try to understand what the writer is saying and does he or she follow through.

PSYCHOLOGY STUDENT

The trouble with English is that there are no answers. There are only evaluations and critical judgments backed up with evidence and strong argument. The ability to make a case through reasoned, logical argument, and the ability to marshal evidence and to read widely in supporting literature is crucial.

ENGLISH PROFESSOR

The student who describes how she is learning to problem-solve in her introductory physics course understands an important strategy in the discipline—to analyze a problem by breaking it down into its elements and then reconstitute or represent the problem in all its complexity. The ability to judge the strength and consistency of logical structures in physics is central to understanding in this discipline. The student in psychology is faced with a different kind of puzzle. "Analysis" has another meaning here; the student must wrestle with contrasting perspectives or theoretical frameworks in order to approach intellectual closure. In addition, he needs to be skeptical and continually search for consistency to validate findings. Knowledge is yet more elusive in English literature. The professor expresses the dilemma in a field in which, rather than physical proof, the processes of argument and judgment provide the structure.

Imagine the predicament of the entering university student registered in courses in each of these three areas of study. To learn in the physics course, the student would first have to recognize that a learning strategy is necessary, then decipher that it consists of careful and intensive analysis of the knowledge base. In psychology, the student would have to change strategies—go outside the problem to find a variety of theoretical solutions and then determine which one best fits the evidence. In English literature, another tactic would be needed—modeling the process of argument itself. The ways of thinking portrayed here have certain commonalities. The student must be deeply engaged. The student must have the vocabulary and theory of the field or be in the act of acquiring them. But each discipline requires a different mindset, and contrasting strategies need to be employed.

To understand what students experience when they are learning the methods of inquiry of a discipline, we can call on two major areas of research: developmental psychology and epistemology, the theory of knowledge, its methods, and validation. Developmental psychology provides insight into student learning and intellectual development; epistemology deals with the search for knowledge in different disciplines. These two areas have been infrequently associated, and one goal in this book is to bring them together in order to understand how a dynamic learning environment might be created. Links between the areas are most likely to be found in a third domain of research: cognitive science. The aim is therefore to understand the process of intellectual development and to consider the role of the disciplines as the primary nurturing ground for this development. We begin by examining what is known about students' intellectual development in university, and then turn to how the disciplines contribute to this development and the kinds of cognitive processes or higher-order learning skills that will be needed.

Student Learning and Intellectual Development

Student learning at the postsecondary level has become a significant international concern as governments recognize the necessity of lifelong learning, yet struggle to find indices of what students learn in college (Ewell, 2001; Miller, 2001). In an analysis of trends and implications for learning and teaching in the twenty-first century, Baxter Magolda and Terenzini (1999) point out that critical, reflective thinking skills and the ability to make up one's own mind are essential learning outcomes in a world in which multiple perspectives abound and right action is often disputed. Important learning outcomes include not only complex cognitive skills but an ability to apply knowledge to practical problems, an appreciation of human differences, and an integrated identity.

Theories that help us understand student learning—particularly higher-order learning, in which the student seeks to understand or construct meaning and thus to develop intellectually—come from four families of research. The first, research on intellectual development, examines how students interpret their learning experience and how their ways of knowing or thinking evolve during the undergraduate years (Baxter Magolda, 1992; King & Kitchener, 1994; Perry, 1970, 1981). A second theoretical approach, based on phenomenological research on students' experience of the learning process (Marton & Saljo, 1976), focuses on their orientation to learning. In a third family of research, work on intrinsic motivation for learning is linked to students' critical thinking and self-regulation (Donald, 1999; Pintrich, 1995; Pintrich, Marx, & Boyle, 1993). A fourth theoretical approach examines students' learning goals in different disciplinary contexts—for example, Cashin and Downey's (1995) study of disciplinary differences in learning goals and student progress toward them.

Research on Intellectual Development

In the 1960s, groundbreaking work on how students interpret their learning experience was initiated by William Perry (1970, 1981). He found that students entering college tend to display a dualistic view in which knowledge is right or wrong and the professor is the authority, then move through relativistic and multiplistic stages where knowledge is uncertain and opinion rules, and finally reach a stage of commitment where some ideas are held to be more valid than others based on evidence. More recent research on intellectual development has focused on changes in students' construction of meaning or ways of knowing, from absolute knowing, through transitional and independent knowing, to contextual knowing (Baxter Magolda, 1992). In Baxter Magolda's longitudinal study, most students—68 percent—entered university in a stage of absolute knowing, considering knowledge to be certain or absolute and conceiving their role as learners to be limited to obtaining knowledge from the instructor. The remaining 32 percent of entering students were in a stage of transitional knowing, considering knowledge to be partially certain and partially uncertain; their role was to understand knowledge. In both stages, students depict themselves as passive recipients of their professors' wisdom.

During their senior year, some students—16 percent—displayed independent knowing; that is, they considered knowledge to be uncertain. In this stage, everyone has his or her own beliefs, and students are expected to think for themselves, share views with others, and create their own perspective. Independent knowing

increased to 57 percent the year following graduation. Only in the year following graduation did a small number of students—12 percent—reach the stage of
contextual knowing, where knowledge is judged on the basis of evidence in context, and the student's role is to think through problems and to integrate and apply
knowledge. These findings suggest that two-thirds of entering students limit their
role as learners to obtaining knowledge, and most will not be actively constructing meaning (independent knowing) until after they have graduated.

How a person solves an ill-structured problem, as well as that person's concept of knowledge and process of justification, are focused on in King and Kitchener's (1994) reflective judgment model. According to the model, some individuals
are in a stage of prereflective thinking, in which they do not conceive that knowledge is uncertain and do not use evidence to reason toward a conclusion. In quasi-
reflective stages, individuals recognize some uncertainty but do not understand
how evidence entails a conclusion and have difficulty in justifying their conclusions. Reflective thinkers argue that knowledge must be actively constructed and
that claims of knowledge must be understood in relation to the context in which
they were generated. Judgments must be grounded in relevant data and conclusions remain open to reevaluation.

The work of these researchers on intellectual development recapitulates the
shift in ethos that occurred in universities during the Enlightenment and the scientific revolution that followed it. Scholars in the Middle Ages assumed a fixed
body of knowledge; they defined that knowledge and were the authorities (Johnston, 1998). The scientific revolution challenged the notion of fixed knowledge. It
was based on the assumption that knowledge is an expanding and open system.
Instead of vesting authority in the church, validity was now found in scientific
measurement and dissent was integral to the process of testing hypotheses. The
shift in ethos changed the role of the university to that of creator of knowledge—
a major transformation in epistemology that, it appears, students must still undergo. Our studies of student intellectual development, however, have shown that,
given the choice, students have relativistic rather than dualistic views, in Perry's
language (Bateman & Donald, 1987). Students describe themselves as transitional,
independent, and contextual knowers rather than absolute knowers, although they
may also discriminate between the role and strategies of the ideal student and
themselves as students (Donald & McMillan-Davey, 1998; Donald, McMillan-
Davey, & Denison, 1999).

The view that knowledge is constructed carries dangers—it could be interpreted to mean that truth is dead and therefore chaos reigns. A more measured
perspective is that we each construct our own understanding of the large bodies
of organized public knowledge that the disciplines represent. This constructivist
view may receive approbation to a greater or lesser degree from members of

different disciplines. We must then ask to what extent disciplinary context determines student views and their development.

Research on Student Orientations

In research on student orientations to learning undertaken primarily in the United Kingdom and Australia, the term *orientation* indicates a combination of an approach to studying, style of learning, and motivation that is relatively stable across different educational tasks (Biggs, 1988; Biggs, 1993; Entwistle & Tait, 1990; Meyer, Parsons, & Dunne, 1990; Ramsden, 1992). Research over a period of fifteen years using two different inventories (Biggs, 1988; Entwistle & Ramsden, 1983) has confirmed two primary orientations: a deep or meaning orientation and a surface or reproducing orientation. A third orientation—achieving, or strategic (competitive and grade-oriented)—has been distinguished but is often associated with a deep or surface orientation. A student with a deep or meaning orientation seeks to relate and reinterpret knowledge. A student with a surface orientation, in contrast, does not seek understanding and tends to use superficial study strategies that rely on memorization and do not lead to increased understanding. An achieving approach includes a desire to excel and achieve top grades, which may or may not increase understanding.

Students may adopt a deep or a surface approach, or both, to varying extents, in response to cues given by the teacher. The cautionary tale to be derived from this research is that students may prefer a deep approach, but when overloaded with course content or evaluated on their knowledge of facts may adopt a surface or achieving approach. We have found that students vary in their orientation to learning depending on their course or program, with students in professional programs being more pragmatic or achievement-oriented and students in pure science more oriented toward meaning (Donald, 1999). Again, the discipline may be providing a distinctive context that aids or inhibits certain kinds of intellectual development.

Research on Intrinsic Motivation

In research on the effect of motivation on learning, students' critical thinking and learning strategies have been related to intrinsic and extrinsic motivation (Pintrich, Brown, & Weinstein, 1994; Pintrich, Marx, & Boyle, 1993; Stage & Williams, 1990). *Intrinsic motivation for learning* is defined as the desire to understand or to learn for the sake of learning; *extrinsic motivation* is a desire to attain an external goal. Intrinsic motivation has also been related to student self-regulation. The term *self-regulated learning* describes students' active control of learning resources (time, study space, peers, and faculty members), motivation (goals and self-efficacy), and strategies (deep processing) (Pintrich, 1995). As students at earlier levels of education learn to self-regulate, or internalize regulation, they have been found to shift from extrinsic to intrinsic motivation (Wigfield, Eccles, & Rodriguez, 1998). The importance of students' motivation, self-regulation, and control over their learning environment for higher-order learning lies in the immediate developmental effect of these processes on learning and learning how to learn. Measures of intrinsic motivation have been shown to be related to a deep approach to learning (Donald, 1999; Entwistle & Tait, 1990; Fransson, 1977; Ramsden, 1992). To what extent are intrinsic motivation and self-regulating behaviors supported and developed in different disciplines?

Research on Students' Learning Goals

Students' learning goals have changed markedly over the last thirty years from intellectual to vocational (Astin, 1998). This presents another kind of contextual problem for student intellectual development because student goals mediate between what instructors intend students to learn and what students actually learn, and vocational goals tend to be negatively related to higher-order learning (Donald & Dubuc, 1999). Learning goals differ substantially across disciplines (Cashin & Downey, 1995). Cashin and Downey, who studied the learning goals of professors and students in over a hundred thousand courses in eight fields, found that despite the rhetoric surrounding teaching higher-order skills like critical thinking and problem solving, many disciplines focus on the acquisition of knowledge. As might be predicted, students report that they make progress in learning what their professors emphasize. The most positive finding from this research is that higher-order learning goals such as learning principles, concepts or theories, and problem solving are, overall, considered important by faculty. Student goals appear to be more closely linked with their professors' goals than with other measures of approaches to learning; they do not coincide to any great extent with measures of their orientation or intrinsic motivation (Donald, McMillan-Davey, & Denison, 1999). Disciplinary differences are most likely to occur for learning goals.

Learning to Think in Different Disciplines

What, then, is the role of the disciplines in contributing to intellectual development? Faculty report that the cognitive processes intrinsic to their fields are often those with which students have greatest difficulty (Lenze & Dinham, 1999). For example, students have difficulty recognizing patterns in mathematics, thinking in another language, or constructing arguments to support hypotheses. Faculty could not explain why students were struggling, but some were aware of disciplinary roadblocks.

To understand what students experience when they are learning to think in a discipline, we must delve more deeply into different disciplinary areas to acquire a sense of the context, how it helps students learn, and the constraints it may put on their learning. The first question we must pose is, What is a discipline?

Definition of a Discipline

A concerted effort began in the 1960s and continued into the 1970s to understand the nature of disciplines and differences between them (Biglan, 1973; Dressel & Mayhew, 1974; Hirst, 1974; Phenix, 1964; Scheffler, 1965; Schwab, 1962, 1978). A *disciplinary area* was defined as a body of knowledge with a reasonably logical taxonomy, a specialized vocabulary, an accepted body of theory, a systematic research strategy, and techniques for replication and validation (Dressel & Mayhew, 1974). Exhibit 1.1 defines basic disciplinary terminology and gives examples.

During the same era, educators endeavored to interpret the requirements of the disciplines for the curriculum (see, for example, Bloom, Hastings, & Madaus, 1971, *Handbook on Formative and Summative Evaluation of Student Learning*). The outcome of these attempts to define disciplines was unnerving. The disciplines were found to be complex and impenetrable—wildly flourishing jungles rather than orderly municipalities. Disciplines behaved more like tribes than communities; territorialism dominated rational decision making, and competition limited access across borders. The sociological characteristics of disciplines often outweighed their epistemological characteristics; longevity, research funding history, and political savoir faire were found recurrently to take precedence in the academic world over the ability of a given discipline to validate knowledge or solve problems. Of greater concern in the disciplines, the process of producing knowledge was not systematically articulated. In *Academic Tribes and Territories,* Becher (1989) described knowledge in the disciplines as a badly made patchwork quilt full of gaps and overlaps. Specialization led to greater fragmentation, as specialists concentrated on their own subdomain and ignored links to others. Postmodernism further damaged hopes of coming to an understanding of disciplinary epistemology as the possibility of central themes, structures, or truths was disputed. This situation led one author to suggest that it might make more sense to think of a discipline not as a coherent domain but rather as a family that provides local metaphors or models (Leary, 1992). With such fragmentation, if we are to provide guidance to our students, the question becomes, Where can we find guiding patterns of inquiry?

Philosophical conceptualizations of inquiry and the acquisition of knowledge provide one entry point for understanding disciplinary differences. I examined four ways of categorizing the process of inquiry. The first, found in the *Paideia Proposal* (Adler, 1982) grouped disciplines by the kinds of skills they promote: communication

EXHIBIT 1.1. SOME BASIC DISCIPLINARY TERMINOLOGY

Definitions of Terms	Examples
Epistemology: Theory of knowledge, its methods and validation	Atomism: Knowledge consists of units that are linked to each other Constructivism: We construct our own knowledge
Discipline: A body of knowledge with a reasonably logical taxonomy, a specialized vocabulary, an accepted body of theory, a systematic research strategy, and techniques for replication and validation	Physics, chemistry
Field: Phenomena studied relatively unrestricted, methods diverse; also, general branch of learning, as in field of study	Engineering, education
Domain: Sphere of influence of a field or discipline; includes recognition of an area bounded but not necessarily restricted	Cognitive domain, scientific domain
Pure: Uses specific models or theories	Physics
Applied: Open to environmental complexity and eclecticism	Engineering, education
Hard, paradigmatic: Logically structured, uses models or theoretical frameworks, has an acknowledged methodology	Physics
Soft: Unrestricted or relatively unlimited field of phenomena; content and method more idiosyncratic, complexity legitimate	Environmental studies, English literature

(language, literature, and the fine arts), measurement (mathematics and science), and critical judgment (the social sciences). Another categorization sorted the disciplines according to their ends, whether rational, empirical, or pragmatic (Scheffler, 1965). In mathematics, the epitome of a rational discipline, deductive chains link general truths and intuition discloses basic truths. Deduction is a process of using general law to infer particular instances. For example, in Euclidean geometry, students apply mathematical laws using diagrams and axioms. Mathematics is a regulative instrument of inquiry. In pure science, the empirical is stressed—natural phenomena are revealed by experience. The relationships among the phenomena cannot be inferred by logic from self-evident truths; they are associations projected as generalizations from past experience. In this inductive process, particular instances are used to infer a general law. In applied science, the pragmatic view involves experimentation in which one actively transforms the environment with the goal of solving problems. Scheffler's view of inquiry is that it is an active process regulated by logic, sparked by theory, and resulting in answers to problems. Different disciplines, however, focus on different aspects of inquiry.

In a third categorization, the taxonomy of educational objectives in the cognitive domain (Bloom, 1956), three levels of knowledge were distinguished: specific facts and concepts, ways and means of dealing with specific knowledge, and general principles. Also identified was a hierarchy of higher-order objectives: comprehension, application, analysis, synthesis, and evaluation. These objectives could then be translated into course instructional goals. The fourth approach, Hirst's (1974) conception of knowledge and the curriculum, divided the theoretical from the practical but introduced concepts, logical structure, truth criteria, and methods to differentiate among forms of knowledge. These conceptualizations of knowledge and inquiry suggested four levels of analysis for the epistemology of disciplines, each building on the previous level (Exhibit 1.2). The most basic level is that of the terms or concepts used to describe phenomena in a discipline. The second level is the logical structure of a discipline, which includes ways and means of dealing with specific knowledge and with principles. The third level is the criteria used to determine validity, and the fourth is the methods or processes of inquiry.

EXHIBIT 1.2. A FRAMEWORK FOR UNDERSTANDING DISCIPLINARY DIFFERENCES

Level of Analysis	Example
Concept: Unit of thought or element of knowledge that allows us to organize experience	Term or phrase that serves a main or linking purpose; ranges from concrete (noise in physics) to higher-order abstract (cultural conflict in history)
Logical structure: Organization of data or concepts showing the relationships between component parts; a schema	Ranges from hard, paradigmatic (physical sciences) to soft, unrestricted (humanities)
Criteria and processes used to determine validity: Standards by which we validate knowledge	Consistency, coherence, accuracy, or precision; use of empirical evidence, conflicting evidence, peer review
Methods and modes of inquiry: Processes of thinking and operations used to describe them	Hermeneutics, critical thinking, problem solving, scientific method, expertise

Disciplines have been most frequently categorized according to the extent to which they are logically structured, or hard, therefore use generally agreed upon models or theoretical frameworks, and have an acknowledged methodology and criteria by which propositions are assessed (Biglan, 1973; Donald, 1986, 1995a; Hirst, 1974; Kuhn, 1970; Toulmin, 1972). Biglan had faculty members sort thirty-six academic areas into groups based on their similarity. He then used a process of multidimensional scaling to produce three dimensions of hard versus soft, pure versus applied, and life versus nonlife that reflect different epistemological organizations. The physical sciences have been described as hard, well-structured, or paradigmatic disciplines (Frederiksen, 1984; Kuhn, 1970). A paradigm consists of a logical structure and governing truth criteria that provide maximum direction to scholars in the field (Kuhn, 1970). In physics, for example, Newton's laws of classical mechanics form part of the curriculum around the world. A prototypical discipline restricts the number and kind of phenomena studied. Less prototypical disciplines do not have a body of theory that is subscribed to by all members of the field. They have been labeled soft, or *unrestricted*; content and method are more idiosyncratic (Becher, 1989; Biglan, 1973; Frederiksen, 1984). In these disciplines, as in the social sciences and humanities, complexity is seen as a legitimate aspect of knowledge; *unrestricted* refers to the fact that the field of phenomena is relatively unlimited.

Whether a discipline is pure or applied also affects the degree to which and the manner in which it is organized epistemologically. Pure disciplines are more likely to use specific models, whereas applied areas are more open to environmental complexity and eclecticism—using the most fitting model or method in a given circumstance (Exhibit 1.1). For example, in physics scientists test theories; in contrast in engineering the criterion of success is what works. Applied areas of study are sometimes described as fields because the phenomena they study are relatively unrestricted and the methods, frequently taken from several disciplines, are diverse. Education, for example, is considered to be a field because it incorporates knowledge and methods from a variety of disciplines, both in traditional subject matter areas such as history or English, and in the social sciences. *Domain* is used in this text to refer to the sphere of influence of a field or discipline, as in the cognitive domain in Bloom's (1956) taxonomy of educational objectives or the scientific domain, and includes recognition of an area bounded but not necessarily restricted.

Members of well-structured, prototypical, or paradigmatic disciplines are more likely to agree on the knowledge structures and methods of inquiry in use. The convergence can extend to the use of a standard textbook. For example, Halliday and Resnick's *Fundamentals of Physics* (1988) in its several editions is recognized internationally as an appropriate textbook for introductory physics courses. Epistemological, linguistic, and curricular convergence are found in physics, in contrast to other disciplines in which agreement on the principal concepts is not readily found. For example, Goldman, Schoner, and Pentony (1980) found wide variation in choice of the most important concepts in political science. Curricular convergence also means that the disciplinary community can claim a high level of validity. Physics meets the three main criteria for validation: consistency, coherence (or internal consistency), and accuracy or precision (Donald, 1990). In summary, there is a wide range of organization or degree of convergence across disciplines, from the way in which concepts are related to the way in which knowledge is validated, and this affects student learning, and more broadly, intellectual development. Each level of analysis reveals differences between disciplines.

Nature of Concepts in Different Disciplines

At the most basic level of understanding a discipline, underlying its logical structure, are the terms or concepts used to describe phenomena in the discipline. In my first attempt to understand disciplinary differences in what students were expected to learn in university, I investigated the structure of knowledge in sixteen courses in various disciplines in the university (Donald, 1983, 1986). I selected model courses—that is, ones in which the professor had been rated highly by students or had engaged in course development procedures. Each course could be expected to exhibit the general characteristics of the discipline, although it would not necessarily be the most typical course. Choosing courses from different disciplines provided the opportunity to discover different knowledge structures and trends across disciplines. The principal research question was: In what ways is the knowledge structure of different university courses alike, and in what ways does it differ?

The basic unit of analysis was the *concept*, defined as a unit of thought or element of knowledge that allows us to organize experience (Exhibit 1.2). Concepts can exist at various levels of generality and abstraction and may be simple or complex. A concept may be a class or category, such as *middle class* in the history course described in this chapter in Figure 1.1, and any given concept exists within a larger framework that may take the form of a structure, process, or larger category. A concept is not considered to occupy discrete space but rather has a center or density of meaning (Deese, 1965). Concepts can, however, be represented as discrete entities—as nodes or clusters of information (Rumelhart, Lindsay, & Norman, 1972). The set of concepts in a course and their relationships form the knowledge structure or core content of the course.

The courses selected for study were in physics, chemistry, biology, entomology, geology, psychology, sociology, political science, education, law, social work, history, English, classics, and philosophy. In each course, one of my research assistants undertook a series of interviews with the professor while making a detailed

FIGURE 1.1. KEY CONCEPTS IN THE HISTORY COURSE "THE UNITED STATES SINCE 1865"

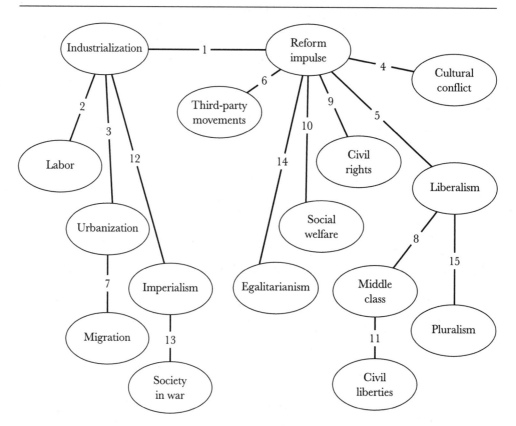

examination of all course material and applying a set of concept analysis procedures to the course content. The method used is described in greater detail in the article "Knowledge Structures: Methods for Exploring Course Content" (Donald, 1983). The first step was to examine the course materials to find any headings, titles, and frequently mentioned items that served a main or linking purpose in the course. The professor selected those that were dealt with in the course and were therefore relevant, then selected from them the most important or key concepts in terms of their main or linking role in the course. The number of relevant concepts ranged from 33 to 170, with a mean of 99. The wide range in number of relevant concepts suggests one dimension of course difficulty: the number of ideas students are expected to learn in a course. Science courses tended to have significantly more concepts than the average, and humanities courses tended to have fewer. One interpretation of this result is that more is taught in science courses, but another potential explanation is that the concepts in science courses are more explicit or specific. This would be consistent with science disciplines being more structured and restricted in scope, and it might thus render the learning task more feasible.

The kinds of key concepts selected by the professors ranged from concrete or measurable one-word concepts such as *noise* to theoretical phrases such as *the first law of thermodynamics*. The number of key concepts ranged across the sixteen courses from seven to twenty (the maximum allowed by the analytic procedures used) with a mean of fourteen concepts. The concepts were tested for familiarity compared with the general student vocabulary, and for how technical or everyday their definitions were. The percentage of technical concepts was higher in the five science courses (83 percent) than in the six social science courses (63 percent) or in the four humanities courses (33 percent). In the matching study that followed during the next three years, students were asked to define the key concepts in a pretest, and their replies were analyzed to reveal areas of knowledge, confusion, and ignorance. For example, in one course students were able to define the terms with everyday meanings but were not able to define terms that had technical or course-specific meanings. Testing and provision of key concept definitions could be expected to be of particular use to students in courses where a sizable proportion of the concepts are technical.

We also examined how concepts were presented in class, how abstract they were, and how general or specific and salient each was. If students could actively manipulate objects or events, as in the use of the concept *rehearsal* in the English drama course, the concept was deemed *enactive,* according to Bruner's (1960) classification (Exhibit 1.3). Bruner (1996) points out that enactive concepts guide activity, imposing means-end or instrumental structures on the world. They are procedural and therefore skills or actions. If the concept was presented in graphic

EXHIBIT 1.3. MODES OF REPRESENTATION

Mode	Example
Enactive: Students can actively manipulate attributes of the actual objects or events	Rehearsal, stage business (English drama); wave shapes (physics)
Iconic: Graphic or image-based; attributes are somewhat isomorphic with the referent	Vibration amplitude (physics)
Symbolic: Language or some other symbol system; attributes not isomorphic	Self-concept (education); logarithmic response (physics)

form or as an image, as *vibration amplitude* was in the physics course, it was labeled *iconic*. Images capture the particularity of events but also serve as prototypes
for classes or categories. They provide preconceptual structures that allow us to
see the typical and the similar.

Concepts presented in language or another symbolic form, such as *self-concept*
in the education course or *logarithmic response* in the physics course, were labeled
symbolic. The most frequent mode of representation of concepts in the courses was
symbolic, but some courses had more enactive concepts—physics and English
drama, for example—and some courses used multimodal presentation. Image-
arousing materials or demonstrations have been found to aid student learning,
so if concepts were known to be difficult to grasp, an instructor could introduce a
series of examples using several different forms of representation.

Another index of difficulty is how concrete or abstract concepts are—that
is, whether they have perceptual or objective referents or not. More abstract concepts could be expected to be less readily understood, because they do not have
immediate referents. The key concepts were rated on a four-point scale from concrete and concrete functional to abstract and higher-order abstract based on the
definition given them by the professor (Exhibit 1.4). For example, *gestures* in the
English drama course, defined as physical language that is intended to show interpretation and reaction, was rated concrete. In the history course *industrialization*, defined as the process whereby other economic systems are superseded by
those where industrial interests predominate, was concrete functional. *Liberalism*
in the history course, defined as a theory advocating individual freedom from government control and a market that is self-regulating, was abstract. *Cultural conflict*
was the only higher-order abstract concept in the history course. It had a defini-

EXHIBIT 1.4. CONCEPT ABSTRACTNESS

Level of Abstractness	Examples
Concrete: Concept based on a concrete or perceptual attribute	Gestures (English drama); vibration frequency (physics)
Concrete functional: Concept based on perceptual attribute that includes use or application	Industrialization (history); noise (physics)
Abstract: Concept without a concrete or perceptual referent	Liberalism (history); feedback (physics)
Higher-order abstract: Concept two steps or more removed from a concrete or perceptual referent, thus requiring inference	Cultural conflict (history); modes of oscillation of a system (physics)

tion of a struggle or controversy among competing groups with distinct values, was two steps removed from having a concrete or perceptual referent, and therefore could be expected to require high inference to understand. Across the sixteen courses, two-thirds of the concepts were abstract, but in the science courses, the majority of concepts (58 percent) were concrete. In comparison in the social sciences only 10 percent were concrete. Similar ratios were found in a study of disciplinary discourse in doctoral theses (Parry, 1998). Abstract concepts might require greater time to represent and explain for successful student comprehension.

The professors rated each key concept according to how inclusive or general it was and ranked how important each was, as measures of its ability to link or organize other concepts in the course. We found that the most important key concept in a course was the most inclusive key concept, had the greatest number of links with other concepts, or was a focal or pivotal concept in the course. These concepts were most often given the highest salience rating, suggesting a dominant role for one or a few concepts in a course. We could suppose that they would be primary contributors to the logical structure of the subject area.

Logical Structure in Different Disciplines

Logical structure is defined as the organization of data showing the relationships between component parts (Exhibit 1.2). A representation of logical structure has been described as a *schema*, a data structure of generic concepts stored in memory and containing the network of relationships among the constituent parts (Bartlett, 1932; Donald, 1987; Rumelhart & Ortony, 1977). Researchers have discriminated between strong schemas such as a scientific theory that consists of general principles and weak schemas such as fuzzy concepts or prototypes in which categories may overlap and relationships may be arbitrary (Anderson, 1984). Strong schemas allow us to predict; weak schemas are precedent-driven. An analogy is the difference between a code of law such as the Napoleonic code, and common law, which is based on precedent and dependent on context.

If we are to understand the relationships between concepts, we need to know in what order and how closely concepts are linked and the character of the linkage. A method of developing this understanding is to build a concept map. Several approaches to concept mapping have been described in the literature. One is content structure maps, in which a subject matter expert shows the principal concepts and their relationships in a domain by drawing links between concepts and labeling them (Pask, 1976; Rumelhart, 1977; Shavelson, 1974). Another approach is graphic representation of the strength of relationships between concepts, where each concept is rated on how closely it is related to another on a scale from 0 for no relationship to 4 for identity (Donald, 1987; Waern, 1972). A third approach is topic- or lecture-oriented maps in which an instructor prepares a master concept map of the ideas to be presented in an instructional sequence (Bogdan, 1977; Cardemone, 1975; Novak & Gowin, 1984; Van Patten, Chao, & Reigeluth, 1986). A fourth approach describes the development of concept maps as a learning strategy (Novak, 1985; Santhanam, Leach, & Dawson, 1998). Novak (1990) points out that the great benefit of concept maps accrues to the constructor of the map, because the process enables the person to make meaningful relationships between concepts. He therefore used maps as heuristic tools when doing research on knowledge construction in mathematics and science classes.

In our study of knowledge structures in different disciplines, we opted for a method based on the closest or most dominant relationships among the key concepts (Shavelson, 1974). Participating professors found this procedure one of the most useful clarification techniques in the study. Each professor was asked to link the two most closely related key concepts in his or her course, link the concept most closely related to one of them, and then continue until all key concepts were represented on the map. For example, in the history course "The United States Since 1865," the closest relationship was between *industrialization,* the most important concept in the course, and *reform impulse* (Figure 1.1). Each of these concepts served as a focal point, with the remaining key concepts arrayed around them. *Labor* and *urbanization* were the second and third closest links to *industrialization,* and *cultural conflict* was the fourth most closely related concept to *reform impulse.* These five concepts were also the most important in the course.

The number of relationships between key concepts could be expected to be a rough measure of the degree of logical structure or strength of the schema. In science courses, the average number of relationships noticeably exceeded the average in the social sciences and humanities (twenty-two compared with thirteen). The format also differed by type of course. The sciences tended to be hierarchical, with branches from more to less important concepts, and with more links between them, suggesting tighter relationships (Donald, 1983). In the social sciences, webs or clusters of concepts linked to a pivotal concept constituted the most common format. In humanities courses, a linear or loose block was more common; concepts tended to stand on their own. We will be examining these relationships more closely in the course concept maps in the following chapters. Generally speaking, however, the analysis of the relationships among concepts suggests that the preferred learning strategy in science courses would be to learn all of the concepts in order to understand a distinct pattern. Students in social science courses, in contrast, would have a looser structure but would have an important learning cue if they recognized a pivotal concept and grouped others around it. In humanities courses, students could be expected to focus on individual concepts and would be less likely to link them in a formal manner.

To determine the nature of the linkage between key concepts, the professors were asked to describe the relationship of each pair of concepts linked in the map. These relationships were then categorized according to a taxonomy of relationships (Exhibit 1.5). Similarity relationships were those between concepts that had some, but not all, of the same characteristics. Three levels were distinguished. Associative relationships were the simplest, in which concepts were contiguous or descriptive of each other—for example, the relationship between *liberalism* and *pluralism*. In functional relationships concepts had a similar outcome or purpose: *reform impulse* and *egalitarianism* have the same objective. Structural relationships showed a taxonomic or hierarchical relationship of a kind or a part. For example, a concern of the *middle class* is *civil liberties*. Among the sixteen courses, the majority of relationships (60 percent) were based on similarity, with 42 percent overall structural. The relatively high proportion of structural relationships gives some support to the claims of cognitive researchers that key concepts can be used as ideational scaffolding because they subsume other concepts (Ausubel, 1968; Novak, 1990).

In dependency relationships, a change in one concept implied a corresponding change in the other. Procedural relationships described steps, order, or sequence. The

EXHIBIT 1.5. TAXONOMY OF RELATIONSHIPS BETWEEN CONCEPTS

Kind of Relationship	Example and Explanation
Similarity	
Associative: Concepts are contiguous or descriptive of each other.	Liberalism and pluralism; in a pluralist society, most reform is of a liberal nature.
Functional: Concepts have a similar outcome or purpose.	Reform impulse and egalitarianism; an objective of American reformers has been to advance the cause of egalitarianism.
Structural: Concepts have a taxonomic or hierarchical relationship, such as subset, inclusion, kind of, or part of.	Middle class and civil liberties; an area of primary concern to the middle class has been the preservation of civil liberties.
Dependency	
Procedural: Concepts are ordered or sequenced as for steps, progression, or prerequisites.	Experimental techniques and analysis of data (biology); none were found in history course.
Logical: Concepts have a logical or conditional order.	Industrialization and labor; the process of industrialization has several effects on the labor force.
Causal: Concepts have an explicit cause-and-effect relationship.	Urbanization and migration; urbanization was a consequence of migration, from country to city and from Europe to North America.

history course had no procedural relationships, therefore an example is shown of the concept *experimental techniques,* which was followed by the *analysis of data* in the biology course. In logical relationships concepts had a logical or conditional order; *industrialization* affects the *labor* force in several ways. Causal relationships showed an explicit cause and effect linkage; for example, *migration* led to *urbanization.* Among the sixteen courses studied, the second most commonly found relationships were logical (18 percent) followed by causal (12 percent) and procedural (10 percent). Dependency relationships, because they are causal or contingent, could be construed as tighter or less arbitrary relationships, thus affirming greater structure in the discipline.

All of the courses used similarity relationships, but significant differences were found in the use of dependency relationships. Science courses had an average of nine dependency relationships, social science six, and humanities four. The kinds of relationships provide cues to understand the thought processes or strategies required to comprehend course material. When the majority of relationships are structural, for example, students can be guided to look for similarities or categories among the themes and subtopics in the course. When the relationships are procedural or causal, the appropriate strategies would consist of considering steps or necessary contingencies. The trends in relationships in the knowledge structures across disciplines revealed clear epistemological differences but also suggested accompanying instructional strategies. Further explanation of this research can be found in the articles "Knowledge and the University Curriculum" (Donald, 1986) and "Learning Schemata" (Donald, 1987).

Criteria Used to Determine Validity

The standards by which we validate knowledge generally include coherence, or goodness of fit in a model or explanation; consistency, or a match with external reality or reliability over time or persons; and accuracy, or precision or discreteness. At the most structured end of the disciplinary continuum, a paradigm consists not only of a logical structure but also governing criteria for validity. Strategies—the sets of rules that guide the search for knowledge—have been described as combinations of experience and reasoning (Thompson, Hawkes, & Avery, 1969). A strategy may put high or low emphasis on experience, and reasoning in a strategy may be either codified—that is, explicit and systematic—or uncodified. The model results in four possible strategies as shown in Exhibit 1.6.

According to the model, a scientific strategy combines high reliance on experience with systematic theorizing. The arts and humanities are considered to rely on a direct strategy that depends on experience but not on a specific code of reasoning. Mathematics and logic use an independent strategy—that is, independent of experience but highly structured or codified. In the fourth quadrant, an

EXHIBIT 1.6. STRATEGIES GUIDING THE SEARCH FOR KNOWLEDGE

High experience	Scientific strategy	Direct strategy
Low experience	Independent strategy	Inspirational strategy
	Codified	Uncodified

Source: Adapted from Thompson, Hawkes, and Avery (1969).

inspirational strategy is low in reliance on experience and is uncodified, representing the opposite of knowledge seeking. Thompson, Hawkes, and Avery conclude that disciplines relying on both experience and systematic theorizing have a double-checking procedure for eliminating error, and can therefore claim a high degree of validity. In disciplines using a direct strategy, such as the humanities, argument and criticism coupled with consistency over time determine the validity of experience. Mathematicians depend on agreement among experts on the logical completeness of their theories.

The social sciences range from codified to uncodified types of reasoning, although for the most part reliance on experience is high. Reliability over time or situations (external generalizability) and across observers is an essential criterion in research in the social sciences. With their heritage in the humanities, Ross (1979) points out that in the switch from philosophy to empiricism, social scientists interpreted the term *science* differently in different disciplines and now find themselves under pressure from newer conceptions of science. Social scientists are trained, however, to discern and formulate patterns that can be expressed in general terms and can therefore create models that can be tested and verified (Rosenberg, 1979). In contrast, because the humanistic disciplines are concerned with phenomena that do not have immediate referents, humanistic truth involves authenticity or genuineness rather than logical or scientific validity (Broudy, 1977).

To test these conceptions of validation criteria and strategies, I analyzed interview data from forty professors in five disciplines—physics, engineering, psychology, education, and English literature—to determine how they validated their work (Donald, 1995a). Each discipline represented a different category according to the Biglan (1973) dimensions of hard-soft and pure-applied. Physics represented hard-pure; engineering, hard-applied; psychology represented social science-pure; education, social science-applied; and English literature, soft-pure. The expectation was that professors in the physical sciences would be logical empiricists, testing theory through observation. Social scientists could be expected to follow the same procedures to some extent, depending on how hard or soft their disciplines were; they could also be expected to speak of testing alternative theories.

Professors in the humanities would be more interested in the test of time as a means of validating experience.

The validation criteria could also be expected to vary across disciplines. Although consistency appears to be an important criterion in all disciplines, its measurement varies. In the sciences it would be with external reality, in the humanities it would be consistency over time and across people, and in the social sciences, consistency would be expected to take the form of reliability over a series of observations. Precision or accuracy could be considered a direct measure of structure or codification, but in less codified or more complex domains the coherence of the argument or the completeness or comprehensiveness of the theory could be expected to be more important.

Considerable cohesion was found between disciplines, but trends were also evident. The greatest cohesion was found in the use of consistency as a criterion (Exhibit 1.7). *Consistency* was used to refer to reliability over time, situations, or persons, and thus proof by means of replicability, objectivity, or agreement. An engineering professor described it in these words:

> Consistency implies that I have done three rather similar experiments; there are differences between the results but they seem to have a trend about them that is comprehensible.

An English professor described consistency as the extent to which an interpretation of a play seems consonant with an interpretation of another play. Consistency therefore involves the idea of matching a conceptualization in the real world, or getting results showing the same trend from a series of cases or experiments.

Coherence or internal consistency was considered important to half the professors, most prominently among psychologists (88 percent), but also by half the engineers and educators. Several physicists pointed out that they would not use the term *coherence* as a criterion of validity because of its specific meaning in wave theory. A psychology professor spoke of building a computer program to model an explanation and discovering only by attempting to build an explicit model that it was radically incomplete and incoherent. An English professor considered coherence the most important criterion, stating that no interpretation of a play is entirely coherent—that is, takes into account every fact about a play—but the ones that take most of the facts about the play into consideration are the ones that are most coherent and therefore most answerable to the criterion of verification. Complexity limits the degree of coherence that can be expected. Some professors held that external and internal consistency were interdependent.

Precision, accuracy, or specificity was named by fewer than half the professors overall, with some saying that precision was assumed in their field or used as a

EXHIBIT 1.7. PERCENT OF PROFESSORS NAMING VALIDATION CRITERIA AND PROCESSES USED IN THEIR DISCIPLINES

	Physics	Engineering	Psychology	Education	English Literature	Total
Criteria						
Consistency, correspondence, reliability, uncertainty	75	88	63	63	63	70
Coherence, internal consistency, parts tested against whole	25	50	88	50	38	50
Precision, accuracy, specificity	63	38	38	25	63	45
Processes						
Use of empirical evidence, reproducibility, performance	88	88	88	75	50	78
Use of conflicting evidence, counterexamples, alternative explanations	25	—	63	—	25	23
Peer review, credibility, acceptability, plausibility	38	13	25	38	50	33

preliminary screening device. In physics, several professors stated that no result is absolutely accurate; there is always some uncertainty. An engineering professor described the criterion in terms of encouraging students to have a concept of orders of magnitude, so that they could estimate within what range an answer should lie. The criterion was used most frequently by physics and English literature professors. English professors sought accuracy in terms of relating textual detail or in whether text was historically sound, that is, whether it could be verified by historical data.

The validation process mentioned most frequently—by more than three-quarters of the professors—was the use of empirical evidence, including experiment, reproducibility, or performance, to test the truth of a phenomenon. Professors talked about judging how good the data are in supporting the hypothesis, about physical evidence, or about getting qualitative and quantitative agreement with observation and experiment. "Does it work?" was another way of phrasing this, or whether analysis produces an explanation that fits the data. Most of the physical and social science professors mentioned the use of empirical evidence. In contrast, half the English literature professors put emphasis on the use of empirical evidence.

A relatively small proportion of professors (fewer than one-quarter) mentioned the use of conflicting evidence, counterexamples, or alternative explanations—that is, the use of deductive logic to test for truth. The use of conflicting evidence was noted only in pure disciplines, and with a majority of the professors only in psychology. The low overall proportion suggests little academic accord with Popper's (1963) argument that a belief is rationally grounded and respectable only if it has been submitted to a crucial experiment designed to falsify it and has succeeded in passing that test. At one time, it was assumed (see Skinner, 1985) that Popper's test of falsification had become part of the scientist's code, but validation processes that rely on empirical evidence had much wider acceptance than a test for falsification, confirming the argument for an inductive process of testing (Krathwohl, 1985).

The third kind of validation process, acceptance by an external authority—either through peer review or in terms of credibility or plausibility—was mentioned by one-third of the professors. Half the English literature professors suggested its use for validation purposes; engineering professors were least likely to mention its use. In English literature limited reliance on empirical evidence may be compensated for by reliance on peer judgment.

We can infer from these results that the process of validation in a pure discipline can be more precise because of its bounded or restricted nature. For example, validation in pure disciplines can employ a deductive thought process with the use of conflicting evidence. Unexpectedly, the differences across disciplines in the validation processes used were greatest between the social sciences and the humanities. Social science professors reported using empirical evidence more than humanities professors, who in turn reported greater reliance on their peers to validate their work.

Methods and Modes of Inquiry Across Disciplines

The criteria and processes for validating knowledge are intrinsically linked to methods or processes of thinking. To understand how students learn to think in a discipline and how structures of knowledge influence teaching and learning, we can look at what is done to promote thinking, and what kind of thinking, in a discipline and more specifically in a program or course. When professors were asked about the extent to which they expected their students to think logically, independently, and abstractly, physical and social science professors expected their students to think logically to a greater extent than did humanities professors (Donald, 1988). Across disciplines, students in first-year courses were not expected to think as independently as students in upper-level undergraduate courses. There was a trend toward greater expectation of abstract thinking in the social sciences, and physical science professors thought that students would be able to reason with abstract propositions more than humanities professors did. Consistent with practice in their disciplines (Broudy, 1977), humanities professors appeared to be looking for something other than logical thought or reasoning from their students; authenticity is important here. The two disciplinary groups most expectant of thinking abilities were in applied fields—engineers, who focused on the development of problem-solving skills in their program but were least interested in abstract thinking, and educators, who had a more general interest in all of the thinking abilities. What processes of thinking or inquiry are important in each discipline?

Disciplines have created distinctive terminology to describe their methods of inquiry. The earliest method was *hermeneutics* to analyze biblical text (Exhibit 1.8). Hermeneutics, or interpretation, is the construction of textual meaning that elucidates the connotations that text explicitly or implicitly represents (Hirsch, 1967). This is accomplished through a dialectic between understanding, which is directed toward the intentional unity of discourse, with explanation, which is directed more toward the analytic structure of a text (Ricoeur, 1976). Hermeneutics is viewed as a circle, in which guess and validation are related as subjective and objective approaches to the text. The first act of understanding is a guess as to the meaning of the text. The transition from guessing to explanation is made through an investigation of the specific object of guessing. One begins by assuming the text is coherent, then develops a framework of explanation that is tested by the facts it generates. The method is thus a process of hypothesizing and then searching for corroborating evidence in the text. Although the hermeneutic approach is espoused most frequently in the humanities, discourse analysis as currently used in the social sciences owes much to hermeneutics.

Critical thinking, a method more generally referred to across disciplines, developed out of the Socratic tradition of disciplined inquiry. Usually defined as a

EXHIBIT 1.8. METHODS OF INQUIRY IN DIFFERENT DISCIPLINES

Method	Example
Hermeneutics: Interpretation; construction of textual meaning through a dialectic between understanding and explanation	Biblical text, English literature
Critical thinking: A reasoned or questioning approach in which one examines assumptions and seeks evidence	English literature
Problem solving: Steps for formulating a problem, calculating, and verifying the logic used	Physics, engineering
Scientific method: Objective methods, replicability of findings, skepticism	Physics
Expertise: Well-developed representation of knowledge, action schemas	Physics, education

reasoned or questioning approach in which one examines assumptions and seeks evidence (Donald, 1985), researchers suggest that critical thinking includes components of logic, problem solving, and abstraction (Meyers, 1986; Sternberg, 1985b). Different disciplines focus on different aspects of the critical thinking process—for example, inferential processes in physics compared with testing assumptions in English (Donald, 1985; Meyers, 1986).

In comparison to critical thinking, *problem solving* is described more specifically and procedurally as a set of steps consisting of formulating or representing a problem, selecting the relations pertinent to solving the problem, doing the necessary calculations, and verifying the logic used to see if the final answer makes sense (Reif, Larkin, & Brackett, 1976). Thus, problem solving includes critical thinking processes but also implementation or testing; the difference between critical thinking and problem solving is analogous to comprehending versus doing. For example, the critical thinker would examine underlying assumptions and infer their effects; the problem solver would continue from this action to create a strategy for dealing with the problem. Problem solving is most frequently used to describe method in the physical sciences, although the scientific method offers a broader conceptualization.

The scientific method consists of universal standards for knowledge claims, common ownership of information, disinterestedness or integrity in gathering and interpreting data, and organized skepticism (Krathwohl, 1985). Popper (1959) claimed that *skepticism*—the active attempt to disconfirm knowledge claims—is how science proceeds, implying deduction, but as noted earlier in the discussion of the use of conflicting evidence, this process is not frequently used. Krathwohl argues that we tend to think inductively, as if knowledge had some degree of certainty, and is tested for generality and strength under varying circumstances. Science is defined by the objective nature of its methods, the replicability of findings, the insistence on empirical demonstrations, and its self-correcting nature; that is, findings are held as tentative until they are replaced by better established knowledge claims. Krathwohl points out that the social sciences tend to interpret these characteristics somewhat differently than the physical sciences. For example, in the physical sciences, objectivity is based on the assumption that a phenomenon exists in the real world and hence is observable or verifiable by scientific methods. In contrast, in the social sciences one attempts to establish reliability between observers—the extent to which phenomena observed by one researcher are seen or perceived in the same way by another. An element of perception or interpretation enters into the process.

A more recent approach to understanding methods of thinking is to examine *expertise,* because the expert is one who has acquired not only a solid base of knowledge but the ability to apply it (Ericksen & Smith, 1991). The expert in a given area has well-developed representations of knowledge or schemas in the subject matter and can relate the schemas in order to operate intelligently. Studies of differences between experts and novices reveal that novices use knowledge of surface structures whereas experts use action schemas (Chi, Feltovich, & Glaser, 1981). Novices represent problems literally; experts use a scientific and mathematical representation (McDermott & Larkin, 1978). Novices become experts by passing through an analytic stage where problem-solving time increases until they develop the representations and strategies characteristic of the expert. Experts recognize patterns and solve problems efficiently and effectively. They have a sense of the context, select the appropriate information, recognize organizing principles, and verify their inferences. They are equipped with representations and thinking strategies or action schemas for applying these representations to problems. What is particularly important about this approach is that it describes the relationship between knowledge and thinking processes, and it further suggests how thinking strategies are developed.

How are these methods or processes of thinking similar or different? Put another way, if thinking processes are to be learned and generalized across contexts or situations—an increasingly recognized need in education—how would this occur? To answer this question, a working model was developed that consisted of a set of definitions of thinking processes (Donald, 1992a). The set of definitions encompassed the thinking processes considered relevant to different domains in postsecondary education and also consisted of specific observable behaviors or operations that required little (low) inference, so that professors from a variety of disciplines could use the model and the behaviors or operations would be observable. The model was developed by creating a comprehensive list of thinking processes from the postsecondary literature, then having instructional experts group the definitions on the basis of similarity and describe the basis of their grouping. This led to a working set of thirty behaviors in six groups of thinking processes: description, selection, representation, inference, synthesis, and verification (Exhibit 1.9).

Comparison of the set of definitions with the discipline-based models shows the working model to be encompassing and observable. As shown in Exhibit 1.9, *expertise* is described by the processes of identifying the context (description), selecting information as needed, and representing, inferring, and verifying. *Hermeneutics* requires inference and verification. *Critical thinking* includes stating assumptions (description), deducing (an inferential process), inferring, and verifying. *Problem solving* includes processes in each of the groups: description, selection, representation, inference, synthesis, and verification. *The scientific method* is described primarily by description and verification processes. Thus each discipline-based model is represented by certain processes defined in the working model of thinking processes as shown in Exhibit 1.9.

A comparison of the models used in the disciplines with professors' models in the classroom revealed consistencies and surprises. Although the following chapters

EXHIBIT 1.9. WORKING MODEL OF THINKING PROCESSES IN HIGHER EDUCATION

Thinking Processes and Behaviors	Description
DESCRIPTION (PS, SM)	Delineation or definition of a situation or form of a thing.
Identify context (E)	Establish surrounding environment to create a total picture.
State conditions	State essential parts, prerequisites, or requirements.
State facts	State known information, events that have occurred.
State functions	State normal or proper activity of a thing or specific duties.
State assumptions (CT)	State suppositions, postulates, or propositions assumed.
State goal	State the ends, aims, objectives.
SELECTION (PS)	Choice in preference to another or others.
Choose relevant information (E)	Select information that is pertinent to the issue in question.
Order information in importance	Rank, arrange in importance or according to significance.
Identify critical elements	Determine units, parts, components that are important.
Identify critical relations	Determine connections between things that are important.

REPRESENTATION (PS)	Depiction or portrayal through enactive, iconic, or symbolic means.
Recognize organizing principles	Identify laws, methods, rules that arrange in a systematic whole.
Organize elements and relations	Arrange parts, connections between things into a systematic whole.
Illustrate elements and relations	Make clear by examples the parts, connections between things.
Modify elements and relations	Change, alter, or qualify the parts, connections between things.
INFERENCE (E, H, CT, PS)	Act or process of drawing conclusions from premises or evidence.
Discover new relations between elements	Detect or expose connections between parts, units, components.
Discover new relations between relations	Detect or expose connections between connections of things.
Discover equivalences	Detect or expose equality in value, force, or significance.
Categorize	Classify, arrange into parts.
Order	Rank, sequence, arrange methodically.
Change perspective	Alter view, vista, interrelations, significance of facts or information.
Hypothesize	Suppose or form a proposition as a basis for reasoning.
SYNTHESIS (PS)	Composition of parts or elements into a complex whole.
Combine parts to form a whole	Join, associate elements, components into a system or pattern.
Elaborate	Work out, complete with great detail, exactness, or complexity.
Generate missing links	Produce or create what is lacking in a sequence; fill in the gap.
Develop course of action	Work out or expand the path, route, or direction to be taken.
VERIFICATION (E, H, CT, PS, SM)	Confirmation of accuracy, coherence, consistency, correspondence.
Compare alternative outcomes	Examine similarities or differences of results, consequences.
Compare outcome to standard	Examine similarities, differences of results based on a criterion.
Judge validity	Critically examine soundness, effectiveness, by actual fact.
Use feedback	Employ results to regulate, adjust, adapt.
Confirm results	Establish or ratify conclusions, effects, outcomes, products.

E: expertise; H: hermeneutics; CT: critical thinking; PS: problem solving; SM: scientific method will examine the thinking processes in greater detail, some generalizations from the study demonstrate the scope of these models and their limitations. The English literature courses were consistent with the hermeneutic model and less with the model of critical thinking. Physics and engineering courses tended to use problem solving rather than the scientific method, possibly because the scientific method has come to be defined in the literature less as a process and more as a set of criteria guiding the process. In psychology, different courses focused on different parts of the working model, moving from description and representation in introductory courses to selection and synthesis, with research methods courses focusing on inference and verification. In teacher education programs, the focus was more specifically on the production of meaningful representations that are characteristic of the expert. In educational research courses, the working model appeared to predominate over any of the discipline-based models. In the general literature, inference is recognized as an important thinking process or is a synonym for it; in contrast, representation is not often described as a thinking process although it is important in the literature on problem solving and on expertise. In the ensuing chapters we will examine why this is so.

Scope of the Book

The discussion so far has pointed to differences between disciplines, often subtle, in the kind of language used, the logical structure, the preferred criteria for validating knowledge, and the most pronounced methods or modes of inquiry. We have also seen that students respond to the learning environment in different ways based on their stage of intellectual development, their orientation, the context of the course, the program, and methods of assessment. Over the years of studying disciplinary differences in learning and thinking, we were collecting data from students about how they learned the concepts and intellectual skills in the disciplines they were studying. In the early 1990s, we began a series of studies with the goal of testing the use and development of thinking processes in specific courses. These investigations were quickly forced to become broader ethnographic studies that described the customs and culture of the classroom. Excerpts from the logs kept by the graduate students who were the participant-observers in these courses alert us to student experience and their interpretation of the learning environment.

We also considered that introductory and advanced courses might reveal different aspects of learning and the learners, so we deliberately sampled introductory, advanced, and where warranted, graduate courses in the disciplines. Thus the database for this book scans not only twenty-five years of research into some eighteen disciplinary areas but research into diverse aspects and kinds of learning in courses.

I also considered it important to understand the sociological context in which the disciplines operate; this led to anthropological and sociological forays into the disciplines that show the academic life space of professors in these areas. In order to provide a focused yet comprehensive perspective on the role of the disciplines in nurturing thinking, I chose areas in which we had collected the maximum amount of data on aspects of the learning experience. These areas of concentration represent kinds of disciplines according to the postsecondary literature—disciplines with varying degrees of structure, pure and applied. I also wanted to be able to make comparisons within the natural sciences and social sciences, and between them. Therefore, in addition to selecting physics as the prototypical discipline and engineering as the applied physical science, I include comparisons with chemistry and biological sciences. Social sciences and humanities courses are given equal billing; four chapters describe different worlds of the human sciences.

We first look at physics, described as hard, analytical, highly structured, concrete, and paradigmatic (Exhibit 1.10). Because of the degree of structure, students report that their learning at times is circumscribed (Donald, 1993); argument does not often challenge existing norms (Parry, 1998). Biglan's (1973) early research suggested that applied disciplines have a different set of rules because they are less restricted in the number and kind of phenomena in the domain. Studying engineering, where knowledge is learned in order to apply it, is therefore contrasted with learning physics. Further contrasts with learning in the sciences, in particular chemistry and the life sciences, are intended to demystify the concepts of paradigm and logical structure. The focus moves from disciplines with evident structure to disciplines with a greater variety and number of structures (Schwab, 1978), and from the microcosmic to the macrocosmic.

EXHIBIT 1.10. HOW THE DISCIPLINES WERE CHOSEN

Discipline	Characteristics
Physics	Prototypical, hard, pure, nonlife, paradigmatic discipline
Engineering	Hard, applied, concrete, nonlife discipline
Chemistry, biological sciences	Pure, nonlife, life disciplines
Psychology	Range of hard to soft subareas; range of pure to applied; life; young discipline
Law	Socratic, ancient discipline
Education	Comprehensive, applied, metadiscipline?
English literature	Interpretive, divergent, critical discipline

Psychology has some characteristics of a hard science, but is noted for its range of hard to soft subareas, and it traverses from pure to applied within the discipline. It is also the home of theory about learning and thinking, so it could be expected to make an important contribution to a theoretical framework for learning to think. It has another singular characteristic among the disciplines chosen for study: it is a relatively young entry into academe. Law, in contrast, is an ancient field, but its strategies for thinking are less well-known. We studied it to determine the extent of its logical structure and consistency and expanded our methods to do so. Another applied social science, but one with a particular mandate, education must recognize and incorporate the paradigms or methods of subject matter disciplines, yet use psychological principles in specific learning situations. Models of thinking in the humanities are represented by English literature; it is a reference for other disciplines in the humanities. Here the challenge is the process of argument itself.

Whatever the discipline, we seek evidence of higher-order learning or thinking, where students attempt to understand or construct meaning and thus to develop intellectually. Higher-order thinking may take the form of problem solving, reasoning, integrating and applying knowledge, coming to conclusions independently, or thinking through different perspectives. It is characterized by being non-algorithmic and complex, entailing uncertainty, having multiple solutions, involving nuanced judgment, and requiring use of multiple criteria and self-regulation and the imposition of meaning and effort (Resnick, 1987). In our studies, the brief working definition of higher-order learning was to analyze, synthesize, and think critically; thinking is defined in terms of the methods or processes of conceptualizing, analyzing, and reasoning.

In the following chapters, representatives from different disciplines provide specifications and elaborations of these definitions according to their own processes of inquiry, with the working model of thinking processes as a reference. Our participating professors also provide insight into how higher-order learning can be aided in each field. Where appropriate, optimal texts and other learning materials are recommended. The emphasis in this book, however, is on the thinking processes important in each discipline. Throughout the text, the voice of scholars and students in each discipline is given precedence; in each chapter I attempt to provide perspective by comparisons with other disciplines and with findings from the higher education literature. In the final chapter I undertake a series of comparisons across disciplines. Contrasts between the sociological contexts in which students learn and the thinking and validation processes they are expected to learn are followed by a summary of the thinking processes most used in the disciplines. The final cross-disciplinary comparison is of the instructional challenges posed. We then return to the original question, how to help students develop intellectually, and the steps that administrators, faculty, and students might take to improve the intellectual context.

CHAPTER TWO

ORDERLY THINKING:
Learning in a Structured Discipline

What is different about physics from many other disciplines is that it attempts somehow to capture an element of truth in the physical world and then tries to proceed in a rigorous fashion to explain from this very simple truth an abundance of things.

PHYSICS PROFESSOR

Physics is the prototype or model discipline. The explanatory power noted in this quotation and the ability to validate knowledge through both experience and theorizing make physics the most coherent of disciplines. In the literature physics is described as paradigmatic, hard, pure, restricted, and analytical. As the physics student quoted in Chapter One said, in physics you have to approach a question by breaking it down into its parts. Physics starts by assuming separate parts that together constitute reality and shows how these separate parts are related (Zukav, 1979). Specific objects, units, or concepts are analyzed and then synthesized so that events can be predicted. This atomistic approach to knowledge increases internal consistency and accuracy; the high degree of logical structure promotes successful explanation and prediction. In physics we could thus expect to find knowledge structures with clear and explicit concepts, and a high level of agreement about methods of inquiry.

To understand how students learn physics, I first explore the disciplinary context and how it affects learning, and then students' experience in a physics course. I examine the concepts, thinking processes, and attitudes that professors consider important for students to develop and students' views of their learning milieu. Fifteen professors participated in the series of studies on learning physics and twenty-three of their students were interviewed. From the examination of the learning context in physics, three instructional challenges arise. The first comes from the structure of physics itself: How can we help students develop the necessary conceptual framework in a discipline that is abstract and counterintuitive? Then, how can we improve students' ability to problem-solve? And finally, what approach do students need to take in order to learn in this discipline successfully?

The Disciplinary Context in Physics

Although the history of physics in the Western world goes back to the early Greeks, modern physics began with the three laws of motion published in 1687 by Isaac Newton, a mathematics professor at Cambridge. The Industrial Revolution in Europe, which began in the second half of the eighteenth century with a burst of inventions and new technologies, made physics essential to the workplace and the economy (Rothman, 1992). During the Second World War the importance of physics escalated as physicists played a crucial role in the development of radar, sonar, and nuclear energy. Postwar industrial development relied heavily on physicists for breakthroughs in communications, transportation, energy, and space sciences. This led to the creation of major laboratories in association with universities (for example, the Cavendish Laboratory at Cambridge University, the Lawrence Livermore at the University of California-Berkeley) and with consortia of universities. The discipline has thus developed in response to specific societal needs, and in the case of some areas of physics in conjunction with the industrial-military complex, with significant research funding coming from defense contracts.

For instructional purposes, the most fundamental area of physics is classical mechanics, which has *force* as a central concept and studies the motion of objects. Other branches include the physics of relativity developed by Einstein, atomic physics, quantum mechanics, nuclear physics, elementary particle physics, thermodynamics, electricity and magnetism, optics and astrophysics. Physics is a cumulative subject to learn, requiring a steady progression from elementary to advanced topics and an accompanying knowledge of mathematics. The curriculum is highly structured, customarily beginning with classical mechanics and moving to electricity and magnetism, optics, and then to more advanced areas. One of the aims of an undergraduate program in physics is to show students how scientific laws, such as the law of conservation of energy, describe which actions are allowed by nature and which are not.

The prevalent philosophy in physics is that the task of the physical scientist is to complete the structure of knowledge in each branch of the science. The premise is that phenomena may appear to be separate entities but are intrinsically unified; the assumption of a single parsimonious system of explanation underlies the scientific method. Although anomalies such as wave versus particle theory occur, higher-order principles are sought to reconcile physical phenomena. Physicists categorize themselves as theoretical physicists, who solve problems mathematically (for example, using differential equations), or experimental physicists, who use laboratory instruments to measure physical objects and phenomena. Experimental physicists often test and verify or falsify the theories produced by theoretical physicists, but theorists have also tested experiments, such as those on cold fusion, finding the results out of bounds. With the advent of computer modeling, in some instances computer calculations have replaced laboratory equipment for purposes of verification.

The questions that lead inquiry in physics are highly abstract—for example, whether there are new particles to be found, if there are other forces to be found, or why particles have the masses they do (see Rothman, 1992). In *A Brief History of Time* (1988), Stephen Hawking began by asking where the universe came from and how and why it began. Some areas that are gaining attention, however, such as the physics of materials, are applied and more practical. Research groups and teams are part of the life of a physicist, but students are normally introduced to team membership only in graduate school. Most physics research is done in small groups, but according to experts in the field big groups are more likely to make headlines (Kleppner, 1985). The cost of doing physical science research is enormous, and decisions are continually made to fund some projects at the expense of others. Physics is therefore a high-stakes, demanding discipline that requires focused attention to problems in a wide variety of areas and calls upon devoted scholarly behavior.

In consequence, the cultural context of physics is known for its selectivity and exclusiveness. Becher (1989) writes that hard, pure knowledge tends to carry high prestige because it involves the search for general laws. The discipline is held to be intellectually demanding and is seen as attracting individuals of high ability. It also promises beneficial applications, which explains the willingness of society to invest substantial sums in research and the well-organized professional-political lobby to obtain funds for research. Other academics view physics as precise, clearly defined, and dealing in pure ideas, but with little relevance to everyday life and with a social organization isolated from other academics (Becher, 1981).

The cultural context renders the world of the physics student challenging but circumscribed, more specified and with more course hours than that of students in many other disciplines. The course-taking requirements for undergraduate majors to meet the standards of the International Union of Pure and Applied Physics include some forty semester hours of physics and an additional twenty hours of mathematics (Nespor, 1994). Physics programs may double this requirement. This means that student time is monopolized early, and first-year physics students report spending many more hours doing problem sets and studying for physics tests than they do for other courses.

The curriculum is hierarchical and recursive; that is, the concepts of physics, first encountered in secondary and sometimes elementary school, are revisited at the undergraduate level and again at the graduate level in increasing depth. Although some students may not recognize the demand for greater depth with each round, professors in our studies were adamant about the need to elucidate and elaborate concepts at each stage. Students may perceive the curriculum to be repetitive, but their professors see it as evolving. When physicists responded to the demand for major curriculum reform in the cold war era after World War II, the curriculum—even at the secondary level, according to one expert—was designed to emphasize ingenuity, stimulating imaginative work, and pressing one's mind to the outer limits (Brandwein, 1962). In response to the demands of the program, students are advised to work in study groups that form the social as well as the intellectual focus of their lives. At the same time, students in hard science programs recognize that they receive a higher level of resources than students in other programs (Neumann & Finaly-Neumann, 1989).

Students' Experience Learning Physics

Given a setting in which the learning task has been designed to be intellectually demanding, what do students undergo in their physics courses? To help us understand better how students learn, and particularly how they learn to think, in our ethnographic studies graduate students acting as participant-observers attended class, laboratories, and study sessions, and kept a log of their experience. The two graduate students who attended the physics course had a background in both physics and instructional psychology and commented incisively in the log on student behavior in class.

The following excerpt is from the log of the third and fourth weeks in an introductory physics course for 150 students beginning a science degree. The course consisted of three one-hour lectures and a two-hour lab each week. Some of the students had a strong background in science and math; others were learning about the discipline of physics for the first time. All students were expected to have a rudimentary knowledge of trigonometry and calculus. They ranged in age from eighteen to twenty-two and 60 percent of them were male.

September 20–September 25

The professor discusses the concept of motion-dynamics this week. The students are expected to read Chapter Four of the textbook, and complete five practice problems and eight marked problems. The lab is on the horizontal interaction between a ball and the floor.

On Friday the 20th, before class begins, the students complain to one another about the length, value, and number of assignments. They discuss whether they are worth doing; the general consensus is yes, 20 percent is a large part of the grade. One student is upset because she has not been able to buy the text yet. A friend informs her that a new shipment of books arrived several days ago.

The professor explains that this week's lectures will be more theoretical than normal because he is going to introduce Newton's three laws. He identifies what he is going to discuss and then begins outlining and defining the idea. He provides many concrete examples from his own life experience or by using objects in the room to illustrate the ideas. The pace is rapid as he moves from introducing what motion is, defining important concepts, identifying particular variables, providing examples, and demonstrating how this represents Newton's first law. He elaborates on what a law is, using scientific language. Then he shows the students how motion is related to force. He asks hypothetical questions but does not provide time for students to respond. No one asks any questions. He uses the same format to develop Newton's second law, giving an operational definition, applying laws to concrete examples, then working through the problems using numbers afterwards.

On Monday the 23rd, the professor develops Newton's third law after reviewing the important points from the previous class. Importance is placed on the language of the scientific method—that is, interpret, method, hypothesis, and the difference between such words as "on" and "by" in physics. He illustrates these ideas with several examples and includes numerical values.

On Wednesday the 25th, in class, we work through four problems concerning motion and force. The professor begins to distinguish three different kinds of force, one of them being friction, which he applies to these examples.

During this week of classes, several students who have asked questions during the lecture have articulated their ideas well. The concerns they have raised indicate that they are learning to question what the professor is saying and writing, and to link new concepts with those they have already learned. The professor talks a great deal during his lectures, turning his back only to write important concepts on the board. He tries to keep eye contact with the students as much as possible. The students, as a result, are fairly attentive. Note-taking seems to depend on the students' seating position in the room. The people at the front watch and listen to the professor more intently than those at the back of the room. Those at the front take down most of what the professor writes on the board and discusses, and they usually do so using a ruler and several colored pens and pencils. The students sitting further back take less precise notes but they usually listen; on Fridays, these students will be finishing up their homework, and comparing it with their classmates' work rather than listening to the lecture.

The pace during the lectures is hectic and the material is fairly complex. Students talk to others beside them on numerous occasions to ask questions, clarify notes on the board, and get important words the professor was saying that they missed. They occasionally ask questions, especially when the discussion is centered on working through problems. Some of the students say they do not have time to do the practice exercises and only complete the required problems that are to be marked. Some have arranged to get together to do their homework. Often students confer before, during, and after class.

In summarizing their learning experience in the course, the participating graduate student observers made the following general observations:

The professor urges the students to question what they are being taught, to take nothing as fact, and to think through problems in terms of the design, measurement, and calculations involved. The questions that the students are posing in class and in the lab indicate that some of them are accomplishing this goal. Other students, who rely on their friends, the tutorial groups, and the professor for assistance with the homework appear to be learning but with great difficulty. A third type of student, who does not ask questions in class and does only the minimal amount of homework, appears to be just getting by.

How do students learn? Notes written on the board are important. If a student cannot read something or is confused about how the professor reached a certain conclusion, he or she will often ask either the professor directly, during or after class, or will ask a neighbor. No one asks for clarification of ideas that the professor has spoken about but did not write on the board. Another way in which students learn is from the hands-on experience in the labs. When faced with a problem, they can reflect on their real experience with the material to help them answer the question. Students also learn from one another as they work collaboratively on assignments and labs. The structure of the course enhances this kind of interaction—that is, labs, tutorial groups, lectures, homework assignments.

An important observation from the log is that although some of the students in the class are able to think their way through the subject matter, more are having difficulty learning. Many students appear to be overwhelmed by the amount they are expected to learn, and have adopted a pattern of learning for the grade—neglecting their reading and the practice problems and focusing on the marked problems. The professor explicitly discusses and models the scientific method; he provides a conceptualization and examples before he engages in problems using calculations. A large proportion of students do not seem to understand the nature of the learning task. Some are able to keep up the pace and can have their questions answered in class; others must rely on tutors, their peers, and additional meetings with the professor. The range of attitudes and abilities in one class suggests the need for a form of triage and alternate instructional preparation. What does the discipline expect students to learn?

The Learning Task in Physics

Given the intellectual demands of the discipline and the disparity between the professors' and the students' worlds, how can students be helped to learn physics? Two professors stated their views.

Learning to do physics is a threshold phenomenon: many students expend a tremendous amount of effort with very little success, then suddenly they will pass that threshold and within a week or two they will not understand why it was all so difficult. It has suddenly become simple. Once they understand the language and the game plan, their intellectual capability is equal to the task and they work very easily and successfully.

The lab adds a little bit to whatever students know beforehand but it is not possible to quantify exactly what they know. They may know some things a little bit better, some experiment that they may have done before in a similar or more elementary form which renders them better informed so that they can do these things better. If they have not seen it, they may take two or three afternoons before they finally see what is going on and what they are supposed to do.

In these professors' perception, learning is a black box, and the solution is for students to expend time and effort. The professors do not expect to be able to explain what the learning task is in the way they expect to be able to explain the universe. Students' perceptions are more task-oriented, but as the following comments and dialog show, at the end of the introductory course students still display the characteristics of absolute knowing, where they think of knowledge as certain (Baxter Magolda, 1992), and they display a surface or reproducing orientation, without understanding (Ramsden, 1992).

I did do a lot of problems in high school but now I just don't have the time. To study for the midterm and the final I redid all the assignments and figured out how each one was done. Then I tried to memorize as many formulas as possible. I didn't rely on the formula sheet in the back of the exam; I felt it was inadequate. I did not read the book or the problems.

This course is from the same textbook, thank God.
Is the final exam 60 percent again?
Oh my—look when the midterm is! It's right after the spring break.
But that's the whole point, then we have time to study.
I can't believe you want to spend all your break studying.

There is actually quite a lot of stuff to learn, the course was very broad, there were a lot of equations; basically, if you can't name them off you are pretty much in trouble. If your background was weak this would be a very tough course.

Because physics is highly defined and developed compared with other fields of study, it might be expected that the learning task would be more clearly structured and immediate than in other disciplines. But the sheer weight of the theory and the fact that it is often counterintuitive mean that the learning pattern for students is intensive, requiring concentration to restructure knowledge. Physicists investigating student learning point out that in addition to having their students successfully learn concepts, they want them to develop a robust knowledge structure and a complex of mutually supporting skills and attitudes rather than a patchwork of ideas (Redish, Saul, & Steinberg, 1998). They want students to develop a strong understanding of what science is and how to do it, and the skills and confidence needed to do science themselves.

For students studying to become physicists, physics professors rate *logic*—defined as the ability to judge the strength and consistency of logical structures in physics—as a very important intellectual ability (Peltzer, 1988). Other abilities—mathematical insight, the ability to attack problems productively in a situation when many approaches are possible, and the ability to think in terms of visual images—are also considered important. Although there is a general expectation in the field that physics students will be able to think logically, our study of the learning task in physics suggested that learning physics also requires the ability to think independently and abstractly (Donald, 1993). For example, professors spoke of the need to understand abstract cause-and-effect relationships and to apply knowledge on the basis of abstract physics principles, although the principles derive their power from confirmation in the objective world. Independent and abstract thought are also necessary to situate physics principles and theories—that is, to recognize the appropriate context for their application.

Student attitudes are less frequently discussed by physics professors, but the general expectation is that students will perform like themselves—as scholars. In a typology of student roles, *scholars* expect to succeed, spend more time studying, and report improvement in their problem-solving skills and critical thinking ability (Astin, 1993). Our comparative studies across disciplines have shown that students in physics programs display these characteristics more often than students in other programs—for example, engineering students (Donald, 1999) or students in arts courses (Donald, 1995b). As the observation of students' experience learning physics shows, however, there is wide variability in their attitudes toward physics and in their understanding of the learning task. To determine more specifically what the discipline expects of students, we examined the concepts and thinking processes to be mastered in physics courses.

Nature of Concepts in Physics

Concepts, the elements of knowledge, are related to each other in a schema or framework that forms the knowledge structure or core content of a course. In physics there are, relatively speaking, many concepts to learn, and they require not only a definition but an understanding of their salient features, including an operational definition (Reif, 1983). In an analysis of physics textbooks, Prosser (1979) found that concepts such as *force* may be defined at both concrete and abstract levels. One of the professors I interviewed described a project initiated by Tobias (1988) in which professors from other disciplines attended introductory physics lectures and gave their outlook on the subject. These professors reported that they found physics difficult not because it was abstract but because it was a mixture of abstract and concrete. One described physics as having an extraordinary combination of the concrete and abstract: an abstract wave passes along a rope, yet the rope is concrete. At the same time resistance from the medium is abstract. The instructor's mind seemingly passes from the abstract to the concrete without effort, but in the nonphysicist's world there is nothing to prepare one for this automatic transition. If experts from other disciplines find the interchange between concrete and abstract unfamiliar, novice students are likely to find it bewildering.

There is a recognized need to provide entering students with a framework for understanding physics (diSessa, 1993; Halloun & Hestenes, 1985; Hammer, 1994, 1996; Mazur, 1997; Redish, Saul, & Steinberg, 1998; Reif, 1983). Reif suggests that physics concepts are building blocks that require substantial ancillary knowledge to make them usable or interpretable. The specification of a concept for Reif includes unambiguous identification, procedural specification in the form of step-by-step identification, application in various instances or cases, and discrimination about where not to use the concept. Learning physics requires a restructuring of knowledge to produce an internally consistent new paradigm (Vosniadou & Brewer, 1987). In research on processing scientific texts, both undergraduate students and experts considered physics definitions, which included explanation, to be more important than facts, which did not (Dee-Lucas & Larkin, 1984). These results confirm the emphasis on coherence.

In our examination of concepts in a general physics course on waves, we found that the majority of fifteen key concepts (53 percent) had technical rather than everyday meanings, and their dictionary definition was a less common one, rendering the learning task more difficult. Two-thirds of the concepts were presented enactively, however, meaning that students could see or experience them in operation, and each class began with a demonstration. For example, the most important concept, *wave shapes*, was presented by means of an oscilloscope so that students could actually see how the wave shapes changed. Other concepts in the course were presented in iconic form—that is, as images, for example *vibration amplitude*, or as symbols, as was *logarithmic response* (Figure 2.1). Thus although the concepts tended to be less familiar, they were presented in class in ways that rendered them immediate to the students, with perceptual referents, and were concrete (66 percent) more frequently than abstract. With this form of representation in class, comprehension

FIGURE 2.1. KEY CONCEPTS IN A
GENERAL PHYSICS COURSE ON WAVES

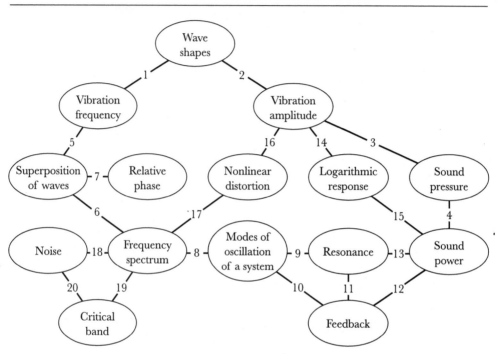

of the concepts would be aided by the mental imagery that relates to things and events familiar to students in their everyday environment (Hewitt, 1983).

More revealing, the concept map of key concepts in the course was hierarchical, with the most important concept, *wave shapes,* at the top of the hierarchy. *Wave shapes* was defined by the professor in part as the detailed time description of how the medium vibrates, the picture normally displayed by an oscilloscope connected to a microphone that is picking up a sound wave. Four additional levels of concepts were aligned below this one in order of importance and inclusiveness. The number of links between concepts (twenty) was higher than the average, with a link to concept ratio of 1.33 (twenty links between fifteen concepts), and there were more causal (40 percent) and procedural (25 percent) relationships between the concepts, suggesting closer relationships (Exhibit 2.1). For example, *sound power* is the result of *sound pressure* oscillations. These findings coincide with earlier research on learning physics that describes the interrelationships between concepts as constituting a significant part of the learning task, and shows concepts occurring in multiple kinds and levels of relationships (Johnson, 1967; Karplus, 1981).

EXHIBIT 2.1. RELATIONSHIPS BETWEEN
CONCEPTS IN A PHYSICS COURSE

Kind of Relationship (Number)	Example; Explanation
Similarity (6/20)	
Associative (1): Concepts are contiguous or descriptive of each other.	Noise and critical band; they are related in the phenomenon of masking in auditory perception.
Functional: Concepts have a similar outcome or purpose.	None in course.
Structural (5): Concepts have a taxonomic or hierarchical relationship such as subset, inclusion, kind of, or part of.	Wave shapes and vibration frequency; vibration frequency is a fundamental component of a wave shape description.
Dependency (14/20)	
Procedural (5): Concepts are ordered or sequenced as for steps, progression, or prerequisites.	Resonance and sound power; power is required to build up the energy of motion in a resonating system.
Logical (1): Concepts have a logical or conditional order.	Modes of oscillation of a system and resonance; the modes of oscillation of a system can be excited by resonance.
Causal (8): Concepts have an explicit cause-and-effect relationship.	Sound pressure and sound power; sound power is the result of propagation of sound pressure oscillations.

Our findings led us to conclude that the close interdependent relationships among the course concepts in the concept map would lead to an all-or-none learning pattern; that is, students would need to understand well the key concepts in a course in order to be able to use them (Donald, 1983). For example, in order to solve problems effectively, students would have to have an in-depth understanding of the concepts and their interrelationships. There is a high requirement for coherence or internal consistency. How do students go about learning physics concepts?

Learning Concepts in Physics

A fundamental notion in dealing with the physical world is that of agency or mechanism—a sense of how events occur or how things work, hence the importance of procedural or causal relationships between concepts. The explanation of how things work according to diSessa (1993) consists of two parts—the phenomena that occur under specific conditions, and the fundamental laws or principles that underlie them. Naive or novice physicists tend to explain physical occurrences in terms of primitive schema or mental models that lack the explanatory power of laws or principles but may resolve individual situations. For example, the notion of pushing objects harder to overcome their greater resistance may be based on the need to modulate one's effort. Learning physics is then a process of modification of these primitive schemas in weakly organized knowledge systems to a denser knowledge organization that allows application of a smaller but more powerful set of fundamental explanatory elements in principles or laws. Thus, one would evolve from a primitive or Aristotelian model in which objects themselves have resistance, to one in which different forces are found to act on an object.

When we asked physics professors what knowledge they expected students to develop in their courses, they tended to speak of the language students needed rather than address the explanatory principles to be developed. One professor pointed out that students may have heard the language but do not understand it, because the concepts are not in our day-to-day lives or general culture. They expected students to have acquired a specific physics vocabulary in their high school courses—for example, to know what is meant by distance, velocity, acceleration, force, molecule, and atom, and to know some mathematics. Students were expected to have the pieces but not the framework for explaining physical phenomena.

The topic of classical mechanics is usually introduced first based on the assumption that because people confront mechanics in their everyday lives, students will have a better chance of recognizing mechanics at work. One of the professors said:

> Physics is an empirical science, so you really need to relate the concepts to experiments. The experiment you do first is kick a ball, swing a bat—they have played baseball. They have more of that kind of experience than they have with optics or acoustics. Mechanics they have studied previously and they have some notions of it or they think they do.

Thus, a primary pedagogical strategy is to begin with familiar phenomena, so that students are ready to develop their own schemas. Do students view the learning process in the same way? At the end of the course, asked how successful they thought they had been in learning in the introductory course in classical mechanics, one student focused on the change in his conceptualization of physics:

> I wouldn't say I learned anything more, but I have gained a deeper knowledge of all the old stuff.

He would appear to have achieved a stage of transitional knowing—where the student's role is to understand knowledge. Another student pointed out that "physical phenomena need a new way of seeing things." Students are therefore building on a previously acquired vocabulary, but looking at it in greater depth and with a new perspective. The approach that students took to their studies had changed as well.

> In physics it's not enough for me to just go and read a book for five hours—I have to do the problems too, and lots of them. The whole way I approach this class is new.

> I find that by thinking more deeply than before about some of the problems I have to do I get through them. So I guess it's more in-depth concentration that I've learned.

In our research on student learning of concepts, we asked students at the beginning and end of term to define the key concepts. At the end of the course, we also asked them to produce a concept map of the key concepts. Students' definitions were scored according to the Wechsler Adult Intelligence Scale (WAIS) vocabulary subscale procedure. If students gave a definition that included the essential features of the definition as determined by the professor, they were given a score of 2. They were awarded a score of 1 for a definition that was not incorrect but showed a poverty of content—vagueness or an example—and 0 for a definition that was wrong, very vague, or trivial. Thus a total possible score in this course would be 30 for the fifteen key concepts. At the beginning of the course, the mean score for students was 5.2 or 17 percent; by the end of the course it had risen to 9.7 or 32 percent. Students' final grades in the course correlated with their key concept knowledge at the end of the course (.31), but more highly with the consistency of their key concept map to their professor's (.55), and with their overall average the previous year (.60).

The professor's stated intent in the course was that it was most essential for students to learn perspectives on the interrelationships of physics and psychophysics (the effect of a physical stimulus on sensation). Thus concept map consistency, which measures knowledge of relationships between concepts, was a better predictor of how well students fulfilled the intent of the course. When I asked the professor how he might explain the closer relationships between students' concept maps and general ability with course achievement in comparison with key concept knowledge, he replied that students in his course were not learning concepts so much as they were learning how to analyze and synthesize. Several of the physics professors in our studies suggested that students had to immerse themselves in problem solving in order to understand. Let us then examine how thinking processes are developed in physics.

The Development of Thinking Processes in Physics

The method of inquiry most frequently described in the physical sciences is problem solving. As noted in Chapter One, this is defined as a set of steps consisting of representing a problem, selecting the relations pertinent to solving the problem, doing the necessary calculations, and verifying if the final answer makes sense (Reif, Larkin, & Brackett, 1976). Student problem-solving ability is a major stumbling block in physics instruction. In memorably demoralizing instructional experiences, physics professors describe students who can produce graphs but cannot say what they mean, top students who can solve all the problems but cannot give an overview or simple derivation, and students of varying abilities who memorize without understanding despite carefully prepared lectures (Redish, 1994). Although physics students score higher than other students in their problem-solving ability (White & Ferstenberg, 1978), an average of 42 percent of students in one study were not capable of consistently using the reasoning skills required to understand the course textbook (Prosser, 1983).

In our studies, we asked professors to use the working model of thinking processes to describe what they were attempting to do in their courses (Exhibit 1.9). In the working model, problem solving encompasses all six groups of processes: description, selection, representation, inference, synthesis, and verification. To test the applicability of the model, nine professors gave their perceptions of how students learned to think in their physics courses: six introductory courses, a general course in astrophysics, an upper-level course in electromagnetism, and an advanced experimental course in nuclear physics. The most frequently referenced or salient thinking processes chosen by the professors to describe what occurred in their courses are reported.

Description

Many of the professors expected that students would come equipped with descriptive skills. The general expectation among professors was that students had the vocabulary but that they needed help in relating concepts. For example, one professor expected that students would already know how to describe a particular parameter or dimension, which suggested that students already had considerable familiarity with the subject area. Another stated that *defining the problem* is an elaborate description.

The professors often talked about identifying the context and stating assumptions as important descriptive processes. *Identifying the context* is a characteristic of expertise. It is a metacognitive or executive process that has a cueing or framing function, calling up a repertoire of experiences and strategies to be used (Donald, 1985). Our physics professors noted that many other skills depend on the creation of a framework for the problem (Exhibit 2.2). *Stating assumptions* was important because physics principles are abstracted from physical phenomena; therefore, what is assumed in any problem solution is critical to the steps and formulas used to solve it. The professors recognized that solutions to many problems depend on students' accurately *stating the conditions,* even though they may not be present in the problem statement. *Stating conditions* is an essential step in the scientific method to establish the inherent limits or scope of the problem.

Physics professors were less inclined to talk about *stating facts, functions,* and *goals.* They talked about stating facts and functions as skills students needed to write examinations, and they preferred to adopt an exploratory mode in which they and their students discovered the goals. However, most analyses of the problem-solving process in physics—for example, the Berkeley studies—focus on stating the facts and setting goals (Heller & Reif, 1982; Larkin & Reif, 1976; Reif, Larkin, & Brackett, 1976). Corroborating this approach, students we interviewed in our studies felt they needed to learn descriptive skills (Donald, 1993). The problem-solving strategy taught to students in the Berkeley studies began with the description of the problem, in which they were to list explicitly the given and desired information. It is a systematic approach to problem solving that encourages students

EXHIBIT 2.2. PROFESSORS' EXAMPLES OF DESCRIPTION USED IN PHYSICS COURSES

Identify context: Establish surrounding environment to create a total picture.	*Identifying the context serves to set up the general framework one is working in.*
State conditions: State essential parts, prerequisites, or requirements.	*Air resistance would be a common condition but this is often not stated in a problem.*
State facts: State known information, events that have occurred.	*Differentiate or discriminate between displacement and distance, and velocity and speed.*
State assumptions: State suppositions, postulates, propositions assumed.	*The assumption might be that you are going to suppress all the rest of the universe and examine only two objects— that the earth and the sun interact with one another, for example, and they interact by gravitational force.*

to examine a problem before blindly calculating, and serves as a basis for the more sophisticated strategies needed to solve complex problems (Reif, Larkin, & Brackett, 1976). Although our professors assumed that students would already have descriptive skills, they acknowledged their importance in the problem-solving process.

Selection

The term *abstraction* has been used to describe the process by which human beings behave or experience not in response to the total environment but to some particular features with the exclusion of others (see Humphrey, 1951). This has high survival value if critical features, rather than noncritical ones, are abstracted. Humphrey notes that the process involves the active neglect of irrelevancies, translated in the learning process as the elimination of errors. In the educational research literature, the process of selection is crucial to performance and is considered an essential learning skill (Sternberg, 1985a, 1998).

In practice, students are often unaware of the need to be selective and lack the strategies to discriminate important from less important material. Undergraduate students after a year of college-level coursework in physics failed to detect consistently the material in texts considered most important by experts (Dee-Lucas & Larkin, 1983). The second step in the problem-solving process advocated in the Berkeley studies was for students to select the basic relations pertinent for solving the problem (Reif, Larkin, & Brackett, 1976).

The processes of selection in the working model consist of *choosing information relevant* to the issue or problem, considering its *relative importance,* then *identifying critical elements and relations.* These processes are components of analytic thinking; in the taxonomy of educational objectives in the cognitive domain, identifying critical elements and relations are the first two steps of analysis (Bloom, 1956). Our professors recognized selection to be vital to the problem-solving process, particularly with ill-defined problems (Exhibit 2.3). They found choosing relevant information and identifying critical elements more appropriate to physics than *ordering information in importance,* which was downplayed because they said that in physics, information is considered to be either important or relevant or not in a problem solution. As in learning to think in general, the process of selecting relevant information is crucial to problem solving.

Representation

Einstein's work in theoretical physics was the product of interplay between concrete perceptual visualizations—imagining himself traveling along beside a beam of light—and the drive toward abstract principles of symmetry or invariance

EXHIBIT 2.3. PROFESSORS' EXAMPLES OF
SELECTION USED IN PHYSICS COURSES

Choose relevant information: Select information that is pertinent to the issue.	*If students choose* F = ma *when they really should be looking at conservation of linear momentum, they will be in trouble. Once they choose relevant information, the rest of the problem solving is arithmetic.*
Identify critical elements: Determine units, parts, components that are important.	*Where the masses and radii are given in different units, a student must learn to recognize this, and take them as an indication of how to solve the problem.*
Identify critical relations: Determine connections between things that are important.	*The first steps the students have to take are to identify the critical elements and relations in the problem-solving context in setting up the problem.*

(Shepard, 1978). Representing physical phenomena in different modes (enactive, iconic, symbolic) is basic to thinking in physics, and it was one of the most frequently described processes for solving physics problems or for demonstrating in class (Exhibit 2.4). Representation organizes experience into a framework. Experts spend more time determining how to represent problems than searching for and executing a problem strategy (Larkin, McDermott, Simon, & Simon, 1980). This reflects the importance of its role in cognitive processing.

Representations result from analysis, and therefore vary depending on the method of analysis used to produce them, the amount of structure assumed in the discipline, and the degree to which they are descriptive or goal-oriented (Donald, 1987). The physical sciences are described as hard disciplines because they assume a strong schema such as a general theory in which laws or principles relate cause and effect. The representation of key concepts in the physics course (Figure 2.1) is consistent with this description—it was hierarchical, with a greater number of links between concepts than there were concepts, and more causal or procedural relationships than in other courses.

The professors considered the process of *recognizing organizing principles* fundamental to physics (Exhibit 2.4). The assumption of a strong schema means that, in the example, *organizing elements and relations* produces an accurate answer in the mathematical sense, not an approximation. Professors and students are expected to *illustrate elements and relations* in their graphs or diagrams. Drawing a diagram of the situation is part of the first step in solving a problem (Reif, Larkin, & Brackett, 1976). In contrast, *modifying elements and relations* appeared to be an advanced skill, expected more of upper-level students and in research activities. Representation was thus central to thinking and problem solving in physics.

EXHIBIT 2.4. PROFESSORS' EXAMPLES OF
REPRESENTATION USED IN PHYSICS COURSES

Recognize organizing principles: Identify laws, methods, rules that arrange in a systematic whole.	*In astrophysics, there are many organizational laws, such as Kepler's laws, laws of areas, conservation of energy, conservation of angular momentum, and so on.*
Organize elements and relations: Arrange parts, connections between things into a systematic whole.	*Students must figure out how to put a problem together: analyzing the information, the problem to be solved, the tools available.*
Illustrate elements and relations: Make clear by examples the parts, connections between things.	*Represent a vibration in some manner that allows you to work with the representation and then interpret the representation to tell what the vibration is doing.*
Modify elements and relations: Change, alter, or qualify the parts, connections between things.	*Modify the conditions in which a system is operating and be able to predict the behavior.*

Inference

Inference—drawing conclusions from premises or evidence—has explanation as its goal; inductive and deductive logic and reasoning are also used to describe inferential processes. There is evidence that introductory physics courses test deductive logic more than inductive, but both contribute to achievement (Enyeart, Baker, & Vanharlingen, 1980). Reasoning is tested via experimentation.

Several of the inferential processes in the model focus on the discovery of new kinds of relations, inherent in the experimental process. However, an example of *discovering new relations between elements,* inferring small mass from high acceleration of an electron, requires deductive logic, not normally a strength of entering university students (Exhibit 2.5). Philosophers of science have tended to separate the context of discovery, as hypothesis generation, from the context of criticism, hypothesis testing (Clement, 1982). Clement examined experts' use of analogy, defined in the model of thinking processes as *discovering new relations between relations,* by asking professors or advanced doctoral students to give a scientific explanation of unfamiliar phenomena. They responded using two methods. One was conservative, to modify or transform an aspect of the problem that was previously assumed to be fixed. The other method was more revolutionary, to make an associative leap to another situation that differed in many ways from the problem posed, recalling a more remote analogy from memory. One of our professors suggested that *discovering relations between relations* shows the unity of physics.

EXHIBIT 2.5. PROFESSORS' EXAMPLES OF
INFERENCE USED IN PHYSICS COURSES

Discover new relations between elements: Detect or expose connections among parts, units, components.	*If students calculate that the acceleration of an electron is very, very high, then they must infer that the mass of the electron must be very, very small.*
Discover new relations between relations: Detect or expose connections between connections of things.	*Analogy shows the unity of physics—students learn that the law concerning electric current flow and the laws of heat flow are the same.*
Change perspective: Alter view, vista, interrelations, significance of facts or information.	*How you view a problem is an extremely important part of solving it. If students choose coordinate systems that have the symmetry of the problem at hand, this helps them see in the most transparent way what is taking place.*
	In astronomy, you must get used to viewing the earth as just one planet in the larger context of the universe.
Hypothesize: Suppose or form a proposition as a basis for reasoning.	*The student is asked to think in a "what-if" manner.*

Categorizing and *ordering* did not evoke much comment from the professors but were considered essential inferential processes. *Changing perspective* was important for simplifying a problem as a way of solving it. For physicists, it appears to be similar to making an associative leap, and could thus be defined as part of the discovery process. Our professors also described *hypothesizing* as a discovery process: What if? All of the inferential processes attempt explanation of phenomena by either expanding or contracting the context of the problem. For our physics professors, the most important inferential thinking processes, because they were the most powerful in the discipline, were *discovering new relations* and *changing perspective*.

Synthesis

In a field that enunciates the goal of unified theory, although not all physicists seek it, synthesis is highly important but is perceived to be beyond the capabilities of the undergraduate student. Examples of synthesis given by the professors were those of experts in the field such as Maxwell's equations (Exhibit 2.6). They suggested, however, that students would be examined on their ability to deduce a certain outcome from assumptions, a matter of inference rather than synthesis. The taxonomy of cognitive objectives describes synthesis as requiring students to draw upon elements from

EXHIBIT 2.6. PROFESSORS' EXAMPLES OF
SYNTHESIS USED IN PHYSICS COURSES

SYNTHESIS: Composition of parts or elements into a complex whole	*Maxwell's equations represent a tremendous synthesis of physical behavior, extending from X rays through light and through electric and magnetic fields and phenomena that appear totally dissimilar. It includes all of optics, for example.*
Combine parts to form a whole: Join, associate elements, components into a system or pattern.	*Find the system or pattern that underlies all vibrations.*
Elaborate: Work out, complete with great detail, exactness, or complexity.	*If we have a difficult problem, we make several approximations that eliminate the effect of certain parameters to simplify in order to do a calculation. Then we introduce the effect of another parameter and start putting things together to make it more realistic until it approaches experience.*
Generate missing links: Produce or create what is lacking in a sequence, fill in the gap.	*We look at missing links and generate ideas in a lab with data, and worry how these data relate to knowledge of the subject.*
Develop course of action: Work out or expand the path, route, or direction to be taken	*We plot a path through a research situation.*

many sources and to put these together into a structure or pattern not there be-fore (Bloom, 1956). This is contrasted with analysis in which one works with a given set of materials that constitutes a whole in order to understand it better.

The physics professors saw several applications of synthesis in their courses. Problem solving, for example, requires students to *combine parts to form a whole.* The process is also important in recognizing systems or patterns, similar to represen-tation. *Elaboration* was needed for the solution of difficult problems. The labora-tory was a venue for synthesis in *generating missing links,* and *developing a course of action* was essential for problem solving and in research. Thus the professors questioned student capabilities for synthesizing, but at the same time acknowledged that the processes were necessary for problem solving and research.

Verification

Verification was regarded as an important skill, but also one that professors thought might be beyond the scope of entering students, often because of time pressure. One of our professors pointed out that his goal would be to lead students to function rather than verify, because verification can be seen as sterile and counter-productive. Even though it is a step in the scientific method, it supposes absolute rather than contextual knowing. A further problem with expecting students to verify their work in a discipline that requires proof by matching evidence to systematic theorizing is that students at the undergraduate level have not yet acquired the necessary theoretical framework to guide their inquiry. In a discipline where the process of validation is most different from lay activity (Thompson, Hawkes, & Avery, 1969), a novice will not yet have developed the capability of confirming the accuracy or consistency of results. Instead, a form of procedural validation is taught to undergraduates in which they check that each step in the problem-solving process is valid and the final answer makes sense (Reif, Larkin, & Brackett, 1976)

Our professors focused on the role of empirical evidence in verification (Exhibit 2.7). They also noted that when theory is taken to be more important than physical evidence, and results do not match the theory, the expectation is that procedural errors led to the discrepancy. In *comparing alternative outcomes,* the question of

EXHIBIT 2.7. PROFESSORS' EXAMPLES OF VERIFICATION USED IN PHYSICS COURSES

Compare alternative outcomes: Examine similarities or differences of results, consequences.	*Newton's laws do not give us the right answer. Why not? There may be various alternatives. Perhaps you have gone to very high masses, or to very small velocities, and you must make appropriate corrections. So you are then dealing with relativity or quantum mechanics.*
Compare outcome to standard: Examine similarities, differences of results based on a criterion.	*The student must find the masses of certain planets, given certain pieces of data, and then verify the results with the quoted masses in the text.*
Judge validity: Critically examine the soundness, effectiveness by actual fact.	*Does this mathematical relationship produce a physically plausible result? Mechanics is taught first because that is where students have more physical intuition.*
	Have you reproduced what the physical world shows you happens every day?
Use feedback: Employ results to regulate, adjust, adapt.	*Researchers may see that something does not work and have to come back and try it again, adjust and adapt.*
Confirm results: Establish or ratify conclusions, effects, outcomes, or products.	*We do this with dimensional analysis or by checking that the numbers are reasonable using rough approximations.*

what theory provides the best explication shows the need to bootstrap; that is, to find the most applicable theory to explain results. *Standards* are supplied by procedures, known measures, and acceptable ranges or limits—a variety of checks. One professor pointed out that another reason they begin by teaching mechanics is that students have a better sense of the limits or plausibility of results in mechanics as a result of their prior experience, thereby aiding them to *judge the validity* of results. *Using feedback* was more an instructional device in problem solving or assignments, but it had universal application in research. The professors saw the possibility of *confirming results* in various ways, through analysis or mathematical approximations, by using instruments such as a telescope and interactively to improve theories. In each example, the respondents made reference to the validation process of matching theory with evidence. Thus they maintained their emphasis on measuring and the empirical (Adler, 1982; Scheffler, 1965).

In summary, the most important thinking processes students need to learn in their physics courses focus on the problem-solving process. Important descriptive processes were *identifying the context* to create a framework for understanding a problem, *stating assumptions* because what is assumed in a problem solution is critical to the steps used to solve it, and *stating conditions* to establish the limits of the problem. Selection is vital to the problem-solving process, particularly with ill-defined problems, as is representation, with experts spending more time determining how to represent a problem than executing a problem strategy. The most important inferential thinking processes, considered discovery processes, were *changing perspective*, for simplifying a problem as a way of solving it, and *hypothesizing* because these processes either expand or contract the context of the problem. Problem solving requires synthesis, particularly *developing a course of action*. Verification processes center on matching theory with evidence. Thus the important thinking processes to be developed are those needed in the problem-solving process, and students are taught procedures to verify their work.

The Challenge of Instruction in Physics

We have seen how students experience learning physics and how physics professors describe its knowledge structures and thinking processes. The question that arises next is, What are the optimal instructional processes for learning physics? Three instructional issues are evident. Because physics is a hard, structured area of study, consisting of strong schemas, principles, or laws, the first issue is how to help students develop the conceptual framework needed. The second is a more general issue of how to improve the ability to problem-solve. Given the lack of student awareness of how to learn physics, the third instructional issue is how to enlighten students about the approach needed to learn successfully in this discipline.

Development of a Conceptual Framework

A student who is working physics problems without a conceptual understanding of physics has been likened to a deaf person writing music or a blind person painting (Hewitt, 1983). Hewitt recommends that students be taught to conceptualize—to conjure a mental image of a physical interaction, process, or concept, to describe it verbally and symbolically, and to distinguish it from other related concepts—before they are taught to compute. There is a marked difference between the expectation among physics professors that students are to gain understanding and whether students actually do (White et al., 1995). White asked first-year students, "When you say you understand physics, what sort of things are you saying you can do?" In response, they talked about being able to explain, but laboratory classes and reports were the only places where they felt the act of explaining was important. No student said that explaining was an important part of problem work or tests.

Although the notions of student misperceptions or preconceptions have frequently been used to describe student learning difficulties in physics, a more enlightening statement of the situation is that most students lack an appropriate mental model for learning physics. In this they do not differ from students in other disciplines (Tobias, 1988). Redish (1994) reports that the most common mental model for learning in his classes is the dead leaves model: Students first write down every equation or law the teacher puts on the board that is also in the text and then memorize them together with the list of formulas at the end of each chapter. Each formula is a dead leaf, and the students' strategy is to sort through their collection to find the appropriate equation for the problem at hand. The second step is to do enough homework and problems to recognize which formula is to be applied to which problem. The third step is to pass the exam by selecting the correct formulas for the problems on the exam, and the fourth is to erase all information from their brains after the exam to make room for the next set of material.

To change this model of learning, Redish suggests that the idea of having students do enough problems will not work, because they are likely to learn to do them automatically using the same erroneous model of learning. Instead he recommends active learning, in which students reorganize their material and pose questions for themselves to answer. Recognizing that it is difficult to learn something we do not almost already know, the instructional strategy of choice is to represent content in coherent and accessible mental models by modifying and extending an existing model. Because students learn by analogy, using touchstone problems that students will reference continually is crucial; these can then be linked to provide the necessary conceptual framework or story line. Redish also recommends giving exam credit for reasoning. The rationale is that to promote understanding, new forms of class activities that promote the organization of content, as well as assessment that requires students to explain concepts and phenomena, are needed.

One approach to creating a mental model in physics is based on the notion of conceptual exchange, considered appropriate in a discipline where there is a major conflict between lay and expert mental models—between Aristotelian and Newtonian physics, or between Newtonian and Einsteinian physics (Pines & West, 1986). Conceptual exchange demands a major shift in framework. The process consists of strategies in three phases. The first phase is *awareness;* this involves experiential and clarification activities and discussion to elicit and compare competing points of view. For example, a set of physics problems on Newton's second law, $a = F/m$, is followed by student-teacher dialogue in which students find that new information and phenomena cannot be integrated into their existing frameworks on the effect of gravity. In the second phase, *disequilibrium,* anomalies or discrepant events are introduced and students are guided to articulate inconsistencies between the events they are observing and their own frameworks. In the third phase, students *reformulate* their frameworks, but Pines and West warn that the scientific theories offered as alternatives must be seen by them to be relevant and useful.

Examples of the new framework must be compelling to the student, as well as analogically extend the existing physical framework. Analogical relations may need to be explicitly developed with models that can be visualized; on the other hand, concrete models may be ineffective if unaccompanied by explanation that provides a mechanism for understanding the phenomenon (Brown, 1992). All of these suggestions imply considerable focused instructional attention to the conceptualization of physical phenomena.

Specific training in understanding that uses programmed instruction has proven effective in helping students grapple with unfamiliar relations. First-year undergraduates given text and a problem set on the gravitational force law as well as programmed instruction to teach them how to understand a relation significantly increased their understanding of the law (Larkin & Reif, 1976; Reif, Larkin, & Brackett, 1976). The programmed instruction consisted of a series of abilities, beginning with characterizing the relation by stating it, giving an example of its application, and listing the properties of quantities in the relation, similar to the descriptive thinking process in the working model. The second ability was to interpret the relation by using symbolic representations. Third, students were to discriminate between relevant and irrelevant information, and situations where the relation did and did not apply, and to discriminate each quantity in the relation from other quantities, and the relation from other relations. Finally, they were to use equivalent forms of the relation to find and compare values. This extensive set of abilities that make up the act of understanding a relation illuminate the level of intellectual demand on students. The abilities require the thinking processes of description, selection, representation, and inference. Once learned, the students were able to apply the method successfully to new relations to be learned.

Among instruments that have been developed to test students' understanding of mechanics, the most frequently referenced is the *Force Concept Inventory* (Hestenes, Wells, & Swackhammer, 1992). In it, students are tested for their understanding of the concept of force; scores on the inventory correlate with a deep approach to learning for college students (Dickie, 1994). Dickie found that over two semesters of instruction, students' scores on the inventory increased significantly. Greater gains in conceptual understanding were also found in courses that used interactive engagement methods, where students participated in conceptual exercises in which they explicitly thought through problems (Hake, 1998). Debate over the use of the inventory to measure student understanding led one physicist to state that it should inform instructors by providing an alternate lens through which to consider student progress (Hammer, 1995). Hammer suggests that instructors need to interview students about their knowledge and reasoning, so that a culture of inquiry is developed in the discipline to aid in understanding how to teach and learn physics.

Improving the Ability to Problem Solve

In problem-solving theory, the problem space consists of the problem solver's representation of the structure of facts, concepts, and their interrelationships that make up the problem (Frederiksen, 1984; Newell & Simon, 1972). Hence the conceptual framework of the student will limit or constrain problem solving. Students who organize and apply their knowledge on the basis of physics principles are better problem solvers (Chi & Bassok, 1988; Zajchowski, 1991). They generate more statements that relate a problem to appropriate principles, and they reflect much greater concern for the accurate representation of the problem. The question then becomes how to help students apply their conceptual framework in the act of problem solving.

Linking changes in conceptual understanding with problem solving may necessitate major restructuring of the course format. In the examples of problem solving given by the professors, they tended to talk about how *they* solved problems in class but rarely about pedagogical strategies for guiding their students' problem-solving process. The most direct response to this pedagogical dilemma is to present a model strategy for problem solving in class, then the solution (Leonard,

Dufresne, & Mestre, 1996). The strategy portion of the sample problem serves as a vehicle for discussing the application of concepts in solving problems. In presenting a strategy, the professor discusses the principles and procedures needed to solve the problem but also attempts to relate ideas from different parts of the course. For Leonard, Dufresne, and Mestre, model strategies consist of three components: (1) the major principles or concepts that can be applied to solve the problem; (2) a justification for why the principles or concepts can be applied; and (3) the procedure by which they can be applied to solve the problem—the what, why, and how of problem solution. Students are encouraged to ask questions during the lecture, many on the strategies, and also to strategize problems before attempting to solve them. Homework solutions are posted on the bulletin board and in the library, and contain clearly labeled strategies and solutions for every problem assigned.

When students in the course were asked to write strategies on their own in an examination, one-third wrote very good strategies, another third wrote reasonably good strategies that showed substantial understanding, and the remaining third displayed major weaknesses in understanding. All of the students' strategies had diagnostic value; they provided the instructors with detailed accounts of the students' conceptual difficulties and what they focus on while solving problems. Students could then be provided with specific feedback to improve their strategies. In comparison with students taught in the traditional manner, who were able to identify correct principles 48 percent of the time, students in the strategies class achieved success 70 percent of the time. Moreover, the weakest problem solvers in the strategies class selected the appropriate principle 85 percent more often than their counterparts in the traditional class, suggesting that the instructional procedure works for less well prepared students. Because of these findings, the instructors decided to require strategy writing for homework and on examinations. At the end of the course, students stated that strategy writing helped them understand what was going on.

Let us examine more closely each step in problem solving for purposes of instruction. The first step is problem description, which depends specifically on the students' having a conceptual framework and strategies for determining the major principles or concepts that can be applied to solve the problem. The problem description can be modeled in class but the underlying processes of identifying the context and stating conditions and assumptions need to be labeled by the instructor. As one student told us:

> He doesn't highlight the important aspects of the problems he does. It's like he does a problem for us in class, but doesn't tell us what's what, and so then you get the homework assignment home, and it's like "What do I do?" It makes the assignments very difficult.

Students need to be walked through the process of selecting the relevant information and governing principles, then illustrating how they are related. Specific training in justifying the principles and relations would include interpreting relations, stating why the relation applied, and why that relation rather than another (Reif, Larkin, & Brackett, 1976). These inferential processes are then brought together in the procedure for solving the problem—the course of action needed to implement the plan and do the necessary calculations. The method of verification professors suggested most frequently was for students to ask themselves if the answer they get is reasonable—that is, plausible or within expected limits. Verification procedures also need to be modeled and explained for students if they are to apply them. What is needed is stage-by-stage formation of the thinking processes (van Weeren et al., 1982).

As with problem-based learning, the role of the instructor then becomes to guide, motivate, and probe students' thinking processes (Allen, Duch, & Groh, 1996). In problem-based learning, problems are introduced with mini-lectures that provide context and point out potential pitfalls and blind alleys. The mini-lectures are selected to provoke, puzzle, and surprise. Students are assigned to permanent working groups of four to seven members that function for the length of the course. The value of groups is described by one of the first-year students in our study who had been asked if anything in particular contributed to her learning in the course.

> We have to do assignments about things after we've done the theory. The assignments are always harder than the examples he gives us in class—I saw the prof for help with the assignments sometimes as often as three times a week. And we worked in a group to do the assignments; and we'd work hard all week just to do this one assignment. This prof was good. Yeah, so it was friends working together, his help, and lots of work that contributed so far. I mean, the in-class work isn't enough, you have to do more and work with friends.

The professor in this course acknowledged the importance of this way of studying and thinking for students.

> When you start a class like this, the students rapidly break into study groups. So essentially they work together. I encourage them to collaborate on the assignments. I tell them, "Spend some time doing it on your own, don't spend two hours working on a problem—that's hopeless, spend twenty to thirty minutes working on a problem, and then if you're stuck go and talk to somebody, discuss among yourselves." These channels have evolved since the beginning of the class, because the students know each other a lot better. There is more of a discussion group actually going on. I can tell as well in class.

These examples highlight the effect of strategies and shared effort in the problem-solving process. In problem-based learning, wrap-up discussions after each problem are used to clarify any remaining questions and to make connections with past problems and identify major principles. The change in role of the instructor is part of the broader approach needed to help students learn physics.

The Approach Needed to Learn Successfully

Where teachers aim to challenge students' conceptions or understanding of the world, and focus on facilitating understanding, students display a deep approach to studying, in which they seek meaning rather than a reproductive attitude, where they endeavor to survive by attending to surface features (Trigwell, Prosser, Ramsden, & Martin, 1998). Orientation to learning and conceptual understanding are linked. For example, students who adopt a deep approach to studying physics draw concept maps with more accurately related concepts (Hegarty-Hazel & Prosser, 1991). But the disciplinary proclivity in science is for professors to lecture, use examinations that require only fragmented knowledge, and distance themselves from their students (Milem & Astin, 1994). This conduct is congruent with their roles as scholars and researchers; lectures mirror the research presentation process. For conceptual understanding and the development of thinking, however, instructional strategies are needed to involve students in classroom discussion, cooperative learning, and other forms of active learning.

In *Peer Instruction,* Mazur (1997) describes how his desire to transfer the excitement of doing science to others and the frustration he saw his students' experience led him to develop an interactive teaching method that engages students by testing their conceptual understanding in a nonthreatening, collaborative process. He first provides a brief presentation on the subject to be discussed. Next, he poses a conceptual question on the subject and asks students to record their individual answer and their confidence in their answer. They then have to convince their neighbor of their answer and record the revised answer. He asks for a tally of answers and takes the time necessary to explain the correct answer so that students understand the concept being developed. Because this active testing format takes one-third of class time, he supplies students with lecture notes at the beginning of the term and asks them to read textbook and notes before coming to class. These methods help students to develop a model or representation of their subject rather than bits of information, as in the dead leaves model.

Parallel to the approach that instructors take is the attitude toward or expectations of learning that students bring to class. Students enter postsecondary education rarely having thought about their capacity to learn or how they did it, and interpret "learning well" as working hard or doing what is needed to obtain a good examination result (White et al., 1995). In research on students' perceptions of learning physics, when students were asked how they go about learning, only 21 percent gave replies that referred to seeking understanding—seeing how principles work or discussing with other students (Prosser, Walker, & Millar, 1996). Few (4 percent) considered physics to be a process of developing models and a language to describe physical phenomena. Instead, students frequently arrive in physics courses thinking that physics is a collection of isolated pieces rather than a coherent system, that physics knowledge is about formulas rather than concepts and principles, and that learning physics is about receiving and storing information from authorities rather than about being responsible for and actively constructing their own understanding (Hammer, 1995; Redish, Saul, & Steinberg, 1998). Even when students have an expectation of coherence, it is difficult for them to synthesize their knowledge, as a student at the end of one of our physics courses noted:

> It's been a very rewarding semester; I feel like I've learned a lot of new stuff. But what I learned—the knowledge—hasn't come together, it's still all in bits and pieces.

This student values finding answers for herself, but at the same time recognizes that she has not yet developed a framework for understanding her coursework. Hammer (1995) recommends that instructors temporarily subordinate traditional content-oriented plans to the epistemological objectives of having students think for themselves, understanding physics as involving their own knowledge and experience, and recognizing the importance of coordinating and reconciling alternative ways of thinking. To assist students in achieving these objectives, he has them experiment and debate their findings to conceptualize them, thus focusing on concepts, coherence, and their active construction of physics principles.

In order to examine students' epistemologies about learning physics, Redish, Saul, and Steinberg (1998) created a survey of students' expectations using the dimensions developed by Hammer and introducing three others. The first was a reality link (that physics concepts are relevant and useful), the second a math link (that math is a convenient way of representing physical phenomena), and the third, effort (that students think carefully and evaluate what they are doing). Tested in introductory courses and compared with experts, students' views were substantially less favorable than those of the experts, with their views on concepts being the least favorable; that is, more than half considered that physics knowledge is about formulas rather than concepts and principles. More threatening, students' views over the semester deteriorated, with effort and the reality link showing the most widespread deterioration. The message is that teachers need to redefine their learning contract with students; students need to be told at the beginning of their college experience that they are expected to make the effort to understand, and that assignments and grading will reflect this approach to learning.

The research on student approaches to learning suggests numerous recommendations for improving instruction that require smaller classes and more interactive lectures. It provides evidence that continued attention needs to be paid to the pedagogy of physics, and that both professors and students need to be aware of the complexity of learning physics and the applicable learning strategies. To accomplish these goals will require early academic orientation activities for students; attitudinal goals need to be considered as part of their introduction to the discipline. In parallel, professorial attitudes of impersonality need to be reconsidered so that the reality of physics is imparted. Recognizing that motivation is essential to learning, Mazur (1997) takes the time to have students consider and discuss what they hope to learn in his course and what they hope to do with their new knowledge. He ensures an atmosphere of cooperation in the class, uses an absolute (criterion-based) grading scale, and provides worksheets that allow students to track their progress in the course.

Optimal conditions for learning include the use of strategies that alert students to the concepts or principles to be discussed—for example, specifying learning goals by asking what would happen in a particular situation, then remarking that that is what they are going to investigate in class (Ferguson & de Jong, 1991). Strategies for helping students create their own frameworks include specifying main issues, confronting or evaluating, relating and formulating expectations, and posing questions that require an answer from students. Pedagogical links have to be established between concepts, principles, and the problems to be solved. The literature on problem-based learning suggests how to organize instruction. Strategies that are useful to students working in groups may need to be spelled out. For example, students may require help in distributing tasks, questioning each other, and resolving disagreements (Barden & Pugh, 1993). Professors may need to devote time and energy to delineate the group process and facilitate group work in their program. What is most striking about learning in this paradigmatic discipline is that it is not easier than in other disciplines, nor does it naturally follow from students' previous learning experiences. This makes it all the more important to focus on student understanding and get frequent feedback from students about the development of their conceptual framework and their learning and thinking strategies.

The Disciplinary Perspective in Physics

In the Preface, three questions were raised to guide consideration of how to promote students' intellectual development in each discipline. The first concerns the kind of learning environment the discipline provides. The second asks what higher-order thinking processes we want students in our disciplines to learn. The third question concerns the optimal ways of cultivating these thinking processes. As the prototypical discipline, physics provides a place of scholarly prestige and high intellectual demand. Although highly abstract questions about the nature of the universe lead inquiry in physics, because it is a convergent, well-organized discipline there is a sense of epistemological solidarity. The environment of the physics student is circumscribed and specified by the number of hours required to navigate physics and mathematics courses successfully, especially the time spent doing problem sets and studying for tests. Because of the high demand on their time and the difficulty of the tasks, students are advised to work in study groups that often become the social as well as intellectual focus of their lives. At the same time, a higher level of resources in the discipline—more research grants and a favorable student-faculty ratio—is reflected in smaller classes and easier access to professors.

Physicists want students to develop a robust knowledge structure and a complex set of mutually supporting skills and attitudes as scholars. The ability to judge the strength and consistency of logical structures, to abstract, and to think in terms of visual images, are important higher-order thinking processes to be developed. Deductive thinking and problem solving describe these processes. Important to problem solving are, first, *identifying the context* or framework for the problem, *stating assumptions* and *conditions* to establish the limits of the problem, *selecting elements and relations* in problems, and *representing* the problem space. Inference expands or contracts the context of the problem. Problem solving requires *developing a course of action* and verifying to match theory with evidence. Thus in physics the thinking processes to be developed are those needed for problem solving—all of the major processes in the working model.

Optimal instructional processes are needed to help students develop a conceptual framework, improve their ability to problem-solve, and develop a more general approach to learning. Class activities that promote the organization of content by means of conceptual questions requiring students to discuss and infer, and assessment that requires students to explain concepts and phenomena, help students develop conceptual frameworks. A powerful instructional process is to help students understand model strategies for solving problems that include a justification for why principles or concepts are applied and the procedure by which they can be applied to solve the problem, then posting homework solutions. The optimal role of an instructor is to be a guide who motivates and probes students' thinking processes. To promote positive learning attitudes, instructors need to take the time to have students consider what they hope to learn in their courses, model and organize how to work cooperatively, and help students track their progress so that they become responsible for their own learning.

CHAPTER THREE

HARD THINKING:
Applying Structured Knowledge
to Unstructured Problems

It is more than trying to teach students to solve well-posed problems, because ultimately they are going to have to solve ill-posed problems—that is, where there is too little or too much information.

STRUCTURAL MECHANICS PROFESSOR

What is the difference between learning a pure and an applied physical science? Engineering uses the theory and vocabulary of pure science but applies it in a professional or practical milieu. The structural mechanics professor in this quotation describes the instructional challenge: engineers deal with unbounded problems and must set the limits of their problem space; differential calculus is foundational. Applied physical sciences could be expected to develop thinking processes similar to those developed in physics, with a primary emphasis on problem solving. But to what extent are the deductive thinking skills needed to work from theory to phenomenon in a pure science relevant in an applied science? Conversely, are thinking processes in an applied science going to be inductive, moving from examples to the general case, or deductive? Does means-end thinking better describe the process? What is the effect of the engineering profession on the curriculum? If applied science phenomena have ill-defined parameters and the methods to study the phenomena are diverse, what does this mean for student learning?

As an applied science, engineering must meet society's needs for design and systems (Sparkes, 1989). In a study of quality in engineering education, Sparkes suggests the need to draw a distinction between engineering and other university subjects in content, purpose, and process. A key difference between scientific processes and engineering processes is that scientific processes are concerned with the analysis, generalization, and synthesis of hypotheses, while engineering processes are involved with the analysis and synthesis of designs, where one reaches decisions based on incomplete data and approximate models. To understand how students become engineers, I first explore the development of the field of engineering, then students' experience in an engineering course. I examine the concepts and thinking processes that students are expected to develop in their programs and what it takes to succeed. Eighteen professors and their students, forty-five of whom participated in interviews, helped to clarify the nature of the learning task. Major instructional concerns are how to help students gain problem-solving ability and design skills. The application of these skills in the industrial milieu also merits attention.

The Disciplinary Context in Engineering

Engineering education developed in response to the needs of the technology-based, industrial corporation (Chandler, 1977; Goldman, 1992; Noble, 1977). Much as the physical sciences responded to the needs of industry, engineering programs responded to a societal demand for engineers to work in growing corporations. By 1985, 80 percent of engineers in the United States were employed in private industries dominated by large corporations in aerospace, defense, energy, electronics, computers, transportation, chemicals, and communication (National Science Foundation, 1986). One-third of engineers were in the defense industry, directly or through subcontracts. A considerable amount of technological activity in the United States is driven by the economics, practices, and performance-driven design values of military applications of science and engineering (Goldman, 1992).

Engineering education must thus be viewed in relation to the global demand for increased technological expertise. This demand creates a tension between industry and education that affects the learning context. For example, recruitment into the profession follows a very different pattern from that in physics. Starting salaries in industry for engineers with a bachelor's degree tend to be more attractive than the financial prospects for graduates of doctoral programs (Becher, 1989). This leads to difficulties in recruitment to graduate education and to correlated shortages of faculty, a general symptom in high-demand technical fields (Fairweather, 1989). Historically, a large percentage of engineers have moved from engineering into management, further weakening the level of expertise available for the education of future engineers but strengthening the industrial-corporate link.

Consequently, in engineering programs there is a continual tug-of-war between the theoretical and the professional. Although research funding in engineering was slower to develop than in the pure sciences, with networks of centers forming only in the 1980s, they have contributed to the conflict (Kash, 1987). The development of research networks supported the trend in schools of engineering to become more theoretical, based on the rationale that change in technology is so rapid that students need a firm foundation in the basic sciences and mathematics. In turn, graduates complain that their undergraduate education was oriented toward postgraduate degrees rather than the workplace, but they also recognize that they received a solid grounding in the fundamentals of engineering (Donald & Denison, 1996).

Does it take a particular disposition to become an expert in this field? Engineering professors have an image of practicality and pragmatism; they are respected as being in touch with reality (Becher, 1989). The image of physics professors is that they live their lives in their laboratories, but engineers display a more diverse pattern: some may be totally absorbed in their work, others consider it important to know when to stop. Engineering specializations—mechanical, chemical, electrical, civil, and computer—add to the diversity. Road construction requires a different set of skills from those needed for robotics. According to Becher, although they may appear to others to be conservative and conformist, engineers tend to think of themselves as hardworking, stable introverts. They extend this view of themselves to their students, whom they see as not very outgoing, burdened by the weight of their course material. They explain their cautious introversion by the need to ensure that what they produce is useful and safe; failures such as bridges falling down are matters of public concern.

Creativity and inventiveness are more descriptive of engineers than the ability to communicate; succinctness rather than elaboration describes the verbal modus operandi of engineers. At the hard end of the disciplinary spectrum, like physicists engineers tend to write in a highly compressed quantitative code for other engineers rather than for outsiders to the discipline. They tend to be more entrepreneurial and cosmopolitan, however, than other academics, because they must attend to the values of the profession (Milem & Astin, 1994). They are more aware of economic life than physicists, if still relatively insulated from the voracious aspects of the market.

The prime function of engineering is to generate products and product-oriented techniques, therefore a broader set of skills is expected to be learned than the focused problem-solving skills of physics. Engineering processes and skills, manual and intellectual, are learned mainly through practice. Reasoning skills rated most important or critical for engineering graduates include breaking down complex problems into simpler ones, reasoning or problem solving in situations where all the needed information is not known, and identifying all the variables involved in a problem (Powers & Enright, 1987). The most dangerous error noted by engineers is applying a formula, algorithm, or other rule without sufficient justification. The knowledge and skills needed in engineering therefore reflect both a high degree of theoretical structure and the procedures and strategies for applying them.

The resulting curriculum problem is to find the time to fit all that must be learned into a limited period—usually four years. There is continual pressure to expand the length of the program. An accompanying problem is to recruit students with the necessary background in science and mathematics. There is also pressure to ensure some exposure to the humanities and social sciences, to ethics and communication skills. According to one of the engineering professors in our study, industry has been asking more and more of university programs—they want students to know all about occupational health and safety, for example, as well as how the profession operates. Cooperative learning programs, in which students spend a semester on campus and then a semester in a work milieu, provide professional training at an early point in undergraduate education but may extend the student's time in the program by several years. In contrast to programs in the pure physical sciences, engineering schools have regularly undergone program evaluation in order to be accredited, and students at different times have received individual accreditation through professional engineering examinations. The profession exerts a degree of authority over program and curriculum.

Students entering engineering programs, then, encounter a beehive of activity, with a reasonably high level of research and consulting activity and a more modest publishing capacity in their department among their professors. There are fewer postgraduate students than might be desired (with exceptions), a heavy course load, and upon graduation excellent job prospects, although they vary across specializations.

Students' Experience Learning Engineering

In our ethnographic study of learning in engineering, the graduate student participant-observer logged his experience in a first-year course in engineering mechanics given in the second semester to 150 students by a professor who had won awards for his teaching. The course consists of two two-hour lectures each week, from 10:30 A.M. to 12:30, with a ten-minute break after eighty minutes of lecture time (11:50 to noon). In addition, tutorials held once a week with a teaching assistant allow students in groups of ten to fifteen to go over assigned problem sets. Students are evaluated in two examinations: an in-class midterm and a final. The following excerpts are from the log of the fourth and twelfth weeks. Note the professor's engagement and how he develops an in-group attitude of engineers versus other disciplines.

January 27

The topic today is energy conservation and equilibrium. The professor uses a number of visual examples to illustrate equilibrium. For example, he pulls a glass ball out from under the desk and asks the class the general question, "If an object was placed on the rounded surface, would it stay forever?" Half the class responds "yes" and the other half "no." He then allows the example to speak for itself: "Yes, it will stay forever, it is in equilibrium." He asks the students to use grandma's language and not lawyers' language to simplify an explanation, which he says illustrates a better understanding. He then places the glass ball on the table and hits the table to cause a vibration without causing the ball to fall. "Stable equilibrium means the system likes to sit there."

The professor tends to lecture to the left side of the class, where the more verbal students are sitting. The class gets very boisterous approximately forty-five minutes into the lecture. Students mention after the class that it is difficult to concentrate close to lunchtime and that it is too long to attend to a lecture of this caliber for more than three-quarters of an hour without a break. A majority of students begin consuming fruit juice and sandwiches at around the seventy-minute mark in the lecture (11:40 A.M.).

The professor is available at break time to respond to students' concerns and questions. The second part of the class is used as a forum for students to take the initiative and go up to the front of the class to solve problems from their problem sets. This approach instigates active learning among the students, since they all help the individual at the blackboard. The professor helps facilitate the learning process by asking open-ended questions directed at the entire class, not just the individual at the board. He says to the class, "It really helps to see other students solve their mechanics problems as they get stuck in similar places, and this is where the class can really make a difference."

February 3

The class begins with the professor laying down the ground rules with regard to talking and making noise: "Strike two. One more strike and I am out of here, and we will have a quiz on Monday. If you know it all and you don't want to listen, then we will go, and we will have a quiz on Monday. What is this earthshaking news that you have to transmit to each other? Elementary courtesy, my friends. I give my best shot, you give your best shot. You don't like it, out! If any of you would like to come up here and concentrate for two hours, try it. Go ahead. I don't want to hear a pin drop."

"We have to learn in engineering to speak concisely, precisely, tersely, and actually. This is our game. Engineering is to make complexity understandable and manageable, which is unlike lawyers, who make situations complex and incomprehensible."

"Math is a tool I use to study physical situations."

"The meat of the thing is doing problems, and I repeat again, doing problems is not to please me, it is the vehicle to practice. If you want to get fit, you go to the gym and you lift weights. The act of doing it is the learning. Getting better. You can't get fit by watching someone lift weights."

"You are not going to go out in the real world and roll marbles down inclined planes. You are going to learn to think and analyze, and take the real-world situation and translate it into an analyzable form. This is practice."

"Engineering mechanics is problem solving. Learn how to solve problems." At this time, the instructor describes a good problem solver as someone who can get at the substance of the problem. "Physicists do the liturgy, engineers do the useful stuff like feed people. Engineering mechanics is solving problems."

April 7

The professor advises students how to study for the exam. "Get to the meat of the problem! Understand rather than remember. The way to study is to give yourself little exams. At first it is painful. Go to the library and pick a book off the shelf, open a page, and give yourself a problem. This is worth gold and diamonds. If you want to learn efficiently, you do a few problems on your own and I will have to tie you back from going to the exam. You will want to get the exam over with, because you will feel confident about it. Throw anything at me! A course like this is three-to-one: one hour lecture, three hours preparation. Before I do a lecture, I have to sit down and sweat out a few problems myself, and that is why I feel confident."

What stands out in these excerpts? The professor models not only the problem-solving process but what it means to be an engineer. He puts a great deal of effort into demonstrating to students that they are part of a profession in which they will be called on to behave in certain ways. He makes somewhat derogatory comparisons with competing disciplines. He identifies with the students. He threatens and negotiates. The students have learned to be attentive; the limitations on their attention appear to be based to a greater extent on their level of hunger than their interest in the topic. Students appear to know when to push hard (when problems are being solved on the board), and passively sit back when theory is being discussed. They are selective; they attend to what they find familiar or will be assessed. They are active, engaged, but pragmatic.

The Learning Task in Engineering

What does the discipline expect students to learn? Much is demanded of engineering students. At entry, they are expected to apply novice mathematical and physical science knowledge to unstructured problems that require a broad range of intellectual skills. Their curriculum is heavier than that of most science or arts students, and in the following quotations their professors recognize the cognitive and attitudinal pitfalls.

> Engineering is a very difficult discipline, a demanding, challenging discipline—and if you haven't got the commitment, you're not going to get anywhere. Engineers are like managers, they work from insufficient data and from aspirations to finished tasks and if you can't plan and organize, you can't do that.

> As there is a drift in engineering toward purely numerical methods and hand calculations with very little exposure to real structural behavior, it is clear that a lot of the failures—dramatic failures—that have occurred in engineering in the last decades have been because people have too little understanding of basic structural behavior. Students believe that what they are doing on paper is an accurate reflection of the way structures behave in reality.

These professors note the vicissitudes of an engineer's life, and what their students will face in the professional world. The transfer of abstract mathematical skills to real-life situations is dangerous, because errors can result in fatalities; learning to be an engineer includes estimating risk and taking the concomitant responsibility. Students' attitudes toward learning are positive, but they perceive the constraints of time and are pragmatic in their course selection.

> Learning to understand is important to me, but so are marks. When I choose my elective course outside of engineering, I choose not the bird [effortless] course but one that will help me the most in the future.

> Learning is the only thing that really interests me. Without the continual bombardment of information (stimulation) things get boring quickly (for example, summer break). It is frustrating sometimes, though, that no matter how hard you work, there always seems to be so much more that could be learned—time always plays a factor.

Students entering engineering programs are expected to have succeeded in previous mathematics and physical science courses; grades in calculus, both in first and second year, are most strongly related to success in engineering coursework (Pike, 1991). Professors in engineering courses expect their students to be able to think logically; most expect students to be able to think independently, but few expect them to think abstractly (Donald, 1988). In response to the demands of their program, the portrait of the engineering senior is distinct. Civil engineering students in their fourth year were found to be tough, practical, realistic, aggressive, and participative (Barker, 1989). Compared with students in arts and sciences programs, they are more self-reliant, willing to take responsibility, act on practical logical evidence, and keep to the point. They prefer to work and make decisions with other people and depend on social approval; they are conventional and go along with the group. In general, they tend to be good at making relationships, are high-risk taking and enterprising, and like to be the center of attention. They prefer learning kinesthetically (actively) more and auditorily less than arts students but nevertheless attend lectures as their main source of schooling, although they have more hands-on experiences in labs than arts students (Zhang & Richarde, 1999). Briefly then, expectations are that engineering students will have mathematical and physical science skills, will be able to act on logical evidence, and will be able to work with others.

Nature of Concepts in Engineering

The first thing that one notices in talking with engineering professors is that language is used in a system or at the service of intellectual processes. For example, one professor stated:

> The engineer has a basically modest vocabulary and should be able to make progress with it. In the field of engineering, the intellectual skills are important.

Most basic as vocabulary is the mathematical and physical science terminology demanded of students in the program. This is used in models of physical systems.

> Students are expected to have calculus, particularly in integration; physics, so that they would understand the concepts of work and force; and some knowledge of mechanics.

As an applied science, an engineering program requires a foundation of the mathematical modeling of physical systems. Mathematics and science are put together so elementary courses are layered with a sound basis of mathematics and science.

Although professors agree that students have to "come to grips" with a whole new set of terms, glossaries of terms are rarely provided. Instead, according to one professor, new concepts are explained as they arise. At the same time, precision in the use of vocabulary is fundamental, both for undergraduates and experts.

Understanding the basic concepts and being equipped to deal with them in a more precise way is crucial.

An expert in the field would be expected to have a precise vocabulary, a precise meaning of words such as *dynamic load*. The expert uses the same vocabulary as a student but in the very precise way in which it is meant to be used.

From these statements we gain the impression that mathematical terminology is supplemented with mechanics and the vocabulary of material structures.

Learning Concepts in Engineering

To what extent is conceptual learning expected of students and how is this learning organized? When we asked engineering professors what knowledge they expected students to develop in their courses, their replies focused on the integration of knowledge into systems or into the problem-solving process.

The terms of the course are defined very carefully. One of the most important things to do is to get the students to define the system they are dealing with so that if you have a complicated system you can break it down into a number of subsets and then deal with those.

The course is based primarily on the process of problem solving where the focus is on procedural knowledge as a basis for successful problem solving. For the first three or four weeks of the term the elementary vocabulary of statics is being acquired through using it, writing it up, and recognizing the significance of terms in the wording of the problem. The strategies are incorporated into a sheet that requires students to (1) estimate the answer, (2) use a checklist of problem descriptors, and (3) rewrite the problem before they begin to solve the problem. For example, students must recognize whether the problem is 2D or 3D. This method makes students recognize the significance of different words. Rewriting the problem ensures that students have absorbed the gist of the problem.

The vocabulary is acquired through using it, writing it up, and recognizing the significance of terms in the wording of the problem.

These quotations describe a learning situation considerably different from that in physics where the emphasis is on learning concepts. Physicists focus on the importance of knowledge structures (for example, diSessa, 1993; Halloun &

Hestenes, 1985; Hammer, 1994; Redish, Saul, & Steinberg, 1998; Reif, 1983), but the concern in engineering is with procedural (how) rather than declarative (that) knowledge. The distinction between procedural and declarative knowledge was introduced by Ryle (1949) to explain the attention paid in ordinary life to people's competencies rather than their cognitive repertoires, to actions rather than to knowledge per se. What is important for Ryle is the capacity to discover knowledge and to organize and exploit it when discovered.

By knowing "that"—knowledge as content, facts, and principles—we achieve stability and access, as in a dictionary. By knowing "how," we derive knowledge about our knowledge and how to apply it (Winograd, 1975). In a two-stage theory of learning, Anderson (1982) posited that students first learn facts, then embed knowledge in procedures for performing skills such as problem solving. He suggested that at least one hundred hours of practice would be needed to move from declarative to procedural knowledge. Our studies and those of Reif (1983), for example, have reinforced the need for embedding knowledge in larger frameworks that include action schemas, in one sense reversing Anderson's posited stages of learning. In constructivist theory, understanding occurs as a result of joining concepts to actions; using information theory terminology, retrieval from memory depends on how well knowledge is encoded in schemas. Similar to the concern with student preconceptions or misconceptions in physics and hence their conceptual ability, engineering professors question the verbal capabilities of their students.

> Precision in their use of words is important; if they are asked what the moment of a twenty kilonewton force about A is, they may answer in a most haphazard way. They have not focused their thoughts and the question arises as to whether engineering students have a default in their ability to write and think verbally, at least in their level of precision.

As students progress through the program, there appears to be a consolidation of concepts rather than an increase in knowledge; learning is viewed as a pyramid in which basic knowledge is synthesized and applied in different ways at the top. Professors' concerns are with the students developing learning strategies that they will be able to apply throughout their professional lives.

> Very little extra vocabulary is added as one goes up the pyramid; all of the base of the pyramid is being used. Climbing is the analogy I would use. You have to go through the same foothills to reach different peaks.

> Learning how to learn is very important; it is every bit as important as actual knowledge, particularly today, when knowledge will be useless in five years.

Thus the action schemas or competencies are foremost. The evaluation of learning supports the approach of consolidating knowledge and being able to apply it. The professors ask students to analyze and synthesize rather than show that they know.

The type of questions asked in the problem sheets and in the exam questions are not so much defining terms or definitions. Rather they are technically based questions—for example, What materials would you use for a specific application? Or, how do you develop this particular property? Or, how is this specific property related to structure?

Given their professors' concerns about conceptual development, how do engineering students view the learning process? One student highlighted a problem with assignments—that they can be quite confusing if the concept or theory behind them is not understood. Another student commented that assignments involve procedures to follow, without a rationale being given for a particular design technique. Specifically, students requested more examples and greater explanation of ideas behind the concepts. Students thus appeared to be seeking greater understanding of the context and more examples to aid them in their integrating tasks. Asked if their learning experience in engineering differed from that in courses in other areas, students noted the demands made on their ability to think.

I have to understand the problem first before solving. For my math course, I don't really have to understand the problem first. You have to know the basics before doing anything.

Here you have to think more before doing anything.

Students echo their professors' concern with the amount of material to be covered in a finite amount of time, and their responsibilities as learners.

Quite often this course is a self-learning course. We get three assignments a week and some material has never been taught in class. It's very fast-paced. The workload is heavy. It's different from other courses.

There's a lot of work. You have to get used to it. It's overwhelming. You have to adjust.

The high demands placed on students are evident in these quotations; the learning task is centered in the kinds of thinking processes developed in engineering courses.

The Development of Thinking Processes in Engineering

In engineering, *problem solving* and *design* are the terms most frequently used to describe the thinking processes needed and developed. In some programs, courses are taught specifically on the problem-solving process (see Adams, 1986a, 1986b). When we asked engineering professors to test the applicability of the working model of thinking processes to describe what they were doing in their courses, they used all six groups of processes: description, selection, representation, inference, synthesis, and verification. Of the fourteen professors who gave their individual perceptions of how students learned to think in their courses, eight taught first-year courses (in structural mechanics, statics, engineering thermodynamics, electromagnetics, circuits and electronics, and chemical engineering); four taught upper-level courses (in structural mechanics, thermodynamics, electrical energy conversion, and materials engineering); one taught a general course in problem solving; and one taught a course in computer science.

What stood out most clearly in the interviews with the professors was their emphasis on the need for students to change their approach—that students had been misled by the criterion of efficiency and needed to learn new ways. Because of this, the task of the professor in an introductory course is difficult.

Whenever there is a way to go through school without thinking, unfortunately that way is taken more often than not by most students. There is no way to force a student to think. However, you can encourage them and try to make it not be that much more efficient not to think. What do I mean by this? There are many times in school when a student can memorize a number of points, get 100 percent on the exam, then forget it all the next week, and basically have learned nothing. In engineering this approach is totally worthless. There is a small set of basic ideas that you have to memorize, but just through using them repeatedly you will memorize them. The student has no choice, you cannot avoid using these basic ideas and they will become a part of long-term memory.

But the real value in engineering is being able to think and apply these fundamentals to new problems you have not seen before. This is what we are trying to train the students to do. I have students who have tremendous marks, and can memorize everything, and they come in and show me that they can do any number of problems. But when I ask them why are you doing this step in this problem, they respond, "Because that is the way you did it." When I ask them why do you think I did it this way, or ask what if I gave you another problem that is similar to this one and another one combined, but not exactly either, the student usually responds, "I can't do it because I have never seen it before." Their knowledge is all memorized and there is no understanding, and what is worse is that there is a tremendous fear even to consider how they would approach a problem they have not seen before.

The idea of thinking was not established as being very important in their minds earlier in their education. I remember when I was in high school, memorizing was the best thing to do—you get the highest marks. You need not waste your time thinking because the exams were geared just to what you could remember. It is also difficult to mark an exam that grades thinking, because there may be fifty good answers to a given problem and they all may be different.

If the students cannot think when they go into the next term, they are probably not going to succeed in their next courses. So I have to try to take them from not being used to thinking about things to being competent and self-reliant at the end of the term. They have to be able to think constructively and have had enough practice to do a reasonable job of it. This is really hard, because (a) the students do not want to, (b) they are not experienced, and (c) their life experience up until now has told them: "Don't think, it's inefficient and you might not get the same marks, you may make mistakes."

Students are not being encouraged to use their brain for other things than memory. The students should be strongly encouraged to think. To the extent that I try to do that in this course, I catch a lot of flack. I tend to ask many questions that have not been asked of them before and the students do not like this. I get many complaints, and the students say: "You are not allowed to ask us questions that you have never asked us before." My response is that is the way it has always been and that is the way it is going to be when you go to work. If the answer is already known, no one is going to pay someone to answer it again. I believe the students would have failed in obtaining an education in engineering or an education at all, if they cannot think for themselves.

When asked if he thought his students had learned new ways of thinking in his course, he said he hoped they had learned that it is worthwhile to think and that they could judge how competent they are at problem solving and feel good about their strengths and take responsibility to correct their weaknesses. He added that he had tried very hard to convince students that studying does not mean what it might have meant in the past. It means understanding, not just being able to repeat or regurgitate what they might have read elsewhere. The examples given of the thinking processes in the working model show what professors' expectations are and how they prompt students to think.

Description

Although professors expected students to have all the descriptive skills to some extent when they entered the program, they least expected students to be able to *identify the context* in which they were working. One professor noted that *identifying the context* is most difficult because students often have not had the real-life experience needed to visualize what the context is. Another commented that the breadth of context will affect the problem solution, and that establishing the big picture is therefore critical in ensuring an applicable solution (Exhibit 3.1). In a vivid illustration of *identifying the context,* one professor examined energy as a resource base from many points of view—scientific or engineering or business or political—and explained that one cannot treat these things in isolation. He used the oil crisis in Canada and how it related to the rest of the world crisis to exemplify the interrelationships of factors. Although Canada as an isolated entity has enough oil, it imported oil from the Middle East to its eastern seaboard because there was no pipeline to that region. Therefore, global political and economic factors affected the energy resources of the country.

Some professors noted that engineers often have to make decisions without having all the *facts*. One of them said that it was crucial for students to know what they did and did not know and to admit it, because later in a job situation, it would be far worse to "blow a month's work time" and then come back and tell their employer, "I am incompetent and I cannot do it." *Stating assumptions* was held to be more important than getting the facts, because it forced the student to examine the underlying principles that would lead to problem solution. *Stating their goal* was important, in contrast to the expectations of physics professors, because engineering students need a plan of action to "see themselves through." This was in distinction to "just jumping in" and saying, "I will figure it out somehow"—considered a dangerous approach.

EXHIBIT 3.1. PROFESSORS' EXAMPLES OF DESCRIPTION USED IN ENGINEERING COURSES

Identify context: Establish surrounding environment to create a total picture.	*A standard strategy in design is to start out with as big a picture as you can, the most context you can, and then focus down to a much smaller one. Depending on how much context you consider, you are likely to come to different solutions.*
State facts: State known information, events that have occurred.	*Often in problem solving there are not facts or you do not have enough time to get facts; you have to base decisions on something else.*
State assumptions: State suppositions, postulates, propositions assumed.	*Students state assumptions in their assignments, then work the problems.*
State goal: State the ends, aims, objectives.	*Students must be able to understand what a problem is telling them (that is, what is given) and asking of them.*

In summary, engineering professors agreed upon the importance of developing descriptive thinking processes in their courses, in marked contrast to physics professors. According to one of our engineering professors, that is because description requires experience and students arrive with relatively little background in the field. He thought that description would be used more often in upper-level courses in projects in which students are given a goal, some context, and a few facts but must then design the project, which requires description and selection.

Selection

Selection is important in both problem solving and design. Students are expected to be able to *choose relevant information,* but the ease and rapidity with which they do this depends on practice and being exposed to a variety of situations (Exhibit 3.2). One professor pointed out that the information can be infinite, say, in choosing a working fluid. *Ordering information in importance* becomes much more critical in en-

EXHIBIT 3.2. PROFESSORS' EXAMPLES OF SELECTION USED IN ENGINEERING COURSES

Choose relevant information: Select information that is pertinent to the issue in question.	*Students must choose the right (most appropriate) Newtonian equation to predict or describe a free-falling object.*
Order information in importance: Rank, arrange in importance or according to significance.	*Ask students to compare driving two blocks to the corner store and driving a car to transport medicine fifty miles from one hospital to another; the idea is that just because something can be done does not mean it should be done.*
Identify critical elements: Determine units, parts, components that are important.	*To select an appropriate material for magnetic application, students would have to know what is the critical part of that application, which materials satisfy this application.*
Identify critical relations: Determine connections between things that are important.	*Humans are put into the larger context to examine how we use resources. For example, the people of the United States and Canada, who represent a very small percentage of the world's population—6 to 7 percent—use over 30 percent of the world's energy resources. How will energy be utilized when, for example, the Chinese want to have the same level of resources?*

gineering because a multitude of phenomena in the real world must be sorted for their relative impact, and students must learn to place a value on alternative pathways. Another demand for this skill would be in report writing. Deciding what are the important components or materials are examples of *identifying critical elements*. *Identifying critical relations* is essential in using equations—for example, in relating temperature to condensation pressures for a solar-powered irrigation system. In the choice of materials or in broader decisions such as energy use, students must weigh different variables and relate them to each other.

One professor pointed out that what to select depends not just on the problem and the available material for solving that problem but also on how the student's individual mind works best. His rationale is that most problems have ten or more different solutions; for him, the best way is not only the way that solves the problem but also the way in which he feels most confident. He tells students that they may have a tremendous grasp of certain tools to solve the problem in one way, and a limited grasp of the tools that are used to solve the problem in another way, and the method in which they have most confidence is the best. People's minds work not just based on what they know but also on how they are used to thinking; certain tools will be much better suited to their thought processes.

In summary, selection appears to be a much more important thinking process in engineering than in physics, because students must learn to deal with problems in which there is a great deal of information. They must therefore learn how much information to take into account and what they can safely ignore. In addition, there are different ways of solving problems, which means that students must also select the pathway they will use to solve the problem.

Representation

Engineers use representation in diagrams, formulas, laws, and designs. Model building, both concretely and mathematically, is central to the task of the engineer. Without building a model, one cannot put the parts of a problem in context and then make the necessary integration to solve the problem or build the design. The catch is to have students *recognize the organizing principles* underlying the problems they are given to solve (Exhibit 3.3). As one professor said, toward the end of their program students may realize that the principle of minimization of energy can be applied widely, but they cannot understand such a principle until after considerable experience. Students *organize elements and relations* in their problem representations and designs. Engineering professors *illustrate elements and relations* in class—cow dung as fuel being one of the more salient. Students, however, not only must *illustrate elements and relations* but also apply them. According to a thermodynamics professor, students would normally be asked to make a sketch of hardware

EXHIBIT 3.3. PROFESSORS' EXAMPLES OF
REPRESENTATION USED IN ENGINEERING COURSES

Recognize organizing principles: Identify laws, methods, rules that arrange into a systematic whole.	*The second law of thermodynamics has fundamental restrictions that say you cannot do this another way or you would be violating a natural law.*
Organize elements and relations: Arrange parts, connections between things into a systematic whole.	*Represent structures as lines, joints as circles, or fixed ends, pinned ends, or symbolism.*
	Third-angle representations and projections of solid objects.
Illustrate elements and relations: Make clear by examples the parts, connections between things.	*Drawing diagrams: students will not be able to solve the problem unless they can isolate the system and show what forces are acting on it.*
	In the Third World the main fuel is cow dung, and the cow is a sacred animal in India. The cow provides fuel and thus there is a practical result to this religious law.
Modify elements and relations: Change, alter, or qualify the parts, connections between things.	*If something did not work—for example if students decided to use water when Freon would have been a better working fluid— they would soon recognize that and then modify their proposed solution.*

components. Then they would draw a plot of pressure versus volume or temperature versus entropy. If they decided to use water when Freon might have been a better working fluid, they would then be expected to *modify elements and relations* to come to a successful solution.

Although students in introductory courses did not emphasize representation as their professors had, student respondents in second-year courses said that it was now "easier to conceptualize what a problem solution would be like" and that they must now "look more at the overall picture and combine concepts." They were thinking more conceptually and visually, and this coincided with their tendency to enunciate clear learning goals (Donald, 1991, 1992b). Both representation and description were developing in the first two years of the program.

Overall, representation acts as a trigger for problem solving, requiring students to incorporate their skills to understand and act. Engineering examples and explanations of the need for and use of representation were highly consistent with those of physics professors in Chapter Two. The centrality of representation to problem solving, whether as model or trigger, is evident in the breadth of examples used in both areas of study.

Inference

Professors emphasized inference as one of the two most important thinking processes in engineering along with representation; students by their second year also recognized its importance. The professors saw it as the step in problem solving where they focus on the implications of their calculations (Exhibit 3.4). For example, one talked about how he stops and stands back from the board, facing the same way as the students, and says, "Well, we got these particular results, what do

EXHIBIT 3.4. PROFESSORS' EXAMPLES OF INFERENCE USED IN ENGINEERING COURSES

INFERENCE: Act or process of drawing conclusions from premises or evidence.	*You have to do a bit of work and then stand back from it and say, "What do I deduce from this? Do I see any new connections that I did not observe before? Do I see any implications arising from my analysis?"*
Discover new relations between elements: Detect or expose connections between parts, units, components.	*There is no fundamental difference between a cow and a human on an energy basis; we all survive on the energy that comes from the sun, that grows the food.*
Discover new relations between relations: Detect or expose connections between connections of things.	*Make analogies between formulas and relationships in electrical engineering, chemical engineering, and stress analysis.* *Deduce particular physical properties from combinations of other properties.*
Discover equivalences: Detect or expose equality in value, force or significance.	*You can burn a pound of butter as fuel and it is actually a better fuel than a pound of coal in terms of heat energy.*
Categorize: Classify, arrange into parts.	*Understand good and bad conductors, hard and soft magnets, and so on.*
Order: Rank, sequence, arrange methodically.	*Rank materials in the order of energy density.*
Change perspective: Alter view, vista, interrelations, significance of facts or information.	*In a project to design something that will make the campus more convenient for blind students, one professor has some students led across campus blindfolded to help them learn what the problems are, not in navigating, but rather in keeping their socks matched or shaving a mustache or not colliding with bicycles or things that move.*
Hypothesize: Suppose or form a proposition as a basis for reasoning.	*To illustrate the solar irrigation pump, you would hypothesize something and if that did not work, you would have to try another solution.*

we infer from them?" He considered it an important part of the lecture process to infer from the algebra that they had completed something students had not seen before so that they could get a better feel for the subject.

Discovering new relations between elements occurs, for example, when in the thermodynamics course the professor has students thinking hard about what working fluid to use. Linking cows and humans in their need for energy is a discovery for many students. Students may *discover new relations between relations* when they apply formulas to specific situations, but they may also see connections between different engineering specializations. In solving trigonometric identities one is looking for *equivalent* expressions. Energy equivalences—for example, between butter and coal—are vivid comparisons.

Similar to expectations in physics courses, professors think that students will already be able to *categorize* and *order,* but *changing perspective* needs attention in engineering courses. One professor explained that a lot of students have never thought about what flipping on a light switch entails—the instant availability of power—and that a lot of backup electric power is needed because it cannot be stored. Another had students lead others blindfolded across the campus in order to have them discover what would make the campus more accommodating to blind students. *Hypothesizing* was considered a more sophisticated skill and so was developed later in design projects; however, one professor stated that many of the physical models that are developed to explain properties in relationships are done hypothetically.

Synthesis

Synthesis is the most essential process in upper-level courses; problem solving and design rely on synthesis to succeed. One professor noted that students move toward it as they progress in their studies and that the overall goal of the engineering program is to produce creative, independent, flexible, and critically thinking individuals who are adept at problem solving and adaptable to the changing needs of the field. For him, this was encapsulated in the process of synthesis. In contrast with physics—physics professors did not expect students to be able to synthesize—engineering students are trained to do so. Students start out with guided synthesis, rather than self-generated synthesis, and their labs are intended to nurture these skills. This means that students have the design process modeled for them and then are given more leeway with greater responsibility in projects (Exhibit 3.5). Projects are the primary means of developing synthesis, and thus the instructional method includes teamwork—the skills needed to work together on a project form part of the curriculum.

Students are expected to *combine parts to form a whole* when they are given problems in which they must first analyze the components of a system, then put the system back together. Less attention was paid to *elaboration,* but instances were found

EXHIBIT 3.5. PROFESSORS' EXAMPLES OF
SYNTHESIS USED IN ENGINEERING COURSES

Combine parts to form a whole: Join, associate elements, components into a system or pattern.	*Writing a program and learning a new programming language such as C.*
	The engineering method has two critical parts: you have to break down a complicated system into components that you can analyze relatively simply, then put it back together. Unless you put it back together, you do not have an engineering solution.
Elaborate: Work out, complete with great detail, exactness, or complexity.	*Students must specify that the object is to pump water using the energy available in the Sahara; then they have to decide what size of vapor engine they might have to use.*
Generate missing links: Produce or create what is lacking in a sequence, fill in the gap.	*Students get a problem that is not defined completely.*
Develop course of action: Work out or expand the path, route, or direction to take.	*Students apply the basic fundamentals until they reach a solution for the whole system.*

where students had to refine or to specify a program or solution. Students may be asked to *generate missing links* in any problem solution but also in design projects. This may cause additional instructional dilemmas. For example, according to one professor, some students will be able to project a likely solution but others can only look at the whole, and some become so involved with the detail that they are unable to look at sizes and structural behavior in a concrete way. Thus some students' personal strategies may impede the design process because they preclude generating missing links. Finally, *developing a course of action* follows from understanding the goal of the project but also requires an understanding of the whole system.

Synthesis is emphasized, according to one professor, because it has a very heavy requirement that you get much more thoughtful about what you are trying to do. The prerequisite in problem solving is to define the problem, and thinking of an easier way or a simpler way or getting around the problem in some way are also strategies for responding to the problem.

Verification

As with synthesis, verification processes are critical engineering skills, and they are actively developed. The emphasis on verification has two sources. One is the fact that engineers deal with a variety of unknowns and hence must approximate reality. The other is that they are liable for their performance or products, and must therefore limit risk to the extent possible. As one professor noted, engineers work in teams, always verifying with each other what they are doing. When discussing the realization of a project with other engineers, one does not consciously say, "Well, what I am doing is verification" or "What I am doing is synthesis," but that is in fact what one is doing all the time. The reason for this emphasis, according to the professor, is that any design must fulfill its purpose—it must be economical, aesthetically satisfactory, and durable. Fitness of purpose is central to good design but the design must also be environmentally sensitive and capable of alteration with good use of materials. Verification consists of ensuring that products or processes meet a variety of criteria.

Verification processes begin to be developed more simply, however, at the board during problem-solving sessions, when a professor turns to the students and asks if an answer makes sense and why (Exhibit 3.6). There are also levels of verification processes—from checking calculations, to similar solutions, to other authorities. Empirical testing in the laboratory is used to verify models or conceptual frameworks. Frequently, they *compare alternative outcomes* by using different materials or substances and seeing their relative effects; computer modeling allows for this kind of testing. Standards or codes govern many engineering procedures and the materials used, so that *comparing outcomes to a standard* is common. As one professor noted, however, in some cases no standard exists; the engineer must have a sense of what would work best or be able to test what would be the best solution.

Considerable emphasis is put on *judging validity* through establishing what would be a reasonable solution or what would work in the real world. One professor explained how validity is judged by saying that in engineering one likes to encourage students to have a concept of orders of magnitude, the boundaries within which the answer to a problem could lie. They dislike people saying, "It's large; it's small"—large and small have no meaning. For example, short time scales vary according to the person using them. Another explained the limitations of *judging validity*: students must carefully examine and estimate the soundness, effectiveness, or support but not by actual fact because most of the problems he gives do not have answers.

Feedback may come from authorities in the field, other professionals, or other members of one's team. Feedback also comes from any real situation. Lessons from failure are particularly striking, whether structures that collapse, performance difficulties, or early deterioration of materials. *Confirming results* occurs when results lie outside a trend and so must be reassessed, or when experiments are used to establish systematic variation. One professor stated that the test of validation is, "Does it work?" He had just been engaged with a student on a very complicated

EXHIBIT 3.6. PROFESSORS' EXAMPLES OF VERIFICATION USED IN ENGINEERING COURSES

VERIFICATION: Confirmation of accuracy, coherence, consistency, correspondence.	*Frequently after a particularly turgid piece of algebra, we look at the answer and say, "Does it make sense?"*
	Checking numbers, checking against previous solutions, checking against what other people think, checking against what other people in the design team have thought, and discussing it endlessly with other professionals.
Compare alternative outcomes: Examine similarities or differences of results, consequences.	*When students try to use one working fluid—for example, Freon—then use a second working fluid, perhaps ammonia, and then a third, perhaps water, and then compare their effects.*
	With computers, you say, "What would happen in this structure if I change beam number 7 to twice the size?" and then watch the implication.
Compare outcome to standard: Examine similarities, differences of results based on a criterion.	*Codes, design rules, and design charts are all standards.*
Judge validity: Critically examine the soundness, effectiveness by actual fact.	*A number may be valid within the confines of the problem but not in real life.*
Use feedback: Employ results to regulate, adjust, adapt.	*Structures that collapse, performance difficulties, early deterioration of materials.*
Confirm results: Establish or ratify conclusions, effects, outcomes, products.	*A result that lies way outside of the trend of other results is reassessed. Finding out how a parameter varies systematically with another parameter, looking for trend curves.*

theory of electromagnetic waves coupling between a whole set of lines, but for them the real thrill was when they built the structure according to these principles and then measured it. The theory, the manufacture, and the testing all gave the same answer. Then, he noted, "you feel you've got it right, or as right as your present extent of knowledge will allow. It is not black and white; the level of correctness is usually within 10 percent in engineering." The manufacturing tolerances they had in the research project and the assumptions of the theory combined to ensure that they were not going to get a perfect answer in this particular instance. Thus verification processes were of great importance, were of many different kinds, and tended to be approximate or within certain limits.

What is most important about the thinking processes students learn in their engineering courses? Acquiring description and selection skills is imperative because students must situate the problem and usually deal with situations in which there is too much or too little information. *Identifying the context, stating their goals,* and *choosing relevant information* are key thinking processes to be learned. Representation of the problem to be solved is also crucial. Among the inferential processes, *discovering new relations between elements and relations* and *changing perspective* received the most attention. Synthesis becomes critical in upper-level courses, particularly in design, as is verification through approximations to reality; accountability for performance makes it so. All the thinking processes warrant and receive attention in the engineering program.

The Challenge of Instruction in Engineering

The engineering professors who contributed their insights to understanding learning in their field emphasized the need for problem-solving skills but were equally concerned with design and quality issues. This led one expert to suggest that most engineering skills require a great deal of calendar time to master; hence a skill that was started in one course will be acquired over a period of years. The unit of learning is not a course but a program plus postgraduate study or experience. The first instructional challenge is then to understand the kinds of instructional and evaluation methods that are or could be used to bring coherence to students' learning experience over their courses.

As a hard applied science, engineers view knowledge as purposive and pragmatic (Milem & Astin, 1994). They are thus less inclined to be concerned with the development of a conceptual framework, as are neighboring physicists, but focus their attention on mastering the environment and developing new products or techniques. Primary challenges for engineering instructors are improving students' problem-solving ability and design skills, but a codicil is needed on the application of these skills in the industrial and larger economic milieu.

To gain an understanding of the resources available to teach engineering and its pure peer discipline, physics, we analyzed the kinds of instructional articles located in the *Engineering Index* and in *Physics Abstracts* in 1985 and 1986. We found four kinds of articles with some overlap between categories. *Conceptualizations* dealt with concepts, theories, or the philosophy behind topics studied. *Experimentation* described pedagogical studies relating learning variables such as the effect of student background on learning outcomes. *Specific practice* described how to teach a specific course or course unit—for example, a demonstration, activity, or assignment. *General practice* included ways to teach in general and multidisciplinary or unified approaches to the subject.

Of 289 articles reviewed in the two-year period in the *Engineering Index,* over half were devoted to specific practice, often with some other category, and another third to general practice, with less than 10 percent focused on conceptualization or pedagogical experimentation. Most articles addressed curriculum and instructional issues, with minimal attention to student characteristics. In contrast, in *Physics Abstracts* the largest group of instructional articles were categorized as conceptualizations, focused on proofs and demonstrations of theory. In the *Engineering Index* problem-solving activities with real, practical referents were stressed.

There was much more general discussion in articles in the *Engineering Index* about engineering education, good professional practice, and changes in practice and standards necessitated by technological change. Engineers were more likely to discuss a variety of teaching methods and their implications, including individualized instruction, audiovisual methods, and computer-assisted instruction. In both engineering and physics, evaluation or assessment articles formed a relatively small percentage as a topic. In engineering, a fairly large group of articles were found on the profession and its present and future needs—what employers wanted, ways to select and train students to keep up with change, and engineering programs in various countries.

Research or experimentation in postsecondary teaching and learning in physics and engineering is often indexed by other educational abstracting services such as *Psychological Abstracts,* but there was next to no referencing of such articles in the *Engineering Index.* Thus articles on engineering in journals on instruction and learning are unlikely to be found by engineers who search using the abstracting services in the field. In those journals referenced by the *Engineering Index* or *Physics Abstracts,* the professor searching for ideas about improving instruction may find a considerable wealth of specific practices that could be applied but relatively little experimentation. A search further afield could be expected to provide more knowledge about the effects of instruction.

Instructional and Evaluation Methods in Engineering

Instructional and evaluation methods tend to differ by discipline and are major influences on how students learn. Because the kind of instructional method affects the kind of learning, and because active learning methods such as cooperative learning or projects are needed for higher-order learning to occur, the choice of instructional method is the first challenge. Instructional methods in engineering courses are for the most part lecture; in a study of thirty-five thousand faculty across disciplines in the United States, 78 percent of engineering faculty indicated that they used extensive lecturing in all or most of the classes they taught, higher than the overall average of 54 percent (Milem & Astin, 1994). Almost half (45 percent) responded that they also used class discussion in all or most classes, compared with an overall average of 70 percent. Group projects were used by 16 percent, matching the overall average, but a higher percentage than in other physical sciences, which averaged 5 percent. Engineering professors reported using cooperative learning (14 percent), more than other sciences, but lower than the overall average of 27 percent. Thus active learning methods were recognized but not used as much as might be expected given the problem-solving tasks of engineering students.

In a study of engineering professors' conceptualizations of their teaching practice, mainly derived from teaching experience, two-thirds of sixty professors teaching first-year courses displayed a *student-directing* conception of teaching (Van Driel, Verloop, Van Werven, & Dekkers, 1997). This conception was characterized by a commitment to help, stimulate, and control students, to meet their students frequently and preferably in small groups in order to stimulate and support student learning. They were concerned with delivering an enormous amount of subject matter in order to maintain a high standard of education, and thus carefully planned and controlled students' learning activities. Another quarter of the teachers adopted a *teacher-centered* approach, in which they imparted information to students and expected students to study hard. The remaining 10 percent were *student-centered,* and were more inclined to promote self-regulated student activities.

Most teachers considered problem-solving abilities to be crucial, but how they incorporated the development of these skills in their teaching strategies was not clear. Teachers tended to be skeptical about whether students were able to be self-regulating, referring to their lack of discipline or the complexity of technical problems that they thought students could not solve without help from their teachers. Thus even when the conception of teaching includes the promotion of problem-solving abilities and self-regulated learning, most professors doubt the feasibility of the approach and do not use strategies to promote student-centered learning. After reviewing the results of the study, the professors formed teams of five to eight teachers to examine their teaching practice and design new first-year courses focused on project work.

The evaluation methods used in a course or more generally in a program set the standards for students. Where students are assessed on their thinking, they tend to develop their thinking capacity. If, however, recognition questions are used, students tend to limit their learning to memorization. In the cross-disciplinary study of instructional practices (Milem & Astin, 1994), engineering professors used competency-based grading more than the average (62 percent versus 52 percent) and more than any other type of grading. However, they tended to grade on the normal curve more than other professors (43 percent versus 22 percent overall), which intensifies competitiveness among students and reduces students' sense of control over their learning. They used multiple-choice questions least of all the disciplines (10 percent versus 32 percent overall). Thus although they might have been leading students to be competitive and weakening self-regulation, they also were using some assessment methods that promoted higher-order learning.

A problem peculiar to engineering is the effect of grading students in their early years on their analytic or problem-solving skills rather than their problem identification and design skills. Students entering engineering programs are immersed in coursework that is heavily weighted toward the sciences and emphasizes analytic skills, and some argue that problem finders who would later on have a great deal to contribute as masters of design are lost before their talents are called upon (Beasley, Huey, Wilkes, & McCormick, 1995). Because engineering requires a wide array of skills both analytic and synthetic, the possibility is that some students are phased out of the program because they are weaker at prestructured and analytic problem solving but excel at integrative thinking. In the study, there were disproportionately more problem finders among students and more problem solvers among the faculty. The results suggest that investigation is needed into means to enhance the success of both problem finders and problem solvers.

Gaining Problem-Solving Ability

How can problem-solving ability be enhanced, and how does problem solving in engineering differ from that in other fields? In the study of the thinking skills expected of students, one of the two disciplinary groups who most expected their students to have thinking abilities were engineering professors, and they focused on the development of problem-solving skills (Donald, 1988). Yet in studies of problem solving in engineering courses, teachers have been found to pay little explicit attention to several phases of the problem-solving process that are important to beginners (Kramers-Pals, Lambrechts, & Wolff, 1982). The most common occurrence is modeling an abbreviated process so that students do not see each step separately. Expertise blinds the professor to the number of steps necessary for a novice to solve a problem.

The skills of problem solving, in which representation and pattern recognition play a major role (Frederiksen, 1984), require thousands of hours of practice (Chase & Chi, 1980). According to Chase and Chi, an important component of the knowledge base is a fast action pattern recognition system that greatly reduces processing load and serves as a retrieval aid for alternative courses of action. Practice creates patterns of lexicons—that is, dictionaries or glossaries, both in images and symbols—and a set of strategies that can operate on the patterns. In engineering, the lexicon is likely to be a set of technological laws, and functional and structural rules (Ropohl, 1997). Ropohl defines technological laws as transformations of one or more natural laws with regard to a technical process. He gives the example of Hooke's law of elasticity, which explains the stretch of material as a linear function of the tension. He points out that engineers are interested not only in calculating the strength of a certain component but in the marginal tension at which the law does not operate, because it is at this point that the component tends to break. In addition, a safety coefficient must be applied. Thus the technological law extends beyond the natural law or laws, which must be used in combination with other data to establish the technological law.

Describing a problem is therefore complex. Frequently a technological law is an empirical generalization derived from practice (inductive inference), as in the laws of metal cutting, and is without a coherent theory to explain the procedure. Functional rules specify what to do under given circumstances (conditions), and structural rules aid the engineer to anticipate the object to be realized through mental images (representations); the blueprint is the language of the engineer (Ropohl, 1997). Thus for the engineering student, problem solving involves not only applying laws but knowing under what circumstances to apply them and how, using a broad set of thinking processes. Instructional strategies may take several forms: coaching, tutorials, and a workshop series, for example.

Coaching. Helping students to understand the nature of problems has become a topic of great interest at recent professional engineering meetings. In one session, professors described how they use thirty-minute workshops to coach students in learning skills to respond directly to student weaknesses (Yokomoto & Ware, 1997). For example, when a need is indicated by students saying an exam was too long or that they knew the material but could not finish, the workshop tasks become coaching the students to approach the problem in the examination more efficiently, by making a list or drawing a cognitive map of everything they know about a specific topic, or having them write step-by-step rules for executing a particular procedure. When students choose less efficient ways to approach a problem, the instructors have them list several different ways to approach it and then coach them to select the most efficient way. When students say the exam was full of trick questions, they have students solve a homework problem that has been rewritten so that what was the unknown is now the given, and vice versa, then ask them to articulate the relationship between the two problems, and to design an inverted problem themselves. The workshops, as in sports and music training, are intended to disclose the learning skills essential for high performance in examinations.

Tutorials. Because he recognized the complexity of the problem-solving process, one professor in my cross-disciplinary study developed a highly structured introduction to problem solving. In his course, problem solving is developed in tutorial sessions where students must learn the component skills by specific practice or drill. They must first select information that is pertinent to the problem by rewriting the problem. They are expected to write down the law; they have to systematically set down the equations that they are using. They then must clarify the parts of the solution: they have to have axes, diagram, equations, and a check as parts of their solution.

The professor also makes his students drill the specific components, the composite skills required to resolve forces, by means of practice sheets. This is a prerequisite to being able to do the problems. The professor noted that he would like his students to be able to do these steps almost without thinking about them, as low-level procedural knowledge that serves as a basis for problem solving. In the tutorial, the professor and two teaching assistants circulate while students work on the drill sheets. Drawing diagrams is one of the component skills; students will not be able to solve the problem unless they can isolate the system and show what forces are acting on it.

The professor breaks down each topic in the course into basic behaviors that students must be able to do pertinent to that particular problem.

> It might be a numerical skill or an analytic skill or a diagrammatic interpretation; there will be something underlying those types of problems and they cannot get started on the problem solution without appreciating it. The terminology, for example, must be known as if it is second nature. In engineering, it is obvious when students have not learned the knowledge structure because they cannot get started on the problem. If you were to give them the diagram or suggest using a certain framework, they would be able to do it, but they cannot supply the framework. The foundation activities, the drills, are therefore crucial.

The instructional design in this course is exemplary for its attention to each step of the problem-solving process. Even when students enter the program feeling well prepared for their engineering courses, they report a difference from their previous learning experience.

> It needs more concentration and much deeper understanding and thinking.

> It needs a lot of hard work. There's a lot of competition.

Asked what advice they would give other students, they recommend a meticulous approach.

> Try to develop a good understanding and not take anything for granted. Go to the tutorials, read the book, and get as much as you can.

These students are aware that learning to solve engineering problems requires energy, practice, and concentration.

Problem-Solving Workshops. Recognition of the complexity of the problem-solving process led professors in a chemical engineering program to develop a series of problem-solving courses that have become an instructional benchmark in engineering education. In a twenty-five-year project that began with Don Woods sitting in on his colleagues' lectures and assessing the learning environment in which problem-solving skills were developed, Woods found that his colleagues carefully modeled the problem-solving process and tried to engage students, yet students did not develop skill in problem solving, even at the doctoral level (Woods et al., 1997). They therefore decided to develop a series of problem-solving workshop courses for the program (the McMaster Problem-Solving Program) in which—because the needs of each cohort differ—students choose the specific skills they will focus on.

Woods and his colleagues based their work on the analogy that instead of being given more fish, students needed to be taught how to fish. In the first-year course on solving reasonably well defined problems, for example, students most frequently choose units in defining the stated problem, analysis, and strategies, as well as self-assessment, stress management, and creativity. By the third year, students tend to choose workshops on asking questions, visual thinking, and group evaluation. Frequently chosen units in the fourth year are self-directed learning, being an effective chairperson, troubleshooting, and coping with ambiguity. In each workshop the students are given explicit activities that allow them to see how they apply the skill in a content-independent domain, let them compare their behavior with a target behavior, and help them to develop the behavior through practice and immediate feedback. Students complete journals for each unit, identify personal enrichment goals, and have two interviews in which they describe the degree to which they have achieved each objective.

Through the series of workshops, students develop thirty to forty skills in approximately 120 workshop contact hours. By the third year, when students have developed problem-solving and interpersonal skills, they work in small problem-based learning groups in which they identify what they need to learn and allocate team resources to solve the problem. Their perceptions of the learning environment are significantly more positive than those of students in other engineering programs in the same institution for quality of teaching, openness to students, freedom in learning, standards and assessment, vocational relevance, and social climate. Elements of the program have been extended to engineering programs elsewhere and to other disciplines, including medicine, nursing, and education, and across the globe in various fields.

Instruction in Design Skills

The thinking processes that design courses focus on are synthesis and verification. One commentator noted that different areas in engineering have very different conceptions of design, and thus instruction in design skills must take into account more than content and timing of the courses. Ropohl (1997) suggests that structural rules concerning the assembly and interplay of the components of a technical system are indispensable in engineering development and design. However, many design rules originate in experience only. In design, the engineer must create novel realities. Thus, according to Ropohl, the engineer has to anticipate the object to be realized and must determine the spatial and temporal details that cannot yet be observed but will have to be created in the designing and manufacturing process. Because images of novel design structures are formed from elements that have been learned by studying hundreds of similar examples, practice is essential. Projects are therefore the preferred medium of instruction.

> In projects, students are left a very open-ended task. The students know what the end point is; the initial points are really what knowledge they bring.

> Project courses put students into design teams where they are given a general problem that they have to define. It is not a problem with a single answer; it is more true to real life. One may be asked to make a proposal for a communication satellite that will allow remote transmissions from a particular medium to a receiver. It is up to the students working on the project to propose a reasonably viable solution to the problem.

In addition to working with general problems for which they must learn what is not relevant, in order to economize effort students in design projects learn about group dynamics. One professor of a design course suggested that engineering students tend to want to do everything by themselves and not to rely on others. However, in these courses, as in the workplace, this is just not possible. Hence, it is important for students to learn group skills, and cooperation is promoted by giving a single grade to the group. Student teams evaluate each other at different stages in the course by doing the assignment and comparing notes with team members. Before they hand in the final product at the end of the semester, they argue, discuss, and organize their work among themselves. Students claim there is a high level of transference of skills acquired in this course—they learn to assimilate and use knowledge.

Challenging traditional course organization, the principles of problem-based learning have been applied to a first-year engineering design course (Smith, Mahler,

Szafranski, & Werner, 1997). Working on the premise that engineering is a social process that identifies a need, defines a problem, and specifies a plan that enables others to manufacture the solutions, cooperative problem-solving groups of two to four students are organized. The format for group work is specified: the group formulates a problem and its solution and puts both on an overhead transparency, then presents the model and the solution. Discussion and questioning of all models follows. Students prepare a project report, and the group's effectiveness is evaluated. The outcome is greater understanding of the design process with recognition of its complex and undefined nature.

The professor's instructional responsibilities in this course were to specify the objectives for the lesson, make a number of instructional decisions on the group roles, materials, and arrangements, explain the task, monitor the learning and intervene when necessary, and evaluate student learning and how well the group functioned. Critical to the procedure is a criterion-referenced evaluation system, in which a set of criteria is used to judge a design, so that students are not placed in competition but instead learn standards for high performance. Gaining insider knowledge about how to think like a member of a profession is a primary objective of this program. Beginning in their first year, these students are introduced to their role as engineers and the processes of design and problem solving are integrated.

As a general approach to improving design courses, instead of using a black box model, in which faculty provide input and students provide output, Millar and Regan (1993) propose a process model based on two premises of successful first-year design courses. First, hands-on experience with the engineering design process provides students with essential knowledge about what it means to be an engineer, knowledge especially needed by those who come to engineering without personal experience as "tinkerers." Second, systematic faculty involvement with the course design process provides faculty with essential knowledge about what it means to be an engineering educator. In the process model of teaching and learning, faculty systematically seek to understand their constantly changing discipline, students, and university environment in order to orchestrate courses that have demonstrable effects on student learning. Faculty work together to assess student learning experiences and respond to them. Millar and Regan found that students resented being treated as producers of course output indicators, objected to course material for which the reason was not made clear, and complained that although they were interested in learning, grading on a curve reduced them to competing with each other. In response, Millar and Regan changed class size, how they conceptualized course content, and how they used class time and graded.

The first step was to reduce class size to a maximum of twenty-five students. This allowed them to create an environment in which students learned in project groups. The groups were challenged to design and build a device that solved a problem posed by faculty—for example, a swing set for a public park or a solar-powered still to produce potable water from saline at minimal cost. Grading was based half on the overall performance of the project group, and half on individual performance on exams. They decreased lecture time, and increased project group time and computer laboratory time, and introduced mini-lectures and "roving" consultants. The faculty who participated in the Millar and Regan study found that students learned more and developed better designs than expected. More surprising to the faculty, students displayed intelligence, motivation, and creativity. The course was more work for faculty but far more rewarding, and it provided them with key insights into factors that hamper and facilitate student learning.

The faculty designated self-assessment as another skill to be gained in design courses. As part of the global trend to reassess the role of engineers for the twenty-first century, greater attention is being paid to students' ability to assess their own work and monitor their performance throughout the design process (Boud, Churches, & Smith, 1986). For example, second-year students were given an extended set of criteria to be considered in judging a design exercise and then asked to assess the extent to which they applied each criterion in their own design. Students had already received detailed feedback on early sections of the project, and their task was to assess their final submission before it was marked. Over two-thirds of the students felt the exercise helped them to pinpoint strengths and weaknesses in their project, and most could see a more effective strategy for the design in light of their experience.

There appears to be general recognition in engineering education of a shift in emphasis from analysis to design, an expansion in the kinds of language used in engineering, and a questioning of the role of the undergraduate degree as the entry-level certification into the profession. The engineering science model is challenged by the need for engineering graduates to be able to operate as practitioners (Dym, 1999). Dym suggests that design, instead of being the capstone of engineering education, should be the cornerstone or backbone; it should be present throughout the program in every year. It should connect incoming students to their mentors, who are seen as coaches and facilitators. Although mathematics is the language for modeling and formulating problems, computing is increasingly used as a language for solving problems. In addition, verbal or textual statements and graphic or visual representations require acquisition of and familiarity with other languages. Dym suggests that because engineering graduates increasingly pursue other careers after completing an engineering degree, the undergraduate engineering degree might more appropriately be considered an ideal liberal arts degree for a highly technological age. Although this vision would not gain ready acceptance in liberal arts colleges, it presents a challenge both inside and outside the field of engineering.

Application in the Industrial Milieu

Many professors commented on the need for students to understand the professional workplace and to acquire the necessary work habits. A more basic understanding, however, is of the relationship between technical objects, the environment, and social practice. Students need to gain an understanding of the ecological and psychosocial contexts in which technical products must be optimized. These questions are usually dealt with in courses on systems engineering, value analysis, or technology assessment. In our study of engineering graduates' evaluation of their undergraduate education (Donald & Denison, 1996), we found that former students gave their job preparation a high rating and acknowledged the importance of developing a sense of responsibility, but suggested that students need to develop their communication, leadership, and teamwork skills.

In spite of the attention paid to these skills in the program, one graduate commented that more hands-on or practical courses were needed; the real world had been "one heck of a shock" to him. We concluded that adequate background in the disciplinary foundations of a profession is a necessary but not sufficient condition for being able to function effectively in a profession. Furthermore, our graduates' comments suggested that the interpersonal skills necessary in the profession are more likely to develop through participation in extracurricular activities than in any formally recognized component of their academic program. Thus the learning milieu extends far beyond the classroom.

Given the demands for engineers who can think holistically, innovate, and work in teams, the paradigm for engineering education has changed substantially in the past two decades. From an emphasis on analytic skills, there has been a shift to creativity because of the importance of design (Lumsdaine & Lumsdaine, 1995). In comparison with the education of the 1970s, when logical and quantitative skills were dominant, Lumsdaine and Lumsdaine suggest that the thinking needs for the twenty-first century include visual, conceptual, and imaginative skills to deal with long-range global problems. This shift appears to have been recognized in the recent greater emphasis placed on broad problem-solving skills, such as self-management and change management, interpersonal and group skills, and in co-operative learning, self-assessment, and early design courses in engineering programs.

The Disciplinary Perspective in Engineering

Engineering programs respond to a global demand for increased technological expertise and provide a learning environment that is in marked contrast to many other undergraduate programs. Although an umbrella for diverse areas—mechanical, chemical, electrical, civil, and computer—engineering professors and students are generally seen as practical and pragmatic. Similar to physics, a high workload occupies student time and students are expected to work in study or project groups. After devoting themselves to mathematics and physical sciences in order to enter the program, students also need to learn ethics and communication skills because engineering is a professional education. Cooperative learning programs, in which students alternate between campus and a work milieu, provide professional training but extend the length of undergraduate education.

What knowledge structures and higher-order thinking processes do engineering professors want students to learn? The engineering vocabulary includes concepts for calculus, physics, material structures, and systems, procedural knowledge in action schemas or competencies that can be applied to a variety of situations. Because the goal of engineers is to generate products and product-oriented techniques, the skills to be learned extend beyond problem-solving skills to design skills, both learned mainly through practice. Engineering graduates need to be able to break down complex problems into simpler ones, reason or problem-solve in situations where all the needed information is not known, and put things back together again. It is imperative to acquire description and selection skills because students must situate their problem and deal with contexts in which there is too much or too little information. Representation of the problem to be solved and inferential processes to solve it are primordial. Synthesis is critical in design, and accountability for performance makes verification essential. Thus, all of the thinking processes warrant attention in the engineering program.

What are optimal ways of cultivating these thinking processes? One approach is to coach students to understand the nature of problems in workshops or tutorials by having them draw a cognitive map or diagram on the specific topic or problem, write the rules for executing a particular procedure, articulate the relationship between problems, or design an inverted problem themselves. Teaching students how to fish is the analogy used in workshops, which may cover such diverse topics as self-assessment, stress management, and creativity. In design projects students also learn group dynamics because they must learn to rely on others. Cooperation is promoted by giving a single grade to the group, and student teams learn to evaluate each other. Courses on systems engineering, value analysis, and technology assessment help students gain an understanding of the ecological context of engineering. Throughout their training, students are being inducted into a profession that values hard thinking applied to unstructured problems.

CHAPTER FOUR

INDUCTIVE THINKING:
Knowledge-Intensive Learning

The goal is to let them make links between what they know out in the real world, and to have them feel that this is part of chemistry.

CHEMISTRY PROFESSOR

Most important in the area of inductive reasoning is the use of inferential skills. It is the use of these skills that indicates how successful a student is in the course.

BIOLOGY PROFESSOR

When professors in the natural sciences talk about learning, they agree on the importance of acquiring knowledge. The chemistry professor quoted here emphasizes relating knowledge to the real world; the biology professor focuses on students' reasoning inductively—that is, using particular instances to infer a general law. Depending on the discipline, learning has different connotations, terminology, and goals. The physics professors in Chapter Two describe learning in terms of acquiring an overarching conceptual framework. In contrast, chemistry professors tend to focus on learning specific content. Biology is organized according to systems, but it is considered by many in the discipline and in other sciences to be highly descriptive; the components of each system must be learned. Are these different approaches to learning inherent and defining, or do the sciences have more in common than the varied terminology suggests?

Chemistry and biology have distinct bodies of knowledge and methods of inquiry, yet they are grouped together with physics as pure natural sciences. Because they are also increasingly linked in general or interdisciplinary programs, such as environmental studies, in this chapter the primary goal is to compare ways of learning to think across science courses. We have seen that the natural sciences employ epistemological strategies that are empirically based yet codified (Figure 1.2). The implicit result is that learning is analytic, going from specific phenomena to explanation; in the process an extensive vocabulary develops to describe elements and relations. We first examine thinking in chemistry courses compared with physics, and next look at biological science courses in comparison with the physical sciences. In the search for optimal learning conditions, we then compare learning in lectures and in seminars from the students' perspective in courses in these two disciplines.

The chapter begins with the disciplinary context in chemistry, looks at students' learning experience in a first-year chemistry seminar, and examines concept learning in a physical chemistry course. The challenge for chemistry educators is to make learning an immense and expanding body of knowledge meaningful. Next, we examine the learning experience in biological sciences, examples of concept learning in biology courses, and the kinds of thinking processes developed in a biology course. We then compare the learning expected across the natural sciences and the optimal instructional methods recommended for each of the four pure and applied science disciplines explored: physics, engineering, chemistry, and biology.

The Disciplinary Context in Chemistry

The principal artifact in a chemistry professor's office is a three-dimensional model of complex molecular structures (Becher, 1989). Chemistry—the study of the composition, structure, and properties of substances and of the transformations they undergo—displays disciplinary features similar to those of its closest relative, physics. It is considered to be hard and pure (Biglan, 1973). It is also abstract: molecular structure is a representational system that connotes physical objects that cannot be seen (Coppola, Ege, & Lawton, 1997). Chemistry has traditionally been divided into three content areas: inorganic, organic, and physical chemistry (Barrett, 1992). The discipline has a huge and growing factual base with approximately sixteen million chemical compounds, primarily in organic chemistry, and growing at the rate of one million per year (D. Harpp, personal communication, March 2000).

Chemistry has its roots in Egypt, where the name of its forerunner *alchemy* was derived from *chemeia*, the Greek term used to describe the black soil bordering the Nile River that produced the food that sustained the people (Barrett, 1992). Alchemy developed a somewhat dubious reputation as the search for ways of turning base metals into gold. Early attempts to classify chemical properties in the Western world by the Greek and medieval philosophers' divided the elements into air, earth, fire, and water. The study of minerals led in the nineteenth century to a more sophisticated periodic table of the elements from hydrogen to uranium. It was not until the twentieth century, however, that understanding of molecular structure allowed a chemical industry to emerge, providing agricultural and pharmaceutical benefits as well as the means for chemical warfare. The development of synthetic organic compounds meant that by 1990, two-thirds of chemists were earning their living as organic chemists.

Disciplines deal with phenomena at different levels of specificity. Chemistry is situated between physics and biology, and it often depends on physics for explanation; that is, chemistry problems may be understood at a more basic or reductive level of discourse in terms of more specific phenomena in physics such as atomic properties. Science generally proceeds by means of reductive explanation—in which phenomena are related to other phenomena at a more basic level of description—and by constructive explanation—in which phenomena are described in terms of more abstract or higher-order constructs and hypotheses on the same descriptive level (Marx, 1963). These types of explanation are complementary, and provide links in and across disciplines. Overlapping interests of physicists and physical chemists have been a common synergistic phenomenon throughout the development of chemistry. In addition to its traditional link with physics, chemistry has links with biology (biochemistry, food science), medicine (pharmacology), geology, and engineering, particularly in materials science.

In Becher's (1989) anthropological study of the disciplines, a physical chemist observed that the physicist's scientific background is based on deductive solutions (law to particular instances), whereas the chemist's is based on inductive solutions (instances to law). According to Becher's informant, when a problem becomes too hard the physicist passes it on to the chemist, and if the chemist finds it too hard, he or she passes it on to the biologist. However, two of my colleagues, one a chemist and the other a biologist, noted that thinking in pure chemistry is deductive, but in the allied applied areas it tends to be inductive, and problem solution sometimes goes in the other direction—from biologist to chemist to physicist to mathematician. There is disciplinary overlap in both knowledge base and problem exegesis.

Across the physical sciences, Becher describes an accompanying hierarchy of intellectual arrogance: physics represents the hardest, most abstract reasoning. Chemists feel defensive in relation to physicists but sanguine in relation to biologists. The large published output of chemists reflects the fact that many topics can be broken down into small components reported in relatively brief articles of no more than four thousand words written by several coauthors, thus leading to a prolific output per investigator of some ten to twelve published works a year. Chemistry professors tend to be independent, yet bond within the discipline. Chemistry is considered to be divergent compared with physics, primarily because problems can be broken down into fragments. There are similar honors, however, chemistry having been included from the beginning in the Nobel Prize lists.

Recent attempts to situate chemistry in a philosophy of science suggest that describing it as a hard but more divergent, inductive, and fragmented body of knowledge is an oversimplification of the epistemological context. Chemical educators debate whether science can any longer be defined as the objective result of inductive inference in which one develops theory by moving from specific empirical instances to the general case (Regis, Albertazzi, & Roletto, 1996). In agreement with constructivist epistemology, they now suggest that chemistry should be seen as hypothetical knowledge fabricated by human beings in their quest to understand and order the world. This more recent depiction of chemistry is at odds, however, with the sheer amount of information necessary to locate the millions of chemical compounds. Chemists operate at varying levels of specificity, from atomic to complex system, and methods of analysis vary accordingly. Hoffman (1988) states that theoretical chemistry is happy if it is right 85 percent of the time on the geometry of a molecule, suggesting soft theory, in which chemists use hints, analogies, facts, and intuition. Do students find chemistry to be hard or soft?

Students' Experience Learning Chemistry

To increase our understanding of the optimal learning environment, we studied students' experience in a first-year academic seminar entitled Why Chemistry? that was offered by members of the chemistry department to a small group of seven to twelve students. Although the course was not a typical large introductory course, it allowed us to gather comparative data on typical versus optimal learning conditions for the entering student. As the demand for more student-centered instruction increases in universities, we considered it important to gauge the comparative effects of different instructional formats. This course offered a test of the effects of academic seminars compared with lectures on student learning and attitudes, and it provided participating professors the opportunity to compare the two formats.

Two of the four professors who gave the course were interviewed at the end of the term to obtain their sense of the learning experience. The first noted that he was used to classes of five hundred, where the emphasis is on presenting the course material and there is no time to talk and get to know people. He also noted that first-year students are not oriented nor do they have the background to engage in discussion. He described the learning experience at the beginning of the seminar in the following manner.

It took two to three weeks before they loosened up, even though we were very casual and very friendly. They were friendly, but they didn't know what to say. They don't really know what is involved in a scientific article; that is, there's background, there are references, there are people who have gone before. The peer review system would be totally unknown.

The second professor described his teaching process in the seminar.

I found invention really caught their attention because everybody who is in science has read about developments—everything from Salk vaccine to the laser—and these are all things that are found in chemistry laboratories or on campuses of universities. They are inventions, and the people who are given a Nobel Prize are considered role models, so when you talk about invention and inventor and innovation, students are interested right away. I had to produce quality material and I assumed the students were of a certain quality themselves. When I gave an assignment to identify five living inventors, they went to the computer and found a Web site that was particularly oriented toward inventors. They came up with things like magnetic imaging; that was very popular.

When asked if he thought the learning experience in the course had been different from that in other courses he had taught, his reply suggested that his instructional approach differed considerably, with an orientation toward how students learn rather than content acquisition.

It is so different from the didactic approach of teaching a course on polymer chemistry or organic chemistry or thermodynamics, where you have to build a mental scaffold of terminology and a way of thinking about the subject. Here it built on their knowledge of the world. They have a personal framework as to how they look on things in life—whether it's a copy or a camera or cooking. They learn quite differently and I think it's probably good to have a course like this.

In this quotation the professor reveals the instructional quandary of the chemistry professor. Chemistry is about substances that are related in complex structures, but students arrive with their own conceptual structure and way of thinking. There is some distance between content- and student-centered approaches to learning, and the professor distinguishes between chemistry as it is normally taught and responding to the students' state of development. This quandary is a tacit but continuing theme in the literature on chemical education.

We asked students in the course to describe their learning experience three weeks into the term, and then again at the end of term. We first asked their reasons for choosing the course. The answers show that students discern differences within the discipline and are aware of the effect of different kinds of instructional methods.

> I wanted to break up the routine of freshman science courses in which each individual does not make a large impact, the ideas are all old, and analytic thought is rarely dominant. I wanted to learn about something new and exciting that will help me to look at applications of things dealt with in the first-year science program.

> Sounded like an interesting course and the small class environment appealed to me. It explores areas of chemistry and science that I would like to know more about through informal discussion. I think this is a more effective method of teaching.

We asked students what they perceived the course goals to be—what students are supposed to learn or develop as a result of having taken this course.

> I think the goal is to understand various aspects of science and chemistry with a critical yet objective eye. Students are to learn about things that are never taught otherwise to first-year students, such as scientific publishing and atomic microscopy. It is an incredible opportunity to learn things that cannot be taught in lecture halls. Students should learn to discern facts, debate, and provide reasonable justified arguments.

What is most striking is the students' attitudes when asked to describe how they go about learning on a day-to-day basis in the course. Instead of depending on lectures to prompt their studies—the norm in first-year courses—they prepare well ahead of time.

> I read the articles and literature that are handed out, highlight items, and write brief notes in the margins to synthesize the material.

> I usually begin reading the material a few days in advance of the class, although in the case of the book we read, I started right away. Preparation does not usually take more than three to four hours.

Thus students do not appear to spend more time than the recommended three hours preparation per class; the difference is that they study before the class, as in

Mazur's introductory physics course (Chapter Two). Also notable from the students' comments is that their preparation is higher order—one mentions synthesizing the material, rare among first-year students in their third week of classes.

At the end of term, students were asked in telephone interviews how their course differed from other courses they had taken. Again, the emphasis on higher-order learning stands out.

> It has given me the opportunity to remember that learning is about internalizing knowledge (analysis, synthesis, and evaluation), rather than about the memorizing that is promoted in lectures.

> Not as much emphasis on grades as on understanding the material.

> I learned to be much more self-learning and self-teaching.

Students had developed positive learning attitudes that allowed them to think about the course materials and to understand rather than memorize. They perceived that memorization was promoted in lectures, but that in their seminar they were able to analyze and synthesize knowledge.

The Learning Task in Chemistry

In early work on how students learn chemistry, first-year university students were found to possess a large body of factual knowledge but many lacked adequate relating concepts or subsumers—general concepts that incorporate and link more specific ones (Ring & Novak, 1971). Those who lacked the linking concepts achieved at a very low level. Conversely, very high achievement in the course was associated with having a high number of facts differentiated from organizing subsuming concepts that facilitated the learning of new material. Successful students had (a) a large repertoire of facts—as did less successful students—but in addition possessed (b) organizing concepts, and (c) the ability to discriminate between facts and organizing concepts. The instructional implication is that teaching facts is ineffective unless students have organizing concepts available *and* recognize them as such. Providing scaffolding in the form of themes and accompanying assignments is an important strategy for helping students learn chemistry.

This is consistent with the constructivist view of learning, in which the growth of understanding involves a learner constructing his or her own private understanding of some relatively large body of organized public knowledge. The approach most frequently taken in the recent literature on chemical education is constructivist. In this approach, the learning process is perceived as an interaction between one's current understanding and knowledge new to the individual; hence a student's prior knowledge is an important determinant in how much learning will occur. We have seen that physics teachers start with mechanics because they consider it the area about which students already know most. In chemistry, however, students frequently lack the requisite experience (Pines & West, 1986). Pines and West cite the example of students learning organic chemistry for the first time, without prior knowledge of benzene; they will not have seen, felt, or smelled it, yet they will be asked to acquire knowledge about its structure and reactions. Their learning in such a situation may not be meaningful or related, and rote memorization, as one of our students suggested was promoted in chemistry lecture courses, is too frequently the outcome. The need to make learning chemistry more meaningful prompted chemical educators to examine how students learn concepts and structure knowledge.

Learning Concepts in Chemistry

In a groundbreaking article in the *Journal of Chemical Education* in 1984, Novak noted the change in the philosophy of science from an empiricist view of learning based on careful observation to one of conceptual schemes in which science is seen as the constant modification and refinement of conceptual models and associated research methodologies. To relate scientific observations to concepts, he described a heuristic device, Gowin's Vee, a V-shaped figure in which concepts on one side of the Vee and empirical methods on the other side interact to produce an interpretation of knowledge. Novak then used Ausubel's (1968) theory of meaningful reception learning in order to discriminate between learning approaches and instructional approaches. Learning approaches extend on a continuum from rote to meaningful, and instructional approaches on an orthogonal continuum from reception to discovery learning (Figure 4.1). At each point on the instructional continuum, students may learn by rote or meaningfully. Lectures and most textbook presentations are located midway on the learning continuum; that is, they could be examples of rote or meaningful learning. Unfortunately, Novak points out, most students learn chemistry in an arbitrary or rote manner, and laboratories may also be undergone in a rote rather than a meaningful mode, with students making observations but ignoring the guiding theoretical framework.

To encourage concept learning, Novak developed a technique of concept mapping for use by students. He had found that although students might be familiar with some key concepts, they lacked understanding of the relationships between them. He therefore instructed students to create a hierarchical structure

EXHIBIT 4.1. EXAMPLES OF LEARNING ACROSS LEARNING AND INSTRUCTIONAL CONTINUA.

Learning approach

Meaningful learning	Relationships between concepts	Conceptual problem solving	Innovative research
	Lectures or textbooks	Laboratory work	Routine research
Rote learning	Facts	Algorithmic application of formulas to solve problems	Trial and error
	Reception learning	Guided discovery learning	Discovery learning

Instructional approach

Source: Adapted from Novak, 1984.

and to label the relationships. Specifically, students had to ascertain what was the most inclusive concept for a topic, then subsume more specific concepts under it. Concept mapping has since become widely used in chemical education, both as an instructional strategy and for assessment purposes (Coppola, Ege, & Lawton, 1997; Nakhleh, 1994; Pendley, Bretz, & Novak, 1994; Regis, Albertazzi, & Roletto, 1996). In the last decade and a half, chemical educators have experimented with concept maps, Vee diagrams, and other forms of graphic representation to persuade students to integrate knowledge in a meaningful way (Foley, 1999; Smith & Metz, 1996). Visualization is an important device in making chemistry understandable.

In our study of concept mapping, the chemistry department elected to have the physical chemistry course investigated (Donald, 1983). This was a "classical" course; the professor noted that the subject matter had been around for decades and the concepts presented in the course are needed by students throughout their academic career. Students were delaying taking the course, however, because of its reputation for being difficult. Examination of the professor's course concept map provided several clues as to why this might be so (Figure 4.1). First, although the theme of the course was *thermodynamics,* defined as the interaction between heat and matter, many other key concepts were necessary to understand this relationship. The number of relevant concepts in the course, 170, was the highest in the sixteen courses we studied, almost double the average. Most of the key concepts in the course (85 percent) were abstract or higher-order abstract, compared with 33 percent in the physics course. Although some of the concepts in the thermodynamics course, such

FIGURE 4.1. KEY CONCEPTS IN AN INTRODUCTION TO PHYSICAL CHEMISTRY

as *heat, work,* and *temperature,* were part of an everyday vocabulary, their definitions were highly technical, which would increase the learning difficulty.

The relationships between the key concepts were based on similarity rather than causality, hence were not as closely or necessarily related in meaning, and were arranged in a looser web structure rather than the tight hierarchical pattern found in physics (Figure 2.1). There were also fewer links between concepts (twenty-three links between twenty concepts—a 1.15 ratio) than in the physics course (twenty links between fifteen concepts—a 1.33 ratio). The closest links in the course (1, 2, 3 in the figure) were between *thermodynamics* and the three laws of thermodynamics. If the normal pattern of knowledge structure in the physical sciences is one of close causal relationships between concepts with concrete exemplars, then students in this course would have to change their learning strategy from that expected in other science courses.

Even though they had achieved high grades in previous chemistry courses, students reported feeling relatively ill-prepared for this course. Student knowledge of the key concepts at the beginning of the course was also low compared to other courses in science, but it increased substantially over the term (28 percent), was the best predictor of students' grades in the course, and correlated significantly with their grade. In the course, students were encouraged to question points they did not understand and were often able to pursue a problem in class until they clearly grasped the professor's meaning (Donald, 1983). We concluded that indicating the substantially different learning strategy required in this course would alert students and therefore alleviate the learning difficulty. In retrospect, this advice could be applied more generally to learning chemistry.

The Development of Thinking Processes in Chemistry

Compared with the emphasis on learning concepts, relatively little is documented in the chemical education literature on thinking processes. Noting that critical thinking had received little attention in chemistry compared with physics and biology, Kogut (1996) gave students assignments that required critical thinking and found that many were unable to justify their answers, nor could they differentiate between fact and assumption, and one-half made assertions without proof. In response to these findings, he developed a set of instructional strategies to encourage thinking skills.

The first is to ask questions frequently that are process-oriented, seek explanations, or require evaluations. He uses examples and illustrations that challenge dualistic thinking and reinforce the notion that science does not have many absolutely correct solutions. He establishes dialogue by means of in-class group assignments and study groups, and by asking students to clarify their questions or to resubmit assignments to support their answers. He models the thinking process in class through data analysis, alternate interpretations, and statement of the underlying assumptions. After incorporating these practices into his classes, Kogut reports that students become active, responsible learners who grow in enthusiasm over the semester; they are challenged to redefine and reorient their conceptual knowledge base, and conceptual errors are more readily elucidated and resolved. Contrary to the expectation that spending time on critical thinking would mean less content coverage, he found that using instructional strategies that facilitated thinking also facilitated content acquisition. Student performance on examinations was excellent, and attendance increased dramatically.

A more formal approach to enjoining students to think as they problem-solve is to prepare assignments that require students to document the problem-solving process. In two papers in the *Journal of Chemical Education,* Mettes and others (Mettes, Pilot, Roosink, & Kramers-Pals, 1980, 1981) discussed a systematic approach to teaching and learning problem solving, based on the recognition that students have to learn to work with the concepts, laws, and formulas they have been taught. They developed a program for problem solving in four phases and described it in relation to learning thermodynamics.

The first phase is analysis of the problem, in which students make a schema to show the data and the unknown. In the second phase, transformation, students determine if the problem is standard and hence can be solved by routine operations, and if not, look for relations between data and the unknown so that the problem can be converted to a standard problem. In the third phase, students execute routine operations, and in the fourth, they check and interpret results. Each phase is broken down into a series of steps. Most important in learning to problem-solve is the transformation of a nonroutine problem.

The steps for transforming a nonroutine problem include writing down possibly useful relationships, splitting the problem into subproblems and choosing the first subproblem to solve, again writing down possibly useful relationships and checking them for validity in this problem situation, and then linking data and the unknown by applying the relationships. Students are given a detailed chart of the steps condensed onto one page for use in their problem-solving groups. They record on a special worksheet that allows teachers to observe the work and give precise feedback as they circulate. A particularly important section of the worksheet is for students' records of key relations. These can then be compared with the professor's, to establish their appropriateness and centrality to the problem-solving process.

More recent attempts to focus students' attention on understanding chemistry include a problems book entitled *Voyages in Conceptual Chemistry,* designed for use with the first-year chemistry course at Harvard (Barouch, 1997). In it students are asked to explore chemistry conceptually by solving puzzles, interpreting observations, and designing experiments. Problems are set at three levels of difficulty: basic applications on one concept, more difficult applications of more than one concept, and problems that involve subtleties or challenge students to synthesize material. Hints are available in the form of questions to aid students' thinking. In another recent text, guided inquiry is used to help students make inferences and recognize relationships between concepts and the questions to be answered (Moog & Farrell, 1999). The books provide learning activities that supplement a regular textbook and give students experience with chemical concepts and principles.

In these approaches to developing thinking processes, carefully designed instructional strategies guide students to question, transform, and interpret data.

Each approach recognizes the centrality of conceptual problem solving both in the classroom and in assignments.

The Challenge of Instruction in Chemistry

In a domain where the danger of information overload is severe, and where in response students tend to memorize rather than attempt to make sense of the subject matter, professors are especially in need of a framework for assessing the effects of instruction. When dedicated professors who had received high teaching evaluations were asked what they perceived to be the greatest difficulties faced by students in the first-year chemistry course, their responses fell into three categories: staff, student, and course-related factors, with student factors being the largest category (Kirkwood & Symington, 1996). Student difficulties included prior learning and experience, cultural shock in adapting to the course and to university, and more commonly voiced factors such as ability, preparation, and motivation.

Course difficulties focused on difficult concepts, content overload, number of students in the cohort, and fragmentation of subject matter. Although the professors attributed only one difficulty to staff—power relationships between staff and students—the professors saw themselves as cardinal in solutions for student difficulties. They identified their own approachability, direction, and teaching methods, particularly concerning corrections and prior conceptions, as important in solving student learning difficulties. Their solutions tended to be general strategies—tutorial, lecture and lab integration, content reduction, and real life application. The professors, even though highly dedicated, had very different views of student difficulties and how they should be overcome. Kirkwood and Symington therefore recommended that the professors discuss these issues in order to produce an aggregate picture to address the needs of students in their program. Changing the disciplinary predilection for independent functioning to a team approach is the first step.

At a more specific level, chemistry professors recognize a common problem among students in acquiring an understanding of chemistry concepts and principles. Where students' expectation and therefore propensity is to learn predominantly by rote, rather than by actively seeking to construct their own meanings for the subject matter, chemistry remains conceptually opaque and students do not recognize key concepts or concept relationships (Pendley, Bretz, & Novak, 1994). Students may be able to answer numerical problems correctly and still not understand the material, similar to the situation in physics and engineering. Students have been found to use memorized algorithms to solve problems more readily than by conceptualizing them (Smith & Metz, 1996). To prevent this algorithmic approach, Smith and Metz developed an instructional strategy of requiring microscopic representation of problems: students, graduate students, and faculty were given a problem and asked to create a diagram of the chemical reaction in it. Undergraduate errors were highly varied. Graduate students and faculty also showed weaknesses in their conceptualization of the problem. The diagrams allowed the researchers to understand the nature of the misconceptions more generally, then to use them as visual aids in instruction.

In another attempt to combat students' algorithmic propensities, assessment methods were changed from a heavy emphasis on mathematical problem solving to a mix of conceptual and traditional problem-solving questions (Nakhleh, Lowrey, & Mitchell, 1996). In addition, they changed one of three lectures to a conceptual problem-solving session in which students spent the first half-hour working in small groups to solve the problem, then spent the next half-hour explaining their solution to the other groups of students. This strategy led to several changes in student achievement and attitude. The first effect was that students felt this was a very worthwhile part of the course—the discussion frequently went to a deeper level than the professor had believed possible. Class involvement increased, and weak understandings of concepts could be corrected immediately. Students reported viewing chemistry in a different way, and learning vital skills in communicating their thoughts. In their examinations, students found the conceptual questions more difficult than the mathematical problems but became more proficient at answering them. The researchers conclude that it is essential to address concepts directly and to provide students with the opportunity to construct knowledge for themselves.

Heuristic devices such as Vee diagrams and concept maps have been used in chemistry labs as organizing tools both pre- and postlab to alert students to the need to reflect on the meaning of an experiment (Nakhleh, 1994). Maps can also be scored to show how many relationships and examples have been learned in the lab, but there appears to be a barrier between students' integrating concepts they learned in a lecture with phenomena they have observed in the lab. Integrating concepts is a more general problem; even very capable students seem unaware that they must actively move back and forth between smaller and larger concepts, constantly checking and rechecking the internal consistency of the picture they are constructing (Coppola, Ege, & Lawton, 1997). In a series of studies designed to match instructional goals with classroom practice, Coppola, Ege, and Lawton found that instructional strategies and examination practices were important in transmitting expectations, both for faculty and for students. They also concluded that they needed to give out the implicit rules and use authentic problems to elicit authentic goals.

A more general recommendation for instruction in the *Journal of Chemical Education* is to use cooperative learning to enhance communication and help students become active learners. In one study, students in general chemistry were divided into three sections: an unstructured cooperative section in which they were encouraged but not organized to cooperate, a structured cooperative section in which they were required to form study groups, and a control section (Dougherty et al., 1995). In the structured cooperative section, students cooperated on their homework and quizzes, and used e-mail communication for which they received credit. These structured cooperative groups had significantly higher student retention and higher performance when compared with students in the unstructured cooperative section, who in turn performed better than the control section.

In a second example of cooperative learning, third-year students were given a set of final examination questions with the course syllabus, then organized in three-day quiz cycles working in small groups on problems and concepts (Ross & Fulton, 1994). As in the Nakleh, Lowrey, and Mitchell (1996) study, students worked in small groups in class and then presented their problem solutions to the rest of the class. Students in other groups asked questions, and the professor gave mini-lectures as needed to expand the discussion and tie together loose ends. To evaluate individual achievement, students took a thirty-minute final oral examination. Effects were wide-ranging: significantly improved thinking and problem-solving skills; ability to think on their feet, listen more clearly, and defend their answers; and more active engagement in their learning and greater satisfaction with it.

These examples follow the pattern of guided discovery learning, where students must assemble their own understanding of the concepts in the domain (Figure 4.1). Although emphasis in the discipline remains on acquiring knowledge, using it actively and meaningfully appears to be the basic strategy for learning chemistry. For professors, creating conceptual problem-solving instruction and assignments top the agenda for helping students learn to think; organizing a team approach to produce such an agenda is the primary challenge, which is taken up in the final chapter of this book.

The Disciplinary Perspective in Chemistry

A synopsis of the learning environment provided by chemistry shows it to be empirically based yet codified and abstract as in physics; the huge, growing factual base of molecular structure consists of abstract representations, and the danger of information fragmentation and overload is severe. Students tend to lack and need to learn how to relate concepts through more general concepts but they also frequently lack background or experience with chemicals or chemical properties. Concept mapping is used in chemical education as an instructional strategy and for assessment purposes because it allows students to visualize and to integrate their knowledge. Attempting to change students' expectation and propensity to learn by rote rather than by constructing their own meanings for the subject matter is a central instructional challenge.

The higher-order thinking processes desired for students are similar to those in physics, but with greater emphasis on inductive learning, going from specific phenomena to the general law. Problem solving is focal, and the optimal ways of cultivating thinking processes in the discipline include exploring chemistry conceptually by solving puzzles, interpreting observations, and designing experiments. Because students tend to use memorized algorithms to solve problems more readily than conceptualizing them, one instructional strategy is to require microscopic representation of problems to diagram chemical reactions. Students working in structured groups in which they cooperated on their homework and quizzes and used e-mail communication had significantly higher performance than students who did not work together. Guided discovery learning, where students assemble their own understanding of the concepts in the domain and use it actively and meaningfully, sums up optimal practice for learning chemistry.

We now enlarge the context of learning in the natural sciences by contrasting learning in another pure knowledge-intensive science but one designated as *life* rather than *nonlife* according to Biglan's (1973) classification. This enlargement of context will allow us to see how general the challenges of learning science are and whether distinctive features appear as we move from a micro- to more macro-cosmic natural science.

The Disciplinary Context in Biology

The biological sciences are classified along with the physical sciences as hard but also as concerned with living or organic objects of study, similar in this dimension to less restricted or more divergent disciplines such as agriculture, the social sciences, or education (Biglan, 1973). Biology is bounded by the physical sciences on the microscopic side, and by the social sciences—particularly psychology, anthropology, and human geography—on the macroscopic side. The discipline is seen by other academics as highly descriptive, and biologists are considered to be more expansive than physicists (Becher, 1989). The central theme in biology is that all living organisms share certain chemical, molecular, and structural features, interact according to well-defined principles, and follow the same rules with regard to inheritance and evolution (Macgregor, 1992). Although the governing concept of evolution has virtually unanimous support in the field, general acceptance of this theory is less widespread because of religious beliefs—one-quarter of the North American public rejects the idea of human evolution, and another third remain undecided (Wilson, 1998). A dilemma in teaching biology is, then, that cultural history may prevent students from arriving at a clear conceptualization of the theory that makes sense of the volumes of data in the field.

As a discipline, biology is seen as a patchwork quilt rather than a seamless cloak, with the living organism at the center; but areas on the outer boundaries are farther apart from one another than in other scientific disciplines (Becher, 1989). Bloom (1988) uses a similar metaphor to describe theoretical frameworks in biology, characterizing them as loosely knit and therefore acting as a guide rather than a tightly woven fabric that provides questions with more bounded or predictable results. This breadth is reflected in the description of the biological sciences. In the *Encyclopedia of Higher Education* (Clark & Neave, 1992), in contrast to one entry each for physics and chemistry, the biological sciences are given eight entries, including biochemistry and molecular biology, developmental biology, ecology and environmental biology, evolutionary biology, genetics, microbiology, neurobiology, and plant sciences. Introducing the discipline as a whole, Macgregor (1992) notes great variability in categorization of the biological subdisciplines over the twentieth century. During the second half of the century the biological sciences fragmented into different departments, going so far as to describe themselves as different disciplines. The trend now seems to be to coalesce into one heterogeneous department that encourages interaction between faculty with interests in different types of organisms. According to Becher, biologists have a contradictory image; they are seen as interesting, serious, committed, and hardworking, yet having time to sit and talk. Biologists themselves expect clarity of communication in their reading, writing, and speaking while tolerating divergent values.

Historical accounts of biology center on Darwin's 1859 publication *On the Origin of Species by Means of Natural Selection or the Preservation of Favored Races in the Struggle for Life.* His observations on inherited variations among species and the fact that some organisms are better suited to survive opened the way to the theory of evolution. The foundational theory of evolution integrates what might otherwise be, according to one biologist, a pile of sundry facts that make no meaningful picture (Dobzhansky, 1973). Witnesses from the field describe biology as being inexact; evidence is incomplete, and although biologists may be attracted by the idea of generalization they are highly conscious of the variability of the material they deal with (Becher, 1989). At the same time, the ecological movement has led biologists from description to explanation, both reductive explanation in which phenomena are linked to more basic phenomena and constructive explanation in which emphasis is on relating different phenomena. One biologist has argued that *consilience,* or coherence, based on the necessity of reductive confirmation not only in biology but across the disciplines, is essential—the explanations that survive are those that can be connected and proved consistent with one another (Wilson, 1998).

Because of the variability of the phenomena studied in biology, research in the field is data driven and inference is valued. In some areas of biology, research funding and activity have outdistanced that in many other fields because of the critical uses to which knowledge is put in the medical sciences, with the rate of metamorphosis of the knowledge base exceeding that of any other field. Overall, however, publishing norms in biology are consistent with those in the other natural sciences, and fewer articles (one to two) a year per researcher are normal; they tend to be longer than those in chemistry (four thousand to six thousand words rather than four thousand words), with an occasional monograph expected. Whereas 80 percent of chemistry papers are written by more than one author, only 40 percent are in the biological sciences. Variation across areas of specialization is high; for example, an annual output of ten short, co-authored articles is characteristic of biochemistry. This is consistent with molecular biology having more predictable phenomena and thus allowing for the construction of a more coherent theoretical framework (Bloom, 1988). On the whole, as members of a more loosely knit science, in their writing biologists are expected to prove they have read everything relevant to their study and to acknowledge the foundation on which they build. Knowledge appears to have a longer life span, double that of physics, according to Becher, but in some fast-moving areas of biology it is very difficult to keep up with areas of specialization outside of one's own because of time pressure and the incomprehensibility of language and logical structure. Biology is thus more divergent in the phenomena it studies, its methods, and its knowledge structures.

Learning Task in Biology

Texts and lectures in biology are dense in terms of the number of facts per page (Ryan, 1988). In comparative studies across disciplines, professors in biological sciences weight gaining factual knowledge and learning fundamental principles, generalizations, or theories more highly than do professors in other fields (Cashin & Downey, 1995). Consistent with their professors, students in the biological sciences report making greater progress in gaining factual knowledge than in other areas. Biological science professors on the whole also rate "learning to apply course material to improve rational thinking, problem solving, and decision making" as less important than professors in other fields. Similarly, students in biological science rate their progress in this area lower than do students in other disciplines. Students report that the amount of work and the difficulty of the subject matter exceed the norm, and that they work harder in biology courses than in others. Compared with students in other courses, they feel that examinations stress unnecessary memorization and that questions are unclear and unreasonably detailed.

The emphasis on knowledge acquisition in biological science stands out in these analyses. The criticism is that rather than involving students in experiences that depict science as a dynamic and continuously changing discipline, textbooks and classroom activities promote a static, consummatory view of science (Bloom, 1988).

In an early discussion of the structure of disciplines, Schwab (1962) noted that biologists and physicists formulate their bodies of knowledge in widely different forms. Biologists ask what system of classes will best organize knowledge and seek data on similarities and differences. Time for the biologist progresses in a linear fashion, from past to future—like time in the common sense of the term—in contrast to the reversibility of time in physical equations. Biological classification is in weak schemas or prototypes, with exemplars at best having many of the properties of the class, as opposed to a traditional logical class in which all members are alike. Biological inquiry also differs from that in the physical sciences, according to Schwab, in its willingness to hunt down diverse consequences of many and various hypotheses. This principal of inquiry is explained by the existence of a greater variety of potential conceptual frameworks for determining validity in biology (Schwab, 1978). For example, biologists may conceive of an organism in several ways: as pairs of cause-effect connections, in terms of homeostasis where an organism is treated as a collection of equilibrium points, or as a feedback mechanism in a systems view. Becher's (1989) biology respondents portrayed biological training as offering a grounding in manipulative skills as in a laboratory, a capacity for reasoning, and an ability to cope with complexity. The potential variety in approaches to understanding could be expected to prompt greater pedagogical flexibility.

Instructional methods, however, parallel those in the physical sciences, with extensive lecturing (81 percent of professors use lecturing in all or most of the classes they teach) and some class discussion (Milem & Astin, 1994). Group projects are used slightly more often than in the physical sciences, but less often than in engineering. Assessment of learning is relatively varied, with greater use of multiple-choice questions, essays, and term papers than in the physical sciences, where more competency-based grading is used. The wider use of multiple-choice questions is consistent with the emphasis on learning facts. Cross-disciplinary studies of the kinds of questions asked in examinations confirm the emphasis on knowledge and relative nonemphasis on critical thinking in biology (Braxton, 1993). In a study comparing the level of examination questions in biology, chemistry, history, and sociology, Braxton found more knowledge-based questions in biology than in the other three disciplines; critical thinking questions were less likely to be asked on biology and chemistry examinations. Other factors that might be expected to affect level of questioning—such as class size and whether the course was designed for majors—did not affect the numbers of knowledge-based or critical thinking questions asked. This suggests that the discipline has a greater effect on the kinds of student learning outcomes than does student selectivity or class size.

Biologists often apply concepts or metaphors from their discipline to describe learning. One metaphor from plant sciences is the mind as rhizome—an underground system of stems, roots, and fibers that grows continuously, changing as it increases connections (Shuh, 1999). In a book entitled *Thinking About Teaching and Learning*, Leamnson (1999), a biologist, defines learning as stabilizing certain appropriate and desirable synapses in the brain through repeated use. The implication is that building new brain connections requires effort and will therefore be inherently difficult work, because students must organize, abstract, and relate. Leamnson suggests that mental circuitry gets burned in when a circuit is used repeatedly in a large variety of situations; thus practice with a multiplicity of specific cases is called for. This approach is consistent with early laws of learning in psychology: Thorndike's (1914) law of exercise states that the use of a given connection between stimulus and response strengthens the bond. The pedagogical strategy in Leamnson's conceptualization of learning is that in order to get the elements of the discipline to pass through new synapses, students must learn the study strategies of outlining, note-taking, and paraphrasing. Leamnson concludes that student-teacher discourse is an essential component of pedagogy—concepts are stabilized through spoken and written articulation. Thus the pedagogical approach in biology appears to be encoding knowledge through practice by means of a series of basic instructional and study strategies.

Compared with other sciences, the conceptual frameworks used in biology are congruent with students' conceptions. In physics, for example, students have a conflict between their own Aristotelian framed knowledge and the Newtonian principles they are taught; in chemistry there is little personal experience in the discipline. But in biology, personal knowledge tends to be consistent with what is to be learned (Pines & West, 1986). Unless one has a religious background that negates the central theory of evolution, learning is an extension and elaboration on or integration with prior knowledge. There may still be misconceptions, but on the whole the learning experience is a confirming one. This conceptual congruence may contribute to students' perception that biology is factual, because they do not encounter the clash of dissonant theory that a physics student would, even though the theory of evolution is highly abstract. In summary, the vocabulary to be learned is immense but is readily organized in systems, and if methods of inquiry are more diverse, disciplinary knowledge is congruent with prior knowledge.

Students' Experience Learning Biology

As in chemistry, we interviewed a biology professor and his students in a first-year academic seminar and asked them to describe their learning experience. The professor's sense of the learning experience in this course in species diversity was based on three goals that recapitulate the varied learning outcomes in biology: to communicate information, to develop students' ability to reason about problems in species diversity, and to synthesize and abstract, using the Web, library, and research.

> I sent them on different exercises looking for information with the task of producing an abstract or a two-page report posted on our electronic discussion group listserv for everybody to read and then talk about in class. Later we talked about how one abstract worked better than another and what the elements were that would have created a better synthesis, a better abstraction of a raft of information.

Asked how he would characterize learning in this course, he described the process in terms of discovery learning.

> The word that came to mind is *autodidactic:* I give the puzzle, you puzzle it out, and I help you puzzle it out. If you need a hint or clue I assist. After the fact I talk it through with you and reinforce the strong parts of your inference.

An inductive, inferential approach to students' tasks leads to synthesis, which some students are more successful in achieving than others.

Students had selected this course because they were aware of the effect of different kinds of instructional methods on their learning.

> I chose this course because although I find science interesting it is usually taught in a completely boring, rote memorization form. This course seemed to involve more discussion and actual understanding. I also thought there would be more individual attention offered since the class was smaller.

> For my education to be complete, I need the opportunity for discussion to challenge and expand ideas and concepts.

We asked students what skills and abilities they hoped to develop in the course. Their answers went well beyond the notion that learning biology is a matter of absorbing facts.

Analytic skills, ability to work and think independently, ability to research and work as a team.

Independent researching skills and the ability to formulate, compose, and present original ideas to a small group who are interested and curious. Oral skills and note-taking ability.

Their response to the question about how they studied on a day-to-day basis for this course was surprising.

There is a lot of e-mail discussion, almost every day, so I end up thinking about this class and its topics quite a bit. When there is reading, I do that and take notes, but the e-mail discussions are the most important part of the outside work.

Reading of text material, pondering, coming to a position of agreement or disagreement. Reading other students' comments from the listserv to understand their opinions and relate mine if necessary.

Comparison with their other courses highlighted the importance of the professor's approach.

I feel there is a great deal of respect from the professor for our own ideas. He is interacting with us instead of throwing material at us to simply accept.

The seminar makes for a far more intellectually and personally stimulating environment.

Notable again from the students' comments is that their learning is active and higher order—analytic skills and the ability to research are combined in an interactive learning experience.

Learning Concepts in Biology

As in physics and chemistry, concept mapping has been used to study the knowledge structures of experts and students in biology. In one study, students in introductory biology used computer-based semantic network software to represent biology topics they were studying, make the relations between the concepts explicit, and define the relations as precisely as possible (Fisher, 1988a). Almost half the relations in the students' representations were structural relations (Exhibit 1.5) in which one concept included another, similar to the percentage of structural relations found in our cross-disciplinary studies. Causal or logical relations (for example, *acts on* or *agent in*) constituted 17 percent of the relations and were highly specific to biology (for example, *absorb* or *be absorbed by, binds to, evolved into,* or *regulates*).

In a study of students' conceptual knowledge of photosynthesis, students mapped designated concepts, then wrote a sentence or two describing the resultant relations between the concepts (Hazel & Prosser, 1994). A greater number of branches and cross-links between concepts correlated with a deep approach to studying, and with achievement. The authors concluded that in order to encourage students to become personally engaged with science concepts rather than learning superficially or by rote, a supportive environment is needed in which tutors are willing to discuss students' maps on an ongoing basis. Both studies point to the importance of instructors and students thinking seriously about what connections are important in describing a domain, and in having students make these explicit.

We studied the key concepts selected by professors in two courses in the biological sciences—a laboratory on cell and molecular biology and a course on general entomology. Both courses yielded concepts of two kinds: substantive concepts, such as the biological system and DNA replication, and processes or skills that students were to develop, such as experimental techniques and design (Figure 4.2). In the laboratory on cell and molecular biology, most of the concept relationships were causal or procedural; this suggested a tighter or closer pattern of learning. However, the strength of relationship among the concepts was relatively low, and the ratio of links (eleven) to concepts (twelve) was low as well (.92) compared with other courses in the natural sciences, which indicated relative independence of the concepts from each other. The concepts were organized hierarchically, with a cognitive process, *analysis of data,* as the most important concept, at the top. *Analysis of data* was defined as a process in which one compares the results of an experiment to those anticipated by the theory associated with the problems being investigated while being cognizant of limitations imposed by the experimental design. The logical-empirical experimental method is encapsulated in this definition.

The parallel study of student learning in the course took place three years after the initial study of course concepts, and during this time the professor added four key concepts: (1) *recombination, deletion, and complementation mapping,* (2) *conjugation,* (3) *restriction enzyme mapping,* and (4) *restriction-modification systems.* Although students knew least about the four newly introduced concepts at the beginning of the course, by the end of the semester they had made the greatest gains in knowledge of them. Student biology background was the strongest predictor of course achievement rather than general ability or specific knowledge of concepts. The study of this course revealed that key concepts are frequently processes, that there is a need to update the knowledge structure during a brief period in this discipline, and that background in the field is most important as a predictor of course achievement.

FIGURE 4.2. INITIAL KEY CONCEPTS IN CELL AND MOLECULAR BIOLOGY

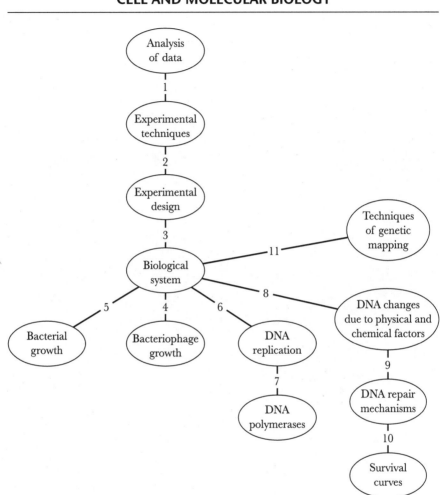

In the general entomology course, which served biological and environmental sciences, students were to learn a different set of skills: information retrieval, how to collect insects, deductive thinking, and manual dexterity with insects. The course had the hierarchical organization expected in science courses; the number and kinds of links reflected the ecological approach taken in this course—that is, a high level of interconnectivity, with thirty-five links among seventeen key concepts (a ratio of 2.06 compared with 1.33, 1.15, and .92 in the physics, chemistry, and cell and molecular biology lab courses, respectively) (Figure 4.3). The course calendar description (a brief summary of course goals) confirmed this connected

FIGURE 4.3. KEY CONCEPTS IN GENERAL ENTOMOLOGY

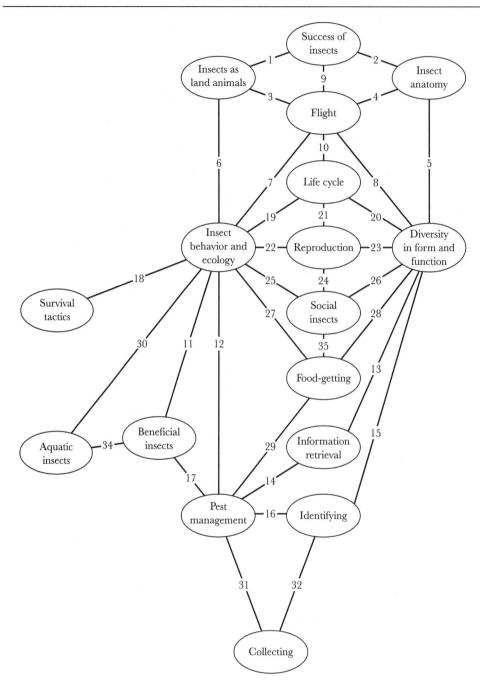

stance, stating that the course stressed interrelationships, integrated pest control, and information storage and retrieval. The professor noted that a basic law of ecology is that everything is related to everything else.

The most important concept in the course, depicted in a superordinate position on the concept map, is *success of insects*; understanding why this is so is the first course objective. The concept most related to other concepts, *insect behavior and ecology* (ten links), defines the relationships between insects and their environment; next most frequently linked, *diversity in form and function,* is an evolutionary concept that relates anatomical adaptations to insect habitat. These central concepts focus students' attention on understanding why and how insects behave the way they do. The professor noted that his approach to building the course was to create a structure of interrelated concepts into which concrete information could be placed. A field trip early in the course allowed students to observe and actively manipulate insects, if the insects obliged.

Students had not had previous courses in the specific subject matter area of entomology and did not feel well prepared for the course, but their knowledge of the key concepts was high compared to that in other courses. This was an individualized course that employed modules (prepared units of instruction)—core modules studied by everyone, and optional modules that students could choose among. Students gained in their knowledge of key concepts by 19 percent even though the concepts were familiar to them at the beginning of the course. *Identifying* was the most frequently accurately defined concept at the end of the course; *flight* showed the greatest gain in understanding.

From these studies, we can say that biological science courses are similar to physical science courses in that they show a hierarchical concept structure, with many close links and causal or procedural relationships dominating (Donald, 1987). The primary difference between biological and physical sciences is that in the biological sciences, concepts tend to be more inclusive, that is, take in a wider range of phenomena. This means that learning is extended rather than restricted, and is consistent with the differentiation of the biological sciences into emergent and ever more diversified areas of study (Macgregor, 1992).

The Development of Thinking Processes in Biology

In a series of studies conducted by the Association of American Colleges to improve the undergraduate major, the biology faculty task force observed that there is an emphasis on courses, bodies of knowledge, and what they want students to know rather than on how they want students to think, solve problems, and work collaboratively (Lattuca & Stark, 1993). In response, the biology task force recommended developing courses that present science as an experience in solving problems and thinking critically. Although the higher education literature describes biological science courses as knowledge-laden and descriptive in nature, the focus on research and other skills in the courses we studied at McGill University indicated that the professors pay considerable attention to the development of thinking processes. In our research project on the thinking processes developed in courses in different disciplines, the biology course selected for study was a laboratory course in the biology of organisms. The professor stated that in response to student feedback he had recently changed the emphasis and direction of the course to use transferable methods such as ecological sampling or histology.

He had created a model of skill progression from basic deductive and inductive thinking to sophisticated skill usage on the biology of organisms. Entering students are expected to use the skills to achieve a particular goal, then extrapolate their knowledge from the specific to the general. The emphasis is first on *identifying the context,* essential for successful extrapolation (Exhibit 4.2). Learning involves progress through alternating patterns of deductive and inductive thinking, with the use of inferential skills, particularly *changing perspective.* The professor pointed out that unless students understand the processes behind the derivation of biological information, they cannot understand the limits of knowledge. He therefore gives them questions to answer in their reports that require creative inference. In biology, inferential and verification skills distinguish the expert from the novice. The final outcome is insight into how biological information is derived. Thus, the focus is on knowledge but from the perspective of its creation and limits.

The Challenge of Instruction in Biology

Knowledge in biology suffers from a history of categorization that students may see as unconnected facts and labels. Some consider the information explosion in the life sciences to be unparalleled by any other discipline (LoPresti & Garafalo, 1994). The challenge is thus to show the integrating principles, as in physics and chemistry, that make learning meaningful. In one attempt to represent biology concepts for beginning students, LoPresti and Garafalo used three higher-order concepts as global organizing themes. The first, *autopoiesis,* denotes the active re-creation of self while maintaining self, a readily demonstrable quality of things that are alive. Using a pair-problem solving method of instruction, students first delineate the differences between the order exhibited by a marble statue and a living person over a five-year period, comparing the consequences of turnover of matter in each case. Students are then asked to read a case study of viruses, and to

EXHIBIT 4.2. PROFESSOR'S EXAMPLES OF THINKING
PROCESSES IN A COURSE ON THE BIOLOGY OF ORGANISMS

Identify context: Establish surrounding environment to create a total picture.

Identifying the context is very important if extrapolations are to be successful (inductive). Problems dealing with weights, measures, sampling.

REPRESENTATION: Depiction or portrayal through enactive, iconic, or symbolic means.

In the lab notebook: charts, graphs, diagrams.

INFERENCE: Act or process of drawing conclusions from premises or evidence.

Most important in inductive reasoning.

Discover relations between relations: Detect or expose connections between connections of things.

What does each parameter tell you about this forest? How do the three parameters differ from one another in their biological impact?

Discover equivalences: Detect or expose equality in value, force, or significance.

In the sampling lab, students are asked to make discoveries about a changing sample and its relation to variability.

They are asked, Can you see other types of questions that might be answered with data or density, frequency or dominance?

Order: Rank, sequence, arrange methodically.

Sample blood cells on a slide to do a differential count.

Change perspective: Alter view, vista, interrelations, significance of facts or information.

Most important in inductive reasoning. Unless students understand the processes behind the derivation of biological information, they cannot understand the limits of knowledge.

Hypothesize: Suppose or form a proposition as a basis for reasoning.

What, if anything, can you predict about a canopy's forest composition two hundred years from now?

VERIFICATION: Confirmation of accuracy, coherence, consistency, correspondence

Influences how other processes are used (deductive thinking).

determine if they are alive. From this exercise, students come to see that organisms are open systems that interconnect with their context.

The other two organizing principles follow from this initial one. *System properties* lead students to view organisms as hierarchies of communication networks. For example, genes network to influence other genes; enzymes network, as do cells. *Self-organization* refers to the ability to respond to changes in the environment contingent on one's store of information, manifested by the regulatory networks that characterize cellular differentiation. To illustrate, information in the cells of the developing fetus interacts to produce different kinds of cells and structures such as organs. According to the authors, one effect of using organizing principles is that the idea that small is more fundamental (the reductive approach) is replaced by the notion that both top-down and bottom-up approaches make important contributions to understanding. Thus both more inclusive and more specific concepts and frameworks serve the purpose of elucidation. The discussions provoked by students' working with these organizing themes alerted their teachers to misconceptions and gave students strategies for constructing their own representations of living organisms.

Another approach to making links between concepts is having students state relations explicitly. Just as writing and outlining clarify thinking, revealing their own organization of ideas allows students to alter and create new forms of organization or stabilize synapses (Fisher, 1988b; Leamnson, 1999). Fisher suggests that graphic network representations promote *chunking*—the creation of meaningful categories in long-term memory that are then more readily retrievable. Her use of semantic networks with students has shown that some students are process-oriented in their thinking about biology, while others are structurally oriented. Process descriptions require many more relations between concepts than structural descriptions. The implication is that process or function demands more higher-order thinking than similarity or hierarchy. Students' network representations provide a basis for clarifying misunderstanding of concepts; misconceptions are evident and can be discussed. Thus, as in physics and chemistry, attention to the conceptualization of knowledge appears to be key to promoting students' propensity to think.

Problem-based learning was developed primarily in the life sciences to help medical students improve their clinical reasoning ability and to make learning relevant to the students. Its use has expanded across disciplines including introductory science programs in order to stimulate students to become actively involved in their own learning (Allen, Duch, & Groh, 1996). Learning issues are identified by the students, and the results of group investigations of these issues focus the discussion. Students make significant use of the library in researching their learning issues, as did students in our first-year seminar in biology.

Powerful metaphors or organizing concepts, and a focus on developing students' skills in laboratories or in problem-based learning are the two strategies that exemplify optimal instruction in biology. Taking students beyond their conception of learning as the absorption of facts is critical. As we have seen in the other natural sciences, a tendency to algorithmic problem solving or rote learning has to be countered by instructional strategies and assignments that require them to approach the learning process as a meaningful challenge. One way of doing this is to create a community of learners. This may require multiple tier planning, as the professor responsible for an introductory biology course for eight hundred students explained. This professor decided to make learning biology an unforgettable experience.

> In the introductory course we use an audio tutorial approach so the lab is open seven days a week; we have tapes to accompany the labs, a multimethod approach. Teaching assistants staff the laboratory and teach the discussion sections, and I give lectures. In the discussion sections, students discuss material that is on the tapes, go over quizzes, prepare for exams; it is a class to highlight, review, reinforce. Lectures are designed to update; I tell them about what happened last week. We have a set of objectives for the course, Helpful Hints, and class observations and critiques by students in a teaching methods course. Every Sunday I do a bionews bulletin to keep everybody up to date.
>
> We have a team, and that's a very important element. We are teaching for twenty years from now. We want our graduates to enjoy biology and be able to read and understand biology articles many years later. We have a lot of motivational things in the course, including a biocreativity contest that they will remember. We have a bio-answers show on television where I go over the answers to the exam on closed-circuit TV; prizes are awarded in a drawing from a fishbowl full of students' names. I go to bio-lunches with students twice a week; students put five or six names in a suggestion box and I call them up for lunch. In my biology course I want students to think about life in a new way, to leave the class saying: I never thought of it that way before. The flavor of our course is very humanistic. A main goal in my course is attitudinal: to learn, grow, and mature.

In the organization of the course, the professor focuses on the undergraduate learning experience but engages his graduate teaching assistants on the front line to ensure that students have immediate access to feedback. He works intensively with twenty or more teaching assistants, giving them a set of teaching notes and resources, and holding regular meetings. They also have a peer videotaping program where every teaching assistant is assigned to another and they videotape and critique each other. Assessment of learning shows a balance between the need to ensure that students have a knowledge base and the need to develop research and communication skills and a positive attitude.

Three major exams are given at night so that there is no time limit. Each is designed as a one-hour exam and they have two hours to write them, for 70 percent of the grade. They are multiple-choice so that we can grade it quickly, get
the basic core of what we need to know about students' grasp of the material,
and because essays did not work with twenty graders and students disputing
their marks. Thirty percent is done in the discussion sections in two in-class
essay quizzes, take-homes, lab reports, and participation.

The first semester is more structured, but in the second semester we are
more flexible. In the second semester students do a cooperative project. We also
do a pig dissection and students have a personal interview on the structure and
function of the pig. A plant project is done in teams, and students design an experiment, report on it, and get a group grade.

We have a distinguished lecture series and the students who attend put their
names on the tickets, put them in a box, and then get *Benefit of the Doubt* credit.
We do that with attendance too. If a student is borderline, we will give him or
her the benefit of the doubt if he or she has attended. In this course the experience is more important than the information. I tell the students that I want them
there to *experience* things and that they are paying a lot to be there for the experience. We made a rule that it doesn't matter what your grade is; if you do not attend class and participate fully, you get an F. Students who get A's receive a letter
congratulating them, and people who get A's both semesters receive a special
wallet-sized certificate of excellence called the Fetal Pig Certificate.

The professor provides numerous incentives to make biology central to the
students both at the undergraduate and graduate level, and noted that a significant number of the senior biology majors come out of this course. The metaphors
used, from fishbowls to fetal pig certificates of excellence, make biology dynamic
and yet familiar.

The Disciplinary Perspective in Biology

Biology is a less restricted or more divergent discipline than physics and chemistry,
hence the learning environment is more expansive. Although biology has a central
theme—that all living organisms share certain chemical, molecular, and structural
features and interact according to well-defined principles—with evolution as a
superordinate concept, theoretical frameworks are more variable, and subdisciplines such as biochemistry and ecology follow different paths. Biology is considered to be inexact; biological classification is in weak schemas or prototypes.
Evidence is incomplete and phenomena highly variable; the process of inquiry con-

sists of a willingness to hunt down diverse consequences of many and varied hypotheses. The ecological movement has, however, led biologists from description to explanation, both reductive explanation in which the links are to more basic phenomena, and constructive explanation in which emphasis is on relating different phenomena. In contrast to physics and chemistry, the conceptual frameworks used in biology are congruent with students' preconceptions. Consilience or coherence, in which the explanations that survive are those that can be connected and proved consistent with one another, is a powerful organizing principle in the discipline.

The higher-order thinking processes to be developed are those needed for a data-driven field; inductive learning is as important as in chemistry. Concept mapping has been used to represent biology topics, make the relations between the concepts explicit, and define relations between them as precisely as possible. Biological science courses show a hierarchical concept structure similar to physical science courses, with many close links and causal or procedural relationships dominating. Concepts tend to take in a wider range of phenomena, consistent with the differentiation of the biological sciences into diversified areas of study. Learning to think involves progress through alternating patterns of deductive and inductive thinking, with the use of inferential skills, particularly *changing perspective.*

One instructional challenge is therefore to show the integrating principles or global organizing themes such as self-organization that make learning meaningful. Optimal instruction includes the use of powerful metaphors and problem-based learning in which students identify the issues and investigate them as a group. Making biology live is the most important goal.

Learning to Think in the Natural Sciences

The natural sciences have varied levels of conceptual coherence—from the hard, paradigmatic in physics through the hard but applied in engineering and the microcosmic, fragmented in chemistry to an emergent context in biology (Exhibit 4.3). Each context affects how students learn to think. In physics, the focus is on the student's ability to represent physical phenomena in different modes, from graphic representation to equations. In engineering, representation is important but must be applied to unstructured problems. In chemistry the fragments must be integrated, whereas in biology concepts are fuzzier and there are multiple modes of explanation, leading to the need to reason in complex situations. Physics, engineering, and chemistry place a priority on learning to problem-solve; in biology more general reasoning and induction are important because of the complexity of the field.

For students entering each discipline the requirements for prior knowledge differ substantially. In physics the prior knowledge expected is extensive—logic,

EXHIBIT 4.3. COMPARISON OF LEARNING
IN THE NATURAL SCIENCE DISCIPLINES

Discipline	Nature of Discipline	What Is To Be Learned	Expectations of Students' Entering Knowledge	Instructional Methods
Physics	Hard, pure, paradigmatic, abstract-concrete, nonlife, highly convergent	Very abstract concepts with concrete exemplars, representation of physical phenomena in different modes, problem solving	Logic, mathematical insight, visual images; conflict between personal knowledge and formal principles taught	*Found:* lecturing, labs. *Optimal:* active learning, interactive engagement, touchstone problems, model strategies, peer instruction
Engineering	Hard, applied, concrete, nonlife	Application of mathematical and physical science knowledge to unstructured problems, design skills, application of skills in the industrial-economic milieu, professional practice	Success in mathematics and physical science, ability to think logically	*Found:* lecturing, some class discussion, project work *Optimal:* computer-assisted learning, cooperative learning, competency-based grading, workshops on learning skills
Chemistry	Hard, pure, paradigmatic, abstract, nonlife, fragmented, variable specificity (from atomic to complex system)	Structure and properties of substances and their transformations, integration of concepts, inductive thinking, problem solving	Very little (they lack experience), concepts have technical definitions	*Found:* lecturing, some class discussion *Optimal:* concept mapping for relationships between concepts, conceptual problem-solving sessions, structured cooperative groups

Discipline	Nature of Discipline	What Is To Be Learned	Expectations of Students' Entering Knowledge	Instructional Methods
Biology	Pure, life, descriptive, emergent, loosely knit, heterogeneous	Substantive concepts, manipulative skill, reasoning, ability to cope with complexity, induction and inference	Congruent with what is to be learned unless religious background negates theory of evolution	*Found:* lecturing, some class discussion, assessment of learning by multiple-choice questions *Optimal:* concept mapping, global organizing themes, problem-based learning

mathematical insight, visual images. These are needed in order to problem-solve. In addition, there is a conflict between what is generally held (lay or Aristotelian theory) about the physical world and what students are expected to learn. The same kinds of prior knowledge are expected in engineering, but the connection between prior knowledge and learning in engineering courses is strengthened because of the application to concrete situations. The preference on the part of engineering professors for students who have had experience before entering the program and the trend to coop programs reflect this emphasis. In chemistry the situation is once again different. Students will not have had prior experience with many chemical compounds; chemistry sets—once popular children's toys—were banned some years ago in many locales because of potential danger. Students will thus frequently lack concrete examples. In biology, in contrast, what is to be learned is congruent with general knowledge, and the challenge is to deal with a vast vocabulary and varied frameworks for organizing it.

Of greater concern to instructors should be the classroom situation, which shows considerable commonality across these disciplines. The mode is to use large class lectures, with some discussion. Labs are frequently not conjunctive with the lectures, and students operate in a rote or algorithmic manner rather than meaningfully. For students to learn to think, what is important is active learning in which they practice relating concepts and problem solving. In all these disciplines, several aspects of the learning situation must be dealt with. First is the knowledge burden, more evident in chemistry and biology because knowledge is not organized there as paradigmatically as Newtonian physics is. Ways of organizing knowledge so that it can be incorporated into a learning schema need to be delineated; the crux is how concepts are related. Professors working with us to create their course concept maps put a great deal of effort into selecting concepts and defining the relationships between them. If it took considerable effort on the part of the professors to explain these relationships, the task is going to be much more difficult for students. The concept of spiraling learning, so that increased understanding of a basic concept such as *force* in physics takes place over a four- or five-year period, gives us some sense of the enormity of the learning challenge.

How do we enlighten? One question that must be dealt with is the level of instructional resources needed to promote active, meaningful learning. Across these four disciplines, examples of optimal learning situations make reference to the preparation and use of learning materials such as worksheets. For faculty, time pressure from research and service eat into potential allocations for course planning and instruction. The professor who had organized the introductory biology course for eight hundred students noted that in his university there is a cadre of a dozen faculty members who teach introductory gateway courses. They meet periodically and try to create an atmosphere of excellence in teaching at the undergraduate level, in which students are important and faculty are concerned with their transition. It is clear that some teaching methods that promote higher-order learning and thinking—for example, peer and small group instruction—can occur in a large group instructional setting. It is the development of learning materials and the assessment of assignments that require the greatest amount of time.

When we presented the results of the concept mapping study to our university community, a professor and an administrator suggested that course credit should be assigned based on the number of concepts to be learned. This suggestion, however, would require major administrative reorganization in the institution, with legitimating proof of the curriculum at the heart of academic program operations. Given what we now know about the importance of organizing and relating concepts in order to problem-solve, we should probably consider assigning credit on the basis of criteria such as the complexity of relations between concepts and the depth of problem solving observed. Students would then know what level of challenge to expect in the course, and that they would be expected to think, and they would be duly rewarded for their accomplishments.

Conceptual problem solving stands out as a method of ensuring that students learn to think in the sciences. Preventing students from plugging in formulas or responding algorithmically, by posing hypothetical cases or demanding a change in perspective in class or in assignments, requires considerable instructional planning. Teams have the greatest potential for organizing learning experiences that ensure students learn to think. We will return to these instructional issues, which are also institutional issues, in the final chapter.

CHAPTER FIVE

MULTIFACETED THINKING:
Learning in a Social Science

Perhaps one of the most fundamental goals is to increase students' general curiosity about the nature of human nature, to make them wonder about why they think, and act, and feel the way they do, and why other people do.

PSYCHOLOGY PROFESSOR

Studying psychology is both liberating and daunting. This quotation illustrates the emancipating potential of study in this discipline; the discovery that psychology is also a hard science with huge archives of knowledge and an exacting methodology can be intimidating. The predominant public view of psychology is that it is a paramedical field—clinical psychologists attend to people who cannot cope or educational psychologists evaluate students having trouble in school. In experimental or academic psychology, however, the subfields and interests extend from the neurophysiological to the social, from pure science to application in all areas of human endeavor, and from the early development of infants to the management of corporations.

This chapter begins with a general comparison between the intellectual cultures of the social and physical sciences, and the perspective of the social sciences on knowledge. Psychology—a social science field whose logical structure ranges from the hard or highly structured to the soft or complex—was chosen as the representative pure social science because of its size and prominence as a field and the extended self-examination it has undergone. To understand psychology as a discipline, I first explore its development as a social science and the various origins of its subfields. Psychology professors are members of an extended family with a brief history of behavioristic patriarchy, and a lived experience of diversity. Students may enter psychology in order to understand themselves but must quickly redirect their attention to the theoretical frameworks and scientific evidence that supports those frameworks.

To witness how students learn to think like psychologists, I examine student experience in an introductory course, then turn to a more advanced course on thinking to investigate how concepts are learned. Eleven psychology professors representing different subfields contributed to the analysis of the thinking processes that students are expected to develop in their courses; forty students were interviewed to understand their perceptions of the learning process. The major instructional challenges are how to link scientific knowledge in the discipline with students' interests, and then how to help students learn the process of research and enter the community of researchers.

The Disciplinary Context of the Social Sciences

The social sciences are intermediary to the physical sciences and the humanities with a wide range of methods and validation processes. As in the physical and biological sciences, the classical goal of the social sciences is to collect precise data obtained through controlled observation (Pelikan, 1992). Social scientists have increasingly relied on research that is primarily quantitative even though hard science methods at times do not appear appropriate to answer important questions in their fields. In response to this imbroglio, there is now recognition of a continuum from hard (as mathematical as possible) social sciences, such as economics and psychology, to soft social sciences that are more closely related to the humanities in presuppositions, methods, and values.

Even when adopting the methods of the physical sciences, the social sciences tend to interpret the characteristics of the scientific method—objectivity, replicability, empirical proof and its self-correcting nature—differently from the physical sciences (Krathwohl, 1985). For example, as noted in Chapter One, in the physical sciences objectivity is based on the assumption that a phenomenon exists in the real or sensible world, and hence is observable or verifiable by scientific method. In the social sciences, one attempts to establish intersubjective testability or interrater reliability, where phenomena observed by the researcher would be seen or perceived in the same way by another observer. Perceptual accord is an added criterion to those of the scientific method.

In the same way as the physical and life sciences grew and differentiated during the twentieth century, the social sciences developed into a variety of disciplines. This development took place primarily in North America, with its logical empiricist and pragmatic philosophy. The institutionalization of the social sciences began at the end of the nineteenth century—the American Economic Association was founded in 1885 and the American Psychological Association in 1892—but in the latter half of the twentieth century, national associations in many countries became linked internationally (Scott, 1992). Internationalization forced social scientists to recognize that knowledge in their disciplines is time- and culture-dependent, which in turn led to an abandonment of the quest for a unifying theory in the social sciences. Attempts to standardize theoretical perspectives—for example, the application of Keynesian economics, in which the state intervenes through monetary policy to maintain employment levels, or of behaviorism rather than phenomenology—have not been widely accepted. Alternatively, bootstrapping efforts in which an eclectic approach is advocated and local metaphors are employed have become common practice.

Learning in the social sciences has likewise been transfigured from a generalist approach, through an introductory text that related questions in the field, to a specialized approach, in which the serious student can claim a close working knowledge of only a limited, specific domain of specialization (Scott, 1992). Specialization and fragmentation in the social sciences mean that professors and students may have difficulty explaining who they are and what their discipline represents. The advent of deconstruction in the social sciences, with its self-critical stance toward both theory and methods, increased debate on the validity of knowledge. Most notably in anthropology, ethnographic authority was severely critiqued inside and outside the discipline and led to an overall questioning of the value of these disciplines. Thus, it has been more difficult for the social sciences to argue for support in the university and from research-granting bodies.

The turbulence of the theoretical and methodological debate in the social sciences is mitigated by the demands of science for systematic investigation. Sutton (1994) points out that however disturbed some parts of the social sciences may be by the new skepticisms, relativisms, and resistance to authoritative doctrine, the academic tenets of disciplined and critical inquiry provide a sense of shared purpose. According to Scott (1992), progress in the social sciences depends on debate colored with tolerance and respect for differences of opinion in a climate where scholars are free to pursue lines of reasoning and approaches to study to their logical conclusions. Psychology developed under the aegis of systematic investigation, and thus it is at the hard end of the social sciences. In practice, however, it takes into account its humanistic, social, and biological foundations (Leary, 1992). Compared with the physical sciences, psychology is regarded as *preparadigmatic*—that is, not operating according to a defined authoritative model. As we shall see, its diverse foundations and its search for appropriate theories render psychology multifaceted and, at the same time, potentially emancipatory.

The Disciplinary Context of Psychology

Although psychology has some characteristics of a hard science, it is noted for its range of hard to soft subareas; in addition, its scope extends from pure to applied under the umbrella of the discipline. The discipline is young compared with the physical sciences, but its antecedents reach back to the beginnings of civilization as a branch of philosophy (Leary, 1992). Defined as the study of consciousness, mind, or behavior (*psyche* is soul, spirit, or mind), it deals with fundamental issues pertaining to human and animal processes. Psychological theories and methods reflect the historical and cultural contexts in which it has emerged, with North American approaches differing from European or Soviet approaches primarily by being more empirical. At the same time, psychological theories have been seminal in the development of other academic disciplines, particularly the humanities and other social sciences.

The shift from philosophy to science came with the experimental study of sensory and perceptual processes—for example, reaction time—in Wilhelm Wundt's psychophysics laboratory in 1879. This began an era of methodical study focusing on the functions or consequences of processes rather than their "essence," as had previously been the case in more philosophically oriented studies. The methods were translated into observation, experiment, measurement, analysis, and theory construction in scientific and professional psychology in North America, which houses a large proportion of psychologists and other social scientists. By 1990, the American Psychological Association had over seventy thousand members in forty-five divisions (American Psychological Association, 1990). Other, more specifically oriented organizations serve large numbers of psychologists in an array of subfields; for example, the American Psychological Society is dedicated to scientific (hard or experimental) psychology.

The subfields of psychology are diverse in their foundations and conceptual frameworks. The biological basis of psychology owes much to Darwin's *On the Origin of Species* (1859), which linked differences in behavior among species to survival effects. Physiological psychology has spawned neuroscience, including research on biofeedback mechanisms, sleep phenomena, and neurotransmitters. The subfield of learning and cognition developed from a focus on habits and conditioning to more complex information processing and problem solving. The area of motivation received early impetus from Freud and focuses on the investigation of drive, incentive, and reward. The study of emotion demonstrates the tension between the universal and the historical or cultural; all cultures distinguish positive and negative emotions, but there are many cultural variations in the objects of emotion, the situations that evoke emotions, and how emotions are expressed. Human development is an integrative area; personality is wide-ranging, reflecting the interaction between "innate" tendencies and situational factors. The subfields of social, abnormal, educational, organizational, political, and clinical psychology at the applied end of the spectrum link with various disciplines in the social and medical sciences. Psychologists make important contributions to the field as the result of many years of devotion to a program of research in one problem area (Becher, 1989).

All of the subfields define knowledge in terms of prediction and control, although knowledge is also viewed as a means of understanding and change, which reflects the discipline's social reform legacy (Leary, 1992). Psychologists are noted for a persistent desire for better theory and practice. This is the result in part of the discipline's entry into academia at a time when the physical sciences held immense political power and a new discipline could gain acceptance only by proving that it had theories and quantitative methods that emulated those of the physical sciences. It also meant that the producers of scientific psychological knowledge had to distinguish their expert knowledge from everyday or common knowledge—more difficult to do in a realm where common sense had served to resolve most controversies. Thus the impetus for establishing psychology as a science came both from a need to meet the criteria of other disciplines and to distinguish itself from custom or culture. This is consistent with conceptions of the position of psychology in the system of sciences. Although commonly viewed as a social science and receiving a large proportion of its research funding from social and human science councils, psychology has also been defined as a branch of physics, a branch of biology, or as coordinate with biology (English & English, 1958), and as such also receives research funding from the natural and the medical sciences.

The scientific aegis led to a preference for striving toward abstract, universal relations and laws rather than understanding concrete, specific situations—the nomothetic over the ideographic approach to the study of human beings. Danziger (1990) notes that this preference for the nomothetic ignored the possibility that a series of specific situations can have structural features in common, and that individual behavior in such situations would show common features across a range of similar situations. He argues that this would make generalization and prediction from one context to another possible, although conditional on the comparability of situations. A more severe criticism of psychological knowledge from the social reform perspective is that it has played an administrative role in classifying, managing, and controlling people rather than emancipating them. The demand for prediction and control led psychologists in the late nineteenth and twentieth centuries to formulate laws or models of learning with varying degrees of adequacy to explain human learning. The models, often based on the training of other species, have had inevitable but unfortunate effects on the general understanding of the learning process because they focus on simple rather than complex learning and have been adopted in different disciplines to justify less than optimal pedagogical practice.

Learning Theory: Models in Use

The generally accepted definition of *learning* as a relatively permanent change in behavior that occurs as a result of practice is based on a reductive model consistent with the concept of learning as association—a connection between a stimulus and a response. In pioneer experimental studies of learning, Ebbinghaus in 1885 conceptualized human learning as a process of memorization through repetition. In order to control for previous learning and hence increase the validity of measurement, he used nonsense syllables such as *glet* or *roit* to study human learning (Woodworth & Schlosberg, 1954). Absent from his reasoning was the realization that he was thus rendering learning nonsensical. Ebbinghaus's conception of learning as memorization was accompanied by a model of measurement that guides much assessment practice today. He postulated that there were four stages of memory: impression, retention (persistence of changed performance), recall (reproduction of once learned items), and recognition (awareness of previous experience). We still speak of what our students have retained, and we set examinations to measure recall and recognition. The problem with this approach is that it circumvents the obligation to test our students' understanding of pattern and relationships.

A second early model of learning focused on the effect of practice. Thorndike in 1914 applied his law of effect, originally developed to explain animal training, to human learning. The *law of effect* stated that satisfaction following from an act strengthens the bond and leads to its repetition, whereas annoyance weakens the bond. Satisfaction and annoyance were conceived in terms of synaptic functions and were thus coherent with biological theory. His *law of exercise*, that the use of a given connection between a stimulus and a response strengthens the bond, is consistent with the associationist model and led to the saying that "practice makes perfect." It is reflected in Leamnson's (1999) biological approach to learning, in which mental circuitry gets burned in, and which also neglects the effects of complexity and higher-order learning.

The first breakthrough in paying attention to higher-order processing was Shannon and Weaver's (1949) information theory, which drew on communications theory to explain how messages or signals are sent and received. The prototype of an information channel is a perfect telephone line in which information transmission is complete, but many information channels do not deliver total output and the receiver is left with some uncertainty (Berlyne, 1965). The receiver may also select information to reduce the uncertainty, and complexity of form influences information transmission. Information theory, in which information is encoded and in the process transformed and actively retrieved, is closer to a model of active or directed learning. Information theory also updated theories of memory: the concepts of immediate or short-term memory and long-term memory were introduced to discriminate between the limited capacity of an individual to attend to streams of data—the magical number seven plus or minus two registering the limits (Miller, 1956)—and semantic or mediated memory.

Attention to what the individual learner brings to the situation came from a more molar approach based in Gestalt psychology, which looked for principles of arrangement, synthesis, or organization. One question was how new knowledge is articulated with already existing knowledge. The answer, which came to underpin educational theory and practice, was the concept of the *apperceptive mass*—an individual's cognitive structure (Bartlett, 1932). In this approach learning depends on discovering relationships between the facts presented and the learner's experience. Prior knowledge will assist or limit the learning of new knowledge depending on whether it is consistent or not. The relationships or logical structures of knowledge are *schemas,* ideas or concepts combined in a coherent plan by an active learner. Another question about learners was *why* an individual learns, which led Tolman (1949), who was both a behaviorist and a gestaltist, to postulate that the organism responds purposefully and selectively to its environment. Perceiving objects as means toward goals, the organism sets up expectations and is capable of inventive learning. Learning is goal-oriented. This more molar approach to learning as exploration was labeled a cognitive theory (Woodworth & Schlosberg, 1954) and is the historical basis for *constructivism,* in which individual learners construct their own understanding of public knowledge.

In the contrast between the atomistic associationist and molar constructivist approaches to learning, do we have a theory paradox equivalent to particle versus wave theory in physics? This brief analysis of models of learning in use provides us with certain insights into our instructional habits in higher education. Association theory gives us an understanding of why professors repeat important concepts in their lectures and courses of study, and why they give students a series of problem sets to solve—practice makes perfect. Association theory also explains the tendency to give frequent tests, based on the laws of effect and exercise, and why students are asked to recall facts, or in the case of multiple choice tests, recognize the best alternative answer. Cognitive theory suggests that students need to identify themselves as explorers or inventors and actively select and organize their own knowledge. Discussion, collaboration, and project work are the pedagogical outcomes of this theory.

What is the learning context for students entering a psychology program? To what extent will these theories affect their experience? When students are asked why they choose to study psychology, they say it is to gain a better understanding of themselves (Cashin & Downey, 1995). What happens when they are introduced to a scientific psychology that requires them to become skeptical investigators? Depending on their background, this introduction to the discipline may be congruent or disturbing.

Students' Experience Learning Psychology

In our ethnographic study of how students learn psychology, a graduate student acting as participant-observer attended lectures during the semester in an introductory psychology course for four hundred students in a large auditorium on

Mondays, Wednesdays, and Fridays from 11:30 A.M. to 12:30. She also participated in one of seven conference or recitation groups where approximately twenty students met with a graduate teaching assistant once a week, and she kept a log of her experience.

One of the most prominent objectives in the course was to establish psychology as a science rather than just a useful tool for understanding one's friends and relations, as the professor explained. The text for the course, *Textbook of Psychology* (Hebb & Donderi, 1987) begins by stating that this is a scientific course. The calendar description (a brief statement of course goals) suggests the dilemma of the entering student who has chosen psychology in order to understand herself:

> Introduction to the scientific study of mind and behavior. Learning, perception, motivation, and thinking are explained in a way which emphasizes the continuity of human behavior and the behavior of other species, and which emphasizes the role of the central nervous system in organizing and regulating behavior.

Assessment of learning in the course is by means of short essay questions, designed to promote student written communication skills. The following excerpts are from the log of the second, fourth, ninth, and final (fourteenth) weeks of the course.

Week of September 9. Conditioning and Learning: Chapter Two

The students arrived early and encouraged others to do so as there were not enough seats for everyone. When asked if they were enjoying the course four out of four students said yes, and three volunteered the information that the professor was an excellent teacher. When asked if they felt comfortable asking questions in class, it was the general consensus that the class was just too large to allow for student clarification. Students rarely asked the professor for information uninvited and they did not talk among themselves during the lecture.

Week of September 23. Nervous System in Development: Chapter Four

Many students found this the hardest chapter and one told me that "it has crushed my dreams of psychology as a bird [effortless] course." The student sitting next to her said that he was in science and just looked smug. Another student commented that as she walked in late from the back entrance and saw the overheads she hoped she was in the wrong class. During the conference (with the teaching assistant) this week nobody spoke a word and students just took notes with intent, purposeful faces. The preclass conversation focused on questions such as "Do you think this will be on the exam?" Later, when they discovered there was a question on the chapter on the midterm test, there were serious attempts to try to avoid the conference that dealt with this question. The students who had more of a science background or who had read the chapter in advance said things like, "Just try reading it; it is not so hard once you spend some time studying it." A few of the students talked after class about Hebb's contribution to psychology (in neuropsychology) and how it was neat to go to a university where psychology had been advanced. They felt that this was the meat of psychology, what made it a science.

Week of October 28. Intelligence and Abilities: Chapter Nine

Preclass conversation was on how students had found the midterm. One student commenting on the tension while waiting for the examination question stated, "I spent the first five minutes just shaking." This week's chapter on intelligence and ability had a high incidence of the thinking process of verification. As students' understanding increases about how the discipline is concerned with precision and consistency in research findings, they are more able to judge the validity of certain arguments. Their understanding of the syntax of the discipline is also improving, and the lectures link more concepts as a result of this and consequently reinforce the same trend. The professor invited the students to question the validity of intelligence testing. He questioned, for example, whether the tests were perfect predictors and noted that they were useful only in certain ways.

Week of December 2. Psychology and Science: Chapter Fourteen

The lecture was a review of all the major theories in psychology from a historical framework. The professor noted when speaking of feedback systems, "This course is too short to go into the very elaborate working out of these ideas that took place after Hebb, and is still taking place today." This lecture looked at the type of work that is presently taking place in psychology. As the professor stated, "If you end up doing psychological research you will be working with some of these theories [that we have seen in the term] or another. There are many different levels of analysis and many different phenomena. In nonlinear systems, for example, small influences can have extremely large effects. The question in psychology is: Can we get a large-scale system that is predictable? This is the type of direction that psychological research may go in." In response to a student question about how one knows about one's self, the professor replied, "We only have partial knowledge about ourselves. No single person is completely aware of his or her mediating processes at one time." His concluding remarks evoked a round of applause from the class.

The participant-observer summarized the learning experience in the following way.

Many students felt this was an outstanding course. After taking such a comprehensive introductory course students would have a clearer idea of the directions and types of research found in psychology as well as the type of work that could be found in the field. To do well in this course the students must go above and beyond what they have been doing for their classes in high school. Students with little or no science background will have a lot of extra work compared to their counterparts. As they are taking Biology 100 concurrently they may find that the scientific aspects of the course get easier as the term progresses. Students looking for an easy course to reduce their workload will not do well. The essays demand more than reiteration of the material in the text. Students will have to make new connections between the concepts and argue their point clearly and precisely. As so much of the mark in the course rests on writing essays, students will not be able to guess their way through the course as they might on a multiple-choice exam. Students whose first language is not English will also have a tough time absorbing so many concepts and definitions.

An important observation from the log is that students in this heterogeneous class discriminate among themselves on the basis of their science background, which is needed to understand many of the concepts and theories in the course. The professor explicitly models a scientific approach to the subject matter, which is cause for consternation on the part of some students. Students appear to put a great deal of work into the course, and are supported in their endeavor; nonetheless, they are expected to think, and to some this is surprising in a lecture course.

The Learning Task in Psychology

For those who want to become psychologists, what does the discipline expect students to learn? Because students for the most part are introduced to psychology in university, it is a good example of developing a knowledge structure and ways of thinking from the most basic level. Although during the latter twentieth century psychology courses were introduced as options in some high schools, their approach and content may bear little similarity to those in university. Studies show no relation between taking psychology in high school and grades in introductory psychology courses in university (Griggs & Jackson, 1988; Hedges & Thomas, 1980; Meeker, Fox, & Whitley, 1994). Meeker, Fox, and Whitley did find a modest but significant correlation between years of science in high school and grade in an introductory psychology course in university.

One objective of the introductory psychology course in university is to demystify the discipline, and particularly to establish methods of creating knowledge and criteria for testing it. Students come to introductory psychology courses with very different backgrounds, as frequently registered in arts programs as in science, and their expectations and performance vary greatly. The research literature explains the effects of these students' diverse approaches. A proportion of them have dualistic epistemologies; that is, they conceive of knowledge as a set of discrete truths rather than having a relativistic (context-oriented) conception of knowledge (Ryan, 1984a). The dualistic conception leads students to perform poorly in comparison with those who approach knowledge by trying to understand or apply it (Schommer & Walker, 1995). Students with relativistic epistemologies consider knowledge to be an array of interpreted and integrated propositions, and produce more coherent essays (Ryan, 1984b). Where assessment of learning is based on essays, students with more advanced epistemologies have a clear advantage.

In addition to epistemological variations, it is widely accepted that introductory psychology students enter the classroom with specific misconceptions about the subject matter (Brown, 1983, 1984; Vaughan, 1977). Attribution research has shown that students have varying perceptions of causality, stability, and controllability—concepts central to the understanding of psychology—which affect their judgment (Russell, 1982). Psychology and natural science students have lower levels of belief in unsubstantiated (for example, paranormal) phenomena than humanities students, but the absolute level of belief is high even among advanced undergraduate students (Gray & Mill, 1990). Does student heterogeneity affect the way courses are organized? One professor of an introductory psychology course noted the importance of inducing verbal precision.

> Many of the words they know they must learn to use more precisely, like *schizophrenia* and *depression* or *multiple personality*. Because psychology is part of the popular culture, students hear these words, which are used inconsistently or vaguely, and they have to learn to use them precisely. For example, to behaviorists there is a huge difference between *reward* and *reinforcement*, where people are rewarded and responses are reinforced. You do not reward a response.

Introductory psychology professors often describe their courses in terms of developing a basic vocabulary. We could therefore expect that early courses in psychology would focus on the development of knowledge structures, but research methods are equally foundational. Course objectives weighted more highly by psychology professors are similar to those of biological science professors—gaining factual knowledge and learning fundamental principles, generalizations, or theories (Cashin & Downey, 1995). Psychology professors award

greater weight to discovering the implications of course material for understanding oneself than professors in other disciplines do. Psychology students con-
cur with their professors by stating that they gained factual knowledge and
learned fundamental principles, and by giving greater relative weight to their
progress in applying course material to understanding themselves. Students in
psychology courses report few differences from other students in rating instructional behaviors but note that they had a higher amount of reading for their
course. General attitudes toward the field are more positive as a result of students' having taken the course than in other courses. These findings are consistent with those of Franklin and Theall (1995), who found that social and
behavioral science students rated their instructors as more effective than did those
in science and mathematics.

Learning Concepts in Psychology

One of the tenets of this book is that concepts—elements of knowledge—are
related to each other in a framework that forms the knowledge structure or core
content of a course (Exhibit 1.2). In psychology as in physics there are many concepts to learn, and they are complex concepts that require not only a definition
but an understanding of their salient features, including an operational definition.
In an assessment of students' knowledge of psychological concepts, understanding the relationships among the concepts predicted course performance (Goldsmith, Johnson, & Acton, 1991). Knowledge mapping has also been used as an
alternative to traditional writing assignments (Czuchry & Dansereau, 1996).
Students' reactions in both introductory and advanced courses suggest that mapping helps them organize and remember information better than a traditional
writing assignment. For example, students create a concept map of terms as
they are introduced in class, then link them and describe the links. This kind of
assignment recognizes the need to provide students with both a vocabulary and
framework for understanding psychology.

In our study of concept learning, we examined the key concepts—those
that serve as main or linking concepts—by making a detailed examination of all
course material and applying a set of concept analysis procedures to the content
of a psychology course on thinking that was designed for undergraduate majors
and honors students. The stated purposes of the course were (a) to communicate accepted knowledge in the field of thinking, (b) to provide an opportunity
to learn about thinking broadly—for example, in animals, language, and computer-assisted instruction, and (c) to illustrate recent ideas about how the brain
might be structured to be able to function as it does. We found that most of the

fourteen key concepts (57 percent) had technical rather than everyday meanings and their definition was one used only in the discipline; thus one learning task would be to acquire a new vocabulary. All of the concepts were abstract rather than concrete—that is, they were without objective or perceptual referents—and half were higher-order abstract (requiring two-step inference). For example, the most important concept was *theories* (Figure 5.1). Consistent with their degree of abstraction, all concepts were presented in class symbolically, via language or some other symbol system, although some graphics or demonstrations were used as well.

FIGURE 5.1. KEY CONCEPTS IN A COURSE ON THINKING

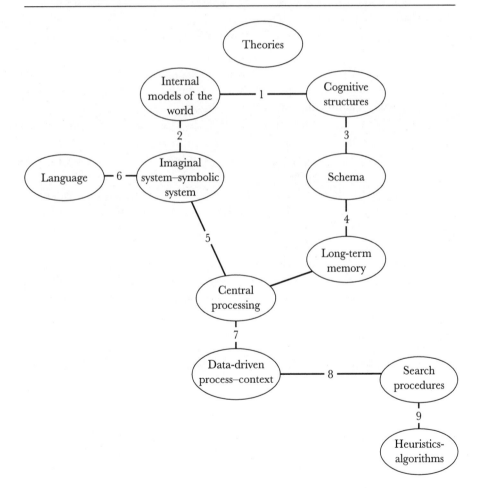

The professor's map of key concepts began with a link between the two most closely related concepts, considered equivalent terms, *internal models of the world* and *cognitive structures.* The professor described these pivotal concepts (the second and third most important in the course) and the fourth most important, *schema,* as representations, as were *imaginal and symbolic systems* and *language.* The most important concept in the course, however, *theories*—defined by the professor as symbolic systems, summaries that allow one to predict, understand, explain—was not linked to other concepts but occupied a superordinate position above them. It too was classified as a representation. Compared with other courses, there were fewer links (nine) between the fourteen concepts, producing a ratio of .62 (the ratio was 1.33 in physics). The linkage was more complex, however, with three sets of paired concepts (*imaginal and symbolic system, data-driven process and context,* and *heuristics and algorithms*) in subgroups. The relationships between concepts in the map were based on similarity; that is, one was a part or kind of the other, rather than being causally related. For example, search procedures are a kind of data-driven process. The concepts designated as representations occupied the upper (more closely related and more important) space in the concept map; thinking processes that were more specific occupied the lower space.

Students in this course tended to feel just adequately prepared, although two-thirds of them had previously taken courses in psychology. Their initial knowledge of the key concepts was low, but over the semester there was a significant increase in key concept knowledge. Concept knowledge at the beginning of the course was the best predictor of final grade, better than students' overall average or the number of courses they had taken previously in the field. Concept knowledge at the end of the course correlated equally highly with final grade. These results confirm the importance of the concepts in this course, whether representations or thinking processes. The best-known key concepts at the end of the course were *long-term memory, algorithms, heuristics,* and *theories.* These terms were used more frequently in class (31 to 70 times over twenty-four recorded classes), but the most frequent term (mentioned 373 times in twenty-three of twenty-four classes) was *language. Language* was used so frequently in class because it is proof of or an operationalization of thinking, and confirms the close relationship between language and thinking, for example, in Vygotsky's (1962) work.

The Learning Process in Psychology

Because learning and thinking are major areas of study in psychology, the professors we interviewed could be expected to provide considerable disciplinary insight into students' learning in their courses. Three of the eleven courses we studied were introductory courses and will be described first, two were advanced courses in psycholinguistics, and five were on thinking or cognitive processes. They give us a sense of the development of abilities in a psychology program. One was a history of psychology course, and it provides an overview of the field.

In the introductory courses, the focus on vocabulary development generally requires a dictionary or textbook glossary: in a glossary of fifteen hundred words, one professor stated, students will not have heard of a thousand. Other terms will have more technical meanings than expected by students. To correct for this, students are expected to purchase a dictionary of psychological terms and to consult it. Some time is spent disabusing students of misconceptions about psychology. Learning tends to be evaluated primarily by means of formal examinations. Final examinations usually cover the work of the entire course. Examinations given earlier in the term may or may not be cumulative; they cover material from the text, other readings, lectures, and discussions during the period preceding the test. In response to the large numbers of students in a class, tests are frequently multiple-choice and require a thorough knowledge of facts and details. In addition, these tests are designed to evaluate students' ability to infer and to apply knowledge to new situations.

> In the multiple-choice test there are four kinds of items. Facts and definitions make up the biggest set of items: when something happened, who somebody was, what something means. The next set of items concerns concepts: for example, the nature of reinforcement or behaviorism. The third set gets at inferences: going beyond what is given in the basic concepts or principles to make inferences and comparisons from one set of material to another or from material in one chapter to another. The fourth set is applications, the use of information applied. For each chapter the percentage of questions might be 40:30:15:15.

Learning is also evaluated formatively (developmentally, ungraded) through questions in class that, as noted in a previous quotation, challenge students to be more precise in their use of language.

> At the beginning of the course I will accept use of the term *nervousness;* at the end of two weeks if students use that term, I will say that I do not know what that means. The shaping leads students to use language more precisely and more meaningfully. Even very bright students will often say things which are superficial or almost meaningless, such as "They were excited about the situation." That conveys very little meaning. What do you mean by "excited?" What part of the situation? What made it new? I attempt to get students to be more

precise in their language usage. The reason for this is that I want the students to be more precise in their thinking, and the assumption is that language and thought go together. If you think vaguely or ambiguously that is how you are going to speak.

Students are expected to participate in weekly conferences or seminars, and although participation is not formally evaluated, in one course students are told that they will not get credit for the course unless the teaching assistant knows their name. Students may also have laboratory work or be asked to participate in experiments. Thus, evaluation of learning is both summative and formative: students receive feedback throughout the course.

The students we interviewed had little background in psychology, although one of them noted that his high school science courses had given him the skills necessary for the course. But in spite of having little preparation for the course, no one felt poorly prepared because a background in psychology was not expected of them. These students interpreted the goal of the introductory course to be to give them one possible approach to the understanding of human and animal behavioral studies—that is, a scientifically, biologically based approach. Another goal was to give them a basic approach in experimental technique and design.

Students spoke of having learned processes (writing up experiments, models proposed for encoding of audio frequencies, how to think critically) more than concepts; these were learned through a combination of lectures, labs, specified reference material, and discussion. This is in notable contrast to remarks made by students in introductory physics courses, who described learning as acquiring knowledge rather than learning methods or skills. One psychology student pointed out that experimental sessions are often not understood until the writing of the report. Asked what advice they would give a student entering the introductory course, two students focused on the workload and the importance of self-regulation.

I would advise people to start working on day one—and that goes for all the courses [in university], not just this one. There's just so much stuff, and it's so fast. The teachers aren't like in high school; they don't have time to wait till 80 percent of the class has got it—it's a one-shot affair, you have to get it when it's there.

A trap that many of the first-years might fall into is thinking that they can get by just with the lectures. They can't: there's a lot of reading that has to be done on your own.

The seven advanced courses in psycholinguistics and cognitive processes are given to smaller groups (from twenty-five to eighty) of second-, third-, and fourth-year students in honors psychology programs or in medical science. The courses are designed as overviews of the theoretical and empirical issues in the area, with comparisons made of the kinds of empirical variables, explanatory concepts, and research findings associated with different approaches. The courses are thus more research-oriented than at the introductory level and place greater emphasis on theoretical models. At the beginning of the course, one professor describes how students are given an idea of what scientific concepts are.

> One starts off by showing students the kind of phenomena you want to explain, and that you have to explain in terms of a model which incorporates mental events, mental processes, and mental representations. The framework is provided by that and by the phenomena and also by describing the way in which one can try to study those phenomena. I try to make students understand why the discipline conducts itself in the way it does, why you need an account of a particular type, and how you set about getting that account.

Even in advanced courses, a great deal of emphasis is put on developing an understanding of the major concepts, according to one professor, because the vocabulary is not as standardized as, for example, in chemistry, and there is a great deal of variability that students have to learn to cope with. Professors consider explanation to be a major goal in psychology courses, and learning concepts is intricately related to thinking processes.

The Development of Thinking Processes in Psychology

Professors in psychology courses expect their students to be able to think logically, independently, and abstractly (Donald, 1988). The way of thinking includes empirical testing, more like physics than philosophy.

> There is something uniquely different about the way psychologists and philosophers think. Psychologists' abstract thinking always has to be reducible to the testable, the concrete. For example, the violation of expectations and the nature of the mind are ultimately reduced to some systematic variation that is in principle testable empirically, through observations, through an experiment. It always comes down to the level of functional reality, whereas philosophical thinking can stay at the level of abstractness and you can talk about the nature of consciousness without saying, "How do you know?" other than through logical reasoning. Psychologists end up with empirical reasoning, saying, "I know because if I do it this way it makes an

empirical difference in behavior. It means I can predict something which I could not before."

The kinds of cognitive processes required of students have been described by researchers in a very specific manner—for example, translating from a nonverbal representation into a verbal form, selecting a certain type of content, giving reasons for the verbalization, and synthesizing or generalizing in a retrospective verbalization (Ericsson & Simon, 1984). Critical thinking correlates with students' perceptions of course difficulty in both social science and biology courses (Garcia & Pintrich, 1992). Demand and rigor in courses in these areas appear to have a positive effect on the development of thinking processes, in contrast to other science courses, where a heavy workload has led to surface learning (Ramsden, 1992).

In our study of the thinking processes learned in different domains, there was a pattern of movement in psychology courses from basic to more complex processes. However, the degree to which a course was concerned with either a content area or method also affected the kinds of thinking processes developed. When shown the model of thinking processes, one professor replied:

No one course would give most of these. Some courses, particularly those dealing with methods, would be more heavily focused on inference or verification. The lower-level courses would be focused more on description and representation, while higher-level courses would focus more on selection and synthesis. Higher-level courses would be more likely to give essay examinations in which those skills would be tested, whereas the more objective, fill-in, multiple-choice tests given at the introductory level focus much more on description and representation. In a lecture class, where typically there is very little give-and-take, where there is a lecture plus reading material format, then the argument might be that what students learn would depend on the way in which the lecture materials were organized.

According to this analysis, thinking processes are developed through a series of courses rather than any one course; the program rather than a course is the unit of measurement for thinking development, similar to the situation in engineering. A second quote confirms the change in students' thinking as they progress from less to more advanced courses. The professor begins by focusing on the development of inference so that students can synthesize and verify.

In the course, one is trying to get students to think for themselves, to be able to analyze information, to be able to evaluate it, to be able to identify data, to be able to categorize it, to be able to identify critical elements and relations and organize it in particular ways and discover relations between elements. What is most important is synthesis and verification. Being able to do these things requires being able to do the previous skills.

In the beginning, you have to ensure that students are getting the facts straight. By facts, I do not mean so much data as argumentation, what kind of inferences you can draw from what kind of data, and the way in which models are developed, the way in which you can legitimately infer from particular kinds of questions what the answer to those questions might be. I assume that by second term they have figured out something of what the process involves of working in this particular discipline and of thinking about its problems and how you are going to answer its problems and develop models. In the second term I hope students would build on that so that their essays would be more critical. They are working on new material, but they would be able to be more critical and more confident about the field, and also have more understanding of what it means to operate in it and to think about it. In the first term one hardly ever sees any critical appraisal.

Thus students are expected to acquire the inferential capabilities in order to think critically or evaluatively. The shift in emphasis over courses in some ways parallels that in engineering, where problem solvers become designers at a later point in their program. By the end of their undergraduate years, analytic reasoning is a priority for psychology students. The reasoning skills that psychology professors consider most important for graduate students to master are the critical analysis and evaluation of previous research in a field, the identification of issues and problems to be investigated or hypotheses to be tested, and the determination of whether conclusions are logically and adequately supported by data (Powers & Enright, 1987). Psychology professors consider the most serious errors of reasoning to be confusing coincidence or correlation with causation, and accepting the central assumptions in an argument without questioning them. There is evidence, however, that when students are taught to eliminate impulsive biases in the testing of hypotheses, they may also learn to give less consideration to generating novel hypotheses (Duemler & Mayer, 1988; Sternberg, 1981). There is a trade-off between coherence and creativity that is similar to the trade-off in engineering between the analysis and problem-solving skills needed in typical entry-level courses and the problem identification and design skills needed to succeed as graduates.

By the end of their program, students in psychology show marked advances in their ability to think. For example, taking psychology courses has been correlated with higher analytic reasoning and mathematics scores on the Graduate Record Examination, taken to gain access to graduate study (Ratcliff, 1992). In another study, over two years of graduate school psychology students made greater gains in intellectual skills than those in graduate programs in other disciplines, in inferential skills, in statistical and methodological reasoning, and in their ability to solve problems (Lehman, Lempert, & Nisbett, 1988; Nisbett, Fong, Lehman, & Cheng, 1987). Students in psychology, medicine, law, and chemistry did not differ in their reasoning skills at entry to their programs, but after two years psychology students had made the greatest gains in inferential skills, followed by medical students, with law and chemistry students showing slight but insignificant improvement. The marked increase in the ability of psychology students to think at both undergraduate and graduate levels, taken together with the focus of psychology professors on developing different kinds of thinking processes in different courses, proves the importance of such a focus for instructional planning. The professors provided numerous examples of the development of these processes in their courses.

Description

In introductory courses, professors considered developing descriptive processes central, although they expected students already to be able to think descriptively to some extent. One pointed out that descriptive processes might be viewed as primitive compared to others, but when entering a new field description is very difficult (Exhibit 5.1). *Identifying the context* was of major importance in testing models, and in particular in social psychology, where the environment is examined as a major determinant of behavior. *Conditions* are important in experiments, logical reasoning, or models of behavior. *Facts* and *functions* are basic to the introductory psychology course. In one author's view, however, a fact in psychology may be defined as a hypothesis on which nearly everyone agrees (Cox, 1997).

Many of the professors talked about the need to *recognize assumptions* and their role in perception and thinking. *Goals* were considered fundamental, whether in experiments, analysis, therapy, or instruction. Thus although descriptive thinking processes were considered basic and likely to be developed in introductory courses, they also were recognized as important for many different activities in psychology, whether experiment, logical argument, or instruction.

Selection

The active neglect of irrelevancies (Humphrey, 1951) is translated in classical learning theory as the elimination of errors. Students, however, tend to be unaware of the need to be selective and do not discriminate important from irrelevant material. One psychology professor said that students would not be able

EXHIBIT 5.1. PROFESSORS' EXAMPLES OF
DESCRIPTION USED IN PSYCHOLOGY COURSES

DESCRIPTION: Delineation or definition of a situation or form of a thing	*To chart new territory you need to make a map to know what is out there before you can build a theory.*
	Can be seen as a very primitive process but also a difficult one when a large new area of research needs to be reviewed.
Identify context: Establish surrounding environment to create a total picture.	*Where models fit into the processes, especially in social psychology training where context is all-important.*
State conditions: State essential parts, prerequisites, or requirements.	*Establish the difference between things that are necessary and things that are sufficient.*
	Contingency is central to behaviorism or to conditions of learned helplessness.
	In an experiment in short-term memory, know that exposure is limited to ten seconds at a time, present a discrete list of items, and ask for immediate recall of that.
State functions: State normal or proper activity of a thing or specific duties.	*State functions of the nervous system, parts of the brain, parts of an experiment.*
State assumptions: State suppositions, postulates.	*Organizing biases influence how people perceive and how they organize materials.*
	Axioms of utility theory, assumptions that justify the application of subjective expected utility theory.
State goal: State the ends, aims, objectives.	*Aims of an analysis, an experiment, psychology, therapy.*

to select when they began but are provided with material in their first lecture to be able to do so. Selection is critical to analytic thinking (Bloom, 1956) and so is developed in many courses and tested in papers, essays, and oral examinations, although one professor noted that creating questions to test selection is difficult. More specifically in psychology, selection is considered critical to the acquisition of new knowledge. Sternberg (1985a) defined three selection processes in a triarchic theory of intelligence as knowledge acquisition components for learning how to solve a problem or learning new facts or concepts: *selective encoding* to determine what new information is potentially relevant, *selective combination* to integrate the information, and *selective comparison* to relate new to old information. According to Sternberg (1987), students high in selective abilities have high test scores and grades. These abilities appear to be distinct, however, and students may have them but not have the creative, synthetic abilities required to carry out research.

Our professors noted that *choosing relevant information* is a complex operation; whether in research or in writing, choices must be made about the centrality of information and how it is related (Exhibit 5.2). Different kinds of information are important in different ways and at different times, so a sense of context is essential. The complexity of psychological information also affects how it is *ordered in importance*, because different criteria will lead to different ranks. Professors noted that psychology requires connections, so that *critical elements and relations* need to be identified together or in tandem. These operations also stood out as meaningful

EXHIBIT 5.2. PROFESSORS' EXAMPLES OF SELECTION USED IN PSYCHOLOGY COURSES

Choose relevant information:
Select information that is pertinent to the issue in question.

In planning research, what do we know and what would be relevant for this study?

What are the things you are going to study and in what way are they related?

How to narrow down the focus, what would be central and what peripheral?

What kind of evidence is essential to make a case, a point, or a derivation, to make the distinction of which information is relevant to this conclusion? Some information is important because it stimulates you to think about something initially, some because it provides a missing link, some because it is useful as the justification or verification.

Order information in importance:
Rank, arrange in importance or according to significance.

What is your criterion? If you have several criteria you can very easily run into the paradoxical state that it is impossible to order something.

In the introduction to an article or to a study, or of results or discussion.

Identify critical elements:
Determine units, parts, components that are important.

Abstract what are the essential units or parts.

In designing experiments.

Identify critical relations:
Determine connections between things that are important.

Stimuli in relation to the viewer, subject, context.

for professors in their own research. Thus, selection processes are complex but essential skills to be learned in psychology.

Representation

Because representation is a major area of research in cognitive psychology—as the choice of key concepts in the course on thinking illustrates—the professors had a great deal to say about the constitutive processes, and one professor puzzled over her role in attempting to situate representation as an instructional activity when it is so central to her life as a researcher. Part of the quandary for psychologists lies in the dual role of representation in cognitive science as data structures and as the process of interrelating structural properties. Students in psychology are customarily asked in their writing assignments and examinations to represent concepts by defining them connotatively—that is, by their characteristics or properties—and then denotatively, by providing examples.

Recognizing organizing principles is an important act in cognitive psychology. It is exemplified in theories. In evaluating research, one must find a larger principle that is superordinate to particular studies. One must also compare and contrast theories or models for their organization and consequences (Exhibit 5.3). The actual *organization of elements and relations* occurs in textbooks as models, in class, and in the study of particular scientists and their theories. Both in instruction and the assessment of learning, the *illustration of elements and relations* is a central strategy, reflecting its importance in the discipline. In contrast, the *modification of elements and relations* occurs less frequently, at more advanced levels. One professor of social psychology, however, started undergraduate students thinking in this manner by having them deviate in some way as part of a project, and then having them observe their own and others' responses to this changed behavior.

Inference

Considered by several psychology professors to be the most important thinking process, inference is modeled in lectures as professors evoke answers to problems and lead students to formulate general principles from the evidence (Exhibit 5.4). Both in class and in their written assignments, students are expected to *discover new relations between elements,* but it is not until more advanced courses that professors expect them regularly to *discover relations between relations.* This process is tested in analogies, and in comparisons between lay and professional or scholarly language. Students are widely expected to *discover equivalences* as a chunking or grouping phenomenon, or in metaphor. *Categorization* and *ordering* were considered part of the basic repertoire, but important to theorization and for the organization of texts.

EXHIBIT 5.3. PROFESSORS' EXAMPLES OF
REPRESENTATION USED IN PSYCHOLOGY COURSES

REPRESENTATION: Depiction or portrayal through enactive, iconic, or symbolic means.	*Define a concept, or contrast visual and verbal representations and give an example of each.*
	A mapping from some external world to a mental world, the mapping of objects and relations in the real world to objects and relations in the representing or mental world. What relations are preserved between objects: a spatial relation where the distance between objects is preserved in the mental representation.
Recognize organizing principles: Identify laws, methods, rules that arrange in a systematic whole.	*View reported research as embedded in the whole rather than having its own existence.*
Organize elements and relations: Arrange parts, connections between things into a systematic whole.	*See the organization that a scientist uses, being honest to that scientist's view. Then you can criticize it, analyze it, and so on.*
Illustrate elements and relations: Make clear by examples the parts, connections between things.	*Use examples, analogies, and metaphors to make personally relevant and clearer what things mean and how they are connected.*
Modify elements and relations: Change, alter, or qualify the parts, connections between things.	*Be a deviant for a day, or think of some fundamental aspect of themselves—the way they dress or talk—and then set about changing it. If being clean is important, be dirty; or change their etiquette.*

Early psychological literature on cognition notes their importance as recoding processes for preventing information bottlenecks (Bruner, Goodnow, & Austin, 1956; Miller, 1956). *Changing perspective* was critical to research in the formulation of new questions and in communication and instruction. Professors talked of simulations in which students had to change their perspective by virtue of their assigned role as a therapist or designer of a robot. *Hypothesizing* was another important skill that was developed in a variety of ways—in class discussion, research proposals, model or framework testing. Thus, inference was pervasive in the psychology class and in what was expected of students in their assignments.

Synthesis

In psychology, synthesis is important in relating to the context and particularly in adapting or shaping it, which involves modification of the environment to make

EXHIBIT 5.4. PROFESSORS' EXAMPLES OF
INFERENCE USED IN PSYCHOLOGY COURSES

INFERENCE: Act or process of drawing conclusions from premises or evidence	*Case histories, demonstrations, material in film or video.*
Discover new relations between elements: Detect or expose connections between parts, units, components.	*Interrelationship between parts and components and different organizing principles.*
Discover relations between relations: Detect or expose connections between connections of things.	*The relation between ordinary language and more technical descriptions of the same kinds of things.*
Discover equivalences: Detect or expose equality in value force or significance.	*Sentences remembered are a kind of integrated structure. Chunking in memory, comprehension, and metaphor rely on equivalences.*
Categorize: Classify, arrange into parts.	*Try to fit problems into certain classes of paradigms.*
Change perspective: Alter view, vista, interrelations, significance of facts or information.	*You are a therapist; you are Pavlov's assistant and you are analyzing data that do not make sense; you are designing a robot based on what you know about the nervous system.*
Hypothesize: Suppose or form a proposition as a basis for reasoning.	*A research proposal starts with a hypothesis about some area in psychology that the researcher has read about and finds interesting.*

it a better fit for oneself (Sternberg, 1987). It is therefore considered by Sternberg to be a different form of intelligence from the critical analysis tapped by most intelligence tests, but it is essential for doing research. One professor spoke of the importance of synthesis in her own research, in designing methods to answer questions and in formulating the questions. Students are expected to *combine parts to form a whole* in comparing constructs such as short- and long-term memory, or in developing their hypotheses (Exhibit 5.5). One professor made a cross-cultural comparison in the use of *elaboration* as a European rather than a North American strategy, although other professors could see its application in word association tests, for example. *Generating missing links* was a common phenomenon, primarily in research and at several stages—in theorization, evidence, or data analysis and discussion. A professor noted that *developing a course of action* was particularly American, in that there is an impetus to put things to work, rather than merely cogitate. Synthesis was thus discussed by the professors in terms of doing research more frequently than as a thinking process to be developed in class.

EXHIBIT 5.5. PROFESSORS' EXAMPLES OF
SYNTHESIS USED IN PSYCHOLOGY COURSES

Combine parts to form a whole: Join, associate elements, components into a system or pattern.	*Prepare an argument about the difference between short- and long-term memory, showing that they are different.*
Elaborate: Work out, complete with great detail, exactness, or complexity.	*A word association test of a concept or series of concepts to see what associations are generated; a more European way of thinking.*
Generate missing links: Produce or create what is lacking in a sequence, fill in the gap.	*Look at research in a given area and try to see what has not been covered or where the inconsistencies are.*
	In the literature or in a theory, you do the study to fill in the missing link.
Develop a course of action: Work out or expand the path, route, or direction to be taken.	*Typically American, psychological, and empirical, and also a part of Jamesian pragmatism. It is a value that is taught throughout, given as a justification that this is linked to some action rather than that this is going to make your mind richer in some vague way.*

Verification

The validation process in psychology is central to theory and method development; hence professors focus on it in both instruction and research. In contrast with students in the physical sciences, psychology students were expected to verify their data and were taught explicit methods to do so (Exhibit 5.6). Because model building and testing is a central part of the curriculum, verification procedures are prominent. Students *compare alternative outcomes* in experiments due to different models, and in one example must bend their minds around alternative outcomes. Experimental design is a process of *comparing an outcome to a standard;* it is built into the research process. The *judgment of validity* is basic to the scientific method; skepticism, criticism, and matching the evidence are implied in the process. Researchers *use feedback* in their research programs at several stages; students are taught by receiving feedback on their activities. *Confirming results* is done in a Popperian manner, according to one professor, by looking for counterclaims, and is thus more likely to occur when a series of experiments have been done. *Confirming results* is not an embedded operation as in physics, where professors spoke of using immediate empirical evidence to do this. An explanation for this difference is that in psychology more descriptive or exploratory research than confirming research is done, hence the limitations on use of this process.

EXHIBIT 5.6. PROFESSORS' EXAMPLES OF
VERIFICATION USED IN PSYCHOLOGY COURSES

VERIFICATION: Confirmation of accuracy, coherence, consistency, correspondence.	*By means of experiment, correlational studies, or systematic observations—in the case of language development, for example.*
Compare alternative outcomes: Examine similarities or differences of results, consequences.	*Different models produce different outcomes. Researchers also need to obtain data in a different form to conform with various models.*
Compare outcome to standard: Examine similarities, differences of results to a criterion.	*In demonstration studies, like Asch or Milgram, the standard is the naive, intuitive conception of the reader or the general public. Built into any experiment is the "compared to what" statement. That is what control groups or comparison groups are all about, or a pre-post measure on the subjects.*
Judge validity: Critically examine the soundness, effectiveness by actual fact.	*How good are the data in supporting the hypothesis?* *Start out with the null hypothesis of no difference.*
Use feedback: Employ results to regulate, adjust, adapt.	*During the pilot phase of the study you get feedback from subjects about whether things are working the way you want.*
Confirm results: Establish or ratify conclusions, effects, outcomes, or products.	*Occurs as more and more people do related experiments or there is a program of research where you build into subsequent studies replications and extensions. Other people who replicate your study build up a set of confirmatory instances, so that what was just an experimental finding begins to sound like a generalization.*

In summary, thinking processes are central in psychology. They are the focus of both the research and instruction of many psychology professors; hence it is not surprising that the thinking abilities of graduate psychology students develop to a greater extent than with students in other programs. The professor's own goals and the disciplinary emphasis on research even at the undergraduate level affect student learning. Selection, representation, and inference are areas of research for psychologists. But the greatest difference between this and other scientific fields examined so far is that psychology professors expect students to verify their conclusions. The demand to test different theoretical frameworks makes the thinking processes central to the learning task in psychology.

The Challenge of Instruction in Psychology

In the study of thinking processes, the professors provided many examples of how they modeled thinking and instructed students, and how these processes develop. We have also seen how students experience learning psychology. Our studies suggest that students need time and specific instruction to learn to think like psychologists. When asked what were the most important things they had learned in psychology, students' responses reflected their recognition of the complexity of the discipline.

> To identify and test all assumptions, to evaluate theoretical material carefully, to construct experiments that rigorously test relationships that occur in a complicated process or system.

> There are no black-and-white answers. For example, in therapy, there is more than one way, and different ways may be equally successful.

To gain an understanding of the resources available to teach psychology we analyzed the kinds of instructional articles located in *Psychological Abstracts* in 1985 and 1986, as we had for physics and engineering. Articles on the teaching and learning of psychology (255) were found in sixty-six different journals, with the greatest number in *Teaching of Psychology*. Although the largest numbers of articles in each of the two years were concerned with undergraduate education in psychology (56 percent), a large proportion of them were categorized as graduate psychology education (38 percent). There is notable emphasis on graduate education in psychology (this category did not appear in physics and engineering); this emphasis reflects the importance of graduate training in the development of psychologists.

Of four kinds of articles, the largest number (36 percent) were concerned with specific practices—how to teach a specific course or course unit, for example, a demonstration, activity, or assignment. Experimentation (33 percent) described studies relating learning variables such as the effect of student background on learning outcomes. Articles on general practice (19 percent) included ways to teach in general and multidisciplinary or unified approaches to the subject. Conceptualizations (11 percent) dealt with concepts, theories, or the philosophy behind topics studied. For example, Gleitman's (1984) article on introducing psychology discussed the importance of providing links between parts of the subject matter as well as to other disciplines.

Most articles, as in the *Engineering Index,* addressed curriculum and instruction issues: the content analysis of leading textbooks, curriculum development, and particular content areas such as cross-cultural psychology, psychometrics, substance misuse, and burnout in professionals. Articles on instructional methods and materials focused on computer use, but supervision, practical uses of writing, experiments, and projects were also included. There were more articles on student evaluation in graduate psychology education than in undergraduate—for example, the evaluation of field placements. Some 42 percent of the articles referred to a branch of psychology, most in graduate education—for example, in school and clinical psychology—but nineteen articles discussed introductory psychology. Thus a fair amount of attention over the two-year period (1985 and 1986) was focused on first-year courses.

This review of resources unearthed a substantial number of articles, but few of them addressed student learning per se. Fewer still dealt with higher-order learning. Most were oriented to specific subject matter, with little attention paid to theories underlying postsecondary learning. We undertook a review of the literature in 1999 to determine if a change had taken place in the last fifteen years; it revealed little additional publication that might specifically aid professors in helping students learn to think, although teaching methods tended to be active and research-oriented. There may be an assumption that learning to think is inherent in the program of study. Published results, however, suggest two major avenues for attention. The first is the challenge of applying science to human experience— that is, structuring common experience in a manner that is meaningful and consistent with scientific principles, but understanding the audience's point of departure or expectations about their learning in the field. The challenge at a more advanced level in the discipline is to help students learn the process of research. At both levels promoting the concept of a learning community is central.

Linking Scientific Knowledge with Students' Interests

How to create a learning milieu that does justice to the scientific study of mind and behavior, and also aids students to locate themselves in relation to the multifaceted discipline of psychology, is a long-standing challenge. In his presidential address to the American Psychological Association, Gleitman (1984) described the first lecture that, as a young professor, he gave in introductory psychology. When he began by saying, "Psychology is the study of behavior," the atmosphere in the classroom became hostile, and when he added, "It is also the study of consciousness," the atmosphere became even more hostile. Having experimented with a variety of beginnings, he finally settled on what he called the *bureaucratic beginning*, "The name of this course is Introductory Psychology. My name is. . . . There will be two midterms and a final." Matching student expectations meant reducing his definition to the terms of assessment.

Gleitman went on to explain that, in his attempts to tell beginning students about psychology, he tries first of all to integrate the course so that students' minds are not as fragmented as he feels so many of psychology's research activities are. Recognizing that psychology is not a neatly organized field, but more like a Hapsburg Empire of the sciences that is always threatening to fall apart, he tries to forge links by presenting topics within overarching categories, for example, "mind as a reflex machine" or "mind as knower." He provides organizing frameworks that help motivate students by adding another perspective on the material, in turn helping them to learn the particulars of psychology. At the same time, he recognizes that the frameworks themselves may be wanting, but reasons that they provide a scaffolding—small islands of coherence in a sea of chaos. He also tries to involve students emotionally with the love of learning by demonstrating it himself.

In response to the rapid generation of information in the field, Makosky (1985) advocates structuring courses by carefully selecting material for inclusion, maximizing student performance and general skills, and preparing them for self-education. As organizing or structuring concepts in the course, she introduces metaprinciples, which have broad relevance, are empirically well supported, and are not likely to be contradicted in the near future. Examples of such global concepts are universal bias (science is not value-free), group differences (variability in human groups is greater than the average distance between groups), or behavioral ambiguity (interpretation of behavior depends on the context). She argues for structuring courses to capitalize on students' background and interests in order to increase their motivation and learning.

Students' interests can be gauged to provide a framework for organizing a course. To illustrate, as part of an effort to create a small classroom atmosphere, Buskist and Wylie (1998) ask students to respond to the following question: What one thing in your life, if you could change it today, would have the most immediate and profound positive impact on your life? Students' written responses, limited to three to five words, are categorized according to problem or issue type—low self-esteem, financial concerns, and emotional adjustment are frequent issues—and presented to students in the following class. Students therefore become aware of the problems their classmates are confronting and see similarities with their own situation. During the term, these issues are linked to the relevant course topics in motivation, learning, development, personality, and stress and coping. For example, the class has opportunities to apply theories and methods of self-control as interventions by developing plans for exerting more control over their diet, exercise, and time management. The teachers become aware of their students' concerns and address them, raising their interest in the basic psychological principles and theories behind them.

A more specific method of capturing student interest and directing it toward scientific knowledge is to have students choose a topic and create a knowledge map of the main ideas on poster board, then mount it in the classroom or hallway where other students can see it and comment on it (Czuchry & Dansereau, 1996). Students in introductory psychology and advanced memory and cognition courses were told that the project could help them study for final cumulative examinations. In class, their instructors modeled their own maps or those of experts in the area; students were encouraged to be creative in making their maps. After completing the mapping assignment, students in both courses rated the method as more interesting and as involving more learning than a traditional paper. This method is also good preparation for membership in the discipline because poster sessions are used as a presentation format by young researchers at scholarly conferences. For example, graduate students prepare a poster that describes their research and then talk about it to others who circulate in the poster room. Making active assignments for skill development such as explaining concept maps or locating and evaluating information from diverse sources (Makosky, 1985) prepares students for lifelong learning as members of learning communities.

Students who have participated in workshops on how to learn psychology shift from having a naive conception of learning as acquiring knowledge, to a more sophisticated conception of knowledge as the abstraction of meaning or a process that helps one to interpret or understand reality (Norton & Crowley, 1995). A professor in our studies attempted to set the stage for advanced thinking by explaining what he saw students' task to be in his course on the history of psychology.

> Now, very often people tell you that you go to university to get knowledge stuffed into your heads. Plato's idea is that you go to university to get stuff taken out of your head. Basically, Plato was right: according to the paradox of inquiry you came to university to exercise your judgment, under supervision.
>
> You are going to be doing more writing. This is going to take a major effort on your part. Getting words on paper, you will have to dig into yourself in ways that you didn't do before. But that is what intellectual life is all about.

This professor is prompting his students to recognize that their learning is a process of active engagement in which they must synthesize and construct knowledge. In response to these instructions, one student said:

> I think the real work was in writing the essay. I tried to think really hard, I mean really deep. I wanted to try and think about things rather than just summarize articles. It was tricky.

The student participant-observer in this course noted that the professor organized the course in ways that developed thinking processes in his students. For example, the weekly conference provided students with a forum to try out their ideas as well as ask questions. The professor tried to provoke students to reexamine their own assumptions and think about what they were studying inside and outside of class. He expected them to come prepared to demonstrate original thinking in class discussions and clear and logical thinking in their essays. Two mini-essays at the beginning of the term gave the students a trial run. The essays required little or no reference materials and so were in fact the first true indications of the students' thinking processes. He periodically referred to the thought processes students should use when writing their major essay.

> Marks will be awarded generously for originality of insight, organization, expression. Not every thought that flows freely through your mind is original. Original ideas have to be backed by careful argument. Marks will not be awarded generously for synopses of other people's writings.
>
> Choose a topic soon. Start reading about and around it. Harvest the ideas that occur to you, make notes of them, and be courageous in following them. Trust yourself to think things through. A good essay says one thing. You do not have to agree with the professor (who actually wants to steal your original ideas).

Clear instruction about what thinking is and about the task to be accomplished, passion for the subject matter, and a sense of humor mark this professor's pedagogy. Thinking processes can be taught by focusing specifically on them or by building them into class discussion and assessment procedures. Students need to be challenged and guided in the process.

But helping students become members of the psychological community may require a broader approach. In a study of undergraduate psychology students' experience, Hawkey (2000) found that development of community membership, involvement, and belonging were longitudinal processes influenced by students' aspirations and obligations as well as structural characteristics of the department and the university. Participation in a research group had the greatest effect in establishing a sense of community membership. Another way to establish a sense of community is to work with the Kuhnian premise that a community of scientists must establish its philosophical stance (Cox, 1997). Cox organizes his history of psychology course around fifty issues that characterize positions held by philosophers, biologists, or psychologists covered in the course. He has students state their level of agreement on a four-point Likert scale from "strongly disagree" to "strongly agree" on items such as "Observations of one's own mental life are valid data for psychology." He discusses the findings in class to show where students agree most and where they vary or disagree with the assumptions. This personalizes their knowledge but also provides an integrative reference for the entire course. The issues are also used to show how positions and theory have changed over time so that students gain understanding of the values of a scientific community, their influence and interpretation. The students as a whole become knowledgeable about evolution, skeptical of determinism, and open to all information—functionalists in the manner of William James.

Learning the Process of Research

Once students have a sense of the field, learning the process of research is synonymous in this discipline with promoting their thinking and problem-solving behaviors. Psychology students who are successful in methods courses such as statistics display more concept-oriented behavior; they make connections between ideas and skills, monitor their activity, and ask more questions about the problem they are attempting to solve (Hauff & Fogarty, 1996). Undergraduates frequently, however, approach research methods courses with trepidation (Brems, 1994). In response to students' fear and avoidance behaviors to psychological research methods, Brems begins early but gradually to introduce research methods into undergraduate courses such as human development, abnormal psychology, and personality theory. She asks students in first-year courses to read research articles but to focus on the introduction section so that they do not become confused by the methods and results sections but learn to recognize how researchers slowly work their way through the relevant literature to develop research questions. Students are then asked to generate simple research questions relevant to a course topic.

In second-year courses, she asks students to focus on both the introduction and the methods sections in the research articles and to start thinking about how researchers go about answering questions. Students are asked to critique the choice of subjects and instruments used in the studies and find out how to do a library search. By third year, student tasks turn to the adequacy of data collection procedures and conclusions drawn from the data. Threats to internal and external validity come up in class discussion. By the fourth undergraduate year, Brems requires critical analysis of research and encourages students to conduct their own research, allowing them to substitute a research project for a term paper. She helps those who choose this option to develop a meaningful research question to investigate that could be presented at a regional psychological conference. Some of these projects have been of publishable quality. By the time students reach graduate studies, they are ready to conduct research and present and publish the results. Brown bag lunches where students can meet informally to discuss research, as well as student clubs, encourage student-faculty interaction concerning research interests, projects, and findings.

In a modified approach to problem-based learning, McBurney (1995) makes his second-year undergraduate research methods course a vehicle for teaching thinking about the research process. Reasoning that research design is a classic ill-defined task, he uses a problem or case method approximately every fourth class period, during which students discuss a problem that requires them to make use of principles from a chapter of the text. Problems may range from the choice of a particular research design to a case of alleged violation of research integrity. McBurney gives out the problem one or two weeks in advance for students to study and encourages them to work in pairs. A group of students are designated to turn in a three- to five-page written analysis at the beginning of the class period in which it is discussed, and they may be counted on to provide the bulk of the class discussion. The analysis contains a summary of the problem, a suggested solution, and reasons for rejecting alternatives. McBurney's role is to pose questions, draw out incomplete answers, and probe inconsistencies. Although students seem somewhat uncomfortable with the ambiguity inherent in the method, and pose many questions about how to solve the problems before they are due, they learn to deal with the complexities of research design by working on these problems.

To provide students with more structure, during the first two weeks of their undergraduate research methods course Wilson and Hershey (1996) ask students to participate in an activity to discover what they already know about the psychological research process. Students are given a response sheet with "Get idea for project" at the top and "Publish the research paper" at the bottom. They are then asked to fill in about twenty typical actions, steps, or stages that characterize the research process. Next, the instructors describe what a script is—a mental representation of ordered actions and events that take place in commonly experienced situations—and ask students to group activities into higher-order categories and generate a name for each category. Students then work in small groups of two to four to compare their event lists and follow this exercise by making a master list, discussing it, and then comparing it with a composite script from expert researchers. Students are pleased and surprised to see the similarity between their list and that of the experts, thus bolstering their confidence. They also have the opportunity to discuss the role of actions often left out of student scripts, such as brown bag presentations or pilot projects. The exercise provides students with an illustration of mental representations, shows them how to monitor their own understanding, and sets an evaluative standard for students to reference throughout the course.

Students increasingly need skill with the Internet in order to do research. In the two-hour laboratory portion of an intermediate statistics course, undergraduate psychology students meet in the computer laboratory to discuss previous assignments and begin the current assignment, although they complete most work outside the scheduled period (Varnhagen, Drake, & Finley, 1997). The course home page presents the syllabus, project descriptions, and data archives for laboratory experiments, on-line help for describing data, and pointers to other statistics sites to obtain information or help. Students can e-mail to the instructor and teaching assistant, access a news group for discussion, and use an electronic form for submitting assignments. Students have been known to e-mail the graduate teaching assistant in the middle of the night and receive an immediate reply. In an evaluation of the course, students rated the communications aspects as extremely useful but used statistics information available on the World Wide Web infrequently. Direct access to the instructor and teaching assistant obviated the need for on-line information. Quality of discussion and student writing skills improved during the term, and students began to discuss topical issues such as when to use statistical techniques and how to examine data before blindly testing hypotheses.

Evident in all of these examples is the need to structure learning experiences so that students actively problem-solve in their courses. Whether in creating a framework for the research process itself, using the Internet to access course information and discuss it, focusing on the substance of research problems in psychology, or inducting students into the process of research, careful planning and evaluation of the instructional process are needed to ensure an efficacious learning experience.

One university links doing research with building a community by having small groups of two to five students in advanced undergraduate courses in research methods design projects to involve introductory students. The projects engage introductory students for one hour in activities such as progressive relaxation, lie detection, basic biofeedback, the study of alcohol use, and operant conditioning (Wesp, 1992). Upper-level students learned their own course material better because of the experience of designing and carrying out activities with the first-year students, and first-year students were also in favor of the activities, which provided them with a wider variety of learning options. The activities also afford more personalized attention to students in a large introductory class.

The American Psychological Association has developed a set of learner-centered principles to guide psychologists in their understanding and facilitation of the learning of others (Alexander & Murphy, 1998; American Psychological Association, 1993). Although intended for education at all levels, psychology departments could be considered to have a particular obligation to put them into practice. The principles recognize the importance of students learning to monitor and evaluate their own performance and invest in the learning process, and of teachers recognizing and responding to both typical and unique dimensions of human growth and development. They also assert that learning is as much a socially shared undertaking as an individually constructed enterprise. This principle provides a foundation for the creation of a community that supports learning in this multifaceted discipline.

The Disciplinary Perspective in Psychology

Although it is a young science with both hard and soft areas of study, psychology is comprised of huge archives of knowledge and an exacting methodology. Students regularly experience shock when they find that the course that was going to help them understand themselves—a central concern to entering university students—is complex and demanding. As a social science, the goal in the discipline is to collect data through controlled observation; verification frequently includes reliability across observers. Psychology is similar to biology in the diversity of its foundations and conceptual frameworks. Knowledge is defined in terms of prediction and control but also is viewed as a means of understanding and change, which reflects the discipline's social reform legacy.

Psychology has provided a series of models of learning, some of which—like the law of exercise "practice makes perfect"—oversimplify the learning task, but information theory and constructivism provide insight into higher-order learning. Thinking processes are the focus of both research and instruction of professors of psychology, and psychology students develop analytic thinking abilities in their programs of study. The demand to test different theoretical frameworks makes thinking processes and particularly verification central to the learning task in psychology.

The challenges in psychology concern optimal ways of cultivating these thinking processes, first by linking scientific knowledge with students' interests by means of powerful metaphors—mind as reflex machine or knower—and second, by introducing students to the process of research that defines the field. Using a question that epitomizes the potential of psychology—"What one thing in your life, if you could change it today, would have the most immediate and profound positive impact on your life?"—instructors have been able to create a pedagogical framework that allows students to link personally important issues to the relevant course topics. This instructional strategy also illuminates the potential of psychology for personal emancipation. The second challenge is to provide students with positive experiences in learning to do research—for example, exercises that help them realize they already know a considerable amount about the steps of the research process so that they are more confident in dealing with design and statistical issues. An underlying principle is to invest in learning as a social as well as an individually constructed endeavor.

CHAPTER SIX

PRECEDENT AND REASON:
Case Versus Logic

Lawyers have to be able to critique judgments by determining what was held and why.

LAW PROFESSOR

Social critics or interpreters of legal doctrine? Reason and precedent vie for ascendancy in the thinking processes of this prestigious discipline. Despite commissions and reviews, the composition of legal education remains controversial, and the critical skills advocated in this epigraph may or may not find a place in the law curriculum. In this chapter, we examine learning in a traditional field established in the medieval universities of Western Europe as one of three advanced faculties with theology and medicine. Students entered legal studies after completing the trivium (grammar, rhetoric, logic) and the quadrivium (arithmetic, music, geometry, astronomy); a broad base of knowledge was considered necessary before undertaking the study of judicial procedure. Modern location of law among the social sciences appears reluctant; legal scholars more frequently compare their discipline to physics, and the path from profession to scholarly discipline in the twentieth century has been erratic.

To comprehend the nature of the discipline, I first explore perceptions of law held by legal scholars and scholars from other disciplines. Law professors joust with three linked paradoxes—or antinomies—that are themes and fault lines running through the discipline. The most general antinomy revolves around the status of law as a scholarly or intellectual discipline, the second the place assigned to values in law, and the third, most specific antinomy, the insularity of the discipline in relation to the university. To decipher how students learn to think like lawyers, key concepts and the thinking processes that students are expected to develop in a course on torts are investigated. In addition, we applied a form of propositional analysis to determine the relationship of concepts to propositions in the course. Three law professors representing different areas of the law contributed to the chapter, and students and other professors also participated in the series of studies. Important instructional challenges concern how to help students build a framework for legal knowledge, how to help them think like lawyers, and how to deal with values in law.

Widely represented in the media, and so more familiar to the general populace than other academic disciplines, law—both civil and criminal—is also more open to question and commentary. Advocacy and adversarial stances render law disquieting to the nonjuridic public. In contrast to the uncomfortable reactions of laypersons, cool rationality is reflected in terms such as logic, analysis, and analogy used to describe the process that law students must learn in order to think like lawyers (Mudd, 1983). A primary objective of studying civil law is to assess which human behavior merits censure or compensation, and a basic criterion is how the reasonable person would act in a given circumstance. In order to determine fault and civil liability, for example, one asks whether the reasonable person would have foreseen a risk (Somerville, 1978; M. A. Somerville, personal communication, February, 2000); based on the outcome, behavior is rewarded or condemned. Because the stakes are high, law is both prestigious and susceptible to criticism.

The Disciplinary Context in Law

Medieval preparation for law owed much to the rhetoric and logic of the trivium. Today the common expectation, promoted by the media, is that rhetoric plays an important role; in contrast, legal scholars focus on logic. The purpose of a legal education, however, has been essentially practical. Law is studied both as a general education for leadership and administration, and as a necessary qualification for professional status recognizing juristic competence (Lewis, 1992). Depending on the country, law is seen predominantly as leading to public service or to private practice. Legal education in continental Europe is directed more toward public administration; Anglo-American or common law education is directed primarily toward the profession.

When viewed as a general education for leadership, the study of law provides a basic university education to those interested in a government career or politics. Lewis points out that this general role has led to a lack of structure in the curriculum that extends to both the purpose and content of courses. Programs are open to disagreement and contention over control and pressure from those who enroll in them, and to external market influences. In contrast to university medical schools, for example, law schools have not provided the same kind of integrated training or exercised the same kind of influence in the delivery of legal services. According to one scholar, the cultural divide between theoretical law school and instrumental bar has limited convergence and therefore coherence in the field (R. Janda, personal communication, June 2000). The division between law schools and the profession has led to two or three stages of learning, the first theoretical or content-based. The second tends to be offered outside the university and supplies the skills needed to practice law, and is either combined with or followed by an apprenticeship in a law practice.

Contemporary programs in the common law countries most frequently prepare students for professional lives in commercial and criminal law—in contracts, torts, and property. Law programs in universities increasingly equip students with clinical—that is, practical—research and writing skills. Entry to programs in North America is guarded by the Law School Admission Test (LSAT), which is designed to test logical ability, particularly deductive logic (Gruber & Gruber, 1982), or the Multi-State Bar Examination (MBE). One dean of law suggests that applicants need training in critical reading, critical thinking, problem solving, and communication, and also should be informed by a sense of history and philosophy (Weidner, 1997). Additional learning objectives are a global, comparative understanding of legal systems and how to work better in teams, an attribute that employers are asking of university graduates in general. The paradoxes or antinomies that law professors must deal with—the nature of scholarship in the discipline, the place of values in law, and how the discipline interacts with others in the university—render the law professor's role absorbing but complex.

Discipline or Profession?

In the university, the status of law as a profession creates a paradox in claims and denials of intellectual activity. According to Becher (1989), the predominant notion that others in the university have of academic lawyers is that they are not really academic. In Becher's anthropology of the disciplines, one respondent described academic lawyers as arcane, distant, and alien, an appendage to the university world. Law schools in the United States often developed independently of universities, and graduates gained their professional qualification through an examination controlled by the bench and the bar rather than through courses of study. Generally speaking, the prestige of private practice has limited the influence of the academy. Law professors in the United Kingdom and in the United States described themselves to Becher as atheoretical, ad hoc, case-oriented, and not particularly scholarly, sharing the anti-intellectual ethos of practicing lawyers. According to Toma (1997), compared with other disciplines legal scholars tend to

be functional and utilitarian in their use of knowledge. They concern themselves with protocols and procedures, and work toward the enhancement of professional practice; they are outward-looking and power-oriented.

Relative to professional law, academic law is abstract and indeterminate
(Morissette, 1988a). Morissette sees academic law as more open to the influence
of other disciplines, such as economics and history. In contrast, professional law
is pragmatic, responsive to recent experience, and service-oriented. The American Bar Association Standards for Law Schools filed by one state bar association
in the United States provide that adjunct faculty may constitute up to 40 percent
of the full-time equivalent faculty (Weidner, 1997). Thus academic and practicing lawyer are functionally interlocked, and perhaps necessarily so, since a large
percentage of students are training to become members of the profession.

More pointedly, the profession dominates the academy rather than the reverse,
as in medicine. Contrary to most disciplines, the legal profession produces knowledge as *rules* through statute and interprets precedent. The doctrine of *precedent*, that
previous cases or legal decisions serve as guides or justification for subsequent cases,
is a primary influence on legal education. The profession, as in medicine, plays
an important role as gatekeeper to the field, determining who will have access; differentiation between discipline and profession is subtle and disputable.

Values or Value-Free?

To North American legal scholars, law is aggressively rational, linear, and goal-
oriented, based on facts, not feelings; success is measured by whether you win or
lose in court or by the dollar amount of settlements (Nelken, 1995). Nelken states
that the profession idealizes the lawyer as the amoral agent of a client's ends—society's hired gun. This portrayal of the lawyer as responsive to special interest
groups runs counter to the idea that everyone has a right to be defended (M. A.
Somerville, personal communication, February 2000) or that social problems
are the basis of law, as one of Becher's (1989) legal respondents claimed. This second antinomy orbits around two questions: Is law moral or is it value-free? What
role do values play?

In the field, the concept of a legitimate legal order guides discourse (Kahn,
1999). According to Kahn, legal order is the coincidence of reason and will, or
popular consent, but because this coincidence is never achieved at every moment
law itself stands in need of reform. Furthermore, law develops through constant
efforts at reform. Although reform is at the heart of the legal culture, Kahn suggests that the legal scholar must give up the project of reform in order to understand what law is. Legal scholars must self-consciously examine the psychological
and sociological meanings of the world understood as *the rule of law*—that is, they

must look at the effects of laws on individuals and societies. He recommends stripping legal scholarship of its moral commitment to the rule of law in order to disentangle itself from the practice of law. Thus a strong argument can be made for scholars to step outside the moral prerogative in order to understand how the discipline functions.

In the teaching of law, as in the sciences, the tradition is that the discipline is value-free. According to Becher's respondents, however, this tradition leaves open the possibility of a critical ideological function: law allows for shades of opinion, even if some aspects are uncontentious and there are shared criteria of judgment. Law professors may use the same database, knowledge structure, technique, and rules for formulating arguments, yet vary in the extent to which they think their curriculum should concentrate on statute and precedent or consider the broader social context. Traditionalists consider themselves to be practicing value-free law (or not to be practicing politically correct law); reformists see a critical function in legal studies as a force for social change. Conflict between abstract justice and concrete demands adds to the complexity of legal life.

One way of dealing with this antinomy is to construct different sets of arguments according to different sets of values: a well-formulated legal argument is considered to be independent of the side of the case it takes (Becher, 1989). More often than not, political stance is acknowledged only after the fact. Despite homage to reasoned logic in the field, legal academics tend to be to the left of practitioners in political views. According to one of Becher's law professors, they have made a conscious decision to turn down the possibility of earning a great deal of money. Compared with other disciplines, the variation in social conservatism places law in its degree of convergence as a discipline in an intermediate position with biology and psychology, where a range of theories and approaches is acknowledged.

As social scientists, legal scholars could be expected to engage in normative work—that is, to concern themselves about what something should be, beyond what something might be. Their patterns of inquiry vary, however. Toma (1997) divides law professors into three paradigmatic groups. More conventional or mainstream *legal realists* focus on understanding the social factors that influence legal principles; they view discovery, truth, and objectivity as goals and regulatory standards even though they recognize that judges operate in a political environment. *Critical scholars* operate from the stance that scholarship should influence specific social change, and that reality is shaped over time by social values. Their role is to be transformative—to change the law and its practice. *Interpretive scholars*, in their attempt to understand multiple realities, employ the hermeneutical and phenomenological methodologies developed in the humanities. In a comparative example of a study of a statute on civil rights, realist scholars might explore the data underlying the decision of the legislature and then analyze how the law applies.

Critical scholars would focus on social forces that afforded certain groups in society influence in its passage, whereas interpretive scholars might deconstruct the text itself.

Legal scholars have traditionally attempted to influence judges, policymakers, and practitioners in their work, but critical and interpretive scholars are more likely to address other academicians and less likely to address practitioners. Because practicing lawyers focus on concrete questions in their daily work, they are little inclined to be concerned with the theoretical issues that critical or interpretive scholars raise. This tends to marginalize the work of critical and interpretive scholars. Although Toma notes that there is an active market for alternative scholarship in law reviews, legal realism dominates law school classrooms.

Insularity Versus Interdisciplinarity

In the university, the discipline tends to be insular, separate from other disciplines, with a specific and focused education. This is despite the fact that students may have a wide range of disciplinary backgrounds. The general absence of interdisciplinary contact between inhabitants of the law school and others on university campuses creates a third paradox when one considers the potential mutual impact of law, humanities, social sciences, and sciences. Possibly because of their insularity, lawyers find it difficult to rank their field in comparison with others, but distinguished academic lawyers are revered for their broad philosophical view of the subject and their range of knowledge, breadth of education, and concern (Becher, 1989). This description suggests an affinity for the humanities, in which larger questions are asked and a philosophical approach is taken in accessible language. Instead, as in the social sciences, a technical and unfamiliar terminology supports insularity and the characterization of law professors as arcane.

Publications have commonly taken the form of student texts on particular topics rather than scholarly analyses of a major field or central theme. Increasing scholarly demands, however, have been voiced: one American law faculty recently announced that every faculty member would be expected to produce a major manuscript every two years (Weidner, 1997). In an era of retrenchment, Weidner contends that the insularity of law schools may lead to their being cut off from their host universities and left to their own financial devices, especially in graduate research universities. He also suggests that in many schools faculty do not get out into the legal community enough. His answer is to work with the bench, the bar, and government agencies by having professors in residence, or by having faculty team-teach with the bench and bar. The profession may compete with other disciplines for the attention of legal scholars, rendering interdisciplinarity more difficult.

Disciplinary Learning Conditions

The learning context for students is highly influenced by the discipline in its professional stance rather than by the university, resembling the experience of engineering students more than of physics or philosophy students. In their teaching, however, law professors may be less inclined than engineering professors to recognize the needs of the profession and take the time to induct students into the profession in their classes (see Chapter Three). Instead, law professors often choose to operate at a high level of abstraction and to decontextualize issues. In the education of lawyers, with content and skills frequently dichotomized, case studies are intended to provide a foundation of knowledge for later practice. This can create a problem for student learning because the combination of abstraction and fragmentation leaves students little imagery to help locate new knowledge and no framework in which to place it.

Do learning conditions have an impact on demand among students to be admitted to law programs? In Europe, demand is not as strong as in the past, but this is in comparison with the relatively large numbers of students who were admitted to law programs in the previous two decades (Lewis, 1992). First-year examinations eliminate a high percentage of those admitted to European law schools. Although law school applications in the United States have declined by almost 30 percent in the last five years, and some law schools have become ferociously competitive for students, law faculties compared with other disciplines have healthy recruitment (Weidner, 1997). The conditions include good employment statistics, negligible research grant funding, and, although some law schools are themselves graduate schools, few students proceeding to master's or doctoral degrees.

Thus the context for a law student consists of a discipline that is highly influenced by professional concerns, in which abstraction and pragmatism vie for dominance. Intellectual and academic demands are to acquire an extensive technical vocabulary and a process of argument, with good employment prospects upon graduation for the successful upper half of the class and variable opportunities for further academic study.

The Learning Task in Law

Law professors describe the knowledge in their discipline as a body of rules, and they see their task as concerned mainly with the descriptive pursuit of ordering this corpus of knowledge (Becher, 1989). At the same time, material constantly arising from new legislation puts knowledge in a state of flux. There is a continued expectation of contention, both epistemologically and sociologically. The study of law has a less evident sense of progression than hard applied knowledge provides engineering since law draws less on pure or academic knowledge but rather depends on practice. Law is distinct from other social sciences in its use of central or overriding concepts, such as *precedent* or *the reasonable person,* and in its method of inquiry or validation processes, which provide structure. For example, in common law, the concept of precedent means that law seeks validation in past judicial decisions. Law students learn an evolving tradition, but Mudd (1983) contends that lawyers still learn contracts, torts, property, and crimes in essentially the same way they did a century ago.

In law, validity is viewed in terms of human authority. In contrast to the sciences, where empirical or objective evidence is given status, legal evidence is lodged in the reports of witnesses. There are four acknowledged sources of law—custom, statute, judicial precedent, and juristic opinion—but these sources are not of equal authority. For example, statute can overrule precedent. Authority is backward-looking, and so law as expounded by judges has a built-in tendency toward conservatism (Watson, 1996). Watson suggests that because of this, several areas of law that are important to its understanding and development are not taught early enough in law programs, particularly underlying principles.

Foremost among the unexamined axioms is that a law, once established, continues. This means that legal institutions, rules, modes of reasoning, and models may survive despite changes in social, economic, and political circumstances. Watson points out that depending on previous systems and borrowing from other systems of law—Roman, French, and British tend to be preferred—raises the issue of the appropriateness of law in the society that does the borrowing. One learning task that has not received sufficient attention, therefore, is the study of the underlying principles and the history of law and how they affect decision making.

Some legal scholars have argued that a lawyer's thought processes are not significantly different from those of other professions or disciplines (Calhoun, 1984; Mudd, 1983). To Calhoun, lawyers, like scientists, are solvers of puzzles and to a lesser extent discoverers, even if, being steeped in statute and precedent, they may not appreciate the importance of transformation or change in perspective. But in law classes, dominated by legal realism, any argument that invokes individual perspectives and values becomes suspect. Calhoun argues that the genius of a trial lawyer lies in knowing when to appeal to logic and when to appeal to value, and thus methods of discovery should be examined more closely in law. More pointedly, if legal education is to be complete, students should be made aware of the possibility of making a successful challenge to a legal paradigm. Human or civil rights cases are prime examples of changes in values. This analysis results in the recommendation that students need to understand not only how to verify within the closed system of law but to challenge precedent and thus experience the excitement of law.

As in other disciplines, the tripartite learning tasks of gaining knowledge, thinking, and attitudes obtain, but the specifications of these tasks in law are distinct. Both tradition and the profession play a major role in setting the curriculum.

Legal Education and Professional Development

The influence of tradition and profession vary according to the history and culture of the host country. In a discipline as ancient as law, conceptions of education have been based on the nature of employment for which legal education is a qualification and the activities that the employment requires, whether civil service or private practice. These in turn determine the knowledge and skills needed for proficiency in the activities, but the effectiveness of the form of education and the availability of appropriate institutions must also be considered. For example, in countries using common law, a linear model of academic, professional, and practical training was adopted and led to distinctions between theory and practice, education and training, and knowledge, understanding, and skill. The linear model fostered noncooperation between those concerned with legal education in England, and a widening gap between academic law and vocational training or legal practice (Lewis, 1992). It also competed with the concept of law as a general education and acted against law schools undertaking the examination of relationships between law and society.

Reviews of legal education have been instituted to deal with this predicament. In a major review of the state of legal education and professional development in the United States known as the MacCrate report, the task force of the American Bar Association concludes that competent attorneys need substantive knowledge, practical skills, and values (MacCrate, 1994; Maurer & Mischler, 1994). Values education is justified in response to the hostility the public feels toward lawyers. The rationale in the report is that entering students need to take the time to consider whether lawyers deserve the negative stereotypes given them by the media as ambulance chasers, con artists, and sharks; the process of critical self-examination needs to begin early in law school. Professional values are delineated operationally as providing competent representation; striving to promote justice, fairness, and morality; striving to improve the profession; and striving to improve professional self-development. Thus skills and values are interwoven.

To illustrate, the skills identified by the MacCrate report as essential before assuming ultimate responsibility for a client—that is, for competent representation—are solving problems; doing legal analysis, research, and factual investigation;

communicating, counseling, and negotiating; handling litigation and alternative dispute resolution; organizing and managing legal work; and recognizing and resolving ethical dilemmas. This extensive list includes a variety of social and managerial skills that to date have received comparatively little attention in law schools. The report identifies problem solving as the most fundamental legal skill and lists some sixty steps, including substeps to be learned. The task for legal educators then becomes to determine how these skills can be taught and the extent to which they can be integrated with the established case knowledge base.

In a review of law and learning in Canada undertaken in the early 1980s, the basic problem of legal education was found to be that, similar to the situation in Western Europe, it had espoused a broad range of goals and opted for no specific structure to achieve any of them (Arthurs, 1983). Dealing with the three paradoxes of scholarship, values, and insularity, Arthurs charged that scholarly or intellectual legal study is diluted and marginalized by the predominance of professional concerns. His argument is that scholarly studies cannot be expected to develop while they remain a peripheral interest of students and faculty members who are chiefly preoccupied with preparation for professional service. Major recommendations in the report are that law schools should avoid narrow vocationalism, intensify efforts to transmit liberal and humane intellectual values, encourage interdisciplinary study, and ensure some exposure to legal theory and research. Furthermore, to respond to the state of insularity, links between law and other university disciplines should be strengthened by appointing some nonlawyers to law faculties, making cross-appointments to and from other faculties, promoting joint degree programs, and accommodating scholars-in-residence from other disciplines.

Consistent with the direction of the MacCrate report and the Arthurs report and also with the linear model of academic training, the Quebec Bar Admission program in 1987 moved from being a comprehensive review of a core curriculum to a skills-training program (Morissette, 1988b). It has six general objectives on which some eight hundred students are trained and evaluated annually after they receive a university law degree and before they article and are admitted to the bar. The program objectives consist of establishing a client-counsel relationship (Counseling), performing legal and factual research work (Research), drafting legal documents (Drafting), acting as a negotiator (Negotiation), representing a client in court (Representation), and managing a legal practice (Management). Research, Counseling, Drafting, and Management are evaluated in written examinations, but Negotiation and Representation are examined using videotaped simulations. Staffing requirements for this kind of program are onerous; if universities were to supply this training, costs would quickly exceed academic budgets. However, the design of the program meets the criteria for optimal learning conditions. The counterargument is, then, can universities afford to do otherwise?

The Teaching of Law

How is law taught? Who are the learners?

Law programs vary between three and six years in length, and even in those designated as undergraduate programs applicants frequently have previous degrees or have spent several years in other programs. Selection processes support the creation of an elite group of upper-middle-class students, although attempts are often made to provide access to the program to students with differing social backgrounds. Instructional method has journeyed from apprenticeship in the common law world to lectures, leading Lewis (1992) to describe law as a cheap discipline, particularly when teaching is given by part-time lecturers. The massive expansion of legal education in Europe was ascribed to the fact that because it was so cheap to provide, no limits were put on the numbers of students accepted into law programs as there were in medical and engineering programs. Entry into a law program can postpone having to make a definitive career choice, or may be viewed as an opportunity to develop complementary expertise to that earned in a first degree. Thus entering students tend to be privileged and sophisticated users of the academy.

Law professors have traditionally made reference to the Socratic process as their primary teaching method (Hartwell & Hartwell, 1990), but this method usually involves grilling a student individually in class and is inefficient in fostering a student's learning. The experience is likely to be traumatic rather than enlightening, while others in the class remain passive, semitraumatized themselves, rather than active learners. The process more likely resembles how a judge grills a lawyer in court (M. A. Somerville, personal communication, February 2000). In contrast, Socratic questioning consists of a systematic series of questions posed by the teacher that purportedly channel students' thought processes in developing new knowledge and guide them to an insight leading to self-discovery (Dillon, 1980). Whether the Socratic method is actually used in law classes, Socrates' method required that teacher and student be involved in a joint inquiry in search of a truth unknown to both. In a law course, the instructor usually has the "new" knowledge and the interaction is likely to consist of question-and-answer exchanges in the classroom. Reference to the Socratic method may thus spring from the level of philosophical abstraction needed to understand jurisprudence rather than from the actual process of inquiry. Students' negative reaction to the method may also derive from the fact that they have strongly applied interests that are antithetical to an abstract philosophical approach.

The most dominant and frequently referenced teaching mode in law is the use of cases. Affecting both curriculum and instructional method, the idea that law should be taught from cases was based on the argument espoused by Langdell, dean of the Harvard Law School in 1870, that law was a science (Watson, 1996). In this view, empirical patterns of social phenomena could therefore be deciphered. The case study method, in which particular cases are analyzed to identify facts and principles, is still used to teach first-year students the fundamentals of law. The problem with this approach, according to Watson, is that in law courses the way cases are taught is not the way science is taught. Instead of an intensive and highly structured learning experience with labs, tutorials, and assignments to explicate lectures as in the sciences, law courses tend to decontextualize legal experience. He argues that law courses use only a few isolated cases, the relationship between cases is not set out, and the theoretical underpinnings and writings of scholars are ignored. The decontextualization that occurs with the use of case studies—with frequent dichotomization of content and skills, because cases are intended to provide a foundation of knowledge for later practice—leaves students floundering. Watson states that the use of cases presents a thoroughly misleading picture of the law to students, and by third year students are widely perceived to be bored by law school.

Law students' learning strategies vary according to the way courses are organized, as one empirical study demonstrated. First-year law students in four courses in introductory law and in private, criminal, and administrative law reported differences in their learning strategies depending on the course organization. In courses that were more related to concrete issues and students' experience, such as private and criminal law, students engaged in more higher-order processing including using knowledge from outside the course and planning their study strategies (Vermetten, Lodewijks, & Vermunt, 1999). In these courses, clear organization and well-developed study materials that suggested ways of approaching the task and provided questions and assignments were associated with higher-order processing and self-regulation than in the other two courses in introductory and administrative law. The four courses provided different learning contexts to which the students responded with different learning strategies; instructional practice had clear effects on how students learned.

Law professors' teaching has been analyzed to reveal behaviors that discourage students from learning (Hativa, 2000a). Hativa studied law instruction in prestigious schools in the United States and Israel and found similar contentious instructional practices. The first was a tendency described by students as "hiding the ball"—asking questions and not supplying answers—so that lack of clarity became the descriptor for the classes. In addition, too little visual information was provided through diagrams or other representations to aid student learning. Another less than optimal behavior found in the courses was lack of organization. Professors did not provide a lesson plan or road map that informed students of their location in the plan and where the lesson fit into the course framework. This meant that information could not be readily encoded or retrieved. Because there was little variety in classroom presentation, students paid insufficient attention to the presentation, thus missing cues. Finally, few immediacy behaviors were exhibited—behaviors that communicate closeness to students or caring about them and that therefore increase trust and support learning. Professors stood behind the desk or podium, rarely moving about the classroom or entering the students' area. As a result of these behaviors, students gave relatively low ratings of teaching effectiveness. The principle emanating from this study is that an adversarial or noninteractive stance is counterproductive to learning.

The effects of contemporary teaching methods in law school on student behavior are illustrated in the following study. An investigation was conducted among faculty and students in a law school situated in a research university to determine why problems were occurring between students and professors (Hativa, 2000b). Students in three parallel classes of 120 students each were not coming to class prepared, and as the semesters progressed, stopped coming to class: attendance dropped to 70 percent by the end of the first year and to 50 percent by the end of the third year. According to self-reports, professors were progressive rather than conservative or authoritarian in their teaching goals. They considered encouraging openness to a variety of opinions and values to be a very important goal, as were developing legal theoretical thinking and promoting creative, original, and innovative thinking. They recognized, however, that in their classes they did not reach these goals. Students' perceptions of whether these goals were achieved in their classes were less positive than their professors'. Students perceived that professors lectured at them but offered little discussion to activate their thinking. Their main complaints were that professors concentrated on covering the material, graded inconsistently, were detached from the students, emphasized theory too much, and were *not* sufficiently open to a variety of opinions and views. The tension created by these opposing perspectives of the academic environment led to disillusionment on the part of students.

The pattern of professors imparting information and students asking for greater interaction resembles that found in the pure sciences. The tradition of lecturing appears to override curriculum and teaching goals. Given the demands of the discipline and the problems associated with contemporary instructional methods, what *would* be optimal conditions for learning law? Beginning at the most specific level, what are students expected to learn in law courses?

Learning Concepts in Law

To understand better the knowledge base that students are expected to gain, we chose a fundamental course in the discipline—torts—which investigates wrongful acts and the responsibility for them. Using the course materials— textbook (*The Law of Torts*, Fleming, 1983), casebook, and examinations—to find potential concepts, we established with the professor that sixty-eight were specifically relevant to the course, eleven of them key (main or linking) concepts (Figure 6.1).

The course is described as dealing with basic principles of intentional torts, negligence, and liability for fault. According to the professor:

FIGURE 6.1. KEY CONCEPTS IN A LAW COURSE ON TORTS

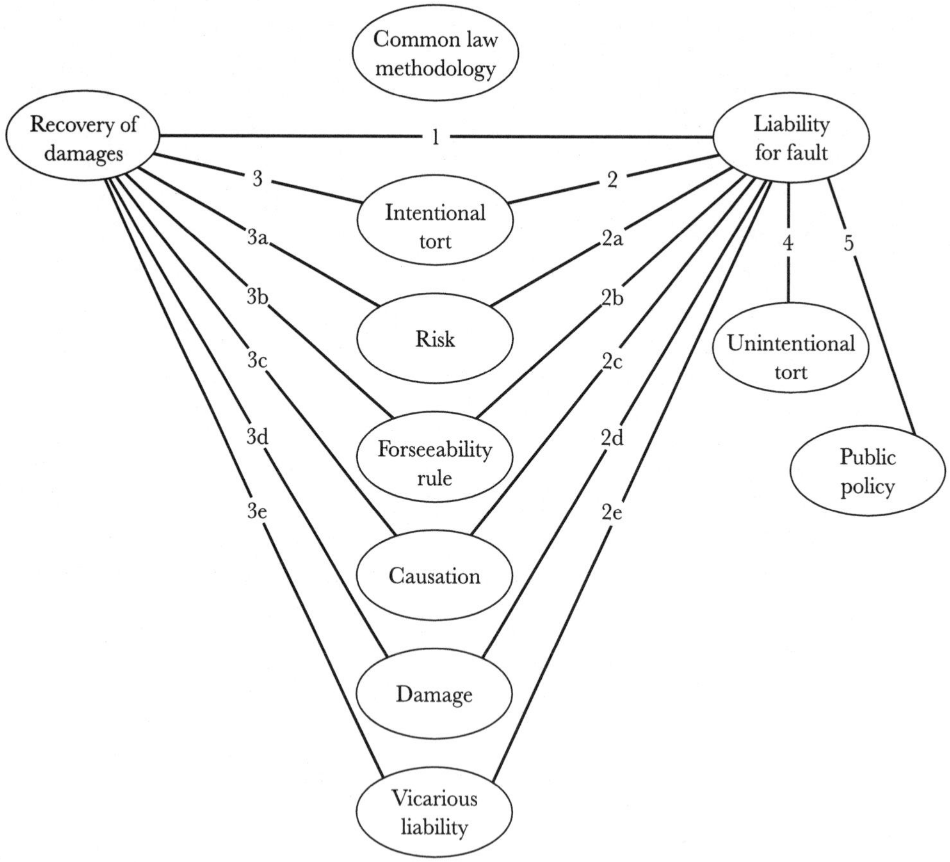

The main goal of the course is to develop students' ability to "do law," which requires a high degree of analytic ability. Although this ability requires understanding and knowledge of the legal system, it comprises much more. Most essential for students to learn in this course is how to think like lawyers. The skills and methods of analysis and procedure are developed through this methodology.

Consonant with the emphasis in the reviews of legal education on integrating knowledge and skills, the most important concept in the course was *common law methodology*. As shown in Figure 6.1, this was superordinate and inclusive of all other concepts in the course, and was given the following definition by the professor:

> *Common law methodology:* A system of analysis by which litigation is determined and which entails the observance of precedent in that determination. The court may find that previously decided cases, though similar, are distinguishable on the basis of their facts, controlling legislation, or public policy.

The next two most important and the two most closely related concepts in the course were *liability for fault* and *recovery of damages,* with *recovery of damages* being contingent on *liability for fault*. As Figure 6.1 shows, the course pivots around these two concepts. The definitions of these terms show their close relationship.

> *Liability for fault:* A tort principle that compels compensatory payment by an actor who has inflicted compensable damage upon another. In such a situation a moral quality is required. That quality is blameworthiness, culpability, fault.

> *Recovery of damages:* Losses suffered at the hand of another are compensable if that other acted tortiously, that is, faultily, and the losses incurred are of their nature, as determined in accordance with common law principles, compensable.

These definitions give us a sense of the complexity and level of abstraction of the key concepts and hence the challenge of learning in this course. All of the key concepts in the course were abstract or higher-order abstract except for one, *damage,* which the professor defined as a more restricted damage—not including damage to the emotions. *Damage* was categorized as a concrete functional concept, perceptually based and including use or application, but the definition shows that it also requires reflection—not all injuries count as legal damage. As in the social sciences in general, students would need to be able to think abstractly in order to succeed in this course.

There were more links per concept in this course than in any other we studied except the entomology course (discussed in Chapter Four), fifteen between the eleven key concepts for a ratio of 1.36 (the ratio in the entomology course was 2.06). The relationships between concepts in this course, as Figure 6.1 suggests, are clear and regular—seven parallel sets of hierarchical and logical relationships follow from the relationship between *recovery of damages* and *liability for fault*. For example, *intentional tort* and *risk* are subcategories of *liability for fault*, and their proof will lead to *recovery of damages*. Understanding the nature of the parallel relationships would aid thinking in this course. The remaining two concepts, *unintentional tort* and *public policy*, are mitigating concepts of *liability for fault*. *Unintentional tort*, or accident, would not be subsumed under *liability for fault* unless injury had occurred. *Public policy* could change or adjust a decision that would affect *liability for fault*.

Compared with student learning in other disciplines, law students made greater gains in learning the key concepts in this course. As described in Chapter Two, we asked students at the beginning and end of term to define the key concepts and scored their definitions according to accepted practice, with 2 for a definition that included the essential features as determined by the professor, 1 for a definition that was not incorrect but showed a poverty of content, and 0 for a definition that was wrong. Students' knowledge of the key concepts was low at the beginning of the course (20 percent) (mean student score divided by two), as it had been in physics (17 percent), but at the end of this two-semester course students displayed a 58 percent knowledge of the key concepts compared with 32 percent in the physics course.

The students' entering average was a better predictor of achievement in the course than knowledge of the key concepts at the beginning of the course; we can infer from this that overall ability is more important than concept knowledge for success. Key concept knowledge did predict achievement in the course; LSAT scores did not. The best known concepts at the end of the course were *unintentional tort* (90 percent knowledge—the theme of the second semester) and causation (77 percent—on which the professor is an expert*)*, even though *damage* (57 percent) and *risk* (48 percent) were most frequently used in class and had the least technical definitions. Students' key concept knowledge at the end of the course was significantly related to their final grade.

Analysis of the results indicates that the tightly structured, logically related set of concepts and the regularity of these relationships provided a solid foundation for learning. Because this course is critical to success in legal studies, there would be considerable incentive to gain knowledge of these foundational concepts. Why students did not have better overall knowledge of them (58 percent) at the end of the course remains a question. Their definitions suggest that these are complex concepts that may require more than one course to learn, much as physics students require several years to come to a deep understanding of a fundamental but complex concept such as *force*.

Since the concepts in torts play an important role in legal studies, we did a further analysis of them to determine what elements and relations were essential for understanding a particular concept and what were common elements among concepts in the course. We used a combination of attribute analysis (isolating essential properties or elements of a concept), feature analysis based on predicate calculus as used in modern logic, and network analysis to determine the structure of relations. From the analysis we developed a schematic representation of the concepts that showed the relationships among them (Figure 6.2). For example, for the concept *recovery of damages* the figure shows that damage caused to person B can be recovered only if person A was at fault to person B. There is a shifting of compensation by making the wrongdoer pay.

After analyzing each key concept, we created a summary matrix that showed common elements among them. For example, *recovery of damages* had the same elements as *liability for fault: damage, person who has been damaged, person causing the damage,* and an *act*. The matrix enabled us to see what the most common elements were among the key concepts—*person causing the damage* and *act*, found in ten of the eleven concepts. *Damage* and *person who has been damaged* were found in nine. These four elements link the key concepts extraordinarily closely compared to other courses, giving further explanation of the logic of torts and of students' gain in concept knowledge. The context and conditions relating to *liability for fault* appear to be where the complexity lies. We therefore decided to explore whether the conditions and context would be rendered clear if we used larger segments or chunks of knowledge than concepts to describe the learning task.

FIGURE 6.2. CONCEPT ANALYSIS OF RECOVERY OF DAMAGES

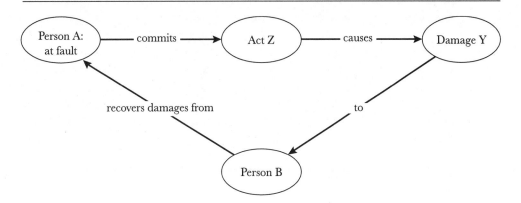

Learning Legal Propositions

We extended our study by applying discourse analysis procedures to the propositions to be learned by students. A *proposition* is a larger unit of analysis than a concept, defined as a statement that expresses relationships among concepts and that has a truth value. Our intention was to compare the concepts in important propositions in the course with the key concepts as means of representing course material. To do this, we worked with the professor to analyze the course material and obtained 182 important propositions from the text, then established that 73 of these were the most important according to her. Three of the most important propositions were the following:

The purpose of the law of torts is to adjust losses and afford compensation for injuries sustained by one person as the result of the conduct of another.

A case of liability has to rest on either an intent to interfere with the plaintiff's interests, or negligence, or strict liability or liability without fault.

Negligence is conduct (both acts and omissions) falling below the standard demanded for the protection of others against unreasonable risk of harm.

The most important propositions contained concepts that were examples of the eleven key concepts chosen in the previous study, such as *liability* or *risk*, but more were new terms that implied the key concepts. Analysis of the relationship between the twenty-five most frequently found concepts in the propositions with the eleven key concepts showed that concepts in the propositions were subcategories of the key concepts—for example, *apportionment of damages* was a subcategory of *recovery of damages* (Donald & Nagy, 1985). Over half the concepts in the propositions implied *liability for fault*; another one-quarter were examples of *intentional tort*. The wealth of language appeared to limit exact usage of terminology.

To establish the level of consistency in the discipline, we asked two other professors who were experts in the content area—having taught the course recently and coexamined in the course—to select the most important propositions from the list of 182 propositions. They made a smaller selection, one-third the size of the original professor's list, but all of their choices were from the group selected by the original professor as important, suggesting conservative consistency in the domain. The 25 propositions agreed on by the three professors tended to be more fundamental principles or definitions (fourteen of them), which employed basic concepts and were more concrete than those not selected. Variability occurred when propositions were abstract, general, or conditional, or were considered to need qualification. Students were also interviewed to determine which propositions they considered important, and they tended to choose those that were most familiar and specific.

We questioned whether the limited agreement about important propositions (one-third) in the course reflected a lack of conceptual convergence in the discipline in contrast to the logically and hierarchically structured relationships between the concepts in the course. The consistency among experts in political science, a pure social science discipline often considered foundational to the study of law, was much lower (Goldman, Schoner, & Pentony, 1980). In political science, ten experts rated terms for their importance in the undergraduate curriculum, and agreed on 11 out of over 20,000 terms, with another 1,075 terms receiving sufficiently high ratings to be considered part of a core curriculum in political science. We can therefore conclude that logical structure, although a primary defining characteristic of a discipline, is specific to the discipline in degree and kind.

What are the implications of this study for students learning law? We have the following facts. The key concepts in the torts course were for the most part abstract and complex. The three professors teaching torts tended to agree on concrete but not abstract propositions. The students in the course agreed on familiar and specific propositions. From these facts we can deduce that abstract concepts will not receive as much agreement in the discipline and therefore will not be as readily taught or learned. Despite these findings, we have seen that the tendency is to teach law at a highly abstract, philosophical level. This is a very specific example of limited disciplinary convergence and its effects on learning. It also suggests that situating concepts concretely through the use of memorable examples or experiences is essential for learning.

The Development of Thinking Processes in Law

Contemporary legal educators have invested great effort in analyzing what it is to think like a lawyer (Calhoun, 1984; Maurer & Mischler, 1994; Mudd, 1983) and in the process of legal analysis (Meldman, 1977; Nathanson, 1994; Somerville, 1978; Weidner, 1997). Although Mudd suggests that there is little consensus in the profession about the meaning of "thinking like a lawyer," he was able to delineate thinking processes to be learned in first-year courses. These include, in addition to briefing cases, the ability to analyze facts and appreciate the shifting legal results produced by factual nuances (evaluation), to separate a problem into its component parts (analysis), to assemble facts into a meaningful whole (synthesis), and to find the features in a problem situation relevant to its resolution (description and selection). Mudd argues that thinking like a lawyer can be seen within a more general framework of thinking clearly and precisely, as in any field.

Law students develop a variety of analytic skills in their programs, just as students in psychology and medicine do. Law students significantly increase their ability to reason using conditional logic (Lehman, Lempert, & Nisbett, 1988). Students in these three disciplines over a two-year period developed causal reasoning schemas or patterns and their associated evidence-checking procedures, and contractual schemas, including permission and obligation schemas, although chemistry students did not. Law students did not improve in probabilistic reasoning, needed for research, as students in psychology did. The law program was supplying students with experience in some kinds of analytic thinking but not in others.

In a discipline that defines itself in terms of legal analysis, replete with logical relationships, what thinking processes would students be expected to acquire? The process of legal analysis, according to Meldman (1977), is the logical derivation of a legal conclusion from a particular factual situation in the light of some body of legal doctrine. This is essentially common law methodology as defined in the torts course (M. A. Somerville personal communication, February 2000). She points out, however, that the conclusion is not objective and is not a given as it is in science but rather chosen from a range of conclusions. So the legal analysis is aimed at persuasion, not truth, except to the extent that the facts are true (to a greater or lesser extent).

Because in common law legal analysis amounts to the invocation of the rule of precedent, the facts in the present case must be seen to be similar to or different from those in the prior cited case, depending on the argument. This involves generalization. For example, the *holding* of a case—that is, the doctrine for which the case stands as authority—is understood in more general terms than the specific persons and activities that were actually involved in the case. Judges in courts of appeal tend to write their opinions in terms of those more general categories, recognizing that their judgments will play a role as precedents for future cases. The logic of syllogism is therefore used to classify a problem, and the logic of analogy is used when a precedent is applied to the problem and the facts fall near, but not within, the scope of a prior holding. Meldman used a computer model to represent problems of increasing complexity, applying it to general and specific cases. Attempts to develop structural models are intended to render the thinking processes used in jurisprudence clear and precise.

Contrasting the problem method with both the lecture and the case study method and assessing it to be more suitable for second- and third-year law students, Ogden (1984) defined three characteristics: problem statements are assigned to students for solution, students use course or other materials to solve the problems, and solutions are discussed in class. The problem method requires students to find their own solution to the problem presented. Problems generally do not have a single correct answer, so students must weigh alternatives and defend their choices. In a study of students' learning of law, Bryden (1984) had first- and third-year students attempt problems in three areas of legal analysis. In the first, *functional analysis,* lawyers seek to understand the meaning or scope of a rule or category according to its purpose. Students therefore need to know the relevant doctrines or policies that apply to the case. For example, when creating a contract to supply goods exclusively, one needs to know if there are statutes that define whether such a contract would be enforceable or not and whether the statutes apply in a given instance. Although third-year students were more proficient than entering students, only half the third-year students displayed functional analysis.

In the second area, *holding* versus *dictum*—that is, a judicial opinion on a point other than the precise issue involved in determining a case—the ability to distinguish the two is considered a fundamental skill of case analysis. Bryden found that in the problems they were given, students did not differentiate between the two. The third area, *statutory construction,* arises repeatedly in classroom dialogue; for example, prohibitory rules may have some permissive implications. Third-year students were more able to delineate the problems than first-year students, but again they missed several of the points in the problems. The author concludes that law school should be teaching students to take account of the procedural context, to perceive and articulate the equities of cases, to recognize situations where functional analyses are needed, and to notice the critical ambiguities in a statute.

In the study of the thinking processes developed in the course on torts, the professor expected first-year students to have all of the intellectual skills in the model of thinking processes (Exhibit 1.9) in a general sense but not in relation to law. She thought that students would be able to describe a legal situation on entry to the course. This involved *identifying the context, stating the conditions and facts* of the case, and *stating assumptions and goals.* She also expected students to have selection skills, that is, to be able to *choose the information relevant* to the case, to *order that information in importance,* and to *identify important elements and relationships.* She called these basic skills (Exhibit 6.1). In contrast, she reported spending some time helping students develop representation skills—that is, the ability to *recognize organizing principles,* to *organize elements and relations,* and to *illustrate and modify* them. This was in order to bring students from a basic level, where they would be able to identify existing laws and methods, to the level of being able to think creatively—to see new possibilities or to outline alternatives in a case. The professor noted that law itself is an organizing principle.

One strategy for *recognizing organizing principles* consists of a series of steps: (a) looking through a criminal code to find instances of a type of crime, (b) defining a concept such as *willfully,* and then (c) distinguishing this or analyzing in order to

EXHIBIT 6.1. PROFESSOR'S EXAMPLES OF THINKING PROCESSES USED IN THE LAW COURSE ON TORTS

DESCRIPTION: Delineation or definition of a situation or form of a thing.	*Look at the facts, look at the issues, look at the results.*
SELECTION: Choice in preference to another or others.	*Choose the information that is relevant to the case.*
REPRESENTATION: Depiction or portrayal through enactive, iconic, or symbolic means.	*Use creativity to see new possibilities or to outline alternatives in a case.*
Recognize organizing principles: Identify laws, methods, rules that arrange in a systematic whole.	*At basic level, identify existing laws and methods. At creative level, identify potential laws and methods.*
	Construct a range of possible decision outcomes or see new possibilities.
INFERENCE: Act or process of drawing conclusions from premises or evidence.	*Analyze the reasons for the facts, issues, and results, and critique these both distinctively and constructively.*
Categorize: Classify, arrange into parts.	*Facts are categorized within parameters, both situational and legal, such as the definition of a tort or crime.*
SYNTHESIS: Composition of parts or elements into a complex whole.	*Which course of action would they choose in presenting a case in order to achieve the outcome they desire?*
VERIFICATION: Confirmation of accuracy, coherence, consistency, correspondence.	*The ultimate verification in law is whether one wins or loses a case.*
	Competent and comprehensive argument and analysis.
Judge validity: Critically examine the soundness, effectiveness by actual fact.	*Persuade the judge to accept your arguments and thus to accept the validity of your case.*

achieve a desired legal outcome. In this instance, students are searching for an organizing principle they can use in an argument. The kind of principle will depend on the desired outcome. The actual thinking process involves sorting, defining, distinguishing, and analyzing to create the organizing principle.

Students learn to use inference when they analyze the reasons for the facts, issues, and results. They have to learn to *categorize* facts in law, understanding that facts are categorized within parameters. Facts in law include those that are situational and those that are legal, such as the definition of a tort or crime.

As in Meldman's (1977) logic of syllogism, students are expected to learn how to categorize both types of facts in order to present and then analyze a case. Students must learn to evaluate which *course of action* they would choose in presenting a case in order to achieve the outcome they desire. Using the logic of analogy, an important legal strategy is to consider the common ground between the plaintiff and the defendant, and then persuade the judge to accept your arguments and thus accept the validity of your case. The professor stated that students' grades reflect the level of inference and synthesis they use to analyze a case, with an A denoting a high degree of both competence and creativity. An A signifies that a student has provided new insights into the case and new ways of structuring it.

This professor took a pragmatic stance toward verification or validation, stating that the ultimate verification in law is whether one wins or loses a case, as had Nelken (1995). She added that students are taught to feel vindicated more by having presented competent and comprehensive argument and analysis than by outcome—winning or losing—because lawyers inevitably must handle unwinnable cases. The strategy for convincing a judge to accept an argument can be categorized most readily within the definition of validity as reliance on or reference to authority, closer to the means of establishing validity in the humanities (Donald, 1990). However, in law this is a distinct type of validation. Rather than resting in empirical proof as it would in the physical or social sciences, or on the authority of peers or the disciplinary canon as in English literature, it is vested in whether an argument can convince a judge.

Asked to what extent a legal expert would be expected to think in the way the model describes thinking processes, the professor replied that a legal expert must be able to use all of the thinking processes in the right order, as in the methodology of legal judgment. This consists of four steps: look at the facts (description), look at the issues (representation), look at the results and analyze the reasons (inference), and critique these both distinctively and constructively by determining what was held and why (verification). These steps follow the order of the thinking model but concentrate on representation, inference, and verification. A final important element is that in law the thinking processes in the model apply equally to both sides of a given case.

From these studies of the process of legal analysis, it is clear that considerable attention has been paid to delineating the steps that must be taken, whether called functional analysis, generalization, thinking processes, syllogism, or analogy. The particularity and the complexity of legal thinking processes are also evident. Much more time could be devoted to explicating the very complex analyses required. To develop these processes students demonstrably need experience in situations where they can test and hone their skills.

The Challenge of Instruction in Law

The issues that law professors face in their teaching are distinctive. Students in law programs are at the same time verbally proficient and adversarial, and to varying degrees have high ideals about society and justice. They are often demanding and confrontational. In a conservative discipline based on an abstract authority, a primary issue is how to provide a framework for learning and the extent to which contemporary teaching methods can serve this purpose. A second issue is the need to develop specific legal analysis skills. A third lingering issue is the paradox of values and their place in the curriculum.

A Framework for Learning Law

The most common contemporary teaching method in law is the use of a casebook in which different types of cases in an area of study, such as torts or property, are abridged or adapted for classroom use. Because case law is used so widely and has some aspects in common with problem-based learning used in other areas of study, it is important to first examine the advantages and disadvantages of this method to see how it could be used successfully. Watson (1996) states that although it is widely accepted that the point of the casebook method is to teach students how to argue about the law, students appear to learn to argue without thinking about the law. He notes that the casebook method is reminiscent of some cases in Seneca's *Controversiae,* but the aim of the *Controversiae* was to teach young Romans the techniques of rhetoric, not law.

The problem lies in the use of a few cases when in fact the law is not contained in a few cases but is usually distilled from many cases, so that if only a few are studied they appear out of context. Without a general framework, students do not get the big picture. They cannot tell to what extent a case reflects general propositions or whether it stands at the edge of a doctrine. It is often impossible to see which facts in the case are relevant. Watson's solution is to set out briefly the concepts and propositions developed in hundreds of cases, then follow this with a discussion of a few cases selected to illustrate the rules, their parameters, and issues raised by borderline situations.

One method to help students integrate their skills using cases is to have them work individually or in teams in greater depth on case studies in which they would assemble and evaluate relevant facts, identify legal as well as social and ethical issues, search out and apply the appropriate law, reach a plan of action, and implement it by drafting proper instruments or making oral presentations (Mudd, 1983). The case studies would increase in complexity from those involving single issues to advanced cases involving several. Cases could be presented to students in written form or using actors as clients, which would permit the development of interpersonal skills crucial to fact gathering and plan implementation. The process would also train students in macroanalysis—the analysis of a multifaceted problem as it might appear in a lawyer's office.

This is essentially the pattern undertaken in Introduction to Lawyering, a course offered by the law school at Union University in New York in the first year of the program (Maurer & Mischler, 1994). It has two aims: to introduce students to essential skills and values of the profession and to provide a broad context for their understanding at an impressionable time in their lives. Stanford University also offers a first-year course on the lawyering process through simulated clinical exercises, small group collaboration, and classroom instruction. Introduction to Lawyering, however, offers large-scale immersion into the legal context. It begins with assignment of students to one of two "law firms" where they will represent either a plaintiff or a defendant in a yearlong legal dispute. They perform the various legal tasks associated with the dispute, confront issues of professional responsibility, and consider the myriad decisions lawyers must make in such a case.

Students experience firsthand the series of decisions necessary in handling a case from initial client interview through appeal. Their assignments include two objective memoranda, a persuasive memorandum to the court and a two-issue appellate brief. Because they are working on a single simulated case in progress, they must prepare for client interviews and negotiations, draft client letters, brainstorm about possible courses of action with their professors, and constantly reevaluate the developing facts to formulate cogent arguments. The course also provides students with a natural setting for encountering and thinking about ethical issues that arise in the context of the hypothetical problem, sending the message that ethical obligations are a constant in the practice of law.

The case is chosen to expose students to a variety of primary and secondary sources of law at the state and federal levels, and to maintain their interest for an entire year. The first case chosen was on employment discrimination based on sexual harassment, an issue that had been covered extensively by the media just before the course began. Students learned the importance of updating authority as courts handed down relevant decisions over the year. Changes in a relevant statute served as a springboard for further analysis of the law and discussion of decision making. The facts of the case also offered issues of potential common law tort liability. Other cases included a housing discrimination issue based on disability and a constitutional issue involving a school dress code.

Students in upper years of the program play the roles of the plaintiff and defendant and are free to adopt any personality they wish, thus providing diverse learning experiences to students in the course. After each simulated exercise in the course, the class engages in a discussion of the performance and suggests ways of improving it, so that students can incorporate new strategies into their repertoire. The course proceeds from client interview and preparation of an objective memorandum, to drafting pleadings, to discovery, where students draft interrogatories in teams, and then to negotiation of a settlement. At the end of the year, students participate in oral arguments based on their appellate briefs. Students noted in evaluations of the course that it provided them with extra opportunities and made them more marketable. Maurer and Mischler conclude that to have a successful law program, there must be institutional commitment to the goal of curriculum integration. What students experienced in this course provided them with a frame of reference into which they could fit the large amounts of information offered in more theoretical courses; both are needed to understand law.

Developing Legal Analysis Skills

Developing legal skills is also a question of curriculum design. One legal scholar suggests that careful analysis of the time-benefit ratio of different methods for improving students' ability to think is needed (Mudd, 1983). For example, assuming that students' ability to think can be enhanced by reading appellate decisions, how many should they read? At what point does the time-benefit curve flatten so that further time spent would have only marginal results? How long would it take to hone the skill of memorandum writing? These questions can be answered through curriculum innovation and evaluation studies. *The Journal of Legal Education,* first published in 1948, and the more recently begun *Journal of Professional Legal Education* provide opportunity for wide-ranging discussion on issues in legal education, particularly directions the legal curriculum might take or developing skills in legal analysis.

To illustrate, in an article on the development of legal problem-solving skills, Nathanson (1994) describes how he and his colleagues created modules in legal skills by following a several-step pattern that began with describing the theory behind the skill, then setting out criteria for effective performance. For example, for legal drafting they devised a guide of important drafting criteria demonstrated with examples that did or did not conform to the criteria. They then gave students practice drafting using factual scenarios with partially completed documents to work on, and finished with feedback on their performance.

When they found that students tended to use lower-level skills such as following precedents, they introduced the notion of using two approaches: linear (applying theories and models in a step-by-step way) and flexible (treating the models with imagination and resourcefulness). The idea of two conflicting dimensions to the performance of a skill was sometimes difficult for students to understand but proved more realistic and meaningful, and hence satisfying. Students showed a consistent preference for practice over lectures. Particularly helpful to them was an all-day joint-venture exercise in which they drafted an agreement and received immediate feedback on it. They were able to transfer learning from this exercise most readily: a memorable framework had been created.

Bridge-building techniques are essential if students are to transfer problem-solving skills. The most important technique is to avoid changing too many features of a problem at one time; changing the legal or transactional context bit by bit allows students to see the similarities yet be sufficiently challenged to use higher-level skills. The professors also found that explicitly referring to transfer in their teaching, and demonstrating how skills can be transferred from one context to another, helped students make the necessary connections. The challenge for legal educators is to sequence and balance the needed knowledge and skills so that students' ability to solve legal problems is extended with every learning activity.

One of the most useful instructional approaches according to students in the traditional course format is the use of computer exercises (Shapiro, 1996). In a course on evidence that Shapiro had taught for eleven years using the same updated casebook, and the leading hornbook or primer in the field, he began to introduce exercises produced by the Center for Computer Assisted Legal Instruction at the University of Minnesota. To improve access on a campus with a limited number of computers available, students who supplied blank disks to the library were issued copies of the exercises that they could take home. When Shapiro surveyed students on their use of course materials, he found not only that they made greater use of the computer exercises than the hornbook or casebook but that far greater numbers of them found the exercises very helpful. One student reported that the exercises were "addicting." Students' examination performance improved with the number of exercises they did. Thus, modifications that challenge students and improve their performance can be made in a course.

Investigating Values

The paradox of value-free law in a normative discipline provokes the most sensitive challenge for instruction. Students need to examine the social context in which they will be working for several reasons. If values are ignored, students are likely to become cynical and disaffected. As one third-year law student stated, "I feel like we learn nothing that affects real people. In school, you quickly realize how the law is geared toward people with money, like successions or trust funds. And the only firms recruiting are the big ones" (LoDico, 2000). Students tend to split down the middle into two camps—conservatives and social activists. In response to this issue, students are given the opportunity as part of their training to do fieldwork in the campus legal clinic or take a six-credit course allowing them to work for a community organization, where they may encounter the frustration of dealing with bureaucracies but also gain hands-on experience in local legal problems.

The movement to reattach law to social values is evident in critical legal studies programs or joint degree programs in law and economics, bioethics and health law, and law and social work that are seen increasingly in North American universities. A wide-ranging intellectual vision of law is often the product of such studies. Transsystemic teaching, where, for example, civil (statutory) and common law are taught together from a varied set of perspectives, also broadens the intellectual sway (R. Janda, personal communication, June 2000). One strength of situating legal education in a university is that it increases the possibility of bringing to bear other disciplines or political outlooks not currently embodied in legal principles, linking with the impartial but critical traditions of higher education generally. Lewis (1992) suggests that trends toward interdisciplinarity may ultimately change law and legal practice.

In *The Cultural Study of Law* (1999), Kahn argues that for scholarship and critical study, an imaginative separation between oneself and one's beliefs is essential. Understanding the constructed character of the rule of law allows one to see its meanings and the possibilities of alternate meanings. Kahn's view is that in comparison with scientific inquiry—a narrative of progress in which the present supercedes the past—law is a collection of interpretive commentaries in constant dialectic. The cultural study of law begins with the recognition that there are competing worlds of experience; the meanings of events are contested in their features and in their frames of reference—aesthetically or politically, for example. Old paradigms do not disappear; shifts occur when internal incoherence is recognized. Although reason operates within the legal order, law's rule is not itself a product of systematic rationality. Thus Kahn concludes that the rule of law is largely the management of a series of tensions bordering on contradictions.

This approach to the dialectic of law has been realized in instruction where skills such as negotiation are developed. The argument for incorporating the study of interpersonal dynamics into the curriculum is that law students need to understand on a practical and personal level how their own values affect the stance they take toward clients and legal problems. Nelken (1995) notes that because more than 90 percent of civil lawsuits never go to trial, even those lawyers who handle lawsuits and not business deals spend a significant amount of time negotiating and resolving disputes. She therefore tries to acquaint her students with the idea that assumptions they bring to a situation may interfere with their ability to represent a client or prevent seeking the information they need to solve a dispute. In illuminating the internal and interpersonal dynamics at work in all negotiations, her objective is to help the practicing lawyer make choices about how to handle the negotiation, and in fact, to behave more rationally.

Another positive outcome of understanding one's own assumptions is in lawyer-client relationships. Clients are often dissatisfied with their lawyers because the lawyer is unable to see the client's emotional self as anything other than an impediment to managing the legal problem. Nelken suggests that lawyers who have developed some understanding of their own internal conflicts will be able to tolerate and incorporate their client's feelings with the legal facts in order to resolve the dispute. Cultural sensitivity in a global economy also calls on the lawyer to understand the subtext or subcurrents, in order to self-regulate and respond more flexibly in negotiations. Thus, values become an integral part of the curriculum, congruent with the role of the social sciences in social reform.

The Disciplinary Perspective in Law

What kind of learning environment does law provide? The learning context is highly influenced by the legal profession; the need to work within a framework of statute and precedent requires that students be verbally fluent, assertive, and rational. One of the contributors to this chapter noted at the end of our conversation that law schools are unruly places where received wisdom and controversy vie for attention.

What higher-order thinking processes are important for law students to learn? Learning to think like a lawyer is a demanding and complex process. A vocabulary of abstract, nuanced terms and principles guide the process of thinking. The methodology of legal judgment consists of looking at the facts, the issues, and the results, analyzing the reasons, and then critiquing these both distinctively and constructively. Lawyers must determine what was held and why. There are various strategies to be learned to produce an argument, and individuals must incorporate a wide range of skills, attitudes, and values into their behavior.

What are optimal ways of cultivating these thinking processes? The challenges for instruction require large-scale attention in the law school to organize a program of instruction that integrates curriculum and meets both scholarly and professional requirements. Contemporary teaching methods such as macroanalysis, in which students analyze a multifaceted problem as it might appear in a lawyer's office, provide a framework for learning. Specific legal analysis skills can be improved by computer exercises or simulations. Finally, students need to examine the social context in which they will be working and determine the role of values in their personal and professional lives, because these will act as guiding principles in their thinking as lawyers.

CHAPTER SEVEN

ORGANIZING INSTRUCTION AND UNDERSTANDING LEARNERS

One of the students' obligations as communicators of understanding is to develop some in-depth understanding of the structures or organizational principles of the disciplines they teach, and then to be able to detect their presence or absence in the text materials they are using in their teaching.

EDUCATION PROFESSOR

Learning to be a teacher is a multilayered endeavor. In this quotation, the professor draws attention to the need for students to be able to interpret other disciplines, then to incorporate their knowledge structures into instructional units that will suit a particular group of learners in a particular culture. The sociological context of education differs from other disciplines in the university because of its fundamental developmental role in society. Education is essential for economic and social development and is a means of emancipation or subjugation, depending on whether students learn to think for themselves or to obey authority. The social importance of education is underscored by its immediate relation to government at several levels—local, state or provincial, federal or central. School boards, commissions, local authorities, and ministries participate in educational decision making and affect the learning context whether in curriculum development or field placements. This is a condition with which other disciplines in the university do not have to contend. In the university, however, the societal importance of education goes unrecognized, and schools or colleges of education must fight for scholarly recognition.

To understand how the discipline of education functions, I begin this chapter by describing the academic context of education, then examine the learning task in teacher education programs. Fourteen professors of education contributed to this chapter; eleven professors responsible for courses in teacher education in six different universities provide their perspectives on how students are educated to become teachers. Scholarly recognition is based in graduate level education, where the focus changes to research training, and three professors of research design give their views of student learning in their courses. Interviews with thirty-eight education students and student reports in a series of research projects provide perspective on their experience.

In this chapter, to distinguish between university students and elementary and secondary school students, *student* is used to denote university student; *learner* is used to denote their students in schools. *College* is used to denote schools or faculties of education. In teacher education programs, examples come from undergraduate and postgraduate programs for elementary or secondary school teachers. The learning task extends across several kinds of knowledge: of the institutional context, educational goals and objectives, attitudes, connecting subject matter to instructional methods, and learners in schools. Students need to learn how to represent subject matter and adapt it to learners, and to design instructional processes that lead to active learning.

Challenges in education programs arise from the need to understand other disciplines in order to explain them, the conceptions of learning that students bring with them, and the exigency for pedagogical expertise. In his classic book *Toward a Theory of Instruction*, Bruner (1966) sums up the challenge for educators: if instruction is effective, learning should be less dangerous or risky or painful than learning on one's own. The caveat for the instructor is that to be used effectively, knowledge must be translated into the learner's way of attempting to solve a problem. In short, educators must integrate subject matter with the state of learners while attending to the surrounding social context.

The Disciplinary Context in Education

As a professional discipline in a university, education has both intellectual and practical missions. Clark (1987) describes this dilemma as facing, Janus-like, in two directions in order to meet the requirements of two constituencies, the academic and the professional. As in other professional disciplines such as medicine or law, education professors must demonstrate scholarship through research and publication in order to achieve legitimacy in the university. At the same time, they are called on to involve themselves directly in the improvement of educational practice. They must therefore devote some attention to schools, school districts, and government ministries that create the policy and superintend the curriculum of the schools.

Defining the metadiscipline of education epistemologically—to what extent is it science, social science, amalgam of disciplines, or profession?—is challenging for several reasons. In the *Encyclopedia of Higher Education* (Clark & Neave, 1992), there is no entry describing education as a discipline, although the relation of teacher education to higher education merits attention. Compared with other academic areas in degree of structure, or hardness, education is located at the soft end of the scale with history (Biglan, 1973). This means that the range of phenomena to be considered is unrestricted and complexity is seen as a legitimate aspect of knowledge. Education is also at the applied end of the pure-applied dimension in contrast with philosophy at the pure end of the scale. Because it is of necessity open to a wide range of phenomena, education is at times referred to as a field rather than a discipline (see Exhibit 1.1). Fields are characterized as being ill-defined at the parameters and not meeting the criteria of a logical structure of knowledge and a generally accepted methodology (Dressel & Mayhew, 1974). One professor described the predicament for educational scholars in the following way.

> Education differs from older, more established disciplines like physics where journals become extremely specialized and people just keep writing in the same one regularly. In many ways education is a less developed but a broader and richer field than physics, so that you tend to cover very diverse areas.

The attempt must still be made to understand the scope and diversity of education. To provide structure, *The Education Index* was developed to list new publications in the domain, and it has many characteristics of a disciplinary taxonomy. However, the fact that the field originated with a focus on the subject matter of other disciplines taught at earlier levels renders the task of defining education more difficult. Vast numbers of search engines are now used to track down educational literature. In the university, educators use a specialized pedagogical vocabulary in addition to having to understand the theoretical frameworks of the arts and science disciplines students are being prepared to teach. Understanding the conceptual frameworks of the subject matter disciplines is a major task. In his explanation of why this is so, Schwab (1978) notes that because disciplines do not have a single structure, clarity is not easily found. Even physics, the most structured discipline, has competing explanations of phenomena. Because the problems in any subject area are too diverse to permit solution with a single pattern of inquiry, a range of methods must be learned. Adding to the complexity, a structure is itself a highly flexible pattern continually adapted to fit particular problems and contexts. Hence, establishing content knowledge in any of the disciplines to be taught—as demonstrated in the previous chapters of this book—is a complicated process itself. The ensuing intellectual process in education demands at the least eclecticism as a strategy.

The sociological definition of education is also uncertain because of varied histories of development and political roles in different countries. For example, in some countries, teacher training was under the authority of local rather than central government and at one time took place in a system of less competitive educational institutions, such as the polytechnics or colleges of advanced education in England. In other countries such as France, aspiring teachers attended one of the *grandes écoles*—the École Normale Supérieure—and were examined to become members of an academy (Judge, 1992). In Japan, teacher education is undertaken by the employers of teachers, and is thus defined and delineated professionally rather than academically.

In the United States and Canada, education is not a federal responsibility but a state or provincial prerogative, intended to be more directly responsive to regional needs and demands but hence more variable. Another effect of this policy is a lack of central determination of the direction education should take in response to national priorities. Thus, various state or provincial education systems do not benefit from the regular attention of federal bodies of legislation. Differences may occur, for example, in entry and teacher certification criteria from one jurisdiction to another. In North America, the trend in postsecondary teacher education in the twentieth century was from local normal (defined as *model* or *exemplary*) schools to colleges of education in state or provincially funded universities. Historically, then, education as a discipline entered the academic world in slippers, somewhat surreptitiously.

Further variation in the field has occurred in teacher preparation for the elementary and secondary levels. For example, in England preparation for elementary school teaching was at one time given in normal schools directly after elementary school, whereas preparation for secondary school teachers was most often an incubation in arts and science without pedagogy. In the past, whether in Europe or North America, specific attention to the process of learning and learners was rare; the foundational discipline that dealt with learning and human development, psychology, did not become a required part of education programs until the second half of the twentieth century in many places in North America.

The perspective held by others in the university of the college of education reflects the modest beginning of this discipline. Described as a social or human service profession in which personal belief affects occupational practice, Becher (1989) attributes the lack of recognition accorded members of this discipline to the difficulty of establishing a strong academic image in a soft field. According to Becher, the discipline may gain some points for utility or social relevance, but education and its proponents will not be held in awe as in the hard disciplines such as physics and biochemistry. To establish a scholarly base and with public recognition of the need for research on effective schooling in North America in the 1960s, colleges of education created educational research departments, and state or provincial governments began to fund centers and institutes that supplied methodological expertise and became models for research in the social sciences.

The ambivalence toward education in the university also results from the subject matter orientation of undergraduate studies in the arts and sciences. According to one scholar, arts and science professors view themselves as central to the process of educating future teachers (Judge, 1992). More problematic for educators, the arts and science professors see themselves as competent teachers without having had pedagogical training and so are inclined to regard courses in pedagogy or other aspects of education, such as philosophy or sociology, as lacking in intellectual substance or practical relevance. At the same time, professors of arts and science are often unwilling to take active responsibility themselves for educating teachers. In the college of education, a further dilemma arises in the relative authority of the subject matter areas and pedagogical foundations, which usually operate as separate departments. Bruner (1966) suggests that for effective instruction to occur, content and the learning process need to be amalgamated. Deciphering the knowledge and thinking processes in education is thus particularly challenging.

Although the central responsibility of colleges of education is teacher education either at the undergraduate or postgraduate diploma level, most graduate (master's and doctoral) programs lead instead toward professional or educational research degrees that require a different set of competencies. This change in orientation creates an additional disciplinary dilemma in colleges of education as teacher education and graduate programs focus on different areas of study, thus limiting disciplinary symbiosis. Graduate programs in education in the past have been directed for the most part at educational administration, counseling, or psychology, diverting attention from the tasks of teacher education. Judge contends that this disjunction in programs created an internal partition in colleges of education, with a resulting depression in the status and quality of teacher education. In addition, the production of new knowledge through research depended on receiving funding as a social science, so that topics in educational research by their necessary specification often did not deal with the untidy problems of schooling and were therefore less likely to contribute to the improvement of schools.

In response to this situation, educational researchers have increasingly focused on teacher education and classroom processes. Educators have also developed strategies for dealing with the apparent lack of structure in subject matter areas. For example, to prepare university students to become teachers, the Holmes Group (1986), a panel of noted American educators, pointed out the importance of providing students in their undergraduate courses with a conceptualization or mental model of their field of study.

Accreditation or review processes for educational programs, most often initiated external to the university by governments, have been instrumental in developing standards and criteria for programs provided by colleges of education. These processes, however, put yet another furrow in the brow. The criteria developed for review purposes are accompanied by claims of government authority that may threaten university autonomy in a way that professional standards and expectations in medicine, law, or engineering have not. Thus education occupies a provocative and perhaps vexing role in the university because it demands more of the arts and science disciplines in understanding their epistemological characteristics and introduces additional program criteria and evaluation processes. At the same time, education as a discipline must meet conditions in addition to those expected of other disciplines as it attempts to interlace subject matter knowledge with pedagogy. How is this done?

The Learning Task in Education

To understand what is to be learned in education we must first deal with some basic philosophical issues. As in law, the aims and axioms of education present a series of paradoxes or antinomies—contradictions between two apparently equally valid principles. The conflict between the potential roles of education as emancipator or subjugator has been noted. Bruner (1996) portrays this conflict more mildly in terms of equipping human beings to operate at their fullest potential versus equipping them to continue and further the culture. The issue of the rights of the individual versus society is most frequently seen in education as a progressive-conservative debate and affects both curriculum and instructional method—for example, whole language versus a return to the three R's in the elementary schools.

Another paradox rests in the nature of the learner and learning; I have termed this the *attributional* versus the *environmental* approach (Donald, 1997). In the attributional approach, the learner is considered to have inherent characteristics and is responsible for his or her own development. The educational institution then has the role of selection or accreditation. In the environmental approach, human abilities are the product of the interaction between the individual and the environment; thus the educational institution carries a greater responsibility to provide a positive environment. For Bruner, the paradox is internally focused on contradictory views about the nature of mind—whether learners must rely on their own intelligence and motivation or whether mental activity is situated in a culturally enabling setting.

A third antinomy situates the modern-postmodern debate for educators: whether there is an established curriculum or how ways of thinking or constructing meaning are to be judged and by whom. The search for authority or for the universal recapitulates the quest for logical structure seen in the hard disciplines in previous chapters; in education, accountability or testing movements are a product of this quest. Deschooling, and the primacy of human experience, exemplify the opposite pole. The experiential approach is based on the premise that most things in learning are not that clear and there are endless numbers of adequate pathways for people to come to understand a subject matter area (Duckworth, 1987; personal communication, October 2000). These issues arise throughout our conversations with the education professors who contributed to this chapter. Given these fundamental paradoxes, how do students in education programs learn to teach?

Expertise is the term most widely used to describe the ability to function in this discipline, based on the importance of educational context and the need for good judgment. As in other professions, teaching expertise could be expected to develop through experience with situations in which the teacher consolidates a framework for action. The learning task in education requires attention to the subject matter to be taught and *how* to teach the knowledge and thinking processes in each subject matter area. Professors of education must understand the subject disciplines they are teaching so that they can engage their students in developing frameworks for elementary and secondary students to learn that discipline. The professors are expected to accomplish this task either while students are learning their subject disciplines or after students have adopted the disciplinary ways and attitudes of a subject matter area of specialization. They thus need to link different models of learning and provide a sufficiently flexible framework to enable their students to engage the next cohort of learners in interpreting disciplinary modes.

Learning About the Educational Context

The interplay between the kinds of knowledge a competent teacher needs creates an intriguing but demanding learning situation in teacher education programs. For example, according to one professor, students are learning to use categories and patterns of understanding that relate to making professional and practical judgments about what to do or what ought to be done in the classroom. At the same time, they have the more basic demand of understanding their own learning in their subject matter areas. In addition to classroom concerns, however, they must understand more generally how educational institutions operate and the limitations of these institutions. Understanding the context is a sine qua non for a teacher. Competent functioning in the institution is the primary goal, and was uppermost in the minds of several professors.

One of the things they have to learn is to think conceptually in an institutional framework; the discourse concerns institutional concerns, not personal concerns. You cannot help people to acquire high skills and competencies in schools as they are, yet at the same time train them as revolutionaries to transform schools into a different genre. The student has to go and teach in a school that may be formal and autocratic, where he or she cannot engage in highly exploratory methods that demand the pupils' own initiatives and freedoms. The course is designed to develop analytic competence to teach in conventional classrooms rather than critical reflection.

At this general level, several goals are superordinate to the classroom situation.

You are trying to get them to be politically conscious about how the system works. There is a notion of what they consider a good teacher to be, and that is part of what goes into the course as well. You are trying to form or change attitudes. You are trying to make your students more aware of issues. You are also trying to make them aware of themselves.

Students must situate their own experience vis-à-vis that of their intended students. For Shulman (1986), knowledge of educational contexts encompasses not only the workings of the group or classroom but governance and financing and the character of the community and culture. One of the professors noted that students entering his teacher education program come from the top 10 percent intellectually and may have to make major adjustments in their expectations of the students they will be teaching and the strategies they will therefore employ.

They might need quite different approaches from those they encountered as students, since the schools they are going to may be very different from those they attended, and the more they get involved in classroom experiences, the more they recognize that is so.

Another adjustment that must be made is in the work ethic or organization brought to the teaching task. This involves personal adjustments at several levels.

The majority of students have not yet come to terms with the sort of discipline that professional work demands. They have to come to terms with what it is like to get to school by 8:30 in the morning and what it is like to still be correcting exercises or preparing lessons until 10:00 at night. This kind of demand they begin to find when they go on school experience. They get completely exhausted by it because they have not been trained to the industry and self-discipline that is demanded of a professional job. We have to turn them from being students of the undergraduate variety into professionals.

Teacher education programs have moved to early immersion in classrooms in order to provide an institutional context as a grounding experience for students. This occurs optimally in conjunction with their pedagogy courses so that they can test what they are learning at the university with their lived experience. One way to relate their understanding of their subject matter area to the teaching process is to focus course learning goals on how knowledge is organized.

Learning Goals and Objectives

In a course for postgraduate students who spend their morning in teaching internships in secondary schools, the afternoon finds them in a seminar where they are called on to relate educational perspectives to their classroom experience. As one of the coinstructors explained:

> This course is focused on issues of knowledge. What is knowledge? How does its character vary across or within disciplines? What is the structure of knowledge as represented in textbooks? How is knowledge organized in the heads of teachers? How is knowledge gradually structured in the heads of students? How do variations in the contexts of learning influence what is learned?
>
> During the ten weeks of the course, four perspectives on subject matter knowledge are explored. First, the class discusses the manner in which a subject and its parts are structured and organized, including written and visual modes of representation. Second, they investigate the nature of knowledge in general, as well as in specific areas. Third, they study the work that psychologists have been doing in the area of cognitive structures. Finally, they explore how contextual factors influence conceptions of ability, understood as the capacity to acquire new knowledge and to apply the knowledge one already holds.
>
> In order to cover these differing perspectives, the class readings include a wide variety of materials in education, epistemology, psychology, and anthropology. In addition, the class discusses the implications of this work for teaching and learning in schools, and students are expected to participate in a number of projects and exercises designed to assist them in testing and applying these ideas in their own teaching. These projects are the most important activities that are undertaken in the class.

The learning objectives in foundations courses in education are extensive and varied. In the study of disciplinary differences in what is taught and in students' perceptions of what they learn, education professors assigned greater importance to developing specific skills, competencies, and points of view needed by professionals in the field (Cashin & Downey, 1995). Students in education reported greater progress than students in other disciplines on several fronts. They agreed with their professors in developing the specific skills and competencies. They also reported progress in learning to apply course material to improve rational thinking, problem solving, and decision making, and in developing skill in expressing themselves orally and in writing. They considered that they had discovered the implications of course material for understanding themselves, similar to psychology students. Education students reported more progress than students in other programs on a variety of objectives. How students develop their insight about their own students and themselves is illustrated by the professor in the same postgraduate course quoted earlier.

> I want the students to understand that their students are not tabula rasa but have their own cognitive organization. I want the students to think about those organizations as they manifest themselves in such things as preconceptions, misconceptions, difficulties that learners have as they encounter new ideas, and the recognition that they have to work with those organized structures in much the same way that a physician has to work with the immune system of a patient. You just cannot assume that everything that is done will have the intended effect; in fact, you can assume that it will not. Therefore what is involved in pedagogy is trying to transact or interact across sets of organized or structured systems.
>
> Inevitably one of the students says, "But we're organized systems too; we have our own conceptions; how does that affect what we see as the conceptions of our students, as well as what we see in a piece of text?" The teacher who is mediating also carries a set of cognitive structures. The substantive goal of the course is to have the students as future professionals develop a conception of what is meant by the knowledge base of teaching. That includes a depth of understanding of one's own discipline. It is not just the organized structures that physics or history or biology comprise but also the grounds on which new structures are introduced and old structures are considered no longer au courant.

For that reason they talk about the work of Kuhn (1970) and his examination of the discipline of physics and more generally about the history and philosophy of science. This professor also wants students to understand that these notions will take different forms in different subject areas. One of the ways they can begin to understand the form these notions take in their subject area is to contrast their discipline with another. Because of the need to understand the nature of knowledge:

The class is just as interested in the physics teacher's grappling with the question, "What does it mean to know a sonnet?" as it is with the English teacher's grappling with the question, "What does it mean to know Boyle's law?" and both of them in turn thinking about what it means to know the quadratic formula, and how knowing takes on very different meanings in these different contexts. At the same time, when pressed, the students come to recognize that there may be more similarities between physics and literature than at first blush they were willing to admit. With respect to the confidence with which one asserts truth in the field, maybe the truth value of Boyle's law at its root has just as many questions surrounding it as the truth value of a particular interpretation of *Romeo and Juliet*.

Another objective in the course is to provide students with a professional vocabulary, for example, Bloom's (1956) taxonomy. It provides a hierarchy of cognitive objectives from knowledge through comprehension, application, analysis, and synthesis to evaluation, but the professor noted that he would let students see its limitations. Notions of *discovery* and *mastery* and cognitive vocabulary are situated in practice; for example, *intelligence* is approached through the question of what it means to say that someone displays particular levels of aptitude in particular settings.

The third assignment in the previous year was a case study of a youngster who was not very smart in class. Each student's job was to study a youngster's records, and then to follow that student around, with the student's permission, to other classes, to clubs, to church, to home, to the athletic fields, with the purpose of identifying a situation or a set of situations in which the youngster was smart. Then they had to try to explain why someone who was smart in some settings was not smart in class. This was a difficult assignment given the time constraints, but was effective.

Learning goals and objectives thus incorporate a wide variety of educational ends with their philosophical and historical grounds. In addition to these educational ends are values or attitudes.

Learning Attitudes

The professors of education stated that certain attitudes are very important for teachers, both for themselves and as learning outcomes for their students. This is another sine qua non in education, because without such attitudes they will not be able to function. The *Taxonomy of Educational Objectives* (Krathwohl, Bloom, & Masia, 1964) was designed to describe levels of attitude development from openness or receptiveness through responsiveness to commitment. In addition to the conceptual framework that students in teacher education programs need in order to deal with the myriad problems that may arise inside and outside the classroom, they need an overarching attitude of understanding and support toward their students (one of my professors described it as "kindness") and determination in the face of what may appear at times to be insurmountable odds. Two professors described these attributes in the following manner:

> Students are expected to show a certain modicum of passion or commitment to their own learning, but more important is their zeal or commitment to their school students' learning.

> Persistence in the face of frustration, if not failure, is critical. An attitude of self-efficacy or self-confidence so that they can look at a piece of instruction that they want to teach, and if they work hard enough, they can get it under control.

Personal attitudes and professional attributes are essential for survival. One professor explained how these characteristics are developed in a postgraduate foundations course.

> One of the themes in the course is knowing about yourself, because it is a very sharp change for the bulk of these people, to come from an undergraduate program into this course. Because the students must make a lot of personal adjustments in that year, the staff give a fair amount of attention to their reflecting on their own opinions and their beliefs and their growth through the year.

Students require self-knowledge as a basis for understanding learners and the instructional process. In our interviews with students in teacher education programs, they talked about their desire to work with children and how important it was to consider what stage of development children had reached in order to understand their capacity to learn. They also noted that the environment in the college of education was substantially different from that in other programs in the university. For example:

> I have found that the philosophy in the education department is not the same as in the rest of the university. The education department tends to value being a true person, human and genuine, rather than the authoritative, condescending nature present in the majority of the other departments throughout the rest of the university. I discovered that I am more motivated and hence work better in a less rigid, authoritative environment.

Students spoke about their course being easy to relate to real life, that they put what they learn into practice right away. They also commented on the level of intellectual activity in the course.

> It's a different kind of material to be studied. It's not just educational material, or about learning; it's more in-depth, like "What's going on in their heads?" and "What's going on in the teacher's head?" and "How does this all come together?" Compared to the other courses I am taking, this one's very much deeper.

According to these students there is both humanism and depth in their courses in education that respond to the cognitive and affective objectives defined in the educational taxonomies.

The Nature of Knowledge in Education

What kind of educational framework do student teachers need to construct? Among educational scholars in North America, the prevalent view of knowledge is as a conceptual scaffold, a foundation for subsequent learning that colors and filters one's school and nonschool experiences (Alexander, 2000; Alexander & Murphy, 1998). The relationship of subject matter and learner is based on a few distinct concepts. The theme expressed by professors in this chapter so far is that what the process of education adds to human development is organization or structure. We could therefore expect that these would be core concepts or principles in the discipline. One professor described the role of these concepts in the following manner:

> Structure is the core concept in the course, the concept of organization, and understanding that subject matters have structures or organizations, although not one to a subject matter. One of the dilemmas in education is that too often those structures are ignored in teaching, so that what gets taught is unraveled from organization to list and from integrated to disintegrated.

In this course, one of the questions students are asked in their assignments is to what extent they reflect on the analysis they do, the kind of lexicon, or more important, the conceptions that lie behind the words. To what extent do students try to understand the relationships between the organizational principles of a unit of instruction in a subject matter they are teaching? What are the preconceptions or misconceptions on the part of learners in response to that material? Do they understand the notion of the learner as an organized system? The instructors look for that kind of analysis in the papers students hand in.

Understanding is an analytic notion: there are structures in the disciplines, people come with structured minds, and the nature of instruction is to modify the structure of understanding in the direction of a conception of the structure of disciplines. This is a process of construction, and there are principles in the philosophy of science and the sociology of knowledge to help one understand where disciplinary structures come from and why and how they change. There are notions in cognitive psychology and in anthropology and other social sciences that help one understand how knowledge is acquired, changed, distorted, and transformed and that the teacher is playing a significant role within this set of structures.

The understanding is of the set of categories for looking at disciplines, at ways of looking at the development of disciplines and sciences and humanities. They read cognitive psychology to get some language for analyzing the way people come to comprehend or not comprehend the disciplinary structures. They also read pedagogical literature to learn ways of categorizing subject matter as distinct from the discipline itself, for useful heuristics for looking at the relationship between a discipline and what you want people to understand with respect to it.

The framework of knowledge to be developed consists of specific theory that will enable student teachers to make rational decisions about their practice of teaching, so that teaching, in one professor's view, is not just a craft they learn from watching someone else but has a body of principles they can apply. Some of these are principles of learning; others concern measurement or curriculum.

You talk about subdivisions of knowledge into propositions, algorithms, images, episodes, motor skills, cognitive strategies, and so forth—all specific types of knowledge. You talk about processing that knowledge, meaningful associations of knowledge; you talk to them about ability, different meanings for the type of ability or abilities by various authors. You tell them about cognitive strategies like keeping your mind on the task, sorting out ambiguities in situations, monitoring how you are getting on, determining what is important and what is not important in situations.

Perhaps the most important point made in these examples is that students need to learn educational concepts as part of a framework in order to solve complex problems in the classroom. The complexity of the knowledge base in teaching led Shulman (1986, 1987) to distinguish seven categories of teacher knowledge needed for expertise. We have already encountered two of them needed for basic survival—knowledge of educational contexts and of ends or goals—and referred to a third—knowledge of learners. Four additional categories of knowledge relate subject matter and pedagogical knowledge.

- *Subject matter content knowledge* refers to the way in which the concepts and principles of a domain are organized, and the methods used to validate this knowledge.
- *General pedagogical knowledge* concerns those broad principles and strategies of classroom management and organization that transcend subject matter.
- *Curriculum knowledge* refers to the range of programs and materials available to teach a particular content area, lateral knowledge of topics being taught at the same time in other courses, and vertical knowledge of topics and issues that were taught earlier or will be taught later in the program.
- *Pedagogical content knowledge* refers to useful alternative forms of representing and formulating concepts and principles that make them comprehensible to others, the conceptions and misconceptions that learners bring with them, and the strategies for reorganizing learners' conceptions.

One might wonder where to begin. Our professors suggested that without subject matter knowledge, pedagogical knowledge cannot be placed in a framework. Subject matter knowledge is crucial, but evidently a much larger framework needs to be built around it in order to teach. Of Shulman's categories of teacher knowledge, four apply across subject matters—general pedagogical knowledge, knowledge of learners, knowledge of educational contexts, and knowledge of educational ends. Three are specific to the subject matter being taught—subject matter content knowledge, curriculum knowledge, and pedagogical content knowledge—and require insight into specific subject matter areas. Each category of teacher knowledge has specific standards. For example, subject matter content knowledge, according to Shulman (1986), not only requires knowing that something is so, the teacher must also understand why it is so. What is the evidence for it? Under what circumstances would its justification be weakened or even denied? The teacher must understand why a given topic is central to a discipline while another is peripheral. The categories of knowledge therefore require different although overlapping strategies to elucidate. How does this occur? Let us take knowledge of learners as an example.

Learning About Learners

In our studies of how students learn concepts, we chose a course for first-year undergraduates in an elementary education program entitled "The Development of Personality and Social Behavior in the School-Aged Child." Using the course materials—three textbooks and extensive readings—to find potential concepts, we established with the professor that ninety-eight concepts were specifically relevant to the course, with thirteen of them key (main or linking) concepts (Figure 7.1).

The course is described in the calendar as dealing with personality, social behavior, and moral development related to the process of schooling with attention to teacher attitudes and practices in responding to the problems of children. According to the professor:

> The course is for elementary teachers of the average child, who may encounter many obstacles to learning—hyperactivity, aggression, truancy, child abuse, sexuality. Rather than focusing on instructional practices, the course is oriented to establishing the atmosphere of the classroom so that it is congenial for learning. In contrast to courses oriented toward methods of teaching subject matter, it is oriented toward sharpening the teacher's perception of the child's growth and social development. It is eclectic in its theoretical orientation.

FIGURE 7.1. KEY CONCEPTS IN "THE DEVELOPMENT OF PERSONALITY AND SOCIAL BEHAVIOR IN THE SCHOOL-AGED CHILD"

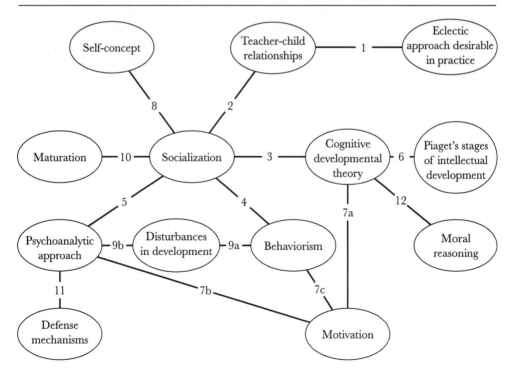

This professor's approach to his course is learner-centered and intriguing, with attention focused on roadblocks he wants students to be aware of when they find that one of their learners is not coping well in the classroom. He has set the problem context in a manner that may disturb teachers in training but will also alert them and make this learning experience memorable. A major assignment in the course is to conduct an interview and do a developmental study of two children, one in the early school years (age five to eight) and one in later childhood (age nine to twelve). An age difference of at least three years is recommended so that comparisons can be made across developmental stages of students' interests, ideas about school, rules, reasoning about right and wrong, fears, friends, preferences, and ideas about the future.

The most important concept in this course is *an eclectic approach desirable in practice*. The professor considered it to be salient and inclusive of all other concepts, but also recognized that it was a technical term rather than familiar or everyday and would not be found in a dictionary. The professor defined it in the following manner:

> No one psychological theory is sufficiently complete to meet all real-life problems. A combination of theoretical approaches appears most useful.

Although chosen first to link to another concept, its final placement was in the upper-right corner of the concept map (Figure 7.1). It thus had an overarching but peripheral role in the conceptual framework of the course. All the key concepts except *an eclectic approach desirable in practice* were closely related in meaning to at least one other concept. The concept that was the primary linking concept in the course—that is, had most links to other concepts (six), and a pivotal or synthesizing role in the concept map—was *socialization*, defined in this way:

> The way in which a child born into a given society becomes a social being—a member of that society.

Socialization had immediate links in the concept map to three theories guiding the course, *cognitive developmental theory, behaviorism,* and *a psychoanalytic approach*. In keeping with the general cognitive developmental orientation in education courses, the definition of *cognitive developmental theory* refers to maturational stages in the development of thought as they interact with environmental experiences to produce or modify cognitive structures. There were fifteen links between the thirteen concepts, for a ratio of 1.15, more than in the psychology course (.64) and showing some of the same complexity as the psychology course, with a double link between two theories (psychoanalytic and behavioral) to *disturbances in development* and a triple link between the three theories and *motivation*.

All of the key concepts in the course were abstract but were presented in the course in a variety of ways. Films and readings highlighted course topics and prepared students for the ensuing discussion. Because students were interviewing two children in their major assignment, they had the opportunity to test new concepts and theories presented in the course; thus instructional practice was varied and multidimensional.

Students entered the course with a relatively high level of knowledge of the key concepts—many of which (six of the thirteen) had familiar dictionary definitions—but student knowledge of the concepts was a prime determinant of how well they did in the course. Among the concepts, students had least knowledge of *an eclectic approach desirable in practice* at the beginning of the course and gained the most. The course assignments that required students to compare the interests and ideas of an early school child and one in later childhood assured that students developed a framework for understanding the school child as a developing human being.

I sent a draft copy of this chapter to the professor of this course, and after reading the draft, he wrote to say that he had developed the course over a number of years, and had been trying to give students some approaches to understanding children. He explained that this was a general course for students who for the most part had no idea of what psychology would look like in the real world, but what students got was his interpretation of the traditional canon. Now, several years later, he said that postmodern thinking had changed his outlook and he would be less comfortable presenting theories such as behaviorism or aspects of an objective reality perceived in the same way by everyone, and would instead emphasize the subjectivity of both teacher and learner.

The need to transact across sets of organized systems is recognized as an important theme, as it is in the course in teaching and learning described previously in this chapter. Teachers need to be concerned with understanding what learners think and how they arrive at their understanding, then how to foster understanding through discussion and collaboration. The underlying principle is that knowledge is what is shared in discourse in a textual community (Bruner, 1996). Bruner suggests that teachers need to make students more aware of their own thought processes and of how they go about learning and thinking. In this course on learners, students had a specific opportunity to discover how two learners were developing, one of the areas of teacher expertise. In what other ways is expertise gained?

The Development of Thinking Processes in Education

In education, thinking or reasoning processes are most often investigated in terms of what distinguishes the expert teacher. In Shulman's (1987) analysis, pedagogical reasoning and action evolve from the comprehension of purposes and ideas through transformation, instruction, evaluation, and reflection to new comprehensions that consolidate learning. An essential capacity is to transform content knowledge into forms that are pedagogically powerful yet can be adapted to the learners' varied abilities and backgrounds. According to Shulman, transformation involves critically interpreting text, representing the ideas in the form of new analogies or metaphors, selecting teaching methods, adapting them to the students to be taught, and then tailoring adaptations to specific students in the class. It is thus a process of organically incorporating subject matter and pedagogical knowledge. Moving from personal comprehension to preparing for the comprehension of others is the essence of pedagogical reasoning. Errors in text must be detected and corrected, materials must be structured and segmented. After instruction, effective teachers retrace their teaching process to compare activities and outcomes, and to ground in evidence their explanations of what occurred.

Research on instructional expertise shows that expert teachers represent an instructional situation very differently from novices (Berliner, 1991). They use higher-order systems of categorization to analyze problems, recognize patterns, and think through problems differently. They are sensitive to particular situations and the social structure, and plan and use time effectively. The expert pedagogue is efficient. Many tasks become automatic, and the expert can therefore reinvest cognitive resources in executive control of planning, monitoring, and evaluating—for example, using classroom feedback to adapt quickly (Sternberg & Horvath, 1995). The suggestion that teachers can be prepared in one postgraduate year to do all these things is at the least incongruous. As one professor commented:

> The question in teacher training is whether you can produce a self-critically reflective student in the period of one year, and how much the demands are such that the student just has to get to grips with the set of basic techniques. The question is whether you *can* develop at the same time a fundamental questioning about whether you ought to be doing something because of some very subtle factors.

The process of reflection is described by another professor responsible for a foundations course in education in the following manner.

> Does it make sense? Does it fit in with your view of how schools should act, what the place of schools is, how teachers should act, how students should behave, how they do behave?
>
> Students are asked to reflect on things to ensure they make sense and understand what this is about, what are the implications. At the start of the year some time is spent getting students to break away from the "soak it up" mold that unfortunately they have acquired very often in their school and undergraduate work. Taking a specific issue—examinations and assessment in schools—

students would discuss the pros and cons of centrally administered examinations and who should be involved in controlling those examinations and the degree of fragmentation of a secondary school curriculum. By the end of the year they should be well on the way to constructing their own views about teaching and learning.

To understand the developmental changes in teachers as they acquire experience, Berliner (1991) adapted a model from Dreyfus and Dreyfus (1986) of five stages of increasing expertise. Student teachers are usually *novices* who learn rules and perform rationally but relatively inflexibly. First-year teachers tend to be *advanced beginners* who note similarities across domains and build up procedural knowledge. Context begins to guide behavior. The *competent performer,* usually after three years of experience, can set priorities and draw up flexible plans to meet reasonable goals and knows what to attend to and what to ignore, what is important and what is not. Those who go on to be *proficient* are adept at pattern recognition and possess a holistic sense of the situations they face—they recognize similarities across apparently disparate situations. A small number of the proficient may become *expert,* able to respond smoothly and appropriately, without apparent effort. Given time limitations, teacher education programs can only hope to begin the process of development from novice to expert.

The professors of teacher education courses were interviewed about their expectations of their students and how they developed thinking in their courses. They expected entering students to be able to think logically—that is, in an internally consistent manner, going either from observations to inferences or from premises to conclusions—and to reason with abstract propositions, as did the physical science and psychology professors (Donald, 1988). In addition, education professors expected their students to be able to think independently. For example, one noted that students are given many assignments that they are expected to do on their own; they are not told how to do them or what the answers are. They are given general guidelines and must proceed either individually, in pairs, or in groups to complete the assignment. The professors related the development of thinking processes to the subjects their students were learning to teach.

Description

One professor's approach was to talk about the thinking processes in a subject area where students had a fairly substantial body of knowledge, since "solving a geometry problem and describing a painting by El Greco are very different processes" (Exhibit 7.1). His rationale was that because students bring with them a relatively fragmented knowledge of their subject areas, a framework for this knowledge base

EXHIBIT 7.1. PROFESSORS' EXAMPLES OF
DESCRIPTION USED IN TEACHER EDUCATION COURSES

DESCRIPTION: Delineation or definition of a situation or form of a thing.	*Describing the process of solving a geometry problem and describing a painting by El Greco are very different processes.*
Identify context: Establish surrounding environment to create a total picture.	*"What's going on?" or "Where am I?" become the basis for problem generation.*
State conditions: State essential parts, prerequisites, or requirements.	*Students use a checklist to ensure that a set of conditions or limited parameters is covered.*
State facts: State known information, events that have occurred.	*Content knowledge of facts.*
State functions: State normal or proper activity of a thing or specific duties.	*Students interview each other about what they understand about their subject and what they hope their students will understand as a result of the teaching they are about to do and that they are going to observe one another doing.*
State assumptions: State suppositions, postulates.	*Talk about the kinds of school students who would find it difficult to understand Darwinian principles of natural selection, not because they fail to comprehend the concepts and principles but because the fundamental assumptions run contrary to their religious ideology.*
State goal: State the ends, aims, objectives.	*What was the teacher trying to teach?* *What was an article trying to say?*

must be developed so that they can transform the subject matter knowledge and create strategies for teaching it. The focus is on relating thinking processes to subject matter content knowledge in order to produce pedagogical content knowledge.

The professors stated that a conceptual framework for the ideal teacher does not exist, and that descriptions of teaching in different teaching *contexts* are needed. *Identifying the context* is an essential process for expertise (Ericksen & Smith, 1991). Berliner (1991) noted that context begins to guide behavior among first-year teachers, after they have completed a preservice program. Students must recognize *conditions* when they evaluate a situation, whereas *facts* were defined as the subject matter "knowledge bytes" to be worked with. One assignment for student teachers is to establish the *function* of their teaching with another student before they begin microteaching—brief practice performances as short as three to five minutes—

after which peers and their professor give them feedback. Students have to *state assumptions* when they consider the background their learners have of theories such as evolution, and how these preconceptions will allow or not allow them to learn the theory. The effects of learners' preconceptions in impeding learning make this a critical issue in instruction. The students may not have a clear sense of their teaching *goals* but would be expected to recognize teaching goals if they saw them in, say, a videotape.

In summary, because students in foundational courses have a fragmented knowledge of their subject matter and a rudimentary knowledge of the teaching process, they can recognize but not yet represent the process of teaching. A major concern is the lack of disciplinary models of teaching available to guide education students to identify the context. Another important issue is how to deal with learners' misconceptions or preconceptions, and their effects on instruction.

Selection

Students in teacher education programs need to develop the ability to *select critical information, order it,* or *identify critical elements and relations* in their subject matter and in their actual teaching practice (pedagogical content knowledge) (Exhibit 7.2). Our professors considered that these processes would have to be developed by having students increase their knowledge and participate in discussion and dialogue with others. This has been done in an introductory educational foundations course where students gained both domain knowledge and thinking strategies (Alexander, Murphy, Woods, Duhon, & Parker, 1997). For example, students increased their use of strategies for selecting main ideas in passages of text, a critical process

EXHIBIT 7.2. PROFESSORS' EXAMPLES OF SELECTION USED IN TEACHER EDUCATION COURSES

SELECTION: Choice in preference to another or others.	*Driven by the knowledge base, so that the more sophisticated the knowledge base, the more automatic and efficient these processes will be.*
Choose relevant information: Select information that is pertinent to the issue in question.	*Through participation in discussion and in dialogue with others, students develop a sense of what are the central features in practical situations.*
Identify critical relations: Determine connections between things that are important.	*Try to see how the parts fit in with the whole.*

for expertise. They also increased their use of strategies for building mental models (representation). At the same time, they decreased their use of less effective strategies, such as rereading the text. Students in this course learned how to select, moving from a state of acclimation or naiveté closer to competency. In summary, the selection processes are important for teachers, but students need practice in developing them.

Representation

The professors considered representation processes to be the most important set of thinking processes in teacher education programs. Representation is central to showing the structure of subject matter and models for portraying it. Library sections devoted to instructional materials in schools and in most colleges of education have been developed to help teachers find ways to depict what they want to teach. As noted in Chapter One, Bruner (1960) introduced three modes of depicting subject matter that affect the ability of any learner to master it (Exhibit 1.3). *Enactive representation* consists of a set of actions appropriate for achieving a certain result; the experience is immediate—students manipulate the objects or events involved, as in experiments. *Iconic representation* portrays by image or graph, somewhat isomorphic with the concept, as pictures or diagrams do. *Symbolic representations* use

EXHIBIT 7.3. PROFESSORS' EXAMPLES OF REPRESENTATION USED IN TEACHER EDUCATION COURSES

Recognize organizing principles: Identify laws, methods, rules that arrange in a systematic whole.	*Make practical principles conscious and critically reassess them.*
Organize elements and relations: Arrange parts, connections between things, into a systematic whole.	*Theories of the middle range, fairly limited postulations of relations between elements, serve as small working models, usually in the form of extended metaphors or analogies.*
Illustrate elements and relations: Make clear by examples the parts, connections between things.	*Consciously use analogy and metaphor to link knowledge structures in learners' heads. Use strategies of analogical reasoning, such as metaphors, analogies, similes, examples, counterexamples, and illustrative stories, to bridge what students already know with what it is teachers intend them to them to understand.*
Modify elements and relations: Change, alter, or qualify the parts, connections between things.	*Look at discrepancies between goals and performance and make recommendations to rectify the discrepancies.*

language or some other symbol system that is not isomorphic with the concept but is governed by rules or laws for forming and transforming propositions. Most models or structures are symbolic, usually language-based, are thus less immediate, and require interpretation.

Our professors noted two stages of representation in their courses that coincide with the two-tiered learning task. One is to learn the general symbol system for organizing ways of thinking about subject matter—a vocabulary that includes principles such as prior knowledge and constructivism that we have used in this book to describe the learning process in different disciplines (general pedagogical knowledge); the other is the application of these principles in their own disciplines and in others (pedagogical content knowledge). (See Exhibit 7.3.) Professors were aware that students come with preconceptions of schooling—because they were good students academically—that may interfere with development of their pedagogical content knowledge and will therefore limit or prevent their adaptation to the instructional situation in which they will find themselves.

The professors gave examples of representation from their own work, one noting that he looks for theories of education in the middle range—small working models—to explain instructional phenomena. For example, he introduced the term *bridging* to explain the phenomenon of teachers trying to teach a piece of textbook material to different kinds of children and building a bridge between where the learners were and where the teacher saw the text as being. *Illustrating elements and relations* is central to instruction, and students learn how to use different methods of representation such as concept maps, diagrams, analogy, metaphor, examples, and narrative to clarify concepts and processes. *Modifying elements and relations* was mentioned as part of an evaluative process of adjusting goals based on student performance. The emphasis in representation is on developing ways and means of clarifying concepts for learners. In the interviews, the professors tended to see the thinking processes as interacting, so that representation was contingent on description and selection, or representation followed description and preceded verification in a process of inquiry.

Inference

Inferential processes are critical for expertise, but the professors doubted their students' ability to infer beyond their experience, and having had little experience, considered that these processes needed to be developed. Students are encouraged in their courses to observe and then consider applications or conclusions from their observations (Exhibit 7.4). An important teaching strategy is to show how *elements are related*, or to provide students with the experience to do so. At the same time, the teacher must be watching for nonverbal cues from learners to determine

EXHIBIT 7.4. PROFESSORS' EXAMPLES OF INFERENCE USED IN TEACHER EDUCATION COURSES

Discover new relations between elements: Detect or expose connections between parts, units, components.	*Make inferences about what behavior means and what the intentions were—motivations, emotions, and understanding—from things that learners said or manifested nonverbally.*
Discover new relations between relations: Detect or expose connections between connections of things.	*A poor analogy is an otherwise great analogy that highlights nonessential elements of what you are trying to get students to understand.*
Discover equivalences: Detect or expose equality in value, force or significance.	*If you had been teaching* Julius Caesar *for several years and no longer wanted to teach it, what would be a legitimate substitute? Of what is* Julius Caesar *an instance in the curriculum? Does it teach a particular body of content, or particular kinds of comprehension or analytic skills, or help students acquire certain social skills so that they can talk about Shakespeare at a cocktail party? What are equivalent pieces of understanding?*
Categorize: Classify, arrange into parts.	*What is the difference between a law in physics and a Shakespearean sonnet?*
Order: Rank, sequence, arrange methodically.	*See things in sequence or in a hierarchy.*
Change perspective: Alter view, vista, interrelations, significance of facts or information.	*Critically examine readings in order to understand emotional and behavioral obstacles to learning and social development.*
Hypothesize: Suppose or form a proposition as a basis for reasoning.	*From theoretical to practical situations.*

if they understand what the teacher is attempting to have them learn. A potential error is to misuse an analogy so that learners, instead of constructing their own conceptualization, become disoriented. One professor described how a teacher had used an example that was not in his learners' background, leading to mass confusion. Relevance is essential for inference to take place. Good exemplars are precious; poor ones are ruinous to learning.

Finding or using equivalences is another important instructional strategy. In one course, students are asked to think about why they would use a particular piece of curricular material by comparing its significance to whatever they would choose to replace it with, for example, what to replace *Julius Caesar* with, and why. *Categorizing* is also important for understanding similarities and differences across and within disciplines. Understanding the basis of classification allows one to substitute new material for old or to make clear the essential attributes of concepts or principles one is teaching. The professors found that students were able to *order* things, but *changing perspective* was more difficult, for example, requiring critical examination of course material so that they could think about how to handle classroom learning problems. *Hypothesizing* was likewise considered a difficult task, particularly making a transition from theory to a practical situation where the theory is to be applied. Thus inference is important, but professors also recognize that it is not easy to explain or acquire and must be carefully approached both in and across disciplines.

Synthesis

Because of the need to apply instructional principles in the classroom, synthesis is important for bringing together all the elements of the classroom situation, including the context, language, and actual steps to be taken (Exhibit 7.5). Students *combine parts to form a whole* when they relate different areas of a child's development to explain behavior. The consequences of interventions or developmental changes need to be *elaborated* in a theory or plan. Students must also infer from their learners' behavior to *generate* explanations of it, then plan instruction to ensure optimal development. Students are asked to analyze videotaped sequences of instruction to explain what *course of action* they would take. Synthesis is thus related to all of the learning activities that prepare students to become teachers, but may develop only after they have been teaching long enough to be described as proficient (more than three years).

Verification

Uppermost in the minds of the education professors was that verification in education is not like that in physics or other sciences. There are several levels of verification, and it requires a long period of time to develop. At one level there are practical judgments student teachers must develop in the classroom based on what has transpired to date and what their instructional goals are (Exhibit 7.6). At another level there is consideration of individual students and their special needs. The process of verification requires *comparing* options and triangulating evidence of what has happened in class. Students need to develop criteria or *standards* for making professional judgments. The questions they must ask concern not only whether things fit together but whether the explanation can help them in the future. Making *valid judgments* is a matter of performance based on lengthy experience and attention to a variety of factors. Students *use feedback* in their assignments and classroom exercises in which they compare notes and provide each other with

EXHIBIT 7.5. PROFESSORS' EXAMPLES OF
SYNTHESIS USED IN TEACHER EDUCATION COURSES

SYNTHESIS: Composition of parts or elements into a complex whole.	*Synthesize all the elements to understand the practical situation in education—judgments in practice—using the language of the teacher.* *Create a new piece of instructional design by putting the different parts of a course together.*
Combine parts to form a whole: Join, associate elements, components into a system or pattern.	*The child's moral and religious development and his or her behavioral developmental level.*
Elaborate: Work out, complete with great detail, exactness, or complexity.	*Explicitly state the consequences of an intervention or the possible developmental changes that might occur based on what has occurred before and the relationships between them in the form of a theory, a set of linked hypotheses, or a plan.*
Generate missing links: Produce or create what is lacking in a sequence, fill in the gap.	*Interpret things that learners said or manifested nonverbally.*
Develop course of action: Work out or expand the path, route, or direction to be taken.	*A behavioral approach or a cognitive approach may be developed toward the optimal development of the child.* *In videotape analysis, the tape is stopped and students are asked, "If that were you, what would you do next and why?"*

their own judgments—for example, in classroom observations. These kinds of exercises also stimulate students to *confirm* their perspectives by examining the evidence and looking for results or outcomes. The process of verification in teacher education covers all the factors instructors must deal with in the classroom, whether they are about curriculum, teaching strategies, or learners' problems. Specific judgments must be made in context, and reviewed when similar circumstances are encountered later on.

In summary, the most important processes for student teachers to acquire include those required for expertise but also for problem solving. Expertise does not explain all of the thinking processes needed by students, nor do terms such as *transformation* or *reflection*, because teachers must actively and specifically problem-solve in the classroom. More global terms such as transformation or reflection, however, include the planning and evaluation processes that take place before and after the instructional

EXHIBIT 7.6. PROFESSORS' EXAMPLES OF
VERIFICATION USED IN TEACHER EDUCATION COURSES

VERIFICATION: Confirmation of accuracy, coherence, consistency, correspondence.	*Question research reports on the treatment of child behavior problems. What are the follow-up reports? How long does a child receive a certain kind of treatment for hyperactivity?*
Compare alternative outcomes: Examine similarities or differences in results, consequences.	*What are the options, the pros and cons, and the research evidence that support a way of doing things so that a teacher can arrive at a decision?*
	Triangulation or convergence on their inferences about what happened in class.
Compare outcome to standard: Examine similarities, differences of results based on a criterion.	*Whether the teaching on a particular videotape is good or not.*
Judge validity: Critically examine the soundness, effectiveness by actual fact.	*Effectiveness of a teaching situation for a set of children, what they are required to learn, and what are the best methods in this particular situation.*
Use feedback: Employ results to regulate, adjust, adapt.	*Role-play and class discussions to develop different perspectives on theory.*
	Students debrief each other after a classroom observation because the observer may have been misreading entirely what the teacher was trying to communicate.
Confirm results: Establish or ratify conclusions, effects, outcomes, or products.	*Different points of view expressed by the students quickly lead them to appreciate the need to defend their own or to find better answers or look for some evidence.*

situation. Our respondents' examples of the thinking processes suggest that student teachers may need a vocabulary that is both more specific and more inclusive than the terminology currently in use in the field. This suggests the need for deep descriptive research into the teaching process to name what is taking place.

Research Skills

Unlike other social sciences, educational research skills are rarely taught before graduate school. Teacher education programs are challenged to produce some level of teaching expertise in a short period of time, and attempts to add research methods to the curriculum have not been welcomed. We have observed that in psychology, research methods are taught at the undergraduate level and are integrated with theory. In law, research skills are being taught increasingly in programs. Similarly, we could argue that to help education students continue to gain the expertise they need, research skills are essential. In the multidisciplinary study of the most important kinds of thinking skills to be acquired in graduate studies, the skills in education were primarily inferential (Powers & Enright, 1987). They included supporting conclusions with sufficient data or information, determining whether the conclusions drawn are logically consistent with and adequately supported by data, identifying central issues and problems to be investigated, and drawing sound inferences from observations. These research skills are similar to those called for in psychology programs but are more general than the skills developed in teacher education programs.

Students entering graduate education programs frequently do not have an undergraduate degree in education and are more likely to have a background in psychology that includes statistics and research design. Those students entering graduate studies from teacher education programs will need to acquire a different set of skills. Some may need help in overcoming math anxiety and in learning to think in the skeptical manner of scientists. The core course in graduate studies in education is research design, which students take early in the program in order to begin planning their thesis. Three professors who teach this course were interviewed to establish what kinds of thinking processes they develop. They also talked about their experience teaching students. What stands out is the tendency among students to use statistical procedures without understanding them, even if they have a mathematical background.

> Students know how to calculate a mean but their intuitions about central tendency are often not very well developed; they are more procedural in their conception. When I get into the reason why you would want to compute a mean and its linkage to a population of sample means or to a population more generally, the students have gone through a lot of stuff but it has not taken. Some of the students are mathematical types who have had lots of math-stat courses; they can prove things at the drop of a hat, but they do not understand them.
>
> There is a lot of fear and anxiety and reluctance. If I can move through all that, I often find that at a deep level the students know the words but not the music.

A notion of causality is central to learning research design—the basis of a research project is the effect of a set of variables on another set. One professor noted that developing a research proposal includes all of the thinking processes in the model;

however, hypothesis testing is central to the task. Another described his course in terms of four topics.

> Topic number one is how you conceptualize a research question. Topic number two is how you bring various design techniques to bear on your conceptualization and building a research plan. Topic number three is a review of the essence of statistical analysis and showing how specific methods of analysis can be used to analyze factorial designs. The next topic is specific techniques of analysis such as analysis of variance, regression analysis, various descriptive analyses such as scatter plots.

This professor uses the metaphor "finding the joints in the turkey"—that is, the variables have to be distinguished so that the problem can be broken down and examined. How are you going to divide your question into a small number of relatively separable components that taken together make up a conceptual framework for your question? This is for many students a new way of thinking, and it may be opposed to the conceptual framework based on relativism that they have been operating with to date. Another professor defined the goal of his research methods course this way:

> To give students a critical perspective on the advantages and disadvantages of methods of inquiry, how appropriate methods are with respect to inquiry into human activities charged with the promotion of human change.

The challenge level of these courses is high. The task is structured more procedurally but less substantively than teacher education courses; it requires a series of skills in decision making about the creation of a study to add to the knowledge base. What kinds of thinking processes are developed in these courses?

Description is a design skill necessary for knowing what questions to ask, making convincing arguments supporting an interpretation of findings, or operationalizing—declaring the methods of observation or investigation used to arrive at the meaning of a concept or theory (Exhibit 7.7). Selection is essential for choosing a topic, defining variables, choosing methods, and reviewing the literature. Representation is used to understand models or paradigms, and in writing and editing the proposal or research project. Inferences must be made about all aspects of the project, from determining what variables will be selected and why, to the hypotheses that will be made. Synthesis follows from inference but entails checks for coherence, which leads into verification. Verification occurs in the monitoring of the project, in dealing with contradictions in results, and in the whole system of controls.

EXHIBIT 7.7. PROFESSORS' EXAMPLES OF THINKING PROCESSES USED IN EDUCATIONAL RESEARCH COURSES

DESCRIPTION: Delineation or definition of a situation or form of a thing.

A design skill for building up a proposal.

Knowing what question to ask when informally looking at data.

Communicating the question and the purpose of the study, and making convincing arguments supporting one's interpretation of the evidence.

SELECTION: Choice in preference to another or others.

Decomposing a complex problem into a small number of relatively independent, nearly decomposable chunks.

Choosing a topic and ordering information in importance when reviewing the literature.

REPRESENTATION: Depiction or portrayal through enactive, iconic, or symbolic means.

Learning a new paradigm.

Editing and rearranging work.

INFERENCE: Act or process of drawing conclusions from premises or evidence.

What are you going to do about your environment? What are your treatment variables? As an experimentalist, how are you going to intervene? What are you going to think about when you select subjects? What are you going to measure and how are you going to measure it? What are all the nuisance variables that you are not particularly interested in but which you need for purposes of control?

SYNTHESIS: Composition of parts or elements into a complex whole.

In a framework that is coherent, the variables tend to interact only within themselves; there is not a lot of cross-talk with factors associated with one process going to the other.

VERIFICATION: Confirmation of accuracy, coherence, consistency, correspondence.

Monitor if the research question is being answered.

Note contradictions in research findings and see why there are contradictions. Is it a problem of methodology? Approach? Different samples? Why would one have contradictory results?

The thinking processes in educational research are more general than in teacher education. In teacher education, many factors must be taken into consideration but there are many instances of proof of success or failure along the way, so that conceptualizations and behaviors can be continually modified. In research, a great deal of abstraction must take place before any proof is available; the investment is immense and the yield risky. The procedural differences between teaching and research alert us to the more general problem in postsecondary education of relating one's teaching to one's research. It increases the need for congruence between what one teaches and what one researches because the processes themselves differ greatly.

In the domain of education, the continuing entreaty is for teachers and other educational practitioners to become active partners and critical users of educational research (National Academy of Education, 1991). While discussing the notion of validity, one of the educational research professors explained the change from the kind of research that was done twenty years ago.

> Many of the things that were coming out in studies of that time didn't make sense to practitioners and just weren't applied in any way. Now the style of research is much more to work with teachers and students in developing the research. The issue of validity is tied up with whether what you end up saying strikes chords with consumers.

Authenticity is one criterion, transferability and ecological validity are others in this applied field. These criteria have changed the pattern of research, requiring training in small-sample, qualitative designs rather than large-sample, quantitative, experimental designs (Berliner, 1991). Case and procedural knowledge and knowledge of complex group settings has gained prominence. Programs of research must be organized to meet the demand for investigation of complex sets of variables.

The Challenge of Instruction in Education

The sheer amount and kinds of knowledge to be learned, and the lack of clear patterns in subject matter content knowledge in other disciplines, present immense challenges to education professors. One intent of this book is to draw attention to how disciplines might provide this knowledge. Another challenge comes in delineating pedagogical knowledge and thinking processes, particularly difficult when they are not generic but contextually dependent. A third challenge is in students' folk pedagogies, epistemologies, or beliefs that may impede their learning. Since students' attitudes can limit how much pedagogical knowledge they acquire, we first deal with the challenge inherent in the attitudes they bring with them.

Folk Pedagogies, Epistemologies, and Beliefs

According to our professors, much of the adjustment students must make revolves around their conceptions of the act of teaching and the nature of learning. Some of these conceptions may impede their professional development, acting like filters through which others' teaching performance is interpreted (Kagan, 1992). Bruner (1996) explains that new ideas have to compete with folk theories that already guide teachers and their students. Folk theories or beliefs are deeply entrenched assumptions about students, classrooms, and subject matter that are not open to critical examination and may exist alongside a teacher's technical knowledge. Although the situation in education has a parallel in what physics professors experience in the incongruity between theory and student conceptions, folk pedagogies can be harmful. For example, one classic folk theory is the attributional theory mentioned earlier that learners either are or are not capable of learning. This theory leads instructors to categorize students and ignore those categorized as less capable, rather than develop strategies to reach them.

Because these beliefs have been found to prevent learning in teacher education programs, Joram and Gabriele (1998) designed a foundations course that targeted four main student beliefs: (1) that experience is the best teacher (and that, therefore, their courses had little to offer them); (2) that they could learn by copying their past teachers (overgeneralizing from their own experience as learners); (3) that learning and teaching are nonproblematic (straightforward and not complex); and (4) that classroom management is the difficult part of teaching (a necessary but insufficient condition that supposes knowledge will be transmitted rather than that learning is an active process). In their course, Joram and Gabriele have students actively question their beliefs and supply metaphors and analogies that allow them to deal with these major questions. They begin with students' main concern—classroom management—and then situate lesson planning as "movement management" within it. They follow this by working with teacher-directed and learner-centered lessons, where students design and present lessons using cognitive theory to aid them in understanding effective instruction. At the end of the course students reported that their attitudes had changed, primarily to an epistemology in which learning is described as an active process and teaching is seen as facilitating this process.

Developing Pedagogical Knowledge and Thinking Processes

The slow process of acquiring expertise—estimated to be ten thousand hours in many disciplines—means that a teacher educator devoting eight hours a day 180 days of the year would require at least seven years. When our professors speak of attempting to bring their students to a state of analytic competence in one year, the enormity of the task becomes clear. To help students in their task, we can look at how different kinds of pedagogical knowledge can be brought together, how students are actually taught in education courses, and what it means to think like an educator.

The first observation is that the general categories of teacher knowledge—general pedagogical knowledge, knowledge of learners, knowledge of educational contexts, and knowledge of educational ends—are usually taught in educational foundations courses. The more specific categories of teacher knowledge—subject matter content knowledge, curriculum knowledge, and pedagogical content knowledge—are usually taught in methods courses. Berliner (1991) points out that professors teaching a foundations course also need grounding in a subject matter area. This is one way to bridge general pedagogical knowledge and pedagogical content knowledge, to require two kinds of knowledge of the professor in the expectation of building a framework for understanding.

Some programs bring subject matter expert and pedagogical expert together to present alternating perspectives on teaching, but we must question the extent to which students are capable of creating a framework of pedagogical content knowledge from two paired but separate ones. This raises another question: How independently or interdependently can different kinds of pedagogical knowledge be addressed? In this chapter we have examples of courses specific to the learner, and others in which learners are one of several topics in a course. We do not know to what extent knowledge of the learner and strategies for dealing with different learners are incorporated into a teaching framework. We do know that if undergraduate students have not yet reached the state of *advanced beginner* in Berliner's terms, little procedural knowledge will have built up.

Educators in universities use active learning techniques far more than teachers in other disciplines (Milem & Astin, 1994). They use class discussion in over 80 percent of their courses, similar to the humanities and double the amount in the sciences. They use cooperative learning in almost half their courses, double that in the humanities and four times as much as in the sciences. Group projects, student development activities, and student-selected topics are also used far more often than in other disciplines, and lecturing is used far less, in 30 percent of courses compared with 80 percent in the sciences. In the study of disciplinary differences in students' perceptions of what they learn, education students reported greater use of teaching methods involving students and they were generally more positive about their professors' instructional methods (Cashin & Downey, 1995). Educators are therefore modeling teaching strategies appropriate for their students.

What it means to think like an educator can be viewed in terms of the kinds of decisions teachers have to make in the classroom. In one study the majority of decisions (50 to 60 percent) were judgments concerning learners, 20 to 30 percent were about instructional procedures, 14 percent were about instructional objectives, and the remainder (5 to 14 percent) were about subject matter content (Clark & Peterson, 1986). Why are so many of the decisions about learners? What does this mean in terms of pedagogical expertise? Are students spending sufficient time in their programs developing knowledge about learners to be able to make sound judgments about them?

Wide concern was voiced by the professors in our studies about all their students need to learn in order to understand where learners are situated. As a young lecturer, one of my own memories is of trying to talk about the learning process while being pelted with questions about how to understand learners and their problems. My students were teachers who were taking a general educational psychology course in the summer *after* they had spent their first year teaching, and what was uppermost in their minds was how to deal with the adolescents in their classes. They needed case studies and some way of organizing the variety of adolescent behavior they were experiencing so that they could deal with it. Interviewing or following a learner as part of a preservice teacher education program is a beginning point for becoming aware of the complexities of individual learners.

Establishing a teaching environment in which students respect each other's understanding, so that they learn to respect their learners' minds even when the learners do not agree with them or are not quite "there" yet, is the quintessential strategy recommended by Duckworth (1987; personal communication, October 2000). In her course entitled Teaching and Learning she has students explain to each other what engaged them in their learning experience in different subject areas from poetry to mathematics so that they come to a realization of how their own thinking brought them to an understanding. She bases her highly interactive classes on the premise that in any subject matter there can be many points of view that inform and enrich your own. Listening to learners explain is therefore central to the pedagogical process at all levels.

Developing ways to understand learners dealing with different subjects requires dedication. One need is to find ways to structure subject matter to enable learners to understand their own thinking processes. This creates a new perspective on lesson planning; for learners to become self-starters they must have the opportunity to construct and be aware of how they have constructed their knowledge. We have seen some of the design questions in producing lessons in different subject areas but have also seen that would-be teachers need to compare strategies across disciplines for providing learners with active learning experiences. Bridging the gap between universals and specific learning experience may be daunting. Educational objectives can be used as starting points; classic taxonomies give examples of appropriate learning objectives in different disciplines; Web-based courses spell out goals for learning more clearly than many would have thought possible. Different disciplinary areas have their own organizations that could aid in delineating frameworks and experiences for learning. The other chapters in this book may offer insights into how learners could construct knowledge in those disciplinary areas, just as this chapter may offer insights into optimal instructional practice for those in other disciplinary areas.

The Disciplinary Perspective in Education

The learning environment in teacher education reflects its fundamental developmental role in society, as education is a means of emancipation or subjugation, depending on whether students learn to think for themselves. Teachers need expertise in many areas: society and the institutional context in which they will be operating; the educational goals and objectives of the subjects they will be teaching; how to connect the subject matter with instructional methods; how to develop sustaining and supportive attitudes; the learners they will be attempting to help. The task is onerous, and insufficient time is allotted to it.

Teaching expertise develops through experience with situations in which the teacher consolidates a framework for action. Students need to hone a variety of thinking processes. They need to learn how to represent subject matter and adapt it to learners, and to design instructional processes that lead to active learning. They must understand their subject matter discipline well enough to explain it, a feat in itself. Equally important is understanding how to translate knowledge into their learners' worlds. Attitudes of understanding and quiet determination are essential.

What are optimal ways of cultivating teaching expertise? Early immersion in classrooms provides an institutional context as a grounding experience for students. In conjunction with their pedagogy courses, students are able to test what they are learning in their courses with their lived experience. One way to relate their understanding of their subject area to the teaching process is to focus course learning goals on how knowledge is organized. Perhaps most important is to gain experience with the kinds of decisions they will be making in the classroom, and to back these decisions with insights about learners.

CHAPTER EIGHT

CRITICISM AND CREATIVITY:
Thinking in the Humanities

In literary study, feeling and imagination are of crucial importance. What ultimately jus-
tifies these elements and activities is the power of literature to delight and move, and in
some small way to change, its readers.

PROFESSOR OF ENGLISH LITERATURE

We enter a different realm of meaning in the humanities. This quotation illustrates the centrality of imagination to learning. In the humanities, learning is concerned with understanding human culture—with aesthetics, where
meaning is found in the contemplative perception of particular significant things,
and synoptics, where meaning is comprehensive and integrative (Phenix, 1964).
One scholar describes the humanities as an initiation into the great stories by which
humankind lives (Sperna Weiland, 1992). Because English literature plays a pivotal role as model to other modern languages in English language universities, I
chose it as the representative discipline in the humanities. When I examined
how students learn to think in English literature programs, two factors struck me:
the diffuse nature of intellectual endeavor in this area of studies and the accompanying variety of approaches to thinking processes. These approaches are most
frequently spoken of as forms of critical analysis, and may be based in aesthetics,
linguistics, philosophy, or the social sciences.

To understand how English conducts itself as a discipline, I begin this chapter by describing the larger academic context in the humanities, then the development of the discipline of English literature. I follow this with an examination
of the learning task in English programs, relating the experience of sixteen professors responsible for courses in English literature from six research universities
in the United Kingdom, the United States, Canada, and Australia. The profes-

sors are experts on different authors or periods—Chaucer, Shakespeare, early to seventeenth-, eighteenth-, and nineteenth-century or contemporary literature; three are experts on literary criticism, one on film. Twenty-four of their students contributed their perspectives in interviews on learning in this discipline. Thinking processes to be developed range from those needed for careful text analysis and dramatic representation to different forms of literary criticism. The challenges that professors face in these programs arise from the breadth of the discipline, the multiplicity of approaches to understanding it, and the particular attention to aesthetics, feeling, and imagination in the field.

The Disciplinary Context in the Humanities

The humanities gained recognition as an area of study in the Renaissance when William Caxton courageously declared the study of humanity a different kind of learning from the study of divinity, thus breaking the monopoly of theology as interpreter of Western civilization (Sperna Weiland, 1992). Early study in the humanities consisted primarily of reading the Greek and Roman classics. In ancient Greek text, *logos*—reason, speech, or word—is the controlling principle of the universe; the study of language, beginning with the classics, was considered a humanizing force in society. The dominant model of inquiry, hermeneutics, was, however, inherited from the tradition of interpreting biblical text. Thus the scholarly origins of the humanities rest in methods of inquiry developed to study both sacred and secular text. The realm of the humanities gradually extended from the classics to embrace the arts from history and philosophy to modern languages. A primary theme is continuing differentiation.

In the academy, the goals of the humanities are both patrician and practical. The burden of society's expectation that the university will equip its graduates with oral and written communication skills falls to the humanities. In the departments, however, these practical goals are challenged or superceded by goals such as gaining a broader understanding of intellectual culture or developing creative capacity (Cashin & Downey, 1995). According to one scholar, the humanities differ from the physical and social sciences by putting faith in the ideal autonomy of the individual (Donoghue, 1998). From the perspective of the humanities, the physical and social sciences conceive of human beings as units subject to forces playing on them from without. The role of the sciences is then to apply methods of observation and calculation to these external forces. In contrast, in the humanities the Promethean view prevails: that we carry the spark of creativity within us. This ontological approach may be particularly enticing and motivating to students of literature. The sacred and the secular, and the aesthetic

and the practical vie for attention in English literature programs. These themes
are foundational antinomies or paradoxes in the field.

The Disciplinary Context in English Literature

In the academic world of the nineteenth century, *rhetoric,* the art of effective or
persuasive speaking or writing, was the focus of student learning in the humanities, and the classics—Greek and Latin—were the major subjects. Literary studies per se gained academic recognition in the last quarter of the nineteenth century
but had to contend with the popular view of literature as entertainment for gen-
tlefolk, to be simply enjoyed or absorbed (Graff, 1987). English developed as a field
of study in North America by subsuming rhetoric and replacing classics as a college subject (Scholes, 1998). In the nineteenth century, the goal in teaching English was focused and practical. Students were required to write, but their
compositions were designed as orations to be delivered before an audience; the
young collegians were for the most part being prepared for the ministry. Con-
gruently, the study of literature was commonly that of sacred Christian texts.

By the end of the nineteenth century, the first division within the discipline
occurred when Harvard split scholarship and composition (Graff, 1987). Rhetoric
became English composition, and students were expected to learn to write according to accepted conventions. This caused the status of writing to plummet;
since everyone knew the conventions, everyone could teach composition (Marius,
1988). At the same time, the principal extracurricular activity on campus was the
literary society. The split between the study of literature and written communication allowed new criteria for English literature to emerge. Literary scholarship
now consisted of the study of language itself (text) and its history (context). The
discipline has swung on a pendulum between text and context ever since (Vendler,
personal communication, October 2000). Text led to canon—the collection of
writings accepted as genuine. In North America the canon was literally the list
of texts set for college entrance examination in English; it had become an area of
prescribed study in schools and colleges.

In the early twentieth century, postsecondary education developed through a
differentiation of fields or disciplines that required focused research and the advancement of theory. This had a particular effect on English literature. The expansion of the disciplines led to a principle of field coverage; colleges in North
America organized themselves into departments corresponding to major subjects
and research fields. Literary studies as a field qualified for department status in the
new research university on the basis of its philological (linguistic) and historical
approaches to literary scholarship (Graff, 1987). The stage was set for conflict as

literary theory challenged humanism and the cultural tradition. The humanists argued that the university's demand for scientific research led to a mechanistic compartmentalization that undermined the ideal espoused by Matthew Arnold, the doyen of English literature, which was of literature as a coherent criticism of life. A further effect of the field coverage principle in the department was curricular compartmentalization.

The historical approach to literature led to its categorization into different historical periods and the interpretation of individual texts within those periods. The field coverage principle permitted instructors to proceed independently in their periods of study without debating aims and methods. It also allowed flexibility in assimilating new ideas and methods; when necessary, another unit was simply added to the aggregate of fields, and avoided paralyzing clashes of ideology. The outcome, however, was that with the need for continued collective discussion removed, conversation about the context and teaching of literature was curbed and the cold war between literary theorists and humanists continued.

In spite of the conflict, in the first half of the twentieth century English reached its academic zenith, only to find itself threatened by demands from the powerful worlds of business and public life. According to Graff, society was asking for reliability and grammatical competence, not critical skills and values antagonistic to those that prevail in the marketplace or the courts. The rise of popular culture distributed through the mass media led to a reduced status of people of letters in comparison with figures in the world of film and television. Further damaging its standing, literature had come to be seen not as representing universal values but as being politically interested. Northrop Frye (1957) in his analysis of Matthew Arnold's Touchstones (1888) pointed out that literary judgments are projections of social ones; Arnold had attempted to replace the biblical canon according to his own political beliefs, with epics dealing with ruling class figures.

English literature is the epitome of a soft—limitless or unbounded—pure discipline. The consequences are epistemological and sociological divergence. In comparison with physics, the prototypical hard, pure discipline, where the core community looks inward for support, dissemination, and social influence, literary studies as a field looks outward. English departments are interpenetrated at many levels by wider systems of literature and culture in which the public and nonacademic institutions such as publishing or journalism participate (Bazerman, 1992). Because of their sensitivity to society, arts and English literature professors in particular may find themselves combination lightning rods and miner's canaries—signaling the inherent conflicts in the university's roles as center for intellectual ferment and developer of society.

Interactions with society and with other disciplines are uneasy since the discipline carries the role of critic. On the positive side, Bourdieu (1988) argues that because of their placement between the two poles of power, societal and scientific, in the university—represented by medicine and law at the societal pole and the natural sciences at the scientific pole—the arts occupy a privileged vantage point for observing the struggle between these two kinds of power. He maintains that in the arts, intellectual renown constitutes the only kind of research or scholarly power that is specifically their own, while their responsibility for the transmission of legitimate culture gives them some social power.

The epistemological practices of the discipline render it vulnerable. The discipline is organized around the production of consensual knowledge arrived at through contention rather than the empirical testing of theories as in the sciences. Thus conflict and challenges to reputation are recurrent themes. Colleagues must cooperate while being responsible for the critique of others' claims for disciplinary standing or legitimacy. At the same time, discourse is divided between the contentious and that which is considered achieved knowledge. The cultural context of knowledge forms part of the discourse, and this rhetorical reflexivity weakens claims of validity and hence influence. In the discipline, scholars tend to be isolated, themselves warring states. Engell and Perkins (1988) note that literary critics' opinions do not group around a few rallying points. Disagreement is more likely to resemble the Brownian motion of particles in which each follows its own separate path even while colliding with others. According to one analyst of the discipline, intellectual life exists between scholars and their computers, and the books they read or skim, not with other scholars (Tompkins, 1996). Tompkins charges that people are isolated from each other by the absence of a culture of conversation. Is the effect of aesthetic sensitivity and disciplinary controversy seclusion?

The sociological organization of the field can be demonstrated by how the Modern Language Association and its bibliography are constituted. The association uses a classification system to divide literature into foreign and nonforeign, language, nationality, and period. However, the categories of language and nationality that may once have been discrete are no longer, and divisions into periods have limited meaning when not attached to nations (Dasenbrock, 1992). The international use of English and the international lives of authors—for example, Doris Lessing or Salman Rushdie—create an even more unwieldy categorization problem. In contrast to citation practice in the physical and social sciences, citations in English literature tend to reference works from previous periods rather than from recent publications. Collaboration is rare: 1 percent of publications in philosophy, language, and literature have more than one author compared with 40 percent in physics or 60 percent in chemistry (Zuckerman, 1988).

Diversity is a hallmark of the field. Scholars in modern languages are less inclined to form allegiances outside their own broad subject area, but many in literary criticism adopt or base their approach on theories from the social sciences—psychology, sociology, or anthropology—creating a sense of open pastureland (Becher, 1989). In contrast with most other disciplines, women have traditionally made a strong contribution in the field of English literature. Specialization in the discipline occurs in the variety of theoretical approaches, methods and language, period and genre. At the same time, the professional language used in the field is highly abstract; although not labeled as jargon, many English texts have extensive glossaries that define terms differently than do general dictionaries, hence a technical disciplinary language is one of the learning tasks. Fish (1995) and others suggest that an appropriate metaphor for humanities departments would be oases or inns for wayfarers who happened to take shelter in the same section of the stacks. Controversy is part of the fabric. Being one of the most divergent disciplines has a cost in other disciplines' perspective of English as politically weak or lacking in intellectual standing. The dearth of collective coherence marks the soft, pure discipline, but allows it commensurate freedom to explore.

What does the state of disciplinary controversy mean for students entering the field? The learning conditions in English departments have been described as a state of tribalism, where different groups of language people tend to be more loyal to their separate languages than to modern languages as a whole (Evans, 1988). This state may render the learning context perturbing if not incomprehensible to students. Humanists in the department take the position that what is important educationally is exploring the impact of big texts on people—criticizing texts helps to tell you who you are. Others claim that effective communication is the real mission of the department, while still others ally themselves with the theories of the social sciences. Evans notes that this tribal multiplicity, if confusing to the university, has enabled the discipline to adapt to a changing environment. For example, when Britain recognized a need for competent linguists in the 1950s, universities moved to improve language training by allowing the effective communications people to devise new courses.

Evans surmises that the field of modern languages is an evolutionary development of classics, taking its essential characteristics of being a multidiscipline, combining macroscopic breadth with microscopic technical requirements in the reading of texts, and its integrative values. The principle of coherence is communication, which involves both symbolic representation and fantasy, because we never know enough and fill the gaps in our knowledge with our imagination. Thus the discipline transcends the cognitive and encompasses affective aspects of interaction and emotion. Students attracted to the area of study juggle perplexity and contention with feeling and imagination.

Students' Experience Learning English Literature

In our ethnographic study of how students learn English literature, the graduate student acting as participant-observer attended lectures during the semester in an introductory course on contemporary English Canadian literature for over two hundred students in an auditorium on Mondays, Wednesdays, and Fridays from 8:30 to 9:30 A.M. He also participated in one of nine weekly conference groups of twenty students, and kept a log of his experience. The course outline states:

> Students will examine representative texts in relation to their historical, cultural, and literary contexts, and will pay close attention to the ways in which Canadian writers experiment with language and form. The course focuses on close reading of the texts, and conferences offer opportunities for discussion and assistance in essay writing and with basic theoretical concepts.

Of the students enrolled in the course, most are majoring in English and 60 percent are in their first year of university. The students range in age for the most part from eighteen to twenty-three, with some older students, and 60 percent are female. The course is held early in the morning, and the students tend to be fairly low key; conversations between them revolve around the hour of the day and the amount of sleep they got the night before. The following excerpts are from the log of the first, second, and tenth weeks of the course.

Wednesday, January 8

The professor begins the lecture by stating that "Watching and Waiting" [Callaghan, 1936] is a good story to begin with as it will give the students an idea of the type of detailed reading and analysis that will be done, as well as the types of themes and emphases placed on topics in this course. The professor states that she begins the semester with three short stories because short stories must be approached in a way that is different from other types of fiction. A short story demands a certain kind of reading, and it is up to the individual reader to determine what type of reading is required. It is also up to the reader to determine what type of role he or she must play in the context of the story when he or she enters into the writing contract with the author. One of the major points for the three stories is how they communicate and construct meaning. There are many subtle nuances in the way meaning is communicated. It can be communicated by the author, sometimes through the text, and sometimes by the readers themselves. One way of communicating meaning is through plot, character, and situation. This framework is used for the first of the three short stories discussed.

Monday, January 13

The professor discusses the third story in the introduction to the course, "Something I've Been Meaning to Tell You," by Alice Munro [1974]. It again falls into the category of having to do with meaning and the way in which one can derive meaning from the story. Typically, one can reconstruct the real shape of things from the ending of a story. This does not happen in this story. The reader is left with questions, and in fact never finds out what it is the one character has been meaning to tell the other. As well, halfway through the story the reader discovers that the narrator's perceptions cannot be trusted, and this casts doubt on the events and meanings attributed to them in the first half of the story. The professor states that this story is meant to make the reader uncomfortable. The notion of reality is radically disrupted, and it is left to the readers to derive what meaning they will from the story. In closing, the professor notes that the tentative and provisional nature of the story that was used here will also be used in the works by Margaret Atwood that students will examine.

Wednesday, March 4

The class begins *Lady Oracle* [Atwood, 1976]. The professor begins the lecture by introducing this novel as a woman's search for identity. She introduces the question "Who do you think you are?" as it was used in a work by Alice Munro. She asks the students for the meaning of the phrase, then relates the question to the novel, saying this is a question that the mother poses to her daughter, Joan, the main character. She next asks the students to identify the main characters' different names, and the students provide them. The professor then talks about identities, and contrasts two characters' searches for identity. The professor reads from the text to justify her position. She lists the two main themes of the novel—self-representation and reflection—saying that we will look at these two themes in the novel. We will be doing this by looking at the various images of mirrors. She asks the students to provide images of mirrors, which they do. With each one, she goes into the text and reads the passage where the mirror image occurs, and then discusses that image. The professor leaves the central mirror image for last. She reads it, and shows how the image provides a framework through which one can view the novel.

The professor then asks the students who, other than the main character, may have written the novel. The students are unable to answer the question, as a large number of them have not yet finished reading it. She asks them to look for that person in their reading of the ending. The professor then looks at the first section of the novel and asks the students to tell her what that first section tells us about the main character, about images, themes, and motifs, which they do. The professor asks the students what kind of book this will be. The students are unable to answer, so she provides a clue by reading a passage. A student then answers the question, saying that it will be a discussion of the main character's life.

The participant-observer's general observations about instruction in the course demonstrate how the professor brings students into contact with the text being studied.

There are many reasons why this was an outstanding course. In class, the professor asks the students questions, forcing them to reason and synthesize the material. She cares about their opinions and wants to hear what they have to say. She has a great respect for her students, and encourages them to share their thoughts. When a student answers a question or gives his or her opinion, the professor always receives it with praise for the student, and then proceeds to comment and expand on it, incorporating it into the lecture. Another outstanding feature was the professor's lecture style. She would adapt it to fit the work that was being studied. Occasionally she would use a straight lecture format, but more often would use a combination of lecture and question and answer. She also used the blackboard to map out events or characters' relationships to one another. She used slides to give us a better idea of the background of the different authors, and on one occasion she brought in taped recordings of a poet's work so that the students would get a better sense of it.

The professor's use of examples was also helpful in the class. If the professor was talking about a specific event or person in a work, she read a passage from it. Doing this helped students to focus on the idea being presented, rather than trying to remember what the event was, or the character to whom she was referring. The professor was able to bring outside information into her discussion of the works. This gave the students a fuller understanding of not only the work itself but also how the work fits into the general themes of the course. The course has a good pace, with the presentation of a new work or author every class, except for the novels, which ran for three to four classes each. Some students were caught off-guard by the novels and had not finished them in time for the lectures on them.

Asked what advice students needed to succeed in the course, the participant-observer pointed out the importance of attending to details but also the active questioning and hunting for pattern in the course material.

There are many skills students need for this course. The first is a good memory. It is important to remember who wrote what, as well as the subject matter of each work. The second is an ability to read critically, noticing patterns of images and recurring ideas or themes. It is also important to be able to synthesize material, to see how each work connects with other works, and also how they connect to the main themes or ideas of the course. The knowledge base is built on from class to class, but it is not always evident that this is the case. For example, in the poetry section of the course, it would sometimes take several classes before one could see how the material fit into the main themes of the course, or how it connected to other works that had been studied. Occasionally, it was not evident how two poets studied connected in terms of ideas, but after studying four, the pattern became much more evident.

Good students are typically alert and active in class, and have at least a mental answer to the professor's questions. Developing analytic skill, and the skill to synthesize material, is helpful for the exams and for writing the essay. Passively taking notes is not a particularly good strategy for this course. It is also helpful to attend conferences as the teaching assistants present material beyond that covered in lectures, which can help students come to a better understanding of the course material.

In summary, students experience a high level of challenge in this course. They are expected to read closely a wide variety of texts; terminology is introduced frequently to explain the writer's strategy. The professor models close reading by examining particular sections of text. She also shows how different kinds of readings or approaches are needed with different kinds of literature—for example, in her choice of the three short stories to demonstrate the different ways in which meaning can be taken from text. The professor provides context for the students, so that they can place and relate to the literature, but maintains a fast pace. Students are required to be actively engaged in class and to develop both analytic and synthesizing skills. The learning task is complex.

The Learning Task in English Literature

What students are expected to learn in literary studies lies in the meaning of the text to the individual. Meaning here encapsulates the intellectual and the emotional. In the opening chapter of *Teaching Literature: What Is Needed Now* (1988), Helen Vendler notes that the attachment to literature found among teachers of English is reminiscent of a reader's early attitude of receptivity, plasticity, and innocence before the text. She describes this state as one in which the text works on us, and our hesitations, pleasures, and self-forgetfulness are the material for all subsequent intellectual reflection; that is what we hope our students will come to know. She goes on to say that professors may have forgotten how unnatural writing is, and expect students to practice an art they are no more trained in than in composing quartets or painting in oils. The solution is to awaken in beginning students the response to the human story told in compelling ways.

Central to her argument is that scholars of English love two things: literature, and equally powerful, language. But she notes that in the American tradition of literary pedagogy, a literature class deals with ethics, sociology, history, or religion rather than investigating an incomparable and idiosyncratic voice. English teachers love different things about literature: a particular age, a single author, puzzle,

argument, rhetoric, social reform. The most useful truth a student can learn, therefore, is that a piece of literature yields different insights depending on the questions put to it. Although major changes have occurred in the discipline—whole
literary genres have disappeared, and there has been a change from the culture of
the letter to the culture of the image—art persists. The mind becomes by its aesthetic inventions. We need to be able to refer our private experience to some identifying frame or solacing reflection. She concludes that an important aim for
English teachers is to give beginning students tales through which they can start
to understand themselves as individuals and as social beings, through myth, leg-
end, and parable.

According to Vendler (personal communication, October 2000), students learn
English at three successive levels. They first encounter the effect or sound of the
text, the voice coming off the page. This is an apprehension of tone, and as they
progress, their hearing is amplified by their increased understanding of language,
so that the expert hears the undersong of etymology. The second level of learning is of the story, the content or matter, and the student's task is to sense the
crucial elements in a play, a poem, or a narrative. The third level is that of genre,
which is the general manner or mode of the text. It is the rhythm or way of composing that is to be learned, in comparison with other rhythms or ways that authors think. Hearing is important because it contains aspects of both logical
structure and momentum or cadence in a work, consistent with the oral foundation of learning. Thinking is a matter of traveling along the line of the artwork in
order to give a wholly adequate response to it, so that the reader does justice to
the author's intent. The learning task for students thus begins with the apprehension of text.

Text and Concepts in English Literature

Taking meaning from text is the essential skill in close reading. Donoghue (1998)
suggests that we must know not just what the words we read and write mean but
determine their status as forces that enter our minds. *Text* refers to linguistic structures that have cohesion, coherence, acceptability, and intentionality; text informs
and has context and intertext as well as pragmatic aspects of communication and
action with other human beings (Van Peer, 1989). *Text* is more inclusive than
the term *concept* used throughout this book and defined as a unit of thought that
allows us to organize experience (Exhibit 1.2); *text* encompasses the idea of logical structure or schema, the organization of concepts showing their relationships,
and further adds to it the effect on the receiver of the communication. Compared
with other disciplines, then, the unit of analysis in English literature is larger
and more complex.

The openness of text structure—the fact that texts do not contain all the elements needed for their comprehension—means that the reader must infer from his or her world knowledge in order to make sense of texts. The reader must also integrate separate textual elements into a general meaning. The background knowledge needed to interpret particular linguistic events is often specific knowledge of particular social situations and participants involved (the context of events) and small-scale social facts or customs, for example, marriage or burial customs (Short & Candlin, 1989). The more internally consistent or coherent the text, the more readily it can be integrated. The more consistent with a real or imagined world that is coherent, the more readily one can infer. Given the openness of text, one of the most important achievements of textual communication is to bridge gaps in time and space. This is not without hazards, for as we saw in the Canadian literature course, the reader must simultaneously make inferences where the text leaves out detailed references to the empirical world while integrating internal relationships that are not explicit.

In introductory courses, students' level of background and technical knowledge can be especially challenging for the teacher. Before students can analyze text, they must go through a stage of familiarization and learn new strategies for deciphering the text. A professor explains the situation in her introductory survey course in early to seventeenth-century English literature.

> I know that the students have heard me use unfamiliar words and I get phonetic spellings of the words in their exams. So I know that they have been listening to the lectures, but they do not look up the words in the dictionary. Very few people ask me what a word means. On some occasions in lectures, when I use a word that I think the students will not understand, I will tell them "This is what the word means and this is the way I will be using it."

A particular problem arises when students must tackle earlier forms of English.

> Many students took one look at the *Canterbury Tales* by Chaucer and said they could not read it, without actually making an effort to try and understand it. A suggestion I would give the student is to find the modern version of the text and read it and then go back to the original text. We try to make the students understand that it does take time to read this kind of literature, that it does take time to get used to the language, but that it is not inaccessible. Some students look at it and just give up, but most of them get the idea that you need to work at it and it is not as bad once you get into it. The teaching assistants say that the students have difficulty in extracting the important ideas from the text. It seems the students have not had practice in making précis [synopses of text] to find

out what the central argument is. Yet, once you point this out to the students, it does seem that everything clicks.

Students were interviewed at the end of the course and asked if they had learned new ways of studying or of thinking in this course. They responded that they had learned both new perspectives and methods.

I have learned to look at things differently—to look at what's behind the surface and not take things at face value. I now look at the whole body of a text more in-depth, and I look for hidden meaning.

I have learned how to analyze other pieces of literature and I now have a larger base to draw from when studying pieces of literature.

I have been exposed to new philosophies and ways of thinking in this course that enable me to understand how people thought in the past.

Students are aware of the need for intensive reading and the potential prize of broad understanding from the study of literature.

Learning Concepts in a Drama Course

At the most specific level, what are students expected to learn in an English course? In our studies of how students learn concepts, we chose an English course entitled "An Introduction to Shakespeare," with sixty-nine students in the course, three-quarters of whom were in their first year of studies. To find potential concepts, we interviewed the professor to obtain the course description, main theme, and all frequently occurring or salient concepts or terms in the course. We found fifty-eight terms were specifically relevant to the course, of which thirteen were key (main or linking) concepts (Figure 8.1).

The main goals of the course are "to make students approach dramatic text and the ways of dealing with such texts, and the use of performance as a learning technique." The course is taught through lectures, group work in the classroom, and practical skill development in a theater setting. Most essential for students to learn, according to the professor, is to be active in a group situation, as well as to interpret plot, action, theme, and characters in order to perform the material. We asked the professor to link the two most closely related key concepts in the course, then to link the second most closely related, and to continue so that all the key concepts were presented on the map. Compared with concept maps in the other courses studied, the ratio of links to concepts (1.0) suggested less

FIGURE 8.1. KEY CONCEPTS IN "AN INTRODUCTION TO SHAKESPEARE"

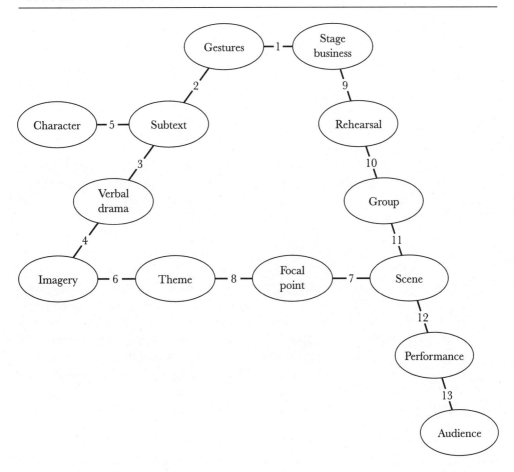

cohesion among the key concepts than in the sciences (2.06 in entomology, 1.33 in physics, 1.15 in chemistry), except for the biology laboratory course (.92).

The most important concept in this course is *performance*, defined as the act of performing, a presentation of a play—an everyday dictionary definition rather than a technical one. The professor considered it to be extremely salient and inclusive of all other concepts, but it did not play a pivotal or central role in relating concepts in the concept map, and was placed at the lower right edge of the map, with the twelfth closest link, to *scene*, the second most important concept. *Scene* is defined as the content of the performance. The placement of these two concepts on the map was explained by their being end products of the course. *Performance* is evaluated in the course by means of a questionnaire distributed to class members for each of the six enacted scenes, so it has a lead role in the instructional conditions of the course.

The two most closely linked concepts were technical terms that suggest the physical action required to perform in this course: *gestures*, defined as physical language that is intended to show interpretation and reaction, and *stage business*, visually expressive performance that extends or modifies verbal performance. In the explanation of their link, the professor noted that both are expressive of meaning, but that gestures are more of an externalization. *Stage business, performance*, and *gestures* were the concepts most closely related in meaning to the other key concepts.

Consistent with the visible performance aspect in this course, nine of the key concepts had concrete definitions; that is, they could be perceived. *Character, theme, verbal drama*, and *subtext* had abstract definitions, hence would have to be conceptualized. In the course outline, along with texts, reading list and schedule of scenes that students are to enact, they are given a list of pointers on their presentation. The first is that there is just one focal point, and they must determine what they want the audience to watch and why. They need to organize and rehearse the movement pattern of the play, keeping visual activity consistent with the overall portrayal. They are also given suggestions about how to use their voice and inflections.

In a course concerned with performance rather than theory, it might be expected that knowledge of the key concepts would not be a central learning goal, but students at the end of the course had a relatively high level of knowledge compared with that in courses in other disciplines, with *audience, rehearsal, character*, and *performance* being the best known. Moreover, their concept knowledge correlated (.41) with their overall mark in the course, higher than did their grade point average the previous year (.34) but not as highly as the general level of achievement in previous English courses (.66). This suggests the importance of these concepts and of concept knowledge in the course, despite the performance orientation. In the study of the use of the key concepts in class, *character* was by far the most frequently used, 122 times in eighteen of twenty recorded classes; in comparison, the next most frequently encountered concepts were *theme*, used 43 times in sixteen classes, and *performance*, used 23 times in eleven classes. In contrast *stage business* was not used once and was least well known by students at the end of the course. Asked to do a concept map at the end of the course, students most frequently linked *performance* and *audience*, showing their attention to the end products of the course.

In this course, concepts that define the goals and activities of the course (*rehearsal, performance*) are central rather than the Shakespearean text students are asked to perform. When the concept map was described in a symposium for professors who had participated in the study, another member of the English department remarked on the use of performance terms rather than the Shakespearean themes.

Was it because this course was an introductory course with emphasis on dramatic skill development? Would theme and figurative language play a larger part if the course were taught in lecture format? How do instructional method and knowledge development interact? Literary theory may supply pedagogical definition.

Literary Theory and Criticism

The relationship of text to theory in English literature parallels in some important ways that of concept to theoretical framework in the social sciences. Theoretical frameworks relate concepts in complex propositions. In his book *The Institution of Theory*, Krieger (1994) defines *theory* as the systematic rationalization of a set of guiding assumptions about the text and its relations to its author, its audience, and its culture at large. Text is seen as an objective stimulus, loaded with structures to be perceived and interpreted. Literary theory treats literature as in some respect a problem and seeks to formulate that problem in general terms (Graff, 1987). Theory then is an instrumental notion referring to a set of procedures to be used in the description, interpretation, and evaluation of literary texts (Verdaasdonk, 1992).

This conceptualization of theory in English literature points to the lack of an explicit or systematic framework that links the terms used in critical discourse to well-defined properties of text. Literary theory may thus provide a working framework for the analysis of text, but the framework consists of open and nondiscrete procedures rather than rigorous method as in the sciences. According to one scholar, instead of defining the context, literary theory opens up new and often socially and intellectually liberating modes of perceiving, however flawed or partial individual enterprises may appear in retrospect (Davies, 1994). The tendency for ideas to migrate from one intellectual context to another and resurface in ingenious novel combinations can be disconcerting but also invigorating.

Literary criticism is defined more narrowly than literary theory as the assessment of the value of literary texts based on traits held and required to be present in texts (Verdaasdonk, 1992). Generally, critical analysis asks what makes one text better than another. Literary criticism arose at the same time as nation-states in the nineteenth century, hence its focus was on the analysis of established masterpieces belonging to the literary heritage of a nation. It is therefore particular to both language and national heritage, although influenced by critics in other cultures. The development of different approaches or forms of critical analysis has taken a dialectic route, with new forms resulting from the insufficiencies of previous ones.

An approach is never absolutely ruled out and may resurface at a later date only slightly altered. One professor in our studies described literary theories as being rather like buses—wait a while, another will come along; wait a while longer, and it will come back with a new look. The passengers on the buses are always changing, as we continually renew and refresh our ideas (D. Bray, personal communication, December 2000). The multitude of forms literary criticism takes reflects the variety of premises that literary theorists make about text and the process of literary analysis. Cowles (1994a) in *The Critical Experience* suggests a professional humility from seeing, first, the range of possible perspectives, and second, that the comparative value of these perspectives depends on one's situation. I created Exhibit 8.1 in an attempt to understand the development of literary criticism, the forms it has taken and their proponents, and to clarify the evaluative criteria used in each approach in order to shed light on the relevant thinking processes required.

Moral and Philosophical Criticism. The principle guiding literary criticism for the past two centuries has been Matthew Arnold's definition of criticism as a disinterested endeavor to learn and propagate the best that is known and thought in the world. In this approach, literary works are treated like touchstones that make us more sensitive to life in all its complexity. The emphasis on determining what is good in the larger sense positions criticism as a philosophical act rather than limiting it to analysis of written text. Arnold, considered the major English critic of the later nineteenth century (Young, 1994), had a wide effect on literary criticism in the English-speaking world and beyond, one proof of which is his extended American lecture tour in 1883–84. He pronounced the commonly accepted aim of criticism, that the main effort is to see the object as in itself it really is; a work

EXHIBIT 8.1. FORMS OF CRITICAL ANALYSIS AND THEIR MAJOR PROPONENTS

Moral and philosophical criticism	Evaluates a work's ideas and values by determining their truth, usefulness, clarity, consistency, complexity—dominant 1500 to 1900 (Plato, Tolstoy, Matthew Arnold).
Historical criticism	Traditional approach to analyzing literature; synthesizes factual data from various sources using rules of scholarly evidence (logic and objectivity) to offer interpretations of literary works—began in 1500s, Renaissance on (Richard Altick, R. H. Miller).
Formalism	Form of the text as an aesthetic object; analysis of meter, genre, plot, point of view, language, particularly irony and ambiguity, symbols, sounds, and imagery, but not history or intent—New Critics 1930 to 1960 (Cleanth Brooks, T. S. Eliot?).

Mythic and archetypal criticism	Uses sacred stories and universal symbols—scapegoat, earth mother, the quest, redemption—to explain text—1870s to peak in 1950s (Northrop Frye, C. S. Lewis). Psychoanalytic criticism uses particular symbols, such as the unconscious and identity, as explanatory principles (1900 on; Jacques Lacan).
Structuralism	The codes, structures, or pattern of a text—signs and semiotics—most influential in the 1960s and 1970s (Ferdinand de Saussure, Claude Levi-Strauss, Roman Jakobsen, Roland Barthes).
Reader response criticism	Focuses on intellectual expectations and responses of the reader; a reaction to the New Critics' denial of reader interpretation; asks what constitutes a valid reading (Roland Barthes, Stanley Fish).
Deconstruction, postmodernism	Reveal the limits or hidden aspects of individual texts by pointing out incongruities; expose the joints and gaps in a text—1970s on (Jacques Derrida, Michel Foucault).
Pluralism	Welcomes the multiplicity of literary theories as they multiply the roles of critics; compares and interrogates literary theories; proceeds from the ethical obligation to understand and respond to each other (R. S. Crane, Richard McKeon, Stephen Pepper).
Rhetorical criticism	Examines the influence of text as a political instrument; based on rhetoric as a cooperative discussion in a community; questioning makes values available for reassessment and revision (Kenneth Burke).
New historicism	Cultural materialism or poetics reads literature as a force within its culture, its social energy (Stephan Greenblatt, Raymond Williams).
Ethnocriticism	Postcolonial movement in which those categorized as "the other" attempt to reclaim their voice and heritage, and move beyond being victims (Edward Hall, Edward Said).
Feminist criticism	By examining text for gender roles, it seeks to end the subordination and oppression of women (Mary Wollstonecraft, Virginia Woolf, Simone de Beauvoir, Betty Friedan, Kate Millett).
Marxist criticism	Based on the principle espoused by Marx that social existence, particularly economic, determines consciousness; text is a consumer commodity that operates according to a set of economic rules (George Lukacs, Louis Althusser).

of literature is an object to be attended to that the writer has put there (Donoghue, 1998). The principal criterion for evaluation of a work of literature in this approach is no less than its bearing on how to live. The thinking processes are therefore those of metaphysics.

Historical Criticism. Historical criticism arose during the European Renaissance and incorporated the use of inductive reasoning and scientific observation in the interpretation of the impact of historical acts on literary text. Its method is a product of scientific method, philology (the study of the structure of language), and biblical hermeneutics (Miller, 1988). Philology developed in the search for a method that would qualify English literature as a scholarly discipline in the research university (Graff, 1987). The main assumption is that the historical context of a literary text must be understood in order to evaluate it. Proof rests in primary evidence, preferably of the most accurate manuscript, and secondary evidence gathered by others on the text (Sorenson, 1994). Essentially, historical criticism considers text itself insufficient explanation and looks for confirming or elucidating evidence.

Formalism. Formalism focuses on a literary work as an aesthetic object—that is, its form as expressed in its genre, plot, imagery, language, meter, and point of view (Cowles, 1994b). Formalism as practiced by the New Critics emerged in the twentieth century as an alternative to the research model that had created a gap between scholars and generalists (Graff, 1987). The New Critics did not think they were turning their backs on the moral and social function of literature, but endeavored to define these functions as they operated in the literary works themselves. Guiding criteria in New Criticism are, first, form—the organizing principle that unifies a work's elements, including the achieved or experienced content—second, irony and ambiguity or paradox, and third, the uniqueness of a text.

Mythic and Archetypal Criticism. Archetypal criticism assumes universal images and patterns, essential and enduring elements that are found in myth and explain meaning in the world. In *Anatomy of Criticism*, Frye (1957), the major proponent of this first potent alternative to the New Critics' formalism, argued that we must approach literature with a conceptual framework similar to a hypothesis in order to explain it. Literature is reconstructed mythology. Archetypes are most frequently natural phenomena such as the sun, moon, and seasons of the year, or characters such as earth mothers and witches, events such as pilgrimages or death and rebirth, or colors and numbers. The approach challenges historical criticism by considering literature capable of transcending authorial intent, and by treating the history of literature not as progressive but as a rhythmic resurfacing of universal forms throughout time. The guiding criteria in archetypal criticism are the identification of archetypes and the tracing of their use. Similar in its expectation of archetypes but focused on Freudian symbols, *psychoanalytic criticism* uses the unconscious, sexual symbolism, and the development of identity to explain text.

Structuralism. Structuralist criticism derived from structural linguistics and anthropology. It examines a text as if it were a language, assuming that the language allows us to make sense of the world but that it is not reality. Our culture provides the codes and conventions that determine meaning and interpretation, give us ways to organize our perceptions and provide context for new ideas and experiences. The approach distinguishes between languages of integrity that function in contexts of their origin, and mythic or manipulative languages that borrow forms for their social liveliness and insert them into new contexts for their propaganda value. Structuralists differentiate themselves from formalists who seek to interpret texts by asking how interpretation and meaning are possible. Structuralists differentiate themselves from archetypal critics by assigning no meaning to codes or symbols outside of the text in question (Cowles, 1994c). The approach is objective and scientific. The guiding criteria for structuralists are, first, the codes operating in a given text, and second, the structural patterns of oppositions such as high versus low or life versus death.

Reader Response Criticism. Reader response critics challenge formalists' denial of reader interpretation. Donoghue (1998) proposes three ways of reading based on the assumptions governing the readings. The first is Matthew Arnold's assumption as posited in moral and philosophical criticism—that the main effort is to see the object as in itself it really is. The second and third ways of reading, in contrast, qualify as forms of reader response. The second, Walter Pater's reading, is of impressions that occur in the mind of a qualified reader provoked by the work of art; for example, the Mona Lisa incites us to a new sensibility. The reader is in sympathy with the object coinciding with what is unique in it and therefore inexpressible. In the third way of reading, Oscar Wilde expresses the role of the reader-critic as heretic, to see the object as it is not, to aspire to an alternative explanation to the given. The work of art is a suggestion for a new work of literature that is the critic's own. These ways of reading lead to interpretive communities that see or formulate texts in the same manner, and the guiding criterion is to be aware of the interpretive community or strategy.

Deconstruction and Postmodernism. Deconstruction and postmodernism assume that language is unstable, based on signs and language systems (as in structuralism) but without an external referent, since the relationship of the signified to signifiers is arbitrary. Thus language has no absolute properties and is experienced as a momentary summation of contextual circumstance. The approach is concerned with exposing the mechanisms by which texts generate meaning while at the same time undermining them with logical contradictions. Schilb (1992) therefore suggests that rather than enhancing students' critical thinking, it may confuse and render them cynical. The challenge of deconstruction lies in its more radical epistemological stance—it demands the power to adjudicate on what is true or false (Donoghue, 1998). It calls attention to gaps and incongruities and therefore opens ways to new readings of a text. The guiding criterion is thus the search for essential but hidden aspects of text.

Pluralism. Pluralism welcomes the multiplicity of literary theories and proceeds from the ethical obligation to understand and respond to each other. The underlying assumption is that if a framework is constructed rather than innate, then any one of them is as employable as another, or each is good for a particular job and may be replaced by another for the next assignment (Donoghue, 1998). The approach grew out of the philosophical pragmatism of William James and posits that the choice of a critical approach depends on the task at hand and one's purposes (Duerden, 1994). The criterion of pluralism is, then, one of best fit of approach to task. The effect of pluralism according to Donoghue has been to end the wars between different approaches only to have the proponents of each withdraw from the arena and set up local constituencies with their own journals, regular conferences, and anthologies to represent the interests of the group. The field is enlarged and each group has room to breathe.

Other Approaches. Other postmodern approaches ally literary criticism with sociopolitical influences. That closest to a traditional form is *rhetorical criticism*, which examines the influence of text as a political or persuasive instrument. Based on a broader interpretation of the Greek concept of rhetoric—as a cooperative discussion in a community, the principal criterion is the consequences of the values in the text for the community. *New historicism* reads literature as a force in its culture, based on its social energy. The examination of social history and the effect of texts within it extends the criterion for rhetorical criticism: cultural effects on text, the effects of text on culture and their interaction. *Ethnocriticism* is a political movement in which those categorized as "the other" attempt to reclaim their voice and heritage and move beyond being victims; the main criterion is a shared story. Ethnocritic processes include the search for cultural metaphors and linguistic classifications. *Feminist criticism* seeks specifically to end the subordination and oppression of women; speaking in a postmodern voice, the main criterion is the abandonment of the regulatory fiction of gender (Houston, 1994). *Marxist criticism* examines text as a consumer commodity that operates according to a set of economic rules. A prime evaluative criterion would therefore be the effect of text on economic bondage or liberation.

A review of the major criteria used in the different forms of textual analysis suggests that they have shifted from the global—the application of ideas to how to live—to the particular—the organizing principle that unifies a work's elements and identifies its uniqueness. Different approaches espouse different ways of expressing this organization: through context, archetypes, codes and patterns of oppositions, paradox, hidden aspects of text, the interpretive community or strategy, the consequences of values in text for the community, the interaction of text and culture, and a shared story, cultural metaphors, and their abandonment—as for gender or economic bondage. From the perspective of organizing principles, the theories are neither discrete nor contradictory; each would appear to add to our understanding of the text. Pluralism recommends the use of the best fit of approach to task. Thus literary criticism appears to deal as much with the representation of knowledge as its evaluation.

In terms of thinking processes, a commitment to close reading may be the nearest thing to a shared principle in contemporary criticism (Rabinowitz, 1992). Although the New Critics' principles of autonomy and unity have been attacked, close reading remains despite problems with its assumption that authors control the details of their texts or that we assign value to what fits our prior conceptions of reading. Close reading, according to Rabinowitz, privileges figurative writing over realistic portrayal of social conditions, deep over surface meaning, form over content, the elite over the popular, and indirect expression over direct. The danger is that close reading may sever the relation between literature and its specific and concrete relation to historical, cultural, and political reality. The tension between the particular and the global continues.

We next look more specifically at how professors of English help students learn to think in their courses. Their examples illuminate the different forms of critical analysis they use in their teaching.

The Development of Thinking Processes in English Literature

The most fundamental terms used to describe thinking processes in English are encountered early in one's education; *the language arts, reading,* and *writing* make up a large part of the curriculum throughout the elementary school years. By the time students reach postsecondary studies, reading and writing have acquired a more complex character that students may presume they know, but do not. Reading becomes close reading of texts, which requires going beyond the text; writing becomes the process of making arguments or creating narrative or poetry. In *Critical Thinking: A Guide to Interpreting Literary Texts,* Manlove (1989) describes close analysis of a text as establishing a rough meaning or direction from within the text, then observing the stylistic peculiarities and fitting the two together with the result that the meaning itself alters and becomes more manifold. Students must pay attention to language, imagery, argument, psychology, and morals. Considerable practice and persistence are needed to find the stylistic features that matter, the patterns they form, and their significance.

To examine the specific thinking processes developed in courses in English, I interviewed sixteen English literature professors about their expectations of their students and how they developed thinking in their courses. In contrast to professors in other disciplines, who expected their entering students to be able to think logically and to reason with abstract propositions, English literature professors described their students as equipped with intuition and sensibility to which it was necessary to supplement logical argument. One described the thinking process in the following manner.

> The student must know what the content of the text is—that is understanding at one level. But to really understand a text, one must start to see relationships; one must see what would be abstracted or generalized as the artistic form of this particular work. What characters are like other characters; in what ways are they alike or different; is there enough likeness to establish a connection; once the connection is established, in what significant ways are they differentiated?

As in other disciplines, the professors were asked to describe with examples how the thinking processes in the working model are developed in their courses. One noted the similarity between the model of thinking processes and the sequence of literary analysis.

> You would start with descriptive activity, then you would proceed through a process of selection, looking for pattern, relationship, significance. You might use strategies of representation along the way. Once you started seeing elements of pattern, you would want to draw inferences; that might lead you on to something else. In the end you would be working toward a synthesis of all the different things that you had come up with and then you would ultimately have to verify that synthesis, to test it back against the work and against the original effort at description, and test even that description: Is it an accurate description of what is there? So that while one would be doing all of these things to some extent at all times, there would be a sequential pattern that would roughly correspond to the suggested list of thinking processes.

The kinds of thinking processes the professors found to be important and the examples of their development were found in courses on Chaucer, Shakespeare, different periods of English literature, film making, and literary criticism.

Description

Sensitivity to language is crucial to the descriptive process in English literature (Exhibit 8.2). According to one professor, the beginning point in the analysis of text is to take students back to the facts of the text; the ability to pose the simple questions is essential to the exploration of complex problems. In order to do this, however, the reader needs an immense amount of information about the history of the

EXHIBIT 8.2. PROFESSORS' EXAMPLES OF DESCRIPTION USED IN ENGLISH LITERATURE COURSES

Identify context: Establish surrounding environment to create a total picture.	*You need to have your sense of yourself as a reader in the present day and remake the reading experience and the relationship between text and reader that may initially have existed.*
	The history, the politics, the science, and the anthropology, the different intellectual modes of that period.
State conditions: State essential parts, prerequisites, or requirements.	*Intelligibility in the work—a matter of social agreement among the interpretive community.*
State facts: State known information, events that have occurred.	*When were Chaucer's works written? In connection with what occasions were some of them written? What is the sequence of his works? What could he or could he not have read?*
State functions: State normal or proper activity of a thing or specific duties.	*The functions that a character has in the work in which he or she occurs.*
	Detailed description, shot by shot, of a short sequence (one and a half to two minutes) that contains twenty to thirty shots from a course film to ensure that sure they understand the mechanics of a film shot in sequence.
State assumptions: State suppositions, postulates.	*Axiomatic statements made knowingly.*
	Emotional intensity of the statement— motives, drives, emotional needs reformulated at a theoretical level.

period in which the text was written to *identify the context*. A professor of Shake-speare noted that part of the meaning in any reading is subject-centered, so he wants his students to explore their role as producers of meaning and how that is linked with the way in which meaning is produced by social and cultural contexts in Shakespeare's age and today. Thus both historical and reader response approaches to literary analysis are called on in *identifying the context. Conditions* of intelligibility of a text reside in the particular interpretive community; thus, working context determines text conditions.

Stating facts is a very complex operation in this field; close reading of the text requires looking behind the surface, as professor and students in the course in early to seventeenth-century English literature noted. *Stating functions* is an important tactic in understanding roles or characters or the range of implication of individual concepts, for example, "gentilesse" or "curtesye" in Chaucer's work. For students creating films, one assignment is a detailed description, shot by shot, of a relatively short sequence (one and a half to two minutes) that contains perhaps twenty to thirty shots from one of the course films. Students must describe the edit and camera movements to ensure they understand the mechanics of a film shot in sequence. *Stating assumptions* is important at several levels: assumptions in the text, assumptions about the critical theory being applied, and those of the reader interacting with the text. Several professors saw this as the most important thinking process, because it determines understanding. *Goals* are less important to the critical process; they are related to the writing of theses or the focus of a course. In summary, *identifying context and assumptions* are considered the most important descriptive thinking processes to be learned in English literature courses.

Selection

Selection assumes a specific role in English literature because of the complexity of text and the processes needed to understand it; different selections must be made according to the form of analysis being used. Whether in *selecting relevant information* or *ordering* it, the organization of an intellectual argument requires high-level processing. Rather than *identifying critical elements* that will be units of analysis as in the sciences, students of English literature must cite relevant passages from a text to support an argument, or understand how small details connect with themes or what their function is (Exhibit 8.3). *Critical relations* extend to the context, to referents, to the place of characters within scenes within acts within plays—multiple levels of relationships. The same demands are placed on understanding a film sequence, why each shot is set up the way it is, or how a scene is related to and generates meaning.

EXHIBIT 8.3. PROFESSORS' EXAMPLES OF
SELECTION USED IN ENGLISH LITERATURE COURSES

Choose relevant information: Select information that is pertinent to the issue in question.	*So many possible patterns have been recorded and observed.*
Order information in importance: Rank, arrange in importance or according to significance.	*How do we judge importance? How do we rank elements in our understanding and reading?*
Identify critical elements: Determine units, parts, components that are important.	*Textual analysis, the ability to cite relevant passages. The kind of argument you can regard as valid relates to specific textual characteristics—passages, characters, elements of plot, ideas.*
	How small details connect with big parts, how different parts relate to the story line, and identify the function in the whole novel. Students look at a novel by Dickens and relate how individual characters function as parts of a story line.
Identify critical relations: Determine connections between things that are important.	*Identify ambiguity and the critical relationship between the "thing" and within the "context" with respect to aesthetics and referents.*
	Analysis of a film sequence: how the parts of it interrelate, why every shot is set up the way it is, the mise-en-scène.

Representation

Unlike science professors, who had specific referents—images or procedures—for representation, the English professors found it difficult to distinguish between description and representation because they thought that the analysis of text requires the two processes concurrently. The text is the representation, and the process of expression or rhetoric is as well. One of the most familiar organizing principles is the structure of a play, in which different acts have specific functions (Exhibit 8.4). Genre and trope (figure of speech) are also major organizing principles. The professors were reluctant to build organizing systems into their curriculum, however, for fear that students would apply them mechanically, thus losing their sensitivity to the text. They also pointed out that frameworks are fictions and thus must continue to be questioned. *Illustration of elements and relations* demands close reading of text to provide examples. *Modification of elements and relations* occurs most frequently in the active production of a play, when a particular staging alters its meaning. Thus the

EXHIBIT 8.4. PROFESSORS' EXAMPLES OF
REPRESENTATION USED IN ENGLISH LITERATURE COURSES

Recognize organizing principles: Identify laws, methods, rules that arrange in a systematic whole.	*The fourth act of a Shakespearean tragedy is almost always less intense than the third and the fifth act; Shakespeare brings his tragedies to an ultimate climax in Act III, where the tragic mistake is usually made, and the consequences are borne out in Act V, with a quiet moment between them.*
	Sonnet, epic, tragedy, or comedy, couplet or stanzaic form, and tropes such as zeugma from Greek rhetoric, where two apparently different nouns are dependent on a single verb, as in Pope's Rape of the Lock, "There thou great Anna whom three realms obey/Dost sometimes counsel take, and sometimes tea."
Organize elements and relations: Arrange parts, connections between things into a systematic whole.	*A specific descriptive framework is a fiction, but it is an attempt to establish a structure that will comprehend the actual works written during a period.*
Illustrate elements and relations: Make clear by examples the parts, connections between things.	*Parts of the subject matter that illustrate the point being made or the argument being offered.*
Modify elements and relations: Change, alter, or qualify the parts, connections between things.	*A particular staging or performance can vary or alter the sense of a play.*

processes of representation occur in different forms from other disciplines and differentially in subareas in English literature. Drama appears to be the subarea that uses representation most, but poetry and text analysis also use these processes.

Inference

Inference is central to English literature but again takes different forms from that in other disciplines. For example, Fish (1995) states that in literary studies, justification is not a chain of inferences, but a circle, and it proceeds by telling a story in which every detail is an instantiation of an informing spirit that is known only in the details but always exceeds them. Inference is essential in forming ideas: to have initial insight into a text, to construct convincing arguments, and to muster evidence to demonstrate the case without distortion (Manlove, 1989). Manlove states, however, that the process is not often described. The first rule is never to take things for granted; rather we must appropriate the work for ourselves and react freely to it, inspecting it in detail, testing its standards and consistency, and looking for irrelevancies. Inference is thus a hunt for possible meanings, an interrogative stance (Exhibit 8.5).

Relationships are the coinage; genre is an expression of different forms of relationship. To develop students' inferential abilities, the professor may ask them to compare two apparently different texts to determine their relationship. According to Manlove (1989), making connections or discovering a common feature

EXHIBIT 8.5. PROFESSORS' EXAMPLES OF INFERENCE USED IN ENGLISH LITERATURE COURSES

Discover new relations between elements: Detect or expose connections between parts, units, components.	*See what would be abstracted or generalized as the artistic form of this particular work, which characters are like other characters, in what ways they are alike or different, if there is enough likeness to establish a connection.*
	The fifth act relates to the preceding four acts in quite strikingly different ways in a romantic comedy, a tragedy, a history play or a late romance, or a problem play.
Discover new relations between relations: Detect or expose connections between connections of things.	*Apparently unrelated works are given side-by-side to discuss and the exercise is to think about relations between them. Are there relations of influence, historical period, technique? For instance, a part of Lacan's essay on* The Gays *is placed alongside Blake's* The Crystal Cabinet—*there is a connection between the problem of articulating separation between the viewer and the object.*
Discover equivalences: Detect or expose equality in value, force or significance.	*In the moral evaluation of characters in* Henry IV, Part I, *when Falstaff plays King Henry IV and Hal plays himself as prince, and then Prince Hal plays his father and Falstaff plays Hal, Shakespeare invites the audience to think about the equivalences between Falstaff and the king, Hal and the king, and Hal and Falstaff.*
	In All's Well That Ends Well, *whether honor and honesty turn out to have the same meaning.*
Categorize: Classify, arrange into parts.	*Generic categories that mean the parts are arranged in different ways.*
	Chaucer's works belong to certain genres: fabliaux, romances, moral tales.

(Continued)

EXHIBIT 8.5. CONTINUED

Order: Rank, sequence, arrange methodically.	*Setting out, in acceptable sequence, an argument of cause and effect.*
Change perspective: Alter view, vista, interrelations, significance of facts or information.	*From temporal and personal provincialism to see that there are alternative visions of experience.*
	Rethink assumptions from the deconstructivist point of view.
Hypothesize: Suppose or form a proposition as a basis for reasoning.	*Analyze a text by creating a series of tentative hypotheses that one then tests against the facts of the text itself and keeps modifying.*

in separate details of a text involves imposing the idea on the material; the truest interpretation will be the one that is least forced. Its effect is to expand and transform our view of the text. More commonly, however, the professors noted the paradoxes or differences in text. Disjunctions or inconsistencies often lead to a deeper analysis and understanding of the text. *Categorizing* is most frequently a matter of determining the genre of a play or poem. *Ordering* is a difficult task given the lack of rules of logic in English literature, but the process of argument requires a sequence of propositions. *Changing perspective* is a foundational goal of literature, to provide insight and see another way of perceiving the world, and explains the powerful effect of deconstruction. A more specific example for students is to learn to use different forms of literary criticism to examine a text.

Hypothesizing, often the initial step in a course, according to several professors, follows the traditional process of hermeneutics or interpretation. As described in Chapter One, the reader-interpreter hypothesizes the meaning of the text, assumes that the text is coherent, then searches for corroborating evidence in the text. Inferential processes are thus central to learning English literature, although they take a particular form that questions rather than confirms an objective reality.

Synthesis

Given the tenets of postmodernism, what is the role of synthesis? One professor noted that with the influence of recent forms of critical analysis, multiplicity and paradox rather than unity have become the hallmark of the discipline. Relationships and patterns come closest to examples of synthesis in English literature courses. The search for form and gestalt also describe the process. In filmmaking, synthesis plays a particularly important role; for example, students must move from the understanding of a single shot to the film as a whole (Exhibit 8.6). They are expected to see the connections among the films of an individual director: how certain themes

EXHIBIT 8.6. PROFESSORS' EXAMPLES OF
SYNTHESIS USED IN ENGLISH LITERATURE COURSES

Combine parts to form a whole: Join, associate elements, components into a system or pattern.	*How do you move from the individual shot to an understanding of a film as an entire system or pattern?*
	Patterns of action in which characters are involved must be apprehended, but then one must apprehend the shape of the action, the causal patterns that may be running it, the patterns by which it is revealed to the reader as far as what the reader's are allowed to know, and at any given point, thematic patterns that are embodied in the action and often act in terms of block structures.
Elaborate: Work out, complete with great detail, exactness, or complexity.	*Let us stop and think what we mean by farce.*
	In film study, every detail is significant, no detail is beneath notice, and all of them contribute.
Generate missing links: Produce or create what is lacking in a sequence, fill in the gap.	*In reading drama, often it is in the things that are not spoken or that are not performed that a great deal is revealed.*
Develop course of action: Work out or expand the path, route, or direction to be taken.	*Develop your own methodology, adapt what you have learned in such a way that you are satisfied with your own interpretation, become a Marxist or a feminist, for example.*

and patterns are consistent throughout a director's work, and how they produce a whole that is greater than its parts. They must use *elaboration* because every detail in a film is significant. In class, particular words demand attention in order to understand their meanings in different situations, a different kind of elaboration. In drama and in literary criticism, students must learn to *generate missing links*, because the gaps or contradictions in text or performance may have considerable meaning. An argument is a *course of action* that students need to learn to develop; an interpretation of a work as a literary critic requires choice of a *course of action* as well. Different kinds of synthesis occur in different kinds of English courses.

Verification

The most common ways of describing thinking processes in English literature—hermeneutics, critical thinking, and literary analysis—include verification. In the validation of their work, in contrast to social scientists, English professors put least emphasis on the use of empirical evidence. Instead they talk of peer review, credibility, and plausibility to describe the process of validation. English professors seek accuracy in terms of relating textual detail or in whether text is historically sound. They refer to writing *exactly* or quoting accurately. One English professor spoke of constantly testing the small things, the parts, against some sort of whole. In discussing the criteria used to validate knowledge, several English professors noted their concern that coherence might limit truth if, for example, in the interests of coherence, conflicting evidence or interpretations were ignored or suppressed. One pointed out that language will never say only one thing. Important literary texts may not be fully consistent and coherent works, and the danger would be in editing out the conflicts and contradictions that are part of them. A self-critical stance, an awareness of the underlying assumptions of one's approach, is an important part of the validation process.

What validation processes do English professors want their students to learn? In the cross-disciplinary study, verification was the skill rated most important for graduates in English literature programs—to recognize central arguments, evaluate, elaborate and develop their implications, and support general assertions with details (Powers & Enright, 1987). For the professors in our study, to find the most coherent interpretation of events in a play is one aim. *Comparing* different interpretations of text and deciding which is most valid is a major task for students (Exhibit 8.7). They must be able to cross from the abstract to the concrete in order to bridge the author's and the reader's experience. They must learn that validity resides in the best possible interpretation, then proceed to produce that interpretation. *Feedback* is used in discussion to examine inconsistencies in an argument or different interpretations of text. Although several professors considered it unlikely that one could *confirm results* given the tentative nature of knowledge in literature, it is important to be able to construct an ordered argument that has made use of all the available evidence. Thus verification processes are valued.

In summary, all of the thinking processes are used in English literature courses. The process of inquiry extends from *identifying the context* in which text is placed to *judging the validity* of an interpretation. Argument requires description, selection, representation, inference, synthesis, and verification. The difficulty is that one cannot call on an objective reality, as in the sciences, to support one's argument. One is bound by text yet must render it explicable by inference. The methods of inquiry most frequently used to describe the process in English literature are hermeneutics, the construction of textual meaning through a dialectic between understanding and explanation, and critical thinking, a reasoned or questioning approach in which one examines assumptions and seeks evidence (Exhibit 1.7). The examples given by the professors in our studies go beyond these definitions to demand a fuller and more detailed set of processes that students must learn in

EXHIBIT 8.7. PROFESSORS' EXAMPLES OF
VERIFICATION USED IN ENGLISH LITERATURE COURSES

Compare alternative outcomes: Examine similarities or differences of results, consequences.	*Look at critical opinions on the same subject and make up one's own mind as to which one is more valid to handle not just the literary text but also the text that is written about it.*
Compare outcome to standard: Examine similarities, differences of results based on a criterion.	*Read back to the abstraction concrete examples from one's own experience; the abstraction works as a middle term between two separated sets of concrete experience, the author's and the reader's.*
Judge validity: Critically examine the soundness, effectiveness by actual fact.	*Validity is in interpretation, which means that a consensus omnium can be arrived at that such and such an interpretation is more powerful and more rigorous and more satisfactory than some other interpretation.*
Use feedback: Employ results to regulate, adjust, adapt.	*Sustained argument will allow difficulties to emerge or inconsistencies in the argument or misconstruals actually to be debated on the spot.*
	You hear someone else say, "Oh, I didn't think that or read it like that."
Confirm results: Establish or ratify conclusions, effects, outcomes, or products.	*Construct a logically ordered argument and one which has not left out an important class of evidence.*

order to succeed in this discipline. The examples of thinking also show us that theories of literary criticism may inform the process of inquiry but in no way delimit it. The most important implication of these findings is that the terminology developed thus far in the discipline to explain thinking processes is insufficient to guide student learning. In fairness to students studying English literature, more detailed attention to the thinking processes required of them is essential.

The Challenge of Instruction in English Literature

The challenges in helping students to learn English literature are evident in the breadth of the discipline, the multiplicity of approaches to understanding it, and the intricacy of the process of inquiry. Added to the burden of inquiry, passion and aesthetics are pedagogical issues for the English professor. Because of the many approaches and the additional affective charge, professors have been accused of having their attention focused on the discipline rather than on their students. According to Schilb (1992), pedagogy can be an unwelcome challenge for many teachers of English literature. The general tendency is to adopt the osmotic theory of education, assuming that students can and should acquire knowledge merely from exposure to certain hallowed texts. Pedagogical strategy is then vested in the authority of the canon. A counterargument to this stance is that having gained some expertise in decoding structures of signification, literary theorists should be intellectually equipped to read their own practices, institutions, and the world as a text (Kecht, 1992).

Forms of literary criticism, if they do not delimit the learning process, can provide potentially useful approaches to pedagogy. For example, formalism, focused on decoding structures of signification, provides an approach for seeking the organizing principle that unifies a work's elements, and ambiguity or paradox in the text—the central tendency and variance around it. The processes espoused in deconstruction are aimed at exposing the mechanisms by which texts generate meaning. Deconstruction has been recommended as a potential source of teaching principles; however, according to Tompkins (1996), the principles do not appear to have yet affected classroom practice or understanding of the student, or how authority operates in the classroom.

One pedagogical issue arises from unwillingness to accept the student as a legitimate voice. The sense is that the young must accommodate rather than assimilate knowledge, that they must be open or opened to the text. Tompkins has argued that the educational process infantilizes students, taking away their initiative, and teaching them to be sophisticated rule-followers. The positing of a generic as well as a passive student, contrary to the principles of deconstruction, would suggest that dominant principles in the field are not being applied in the classroom. However, practice appears to be more student-oriented than in other disciplines. Discussion is used in classes 80 percent of the time, twice as often as in the natural sciences and as frequently as in teacher education; in contrast, extensive lecturing is used half as often (36 percent of the time) as in the natural sciences (Milem & Astin, 1994). Cooperative learning, where students work with each other on projects, is used more (28 percent) than in the natural sciences (12 percent), although not as much as in teacher education programs (47 percent). Students tend to be evaluated more by essays than in other disciplines (58 percent of the time). These comparative figures suggest that humanities students benefit from more student-centered instructional and evaluation methods but that not all students experience these methods. What does the structure of the discipline say about potential pedagogical approaches?

Breadth of the Discipline

The danger of breadth in a discipline is that in attempting to embrace everything, one may end up with nothing (Fish, 1995). The antinomies in English literature both drive inquiry and frustrate it. Beginning with the debate over sacred versus secular text, unresolved quarrels dot the highway. Understanding the English literature of previous centuries requires an understanding of biblical references, which students increasingly lack. To compensate, courses in the history and explication of biblical text are frequently added to the curriculum. Students arrive without background in the classics; particularly needed is mythology to understand text from previous periods of literature.

The antinomy between the aesthetic and practical has been most frequently dealt with by cordoning off English composition courses so that they are taught by adjuncts, often in different programs of effective written communication. A more holistic approach is to require written work of students in their courses that meets the standards of effective communication. This increases the workload of professors and teaching assistants, but contextualizes the writing process. The third antinomy, text versus context, must be responded to more specifically, in each course. Identifying the context is the first step in the process of inquiry, and students frequently arrive with little experience in the universe of English literature in earlier periods. Thus, in addition to gaining biblical and classical background, students need particular historical background to understand text.

At the level of text, the challenges are more fundamental. Two proverbial questions arise from the amplitude of the discipline: What is legitimate text, primary or canon? How does one teach literary theory? The first question must be answered each time a course is given. Miller (1988) suggests that most professors in English literature departments still assume that their chief responsibility is teaching students how to read primary texts. There is, however, widespread disagreement about what the primary texts should be. The canon conflict reflects the controversy inherent in a multicultural society with diverse values and approaches (Graff, 1994). This raises the larger pedagogical issue of how institutional discourses become readable to people not already initiated into them.

Most English departments have responded to the question of legitimate text by maintaining survey courses that introduce students to previous periods of literature, as in the course on early to seventeenth-century English literature. The professor in that course endeavored to explain terms and provide background that allowed students to explicate the text. They in turn recognized that this was hard work. Other courses, as in contemporary Canadian literature, expand the breadth of the discipline by putting students into intellectual contact with living authors and showing the different ways in which meaning is produced in contemporary text. The acceptance of plurality and diversity leads to an ever-expanding curriculum limited only by student receptivity. Although the approaches to curriculum of historical categorization and potential expansion do not resolve the issue of legitimate text, they are pragmatic and feasible responses to a questioned canon.

The second question—How does one teach literary theory or criticism?—is equally difficult to answer. Miller (1988) suggests that in the discipline, in addition to widespread disagreement about what primary texts should be, proliferating critical theories provide incompatible guides to reading. Literary theory requires a shift from the interpretive process of identifying the meaning of a work of literature to a more abstract level where one asks how that meaning is generated. The student must be equipped with considerable analytic power to be able to move into the world of literary theory, and such courses tend to be found at senior levels of undergraduate study or in graduate school. Explanation for this curricular placement lies in the need for students to acquire methods of thinking about text—discovering meaning—before they proceed to literary criticism. The primary pedagogical paradox is that the abstraction of theory or criticism removes it from the world of the student (Fish, 1995). In contrast, with conflicting critical theories the works read in class become examples demonstrating the effectiveness of the competing theories. Critical theory thus liberates by unmasking ideological assumptions. After introverted focusing on the close reading of text, the student may be oddly equipped for this new extroverted role of critic but must still dare to soar.

The common approach to teaching literary theory, according to Myers (1994), however, is the taxonomical survey in which the contents of differing bodies of doctrine are treated as facts, not theory. But all verdicts about literature and literary standards are open to interrogation. Another way of teaching is to abridge and combine theories into a strategy for the interpretation of text, but this is the abandonment of theory. One reason for the ascendancy of theory has been the success of its attacks on established norms of interpretation. For example, deconstruction called into question the New Critics' presumption of unity, coherence, and pattern in literary text. Literary inquiry is always conditional. Myers holds that any approach to teaching is flawed if it relaxes into an uncritical pluralism.

Political or radical teaching recognizes the principle that the role of theory is to be oppositional. A theory is an argument and requires reengaging in controversies. The special role of theory is to let the air out of critics' assurances that the terms they use have an objective reality, to oppose cultural authority. Literary theory is a demand for proof and further defense. Davies (1994) notes that in teaching, one fundamental perplex is how to navigate between the Scylla of reductive simplification and the Charybdis of unassimilable elaboration. The danger of simplifying things is that close scrutiny of textual detail may be replaced by uncritical opinion.

The university context also plays into pedagogical strategy. Literary criticism operates in the larger world of academic freedom in the university. Graff (1994) suggests that ideological contention in the university seems a sign of democratic vitality rather than a symptom of disarray, relativism, and declining standards. He notes that the humanities have become the site of the most radical cultural transgression without ceasing to be a bastion of traditional values. In the liberal-pluralist rhetoric adopted by universities, the university is seen as a site of infinitely multiplying differences that never need to be confronted because in the end they conduce to common goals. However, the students become the battleground of the university's increasing ideological contradictions. One practical response is to create a theme during a semester that opens out into diverse lines of inquiry, such as interpretation across the disciplines or the politics of representation, leading to an intellectual community in which students live the language.

Passion and Aesthetics

Classic Apollonian and Dionysian arguments are made for the relative importance of cool cognition versus heated passion in the learning of English literature. The Apollonian argument proceeds in the following way. If features of literary language are to be properly investigated, this should be done in a scientific manner, involving bold hypotheses and a process of providing examples and counterexamples. These steps would lead to refinement of the hypotheses and setting up provisional analytic models of sufficient predictive power to provide for a process of continually refined and theoretically self-aware analysis (Carter, 1989). The organization of the curriculum so that students become aware of the processes of inference readers employ in order to understand texts—getting to know how texts work—is done by juxtaposing different examples of the same genre (Short & Candlin, 1989). Making sense of a poem involves an assumption that the meaning we arrive at fits with the rest of the text, forming an organic and interpretive whole. Density of meaning and being able to infer from the text are also important criteria. Schilb (1992) raises a limitation of this approach: the assumed intrinsic validity of particular aesthetic talk may have the effect of rigidifying course content and focusing on it rather than on the ways in which students might incorporate it.

In rejoinder to cool cognition, the Dionysian argument asks: What is the source of excitement that hangs over literature? One response is the provocation of our deep-seated assumptions. Putting the reader in nearer relation to the text, interpenetrating rather than observing, is a process of living through a work (Manlove, 1989). The experience of the work is a dynamic and mobile one, an exploration that evokes pleasure. Tompkins (1996) also questions the idea that the suppression of passion makes for intellectual development, arguing that if people care about ideas and have an emotional stake in them, they find the best arguments, hang in when the going gets rough, and feel the excitement and intimacy of real exchange. She claims that we need to comprehend the relationship between the subject matter and the lives of students. For example, in class discussion, the initiative, creativity, energy, and dedication that are released when students know they can express themselves freely are proof that they need to feel a connection between the subject matter and who they are for knowledge to take root.

The antithesis to this argument is that students might then favor the easier flair for being spontaneously righteous and indignant accompanied by an impatience for the slow work of reading (Donoghue, 1998). In other words, fierce rhetoric would overcome quiet logic. Synthesis of the argument lies for Donoghue in the purpose of reading literature—to exercise or incite our imagination, particularly our ability to imagine being someone other than ourselves. This is a training in sensibility, perception, judgment, and analytic skill to understand the direction and force of sentences, thus not of propositions but of actions, a going out from oneself toward other lives. He notes that if English literature were taught as a second language, teachers would be more responsive to the mediating character of the literary language, its opacity. He concludes that we need a recovered disinterestedness in literature, the perfection of standing aside; to read merely to have our political or other values endorsed or to find them abused by a work of literature is vain. Aesthetics, rather than connoting moral lassitude, political irresponsibility, or decadence, is the comprehensive, lived experience of reading, a necessary discipline of attention, a space where the immediate pressures of ethical and political decisions are deferred. It means paying attention to objects that ask only to be perceived. The term poetics could be used instead of aesthetics, to mean the inductive study of works of literature with a view to understanding the principles of their working.

Pedagogy specific to English literature according to our professors included modeling close reading, following the steps of an argument, and employing different forms of literary criticism to understand better authorial intent and audience reception. Understanding the context and text references and assumptions are major teaching and learning challenges, especially when entering students have little literary background. Even though students will have had more previous courses in English than in any other discipline, introducing the field or its subfields appears to be the most frequent teaching experience. Exploring a theme or archetypes and deconstructing the text are recommended broad strategies. Finding a way to develop a more specific terminology to explain thinking processes in the discipline is essential to guide student learning. More detailed attention to the thinking processes required of students would require a collaborative process on the part of professors, but might yield enormous pedagogical benefits.

How might one begin this process? One professor suggested that to guide students to think in the humanities, there is a clear need to help them find patterns (Wilkinson, personal communication, October 2000). Given complexity, one must look for evidence from which one can draw conclusions. Students therefore need to be equipped with tools to aid them in their search, but at the same time need to examine their assumptions or preconceptions and broaden their approach to text. One of the most powerful tools is to formulate a question, and focusing on a paradox or irony in text will often raise the question. We also need to monitor student understanding, provide them with feedback, and coach them when they come up short, all labor-intensive processes. Informing the process is the aim of helping students to hear the cadence yet be able to respond to it and recognize its origins and limitations, to be in sympathy yet able to respond cogently.

The Disciplinary Perspective in English Literature

To promote students' intellectual development, the kind of learning environment needed in English literature is one that helps students understand human culture and integrate meaning. This is not an easy task in a limitless or unbounded discipline permeated by a wider public and nonacademic culture. The discipline is organized around the production of consensual knowledge arrived at through contention; text and context are central concepts. The aim of giving students tales by which they could start to understand themselves as individuals and as social beings must vie with the disciplinary bent for cold criticism.

What higher-order thinking processes do students in English literature need to learn? Text encompasses the idea of logical structure, schema, or organization, and the effect of the communication on the receiver. Although a wide variety of approaches to thinking may be modeled—aesthetic, linguistic, philosophical, psychological, or sociopolitical—thinking in the discipline can be summarized as close reading, traveling along the line of a particular work in order to respond to it, doing justice to the author's intent. In English literature courses, the process of inquiry extends from *identifying the context* in which text is placed to *judging the validity* of an interpretation. The processes needed to succeed in this discipline go beyond hermeneutics and critical thinking to a fuller and more detailed set of thinking processes.

What are optimal ways of cultivating these thinking processes? Forms of literary criticism provide potentially useful approaches to pedagogy. Exploring a theme or archetypes and deconstructing the text are recommended broad strategies. Formalism helps to find the organizing principle that unifies a work's elements and ambiguity or paradox in the text. Deconstruction exposes the mechanisms by which texts generate meaning. One way of creating an intellectual community in which students live the language of literary criticism is to work within a theme, such as the politics of representation, leading students to connect different aspects of the subject matter. Close reading, following the steps of an argument, and modeling different forms of literary criticism help students understand authorial intent and audience reception. Students need to be helped to find patterns and to search for evidence in order to draw conclusions and formulate their own questions.

CHAPTER NINE

LEARNING, UNDERSTANDING, AND MEANING

One important part of learning in the university is that students talk to each other and test each other's understanding. You can listen to a lecturer expounding on a subject and you can understand it as it goes along, but when you come to discuss it with someone else or to try to apply it to problems or to an experiment, to work with it, you might find that you do not know it as well as you thought. Having to cope with someone else's uncertainties is a stringent test of your own understanding.

PHYSICS PROFESSOR

Thinking processes are the most important thing students would pick up from the course, and yet they are probably the least explicitly examined for or taught. The procedure of learning is a process of constant reexposure and gradual growth in the facility with which one is able to think.

ENGLISH PROFESSOR

The English and physics professors quoted here present us with the ultimate challenge in this book: how to encourage understanding and change the learning context so that it becomes more supportive of higher-order learning. In the previous chapters we have seen ways in which the disciplinary context may aid learning or constrain it. We have seen how higher-order learning might be promoted in different domains. We also recognize that each discipline or discursive community presents a competing way or ways of giving meaning to the world. Students will therefore learn different ways of organizing and explaining their experience depending on their decision to concentrate on one discipline rather than another. They may become contextual knowers and constructivists because of their varied experience, or they may turn away from the apparent chaos to a non-intellectual life. Their learning will depend to a great extent on the message that faculty and institutions give them about the nature of intellectual endeavor.

This chapter begins with a comparison of learning across the disciplines examined in the social sciences and humanities, paralleling that done for the natural sciences in Chapter Four (Exhibit 4.3). Then overall comparisons are made of the sociological contexts provided by disciplines and the thinking and validation processes students are expected to learn. I examine and compare the thinking processes used generally in the disciplines and respond to issues raised in the previous chapters about the relative importance of the thinking processes. The final cross-disciplinary comparison is of the instructional challenges each discipline presents. I conclude with a discussion of steps that administrators, faculty, and students might take to improve the intellectual context, and the perspective of students on their learning.

Comparison of Learning in the Social Sciences and Humanities

Complexity, antinomies, and diversity characterize the four disciplines investigated in the social sciences and humanities: psychology, law, education, and English literature. Each deals with phenomena at a broader or more inclusive level than do the natural sciences. Scholars in these areas ask questions that require multifaceted answers. Why do people behave in the way they do? Who is responsible? How can we help people learn? What is genuine authority? These questions are abstract yet socially driven; human, subjective experience is the genesis of study.

What do these disciplines have in common and what differentiates them? What is to be learned by students entering these fields? (See Exhibit 9.1.) In psychology, students must learn methods of empirical analysis and theory construction. In law, the methods of analysis depend on a history of practice that must be learned. In education, students need to understand the disciplines they are responsible for teaching, and how to design instructional practices to fit learners' needs. In English, students must analyze texts for their meaning and apply an aesthetic criterion in addition to others.

The social sciences and humanities share an emphasis on conceptual frameworks or questions rather than on specific concepts, as in the natural sciences. Human science concepts are more inclusive, particularly in the humanities. There are more varied reasoning processes than in the natural sciences. Reasoning results in the creation of theoretical frameworks, as in psychology, or application of a precedent in law. A student's reasoning path in education leads to a plan of action in the classroom. In English literature, argument and interpretation mark the reasoning process.

EXHIBIT 9.1. COMPARISON OF LEARNING IN
SOCIAL SCIENCE AND HUMANITIES DISCIPLINES

Discipline	Nature of Discipline	What Is to Be Learned	Expectations of Entering Students	Instructional Methods
Psychology	Ranges from hard to soft, highly structured to complex; multifaceted, pure to applied, young, preparadigmatic; intermediate convergence	New abstract vocabulary, theoretical frameworks; analytic reasoning; research methods: observation, experiment, measurement, analysis, theory construction	Ability to think logically, independently, abstractly	*Found:* lecturing, seminars, discussion, reading reference material. *Optimal:* applying science to human experience, problem solving, organizing conceptual frameworks
Law	Ancient advanced faculty, insular; soft; applied, profession dominates academy; intermediate (limited) convergence	Abstract technical terminology; logic, analysis, analogy; how the reasonable person would act; statute and precedent; professional practice, skills and values	Ability to describe a legal situation, choose information relevant to the case, think logically	*Found:* Socratic questioning in lectures, casebook. *Optimal:* open to a variety of opinions and values, teams working on case studies, joint venture exercise, computer exercises
Education	Soft, applied, comprehensive, diverse; metascience science, social science, amalgam of disciplines, or profession?	Understanding the conceptual frameworks of the subject matter disciplines, the institutional context, how to represent and adapt subject matter to learners, how to design instructional processes for optimal learning	A relatively fragmented knowledge of their subject areas; ability to think logically, in an internally consistent manner, independently	*Found:* class discussion, cooperative learning, group projects, student development activities, student-selected topics. *Optimal:* interviewing or following a learner, constructivist framework, apprenticeship

(Continued)

EXHIBIT 9.1. CONTINUED.

Discipline	Nature of Discipline	What Is to Be Learned	Expectations of Entering Students	Instructional Methods
English literature	Soft, unbounded, pure, argumentative, interpretive, divergent	Technical language, assessment of value of literary texts, decoding text, training in sensibility, modes of perceiving	Intuition and sensibility rather than logic	*Found:* lectures, tutorials, group work, performance *Optimal:* reengaging in controversies, semester devoted to analysis of inquiry processes

The instructional methods demand input and creativity from students. There is more discussion, more emphasis on experiential learning with cases or projects, and the kind of performance demanded differs from that in the natural sciences by being more comprehensive. Students take on roles as researchers or therapists, lawyers, teachers, or critics in their course activities; situational learning and apprenticeship are important parts of the instructional context. Professors in these disciplines, and especially educators, are more likely to use instructional methods that require cooperative, collaborative learning and performance. At the same time, because of the looser disciplinary structure, students may not as readily distinguish what the learning task is in the social sciences and humanities, and how much is expected of them (Exhibit 9.1).

The difference in the degree of structure in the learning tasks is reflected in the variation in student work habits we found in our cross-disciplinary research. When surveyed three weeks into the term, science students were spending much more time on their studies than arts students. By the end of term, however, arts students were putting in the same number of hours or more. There was a gradual increase in pressure to perform in the social science and humanities courses, primarily because of assessment methods. In the natural sciences, problems and labs had to be completed and handed in early in the term, frequently on a weekly basis. This meant that students could not procrastinate. In the arts courses, however, performance was required often for the first time at midterm, six or seven weeks into the course. Larger class sizes contributed to the sense of intellectual anomie. Thus arts students could remain relatively oblivious to the demands of their course only to discover halfway through it that much more was required of them. This raises questions of our responsibility to inform our students about the demands of their courses and how we prepare them for their task as learners. These questions are part of the larger issue of creating an intellectual context to which we will return.

Comparison of the Sociological Context Across Disciplines

In this book we began each analysis of a discipline with an assessment of the context in which professors teach and students learn, viewed from without and within. The context provided by a discipline differs in many ways sociologically: in relative power or status in an institution, attitudes toward political and social issues, economic status, degree of social convergence or divergence, how concentrated the research pattern, the personalities of members, and how closely the discipline adheres to core academic values. Comparisons along these different dimensions produce conflicting rankings that enrich the portrayal but also show the complexity of relationships among the disciplines.

The most frequently studied sociological dimension across disciplines is the power conferred by research scholarship, but other dimensions have been found to affect student decisions about the path they will take. In his study of French universities, Bourdieu (1988) posits that power is distributed along two axes, scientific and social, with the principal continuum being that of scientific activity measured by the amount of time professors spend on research and their conception of scholarship. The greatest difference along this continuum is between the natural sciences and the social sciences and humanities; a greater proportion of time is spent in research than in teaching in the natural sciences and a greater proportion of time is spent in teaching in the social sciences and humanities.

The characteristic that shows the greatest social differentiation between disciplines in Bourdieu's study, however, is one that has been rarely considered by other postsecondary researchers: the socioeconomic and educational status of professors' families, which he calls intellectual capital. To illustrate, in France professors of law and medicine have substantially higher inherited intellectual capital than professors in science and arts; that is, the more educated the family, the more likely the offspring are to pursue occupations in the professions that developed from the ancient advanced faculties. For Bourdieu there are two competing principles of legitimation in the university: sociopolitical power, and the autonomy of the scientific and intellectual order. Applied to students' choice of entry into specific fields, the higher their family's socioeconomic and educational status, the less likely students are to pursue a program of study in the physical sciences.

The outcome, given general rising economic status, could be calamitous for the sciences and science-dependent industry. This is an issue that undoubtedly requires further study.

Disciplinary attitudes toward political and social issues range from progressive or liberal to conservative, but political inclinations in disciplines are consistent across national borders and time with few exceptions. Academics tend to be more liberal or to the left than the average citizen. In the university, the social sciences are farthest to the left, followed by the humanities (Huber, 1990). The natural sciences fall in the middle, with physics to the left of chemistry; engineering and medicine are on the right. Law, the exception to this disciplinary rule, appears at the right in Europe, but on the liberal wing in the United States. Huber points out that political tendency is associated with both inherited and current economic status, and in the university salaries vary according to opportunities for professional practice or funded research. This has a confounding instructional side effect. In disciplines where more external funding is available, there tend to be fewer students to care for. For example, similar to the relative size of research funds available in North America, Huber found the percentage of external funds to academic staff in Germany in the humanities to be .4, whereas in the natural sciences it was 1.3 and in engineering it was 2.4. The student-staff ratio in the humanities was 20 to 1, while in the natural sciences and engineering it was 10 to 1 and 11 to 1, respectively. Thus in disciplinary areas with greater numbers of students, there is less external financial support.

Students entering these disciplines would, therefore, encounter different contexts both in potential access to professors and in social and financial support. If they choose the sciences, in addition to smaller classes and greater opportunities for financial support they may also be more likely to experience the support offered by *social convergence*—a sense of commonality or collective kinship, mutuality of interests, shared intellectual style, and consensual understanding of principles. This dimension is distinct from the degree of epistemological structure across disciplines. Physics may be one example of social convergence, but Becher (1989) notes that history also is sociologically convergent because its members share a strong tradition of intellectual kinship. He classifies law, chemistry, and biology as occupying intermediate ground, and engineering and modern languages as divergent—the engineers because they lack a collective view and those in modern languages because they advocate conflicting theories. Thus despite differences in external funding in their disciplines, rugged independence may of necessity characterize both the successful engineering student and the student of English literature.

The concentration of research resources in specific areas of study in a discipline— for example, in consortia or centers—adds another criterion for discrimination among the disciplines, although more likely felt only at advanced levels of study. The harder the science, the more concentrated the research resources, with physics at the pinnacle and biochemistry also qualifying, according to Becher. He found, however, that concentration of major resources and research activity was rare outside of physics. In most disciplinary areas undergraduate students are not likely to be immediately affected by a pattern of concentrated research, but the prestige attached to recognized scholarly activity could be expected to filter down. At the graduate level, students would be likely to receive fellowships or funds to present a paper or to witness how the discipline operates at annual meetings depending on the disciplinary resource level. As funding for natural science research consortia increases, we could expect differences in practices between physical and social sciences and humanities to be accentuated.

In his anthropological study of the disciplines, Becher found that professors described themselves in terms of personal characteristics: engineers identified themselves as practical and conforming, biologists as gregarious yet committed. Law professors were regarded by others as distant if impressive. Students also describe themselves in terms of their personal proclivities. In one multinational study, undergraduate science students saw themselves as more introverted than extroverted, more task-oriented than people-oriented, tough rather than tender-minded, more interested in ideas, and able to communicate better in diagrams than in words (Woolnough et al., 1997). In most countries science students saw themselves as cleverer than nonscientists, but in Japan the reverse occurred. According to the authors, a scientific home background and a student's ability and personality predicted whether he or she would continue in science programs, thus perpetuating the stereotype.

The final sociological dimension discriminating among disciplines is proximity to core academic values. For Clark (1987), academic values reside in scientific scholarship and in a liberal education; the most scientific among the sciences and the most enduring established humanities define what is scholarly. According to this analysis, students in physics and chemistry or in history and English literature would enjoy the greater scholarly prestige of their disciplines than students in the social sciences or professions. Academic longevity provides status, and pure disciplines a form of intellectual coinage. Thus the relative longevity of English literature as a discipline might balance its questionable political clout due to epistemological divergence. Other characteristics, such as personal meaning or social utility, are often greater factors in students' choice of disciplines such as psychology or education.

To what extent do these sociological differences affect learning? Learning should be aided by convergence in a discipline, because convergence reinforces learning from one course in the program to the next (Exhibit 9.2). Whether higher-order learning more readily occurs in convergent disciplines is a question that merits and requires further study. More prestigious or better-funded disciplines could be expected to provide higher extrinsic motivation and more resources to students.

EXHIBIT 9.2. COMPARISON OF THE
SOCIOLOGICAL CONTEXT ACROSS DISCIPLINES

Discipline	Context
Physics	Convergent, well organized Concentrated research groups and teams; enormously costly High prestige from effect on communications, transportation, energy, space Selective and exclusive
Engineering	Divergent, pivots about the technology-based, industrial corporation Entrepreneurial and cosmopolitan Practical and pragmatic, conservative, conformist, hardworking Stresses utility and safety
Chemistry	Second in intellectual hierarchy to physics More divergent than physics Biochemistry is area of most concentrated research Agricultural and pharmaceutical benefits
Biology	Intermediate convergence Expansive but fragmented Tolerates divergent values Serves medicine
Psychology	Young; wide variety of subfields and interests A science, but affected by culture Has role of social prediction and control Potentially emancipatory
Law	Prestigious, traditional Limited convergence; profession dominates the academy Insular, atheoretical, ad hoc, case-oriented, functional, utilitarian Responsive to recent experience and service-oriented; question of critical ideological function
Education	Fundamental societal role; transformative Interprets other disciplines Highly accountable High social utility and relevance
English literature	Divergent and diverse, resistant to categorization Conflicts in role between sacred and secular, aesthetic and practical Is interpenetrated by wider culture Characterized by intellectual ferment

Social relevance or utility may also be motivating to students. The disciplines in this analysis that could be expected to have more difficult learning tasks, however, are the divergent, such as English literature, and those that have multiple or extended goals. Thus the applied fields—engineering, with design dependent on problem solving, and education, with a two-tiered task of persuading the young to learn other disciplines—may have this distinction.

Some sociologists of higher education have argued that the social structure of a scholarly community produces its intellectual characteristics (Fuchs, 1992). For example, because of the indistinct boundaries and loose internal control systems in the humanities, hermeneutic and interpretive orientations are found. Does this imply that the social structure and thus the epistemological structure of disciplines can be altered? Attempts to change the way disciplines operate have had effects on the learning context; in my own experience, establishing a separate grants committee for educational research meant that more funding became available to investigate educational questions and to support students. Braxton and Hargens (1996) note the difficulty of ascribing cause to social-epistemological interaction. If cause *could* be ascribed, the sociological context would probably have a greater effect on professors than on students, or context may affect students only indirectly. Thus although the sociological characteristics of disciplines provide insights into the learning milieu and forewarning, factors likely to have greater impact on learning reside within the disciplines. We therefore turn to an examination of epistemological characteristics across disciplines in a comparison of the thinking and validation processes.

Comparison of Thinking and Validation Processes Across Disciplines

Thinking in different disciplines shows conspicuous trends from deductive to interpretive. At the most structured and delimited end of the continuum, deductive reasoning is used—inference based on a general law or premise leading necessarily to a conclusion. Less structured disciplines tend to use inductive reasoning, moving from the particular to the general and based on frequency of occurrence or probability. Further along the continuum are specific cases and arguments built around the cases (Exhibit 9.3). The methods essential for understanding are specific to each field. In physics, engineering, and chemistry, for example, the problem constitutes the framework for thinking but the process of thinking varies. The unknown in physics comes in the form of hypothesizing potential situations. In engineering one must solve a problem without having all of the information needed;

EXHIBIT 9.3. COMPARISON OF THINKING AND VALIDATION PROCESSES ACROSS DISCIPLINES

	Terms Used to Describe Thinking	Examples of Thinking	Validation Processes
Physics	Problem solving, analysis and synthesis, visualization, deductive logic	Experimentation, scientific explanation, what if?	Matching evidence to systematic theorizing A reasonable answer, plausible, within expected limits
Engineering	Problem solving Design Mathematical modeling of physical systems	Problem solving where all the needed information is not known Using procedural knowledge	Does it work? approximate or within certain limits
Chemistry	Deductive and inductive problem solving	Transforming a nonroutine problem Guided inquiry	Experiment—range of methods of analysis match varying levels of specificity
Biology	Inductive, phenomenological, inferential, Uses powerful metaphors	Varied consequences of various hypotheses Regulatory networks	Questioning results and conclusions
Psychology	Skeptical investigation Research methods— experimental technique Understanding oneself Analytic reasoning	Writing reports Evaluating previous research in a field Identifying problems to be investigated Questioning assumptions in an argument	Interrater reliability Empirical testing
Law	Thinking like a lawyer Solving puzzles Legal analysis using syllogism and analogy Factual investigation	Analyze facts, appreciate the shifting legal results produced by factual nuances Derive legal conclusion in the light of legal doctrine	Human authority Evolving tradition Legal evidence Witnesses Logic versus value Winning a case— convincing a judge to accept an argument

	Terms Used to Describe Thinking	Examples of Thinking	Validation Processes
Education	Pedagogical reasoning Expert processes Transforming text Evaluating Reflecting	Representing ideas in the form of new analogies or metaphors Specific problem solving in the classroom	Practical judgments Comparing options and triangulating evidence Authenticity and utility Ecological validity
English literature	Hermeneutics Interpretation Literary analysis– criticism Imagination Rhetoric	Close reading: taking meaning from text Bridging gaps and integrating textual elements Analyzing the organizing principle that unifies a work's elements and identifies its uniqueness	Critique of others' claims Rhetorical reflexivity weakens validity Peer review, credibility, and plausibility Testing the parts against the whole

the problem solver must extrapolate. In chemistry the thinking process is a matter of transforming problems into a recognizable structure. In each of these disciplines, however, structure and procedure prevail.

In biology and psychology, the methods employed are more varied, appropriate to the greater variation in phenomena studied; hypothesis development and testing are central. The concept-mapping research revealed a lower ratio of links to concepts in the biology and psychology courses (.92 and .64, respectively) than in physics and chemistry (1.33 and 1.15, respectively), which indicates a looser or more data-dense structure in the biological sciences and psychology. In these disciplines the problems or hypotheses must first be identified, and various consequences are possible based on the framework or system applied. At this intermediate level of structure, methods of thinking include a review of possible frameworks from the literature, and proof of thinking is found in the reports written by students on their labs or experiments.

Law and education also require multifaceted puzzle solution and transformation. The examples of thinking shown in Exhibit 9.3 illustrate the need to recognize the particular situation and respond to it. In law this takes place in a larger framework set out by statute and precedent; in education the subject matter discipline and pedagogical knowledge provide the framework. These applied social sciences do not lack structure: in the concept maps, the ratio of links to concepts parallels that of the physical sciences, 1.36 in law and 1.15 in education. From our examination of the structure of knowledge in law and education, *statute* and *precedent* are more codified forms of knowledge than the pedagogical content knowledge that links the instructional process with different subject matter disciplines. The would-be teacher has a more difficult search for a framework to apply.

At the least structured and most inclusive end of the continuum, varied forms of criticism supply potentially conflicting frameworks for thinking. In English literature, the hunt appears to be wide open, with a variety of perspectives to work from, but at the same time attention to historical accuracy and aesthetic sensibility are demanded. The logical structure displayed in the concept mapping research showed a ratio of one link per concept, thus structure is balanced by data. Given this context, the student must focus on the text while scanning for modes of interpreting it, then compare the effects of different forms of criticism or synthesize the results from different perspectives.

Differences between the pure and applied disciplines reside primarily in the necessity in the applied areas of building active models or frameworks. The function of application is to put a theory or model into practice, and this requires situational learning in which students have the opportunity to test their own cognitive frameworks or structures in a context where they must perform. Thus in engineering programs, learning in design or project courses is evaluated by means of student products, whereas in law, moot court and joint venture exercises are venues for testing skills. In education, students must show how they have tailored their own learners' experiences in the classroom; in English drama, performance describes the central outcome. The combination of being a hard and applied discipline puts greater performance pressure on engineering students, as engineering students and professors commented.

The different validation processes used in the disciplines show a trend in where authority resides—from the objective empirical to peers. In more structured disciplines, evidence is matched to theory. Psychology occupies a middle position, where empirical testing and interrater reliability are both used as proof. Further into the human sciences, proof rests in evidence that will convince an authority in law, or test results in education, or in internal consistency rendering work plausible in English literature. In engineering and in education, one major criterion equilibrates the empirical and the judgment of others: Does it work? In law and in English literature the criterion is more specifically oriented to convincing others of one's case. In our studies of the validation processes used in the physical and social sciences and the humanities, differences were statistically significant; the thinking processes *are* particular to each discipline. However, consistencies in the use of certain specific thinking processes across disciplines suggests that there are thinking processes a student in any discipline needs to acquire.

Greatest agreement across disciplines was found in the importance of students' learning to *identify the context* and *state assumptions,* and *change perspective,* and their learning the selection, representation, and synthesis processes (Exhibit 9.4). *Identifying the context* may include setting up the general framework for a problem, recognizing what kind of problem they are dealing with, finding where a framework fits the processes being studied, or recognizing the history of the period in which text was written. *Stating assumptions* is critical to solving a problem, recognizing bias, perspective, or the framework being applied, or considering the steps to be taken or individuals to be taken into account. The general importance of *changing perspective* is consistent with the need for a constructivist or postmodern approach to knowledge.

All disciplines acknowledge that because of the abundance of information and phenomena, students must learn to select. Representation describes the structure in each discipline. The general importance of representation as a thinking process lies in its providing conceptual frameworks. Because these are tacit in some disciplines, representation may not be talked about as frequently as inference is, but it is essential to constructivist thinking. Synthesis plays a particular role across the disciplines. It results in laws in physics. Engineering professors approach synthesis as a goal for their students, training them in design skills in team projects. In education, synthesis is important for bringing together all the elements of the classroom situation. In English literature, although multiplicity and paradox are the hallmarks, the search for form is central.

Are these more general thinking processes? They originate in different methods of inquiry or conceptualizations of thinking; for example, *identifying the context* is the mark of the expert, whereas *stating assumptions* is a defining characteristic of critical thinking. Selection has been cast in the more general role of defining intelligence, while representation and synthesis are found in the problem-solving literature. *Changing perspective* and *confirming results* are found more generally in methods of inquiry—in expertise, problem solving, and critical thinking (see Exhibit 1.9). The general agreement on the importance of these thinking processes suggests that they are foundational to postsecondary learning. What if professors in the different disciplines advised students that these were processes they needed to learn whatever course of study they were pursuing? What if these processes were deliberately taught and assessed in each course?

Trends across disciplines in representation parallel the degree of structure in them. In *organizing principles,* there is a continuum from strong to weak schemas—from laws in physics, models in engineering, theories in psychology, small working models in education, to the questioning of structure in English. Professors could

EXHIBIT 9.4. MOST IMPORTANT THINKING
PROCESSES USED GENERALLY ACROSS DISCIPLINES

Process	Definition
Identify the context	Establish surrounding environment to create a total picture.
State assumptions	State suppositions, postulates, or propositions assumed.
SELECTION:	
Choose relevant information	Select information that is pertinent to the issue in question.
Order information in importance	Rank, arrange in importance or according to significance.
Identify critical elements	Determine units, parts, components that are important.
Identify critical relations	Determine connections between things that are important.
REPRESENTATION:	
Recognize organizing principles	Identify laws, methods, rules that arrange in a systematic whole.
Organize elements and relations	Arrange parts, connections between things into a systematic whole.
Illustrate elements and relations	Make clear by examples the parts, connections between things.
Modify elements and relations	Change, alter, or qualify the parts, connections between things.
Change perspective	Alter view, vista, interrelations, significance of facts or information.
SYNTHESIS:	
Combine parts to form a whole	Join, associate elements, components into a system or pattern.
Elaborate	Work out, complete with great detail, exactness, or complexity.
Generate missing links	Produce or create what is lacking in a sequence, fill in the gap.
Develop a course of action	Work out or expand the path, route, or direction to be taken.
Confirm results	Establish or ratify conclusions, effects, outcomes, or products.

use these examples to explain the nature of organizing principles in their discipline in contrast to those in others. Types of illustration show a slightly different pattern. Physics uses graphs, engineering has similar but more extensive systems, and psychology has metaphor and examples, as does education, along with stories that link and relate. In English literature, the process is reversed, because representation is in the text rather than superordinate to it as in other disciplines. Inference also varies depending on the degree of structure in the discipline, with physicists doing experiments, engineers solving problems, psychologists formulating general principles from evidence, and English literature searching for possible meanings. Verification processes differ so much that they are defining characteristics of the disciplines. The degree of structure and the need to develop thinking abilities are themes that continue in the challenges to instruction.

Challenges to Instruction Across Disciplines

Distinctive challenges are raised in each of the disciplines investigated in this book, but there are also points of convergence. Improving problem solving is important in the physical sciences; physics professors consider that students need to conceptualize, then develop problem-solving skills (Exhibit 9.5). Engineering professors consider problem solving the first challenge. In chemistry, dealing with information overload and the student response of memorization precedes the challenge of problem solving. The same problem of information fragmentation and overload must be dealt with in biology, but higher-order principles such as *system properties* provide for the possibility of categorizing, or chunking. In psychology, the same kind of organizing concepts, such as *universal bias* or *mind as knower*, serve to contextualize. Both disciplines take varied approaches to improving reasoning processes, psychology pointedly introducing students to the research process at the undergraduate level.

The social sciences and humanities deal with paradoxes or antinomies. Less structured disciplines are not merely fuzzy; they have contradictory principles or values that are continually in question and hence require perspective. In psychology the stances tend to be treated as variation or diversity on a continuum (mind as a reflex machine or mind as knower), but in law and education values are more likely to be polarized (the basics versus progressive education, for example), whereas dispute defines English literary criticism. Since law and education operate as both disciplines and professions, they must develop complex frameworks for action and specific skills that allow practitioners to solve problems in particular situations and to develop the judgment to apply appropriate strategies. Education has perhaps the most enormous challenge: to understand the other disciplines and

EXHIBIT 9.5. COMPARISON OF CHALLENGES TO INSTRUCTION ACROSS DISCIPLINES AND RESPONSES TO THEM

	Challenge	Response
Physics	Develop a mental model for learning	Active reorganization of material; conceptual instruction
	Improve the ability to problem-solve	Teachers model strategy for solving the problem; working groups, wrap-up discussions
	Enlighten students about successful learning	Active testing, collaboration, debate of findings
Engineering	Gain problem-solving ability	Student-centered, project work, workshop courses; teach students "how to fish"
	Gain design skills	Practice on open-ended projects including group dynamic skills, self-assessment, using a set of criteria to judge designs
	Application in the industrial, economic milieu	Ecological and psychosocial contexts in which technical products must be optimized; communication, leadership, and teamwork skills
Chemistry	Deal with severe information overload	Integration of tutorial, lecture, and lab; content reduction; real-life application
	Deal with rote and algorithmic propensities	Microscopic representation of problems, opportunity for students to construct knowledge for themselves, Vee diagrams, concept maps
	Improve problem-solving skills	Assessment by a mix of conceptual and traditional problems, structured cooperative learning for homework and quizzes, use of e-mail
Biology	Connect facts and labels	Show the integrating principles that make learning meaningful, such as *system properties*
	Improve reasoning ability, make learning relevant	Problem-based learning
	Make learning process a meaningful challenge	Create a community of learners

Psychology	Link scientific knowledge with students' interests	Metaprinciples; global concepts; questions such as, "What would you change in your life?"
	Learn the research process	Gradual introduction, script for doing research
Law	Build a framework for legal knowledge	Work in greater depth on case studies; model legal process through simulations
	Develop legal analysis skills	Modules, bridge building, computer exercises
	Investigate values	Fieldwork in legal clinic, instruction in negotiation
Education	Deal with folk pedagogies, epistemologies, or beliefs	Actively question beliefs to change attitudes
	Develop pedagogical knowledge	Long-term process; interviewing, following a learner
	Develop thinking processes	Respect others' understanding, their learners' minds
English literature	Cope with breadth of discipline	Legitimate text, primary or canon
	Cope with multiplicity of approaches	Demonstrate effectiveness of competing theories
	Combine passion and aesthetics	Read to imagine being someone other than ourselves, training in sensibility

introduce young learners to them. The scope of the challenge in education is matched by the illimitable realm of English literature in the choice of what is to be studied and the multitude of approaches. Ferment is most prominent in literary studies, but some energizing force must be present in order for students to learn in any discipline.

Each discipline has suggested ways of dealing with the challenges to instruction, and these approaches or strategies could prove useful in others. Given the need to help students establish a scholarly approach to learning, optimal approaches are those that integrate learning experiences so that students can see the consequences of their learning and actively problem-solve to complete a task. This may occur in a workshop, laboratory, field situation, or simulation exercise. Another optimal approach is to use a work, study, or problem group where members must define, organize, and resolve a problem. A third is a contextualizing experience where students have the opportunity to see a panorama of possibilities, such as standing issues in psychology or the metaprinciples or theories that shape the field. When students must make choices about where they themselves stand, whether in solving conceptual problems in a physics class or in a pedagogical situation, they actively invest their energies. An exchange of methods across disciplines may not only vitalize instruction but acknowledge that students are studying in several of these areas at the same time and that the challenge to help them develop intellectually is a general one.

Helping Students to Develop Intellectually

Creating an environment that will alert students to the possibility of higher-order learning and then sustain their endeavor requires strategies on several levels. A survey of the educational environment students encounter in postsecondary institutions explains why. The learning environment is not the classroom but the entire campus, and with the increasing use of technology and distance learning it extends well beyond the campus. Undergraduate students report to us that their learning takes place when they do their assignments, not in the classroom. On the traditional campus, in addition to approximately fifteen hours per week in classes of varying size and constitution, learning settings include the library, laboratory, computer cubicle, cafeteria, work or field placements, and the student's own room. To assist students to develop intellectually we need to create a learning context that is sufficiently coherent to be manageable and supportive for them, and to explain to them how it functions.

Accomplishing this requires focusing attention at three levels: the institution, faculty, and students themselves. At the level of the institution, policies are needed to establish a supportive learning context (Exhibit 9.6). Faculty have the responsibility of showing how knowledge is organized in their discipline and how they think, and then interacting with students to ensure higher-order learning outcomes. Students need to become aware of their role and responsibilities as learners. Some of the strategies suggested here have received support in the higher education community, but others have not yet been widely entertained and may entail considerable adaptation.

Understanding the Institutional Context and Ensuring a Supportive Learning Community

Students need a sense of the goals of their college or university and the program they have chosen. Knowledge about the institution and its programs, and about ways of getting things done, is usually tacit, briefly introduced in hazily

EXHIBIT 9.6. CREATING AN INTELLECTUAL CONTEXT

Understanding the institutional context and ensuring a supportive learning community:
Clarify institutional educational objectives, and the character of the community and culture. Instill a sense of the importance of scholarly learning and a sense of community.

Providing the disciplinary context and promoting higher-order learning:
Provide an overview of the discipline, the way in which the subject matter is organized, and the methods used to validate this knowledge. Explain specific educational goals and purposes. Organize, manage, arrange learning activities to achieve higher-order outcomes. Respond to student conceptions, misconceptions, aptitudes, attention, motivation, and stage of development.

Helping students to become autonomous, committed learners:
Create a context for students so that they understand that their learning depends primarily on the quality of effort they put into their work, and show them how to accomplish this. Assess their understanding and competence; monitor their performance.

---

remembered orientation sessions or learned by word of mouth. Web sites and home pages increasingly supply information about the institution, but they rarely tell students where they fit in. Awareness of the campus climate means not only being up-to-date on campus issues and policies but participating in the governance of the institution. Students need an explanation of why they should and how they can actively participate in campus governance and more generally in the campus community. We know that involvement and integration into an academic community has a major effect on student achievement (Pascarella & Terenzini, 1991, 1998). However, according to the National Survey of Student Engagement (NSSE) (Indiana University, 2000), most first-year students (60 percent) in American universities spend five or fewer hours per week in extracurricular activities, including participating in organizations, campus publications, student government, a social fraternity or sorority, or intercollegiate or intramural sports, and seniors spend even less time on these kinds of activities. If extracurricular activities are vital to student learning, then an effort must be made to explain their value.

Although the idea of the learning community in higher education has been promoted over the last decade, students' sense of community does not reflect this effort (Hawkey, 2000). The primary reason for learning communities is that they promote relationships and provide a psychologically manageable environment (Davis & Murrell, 1993). In a psychologically manageable environment, students perceive that learning in general and their own development in particular is supported. As part of a research project, I explored how institutions develop policies to guide campus practice (Donald, 1997). One university had pledged to support scholarly learning as the central mission of the university. Each fall, students are greeted at a convocation in which the values of the institution and the expectations for students and other members of the community are spelled out. Instilling a sense of the importance of a learning community is a challenge for the entire campus.

Another reason to promote a supportive learning community is that students often arrive on campus newly independent and ready to test their newfound independence from family and hometown constraints. Although this independence is consistent with their stage of development and the amount of knowledge they have acquired, it means they are less likely to approach authorities or inquire about the context. At the same time, students frequently lack the strategies needed for independent learning, so their own desired independence may work against their success in learning. It is therefore important to create a sense of relatedness among learners, and an openness to experience and to others. This is consistent with the recognition that the student learning environment extends beyond an individual course. The sense of being a member of a learning community can be aided by block-scheduling, so that students take a series of classes together (Tinto, 1998), or by organizing themes that link courses within programs. In programs, frequently found ways to ensure supportive learning communities include department colloquia in which members talk about their research to others, brown bag lunches at which professors and students debate important issues, research teams that include students in collaboration on specific projects, and first-year seminars that introduce students to the educational context more generally.

Policies that support student participation in the learning community are a first step. Giving an institution a soul is not easy, but historical markers, the presence of alumni, and an expectation of participation in campus activities alert students to the larger context. In a review of the results of the national survey of student engagement, Kuh (2001) maintains that academic policy can directly influence practices that contribute strongly to student engagement, such as requiring capstone courses, creating higher expectations, and enhancing student satisfaction with the learning environment. He also notes that day-to-day behaviors like student-faculty contact are harder to change, and that active and collaborative learning require more fundamental changes in campus cultures.

Service learning, where students combine some form of community service with their course or program requirements, has proven useful in promoting both engagement and thinking skills (Eyler & Giles, 1999). The opportunity to test theories and conceptual frameworks in a community setting, as in the law program described in Chapter Six where students could elect to work in a campus legal clinic or with community organizations, enables students to understand and apply knowledge. Positive outcomes include changes in perspective, high engagement, reflective practice, and citizenship. According to one of our professors who held a first-year seminar on community and social welfare, students learned thinking processes by "looking at the world around them and trying to figure out what was wrong with it and why, and what you do about it. Students met dynamic people in the community centers and in the community organizations that led them to ask these questions." A critical feature ensuring the success of service learning courses is that they integrate course content with community activities. In the community and social welfare course, for example:

> Students had to read materials on the welfare state, poverty, and community. They then discussed the text in class each week. They also had to go out in groups of three or four and do neighborhood walks, to meet people in the community clinic, and in the community organizations, and report on what they had done. They had to do problem-solving exercises around community intervention. They were able to learn about what people do in relation to poverty—how people intervene in the lives of the poor at the community level.

In an assessment project designed to evaluate the effectiveness of university practice and find ways to improve it, Harvard students made numerous suggestions about what academic leaders could do to improve student life on campus (Light, 2001). One overarching suggestion was that a policy of inclusion is essential for students to learn from each other. Because students are assigned to their residences in mixed groups, they learn to respect and learn from diversity and extend that principle to their intellectual development. Students strongly advocated that academic leaders convey to incoming students that they have a once-in-a-lifetime opportunity to experience a new set of people and a new set of ideas that may challenge their own. Harvard sends incoming students a booklet of essays about students' experiences finding common ground there, and how others have transformed the process of living together into a great learning experience. Attitudes are a crucial part of the experience; Light suggests that students should assume goodwill on the part of other students, and try to understand how other people think and how they think about themselves. Central to ensuring a community is a shared understanding of the process of learning. This leads us back to the question of what models of learning we are using and how much consensus there is in and across programs of study on the nature of the learning task.

Providing Disciplinary Context and Promoting Higher-Order Learning

In the review of models of learning in use in Chapter Five, I raised the question of whether we have a theory paradox in postsecondary education between atomistic associationist and molar constructivist approaches to learning. Association theory gives us an understanding of the importance of using key concepts in lectures, and also why students benefit from practice with a series of problem sets to solve and from frequent tests. Constructivist theory suggests that students need to actively select and organize their own knowledge, and hence need discussion, collaboration, and project work. The disciplines send a deeper and more demanding message that only faculty can deliver about scholarly inquiry.

Faculty of necessity must play an important role in formulating an explanation of the context and process of scholarly inquiry, how it governs their lives, and how students have the opportunity to engage in this process. Implementing this principle requires successfully negotiating numerous impediments in the academic world—time limitations, a surfeit of priorities, the demands of specialization, and academic freedom, to name a few. But our students tell us that without our taking responsibility to build a scholarly community, they will flounder. One of my earliest academic learning experiences occurred when, as a new professor at the university's center for learning and development, I was responsible for evaluating some fifty courses given in a modular format and thus self-paced and designed for independent learning. Students reported that above all they wanted contact with their professors and guidance in the pacing of their work. The lesson learned is that the need for contact is fundamental and must be taken into account when programs are planned and student-staff ratios are considered.

In the previous chapters the premise guiding discussion has been that disciplines provide homes within the larger learning community because they determine the discourse: the domain or parameters of knowledge, the theoretical or conceptual structures, and the mode of inquiry. Disciplines provide examples of systematic scholarly inquiry, and therefore serve as scaffolding for students in the process of exploring different ways of constructing meaning. In disciplines, faculty need to explain the main principles and tenets governing their field of study, describe how they establish and validate knowledge, and show the necessity for engaging in further research and discussion. Modeling inquiry in the discipline and explaining how theory is developed and tested is foundational to students' intellectual development.

This has important implications for how instruction is provided. The instructional dimension that has the highest correlation with student learning is teacher preparation or course organization (Feldman, 1989, 1996). Setting the syllabus, defining how the subject matter will be taught, and evaluating the results of students' attempts to learn in higher-order learning situations require more attention and resources than have previously been allocated to these tasks. Over the years in many disciplines the general trend has been for course content to become more specialized in accordance with, for example, the field coverage principle in English literature, and learning outcomes may not cohere with those in other courses or with higher-order learning objectives. Although at one point educators called for increased coherence and the provision of an overview of the disciplines

(Holmes Group, 1986), the means for accomplishing this are not readily available. One effect is that reviews of instructional programming may uncover more gaps than connections, and will necessitate fundamental program reconstruction.

To determine the scope of the discipline and its meaning for students, discussion of the concepts and methods of inquiry may need to be couched in a series of more general questions about the discipline itself. For example, What does the discipline do and how does it accomplish it? What questions does the discipline ask and how are these questions related to those asked in other fields? What are the guiding theoretical frameworks and ways of thinking? Schwab (1978) suggested in his analysis of the structure of the disciplines that the variety and number of structures in a discipline increase as one moves from the more specific (mathematics, physics) to the more inclusive (psychology, social sciences). He therefore asks educators to consider which elements of the more specific or reductive subject matter are constituents of their subject matter as a way of producing systematic knowledge across disciplines.

Another approach to defining a discipline is to ask: How does the expert in the discipline function? What effects does the discipline have on other disciplines and in the larger community? What are the unknowns? These are questions that members of most disciplines might find daunting to answer, and the analysis in this book has only begun the process, at the risk of creating chapters that are long, dense, and arduous for the reader. One professor commented that the process of determining the scope of a discipline would be expensive, time consuming, and labor intensive. Undertaking the process as a program of long-term research might be a viable approach.

A faculty team in the discipline or representative department could set out to determine the scope, knowledge base, and inquiry processes in courses and programs (see Bess, 2000; Donald, 2000). One might begin the discussion with how the main concepts and principles in the introductory course relate to other ideas in the field of study, and how to aid students to make these connections. In the survey of student engagement (Indiana University, 2000), just over half (53 percent) of the first-year students and 63 percent of the seniors reported that their coursework emphasized synthesizing and organizing ideas, information, or experiences into new, more complex interpretations and relationships. The definition and promotion of higher-order learning outcomes need to be discussed by program planners, from thinking through problems, developing reasoning skills, integrating and applying knowledge, developing creative capacities, more generally gaining a broader understanding of intellectual activity, and developing communication skills and self-understanding.

Planning involves examining and critically interpreting the materials available, detecting gaps, a lack of coherence, or antinomies, and determining where further research and discussion are needed. In our studies of knowledge structures in courses across disciplines, one of the most useful steps according to the participating professors was the creation of a concept map showing the relationships between major concepts in the course. We have used these methods to advantage in our course design workshops with professors from a range of disciplines. An extension of the techniques of determining the knowledge structures and skills to be developed in a course to the related courses in a program would provide learning coherence for students and professors. Research of this kind in a chemical engineering program led to redesign of the program with very positive results (Woods et al., 1997). A more difficult task, but worth the effort in terms of student learning, is showing students how different parts of the university or different courses in a program interact. These activities may also be disruptive in an institution, because they call on professors to add a broad planning function to their repertoire.

For the individual instructor, learning outcomes provide direction for the instructional strategy. If the learning outcome is gaining factual knowledge or learning fundamental principles, generalizations, or theories, for example, lectures and reading may be efficient methods to use. If the outcomes are higher order, however, such as problem solving or decision making, other methods that require students to manipulate the concepts or principles actively are needed. Light (2001) points out that if students are spending two to three times more time on their readings and assignments than in class, we should be paying far more attention to the details of homework assignments. A basic principle in the guidelines for learner-centered education is that relevant learning tasks of optimal difficulty and novelty are needed to stimulate curiosity, creativity, and higher-order thinking (American Psychological Association, 1993). Making learning goals transparent is the first challenge.

Students prefer teaching strategies that call for active and challenging learning in which they are involved, learning is connected to real life, and there are opportunities for mutual responsibility (Baxter Magolda, 1992). Yet, despite calls for reforming undergraduate education in the United States, in the ten-year period from the mid-1980s to the mid-1990s, the amount of active learning reported in American universities decreased or remained unchanged (Kuh & Hu, 2001). Over the same time frame, faculty contact with students tended to increase, but peer cooperation was unchanged. The survey shows that less than half (42 percent) of first-year students work with other students on projects during class often or very often (Indiana University, 2000).

Active learning techniques have been shown to have a powerful impact on student learning (Bonwell & Eison, 1991; Silberman, 1996). Methods of active learning range from team-building strategies and on-the-spot learning assessment strategies to modified lectures, class discussions, peer teaching, and independent learning. One particularly effective teaching method, according to students, is to organize classes around a controversy—for example, rent control or euthanasia—or conflicting theories and have students create opposing arguments (Light, 2001). Disciplinary antinomies are ideal candidates as centers of controversy. This method of structured disagreement brings out the best ideas for both sides and heightens student engagement.

Use of the new media and technology allows students to learn in a framework of situated cognition: students learn at a higher level if they are given problems or learning goals in a particular context so that they develop thinking abilities that can then be applied elsewhere (Brown, Collins, & Duguid, 1989). For example, engineering students have been asked to solve problems of access to campus buildings. The concretization of the learning goal enables them to develop models and frameworks that allow them to operate at higher levels of understanding, by beginning in a context and then expanding from it. Most important for student learning is their ability to use the new media to gain access to a variety of information sources to explore and then build their own conceptual frameworks. This adds another dimension to the professor's instructional role—evaluating available additional information sources.

In the classroom, building a sense of community means ensuring that examples are inclusive or representative of gender and ethnicity, and taking a flexible approach to the variety of learners in a class to get their attention and help them become active learners. Adaptation requires continual monitoring and insight into where students are having trouble learning. Ways to monitor learning include one-minute papers, in which students say what they are most puzzled about or would like clarification on, or what needs further discussion, as well as tutorials, question periods, and frequent brief tests with feedback to tailor instruction to student needs. Classroom assessment projects systematically allow instructors to enunciate their understanding of their teaching and learning goals and the ways in which they can assess how well they are achieving them (Angelo & Cross, 1994). For example, an instructor might choose to investigate the effects of providing students with the criteria on which their projects would be judged, and then have them judge the projects on those stated criteria. Afterward, the instructor would compare this method with others for the degree to which students achieved higher-order learning goals and improved attitudes toward learning.

Students remember professors who go beyond explaining the principles in their field to convey how those in the field think: how physicists think or how psychologists think (Light, 2001). In classes where professors ask questions or pose problems that help students learn to think like chemists or lawyers, students focus their learning and put it in context. Light describes how one professor noticed that a hush fell over the room whenever he began to talk about how he approached his work. Students were engaged and intent. Learning is also unforgettable when professors encourage students to disagree constructively with what they are saying. Posing a question such as "What is wrong with what I have just said?" may startle students but will show them that they are expected to think and to question. The invitation to enter into the debate asks students to take significant responsibility for their learning and their performance.

Helping Students Become Autonomous Committed Learners

Because postsecondary learning requires approaches or strategies that students may not yet have acquired, students need to be ready and willing to invest personally in learning, to be open to and aware of the changes that must take place in their way of thinking in order to develop intellectually. We know that the most important factor accounting for success in college after entering grades and Scholastic Aptitude Test scores is the quality of effort students put into their work, their productivity or perseverance (Pace, 1982; Willingham, 1985). Generally speaking, students need to be told that their own effort is the greatest contributor to their learning. One of the main reasons students get into trouble academically is the inability to engage with one piece of work in depth for hours at a time (Light, 2001). Overcommitment to other activities and poor time allocation for assignments spells disaster. Students must also constantly refine their thinking skills, and they must know that this is part of their education. My brother, five years my senior, gave me invaluable advice when I was setting off to college: to be aware that each year would be a new and more challenging learning experience. We need to tell our students this secret. Because students may lack a clear understanding of what the knowledge base and skills are and what their responsibilities as learners are, deliberate student advising is essential.

For students to control and organize their learning, they need first to have an understanding of what learning is, then have specific learning outcomes explained to them so they can strive toward them. Approaches that enable students to evolve in their intellectual functioning include providing them with a guiding analogy for learning, then modeling the strategies they need to use in order to understand and assess their own thinking. The choice of a specific approach should be predicated on the principle of supporting students' higher-order learning and progress in thinking. Individualized, problem-based, inquiry-based, experiential, and cooperative or collaborative learning methods all contribute to higher-order learning. We have seen that these methods are used to some extent in all disciplines, but that the social sciences and humanities use them more than the physical and biological sciences (Milem & Astin, 1994). At the same time, as we saw in the challenges to instruction in physics for conceptual learning, there is no less demand for higher-order thinking in the natural sciences.

The assessment process in courses and programs has a great effect on the way students approach learning. Often it tells students what they do not have to learn, especially if evaluation methods are limited to testing fragments of knowledge. The use of multiple-choice questions in large classes where the supposition is that the learning goal is the acquisition of knowledge has wreaked havoc on higher-order learning. Students in these classes learn not to think, but rather to memorize unrelated bytes of information. Yet questions that require thinking can be posed in a multiple-choice format in their instruction. Preferably, assessment is a process of evaluating student learning and development to improve learning, instruction, and program effectiveness. The kinds of assessment methods that require higher-order thinking are essays, presentations, and competency-based grading; grading on a curve has an insidious effect. Despite its dampening effect on students' attitudes toward learning—by indicating that students are not in control of their learning—22 percent of faculty still grade on a curve in all or most classes taught, with as many as 43 percent in engineering courses (Milem & Astin, 1994). This is evidently an area for program reconstruction.

Study strategies couched in principles of autonomous and lifelong learning, and explained as essential ways of taking charge, may be the most efficient approach to helping students take the necessary responsibility. Learning contracts offer a concrete example of taking responsibility; students choose certain pathways or options. They may opt for a specific grade based on a work plan that they design themselves. In the Harvard assessment project, most of the students said they learned significantly more in courses that are highly structured, with relatively many quizzes and short assignments (Light, 2001). Getting quick feedback from the professor is crucial so that students can revise their work. Homework assignments that are so challenging or complex that students must collaborate promote engagement and change the individualistic campus culture.

Self-assessment strategies help students build active and meaningful relationships with the material they are studying (Kusniac & Finley, 1993). Student self-assessment has the effect of personalizing students' learning and allowing them to take ownership of it while creating a sense of community (Eaton & Pougiales, 1993). Kusniac and Finley describe self-assessment as consisting of an attitude of inquiry, requiring integration of learning from other courses and previous understanding or experience, which in turn creates meaning and relevance in the learning situation. It is self-directed; that is, students identify the questions that emerge for them and become conscious of themselves as learners, and they then connect more actively with the learning context. The context may include entire courses or programs, or specific exercises for planning learning or reflecting on it, as in journal keeping or one-minute papers on what was learned in class in the last hour, which in turn aid the instructional process of adaptation.

University students rate a commitment to learning as the most important criterion of their own quality (Donald & Denison, 2001). They also rate an ability to analyze, synthesize, and think critically and a commitment to lifelong learning as highly important. In addition to recognizing the need for lifelong development, graduates should be capable of finding things out for themselves through disciplined inquiry and by applying what they know to solving problems to improve society. They should be able to use insights and methods derived from various fields of study and practice, and to explain what they know to colleagues and to members of the public. We can expect the learning goals of postsecondary education to expand rather than contract in the twenty-first century.

Creating a stimulating intellectual context for student higher-order learning may be the ultimate goal of this book, but the principal substantive value may lie in the portrayals of the disciplines that allow professors to compare how they see the context in which they operate. Creating a stimulating intellectual context for the members of an academic community is a more difficult, perhaps Herculean task. One question that the findings in this book raise is to what extent the disciplines have stated ends. It was not an easy task to decipher the epistemological principles the disciplines use to define themselves; much fuzziness remains at the edges. Does a discipline, of necessity, require us to remain in its boundaries in order to represent it, or do disciplinary boundaries limit perspective and argument? As an educational evaluator I have attempted to explain to my students the difference between working with the set objectives of a program or evaluation or broadening the scope of investigation to all effects. The evaluator must make a choice of operating within or beyond the given context, as an internal or external evaluator.

Each of the disciplines studied in the book shows evidence of the importance of students learning to change perspective. Postmodernism demands that we move outside the context, but at the same time we must be able to explain that context to the next cohort in our discipline. The antinomies—contradictory but valid principles raised in the social sciences and humanities—demonstrate the fault lines in these disciplines. Antithetical forms of literary criticism are like tectonic plates sliding past each other or colliding. One of the themes arising in this book that struck me as most intellectually stimulating was emancipation, that state of energy that arises from a sense of knowing, a broad perspective, and action schemas that allow us freedom to choose.

If we look at what the students encountered in their courses and what they tell us in the series of studies, it is clear that they rapidly become aware of the challenges they face: in their words, the need to develop their approach to learning, to think longer and deeper, to bring their knowledge together. In Chapter Two, we observe that physics students learn from one another as they work collaboratively on assignments and labs, and in tutorial groups. They note that it is not enough to read the book; the assigned problems require a new approach. They have to think more deeply than before about problems to get through them, and learn in-depth concentration in the process. In engineering, students are aware that in comparison with their previous experience of education, their university courses require greater concentration, more hard work, and much deeper understanding and thinking.

In psychology, students said that the most important things they had learned were that different theories can account for the same results with the same validity and that they therefore have to learn to identify and test all assumptions, evaluate theoretical frameworks carefully, and construct experiments that rigorously test relationships that occur in a complicated process or system. In education, students noted that they were studying a different kind of material in greater depth, trying to ascertain what is going on in learners' heads, in the teacher's head, and how the learning experience comes together. In English literature, students said they had learned to look behind the surface and not take things at face value.

At an international conference on reconstructing higher education held at Columbia University in June 2001, a student representative entered a plea for transparency of quality—that is, universities should be able to show the public what they are accomplishing and communicate how this is done. Our students can tell us a great deal about their learning experience and directions we might take to improve it. There is substantial convergence in the need for deeper understanding of the disciplines. The continuing challenge is how to draw on the expertise of scholars to improve postsecondary education.

REFERENCES

Adams, J. L. (1986a). *Conceptual blockbusting: A guide to better ideas* (3rd ed.). Reading, MA: Addison-Wesley.

Adams, J. L. (1986b). *The care and feeding of ideas: A guide to encouraging creativity.* Reading, MA: Addison-Wesley.

Adler, M. (1982). *The Paideia proposal: An educational manifesto.* Old Tappan, NJ: Macmillan.

Alexander, P. A. (2000). Toward a model of academic development: Schooling and the acquisition of knowledge. *Educational Researcher, 29*(2), 28–33, 44.

Alexander, P. A., & Murphy, P. K. (1998). The research base for APA's learner-centered psychological principles. In N. M. Lambert & B. L. McCombs (Eds.), *Issues in school reform: A sampler of psychological perspectives on learner-centered school* (pp. 25–60). Washington, DC: American Psychological Association.

Alexander, P. A., Murphy, P. K., Woods, B. S., Duhon, K. E., & Parker, D. (1997). College instruction and concomitant changes in students' knowledge, interest, and strategy use: A study of domain learning. *Contemporary Educational Psychology, 22,* 125–146.

Allen, D. E., Duch, B. J., & Groh, S. E. (1996). The power of problem-based learning in teaching introductory science courses. In L. Wilkerson & W. H. Gijselaers (Eds.), *Bringing problem-based learning to higher education: Theory and practice* (pp. 43–52). New Directions for Teaching and Learning, no. 68. San Francisco: Jossey-Bass.

American Psychological Association. (1990). *Yearly membership of the American Psychological Association.* Washington, DC: American Psychological Association.

American Psychological Association Presidential Task Force on Psychology in Education. (1993). *Learner-centered psychological principles: Guidelines for school redesign and reform.* Washington, DC: American Psychological Association, Mid-Continent Regional Educational Laboratory.

Anderson, J. R. (1982). Acquisition of cognitive skill. *Psychological Review, 89*(4), 369–406.

Anderson, R. C. (1984). Some reflections on the acquisition of knowledge. *Educational Researcher, 15*(9), 5–10.

Angelo, T. A., & Cross, K. P. (1994). *Classroom assessment techniques: A handbook for college teachers.* San Francisco: Jossey-Bass.

Arnold, M. (1888). *Essays in criticism.* (2nd series). Oxford University Press.

Arthurs, H. (1983). *Law and learning.* Report to the Social Science and Humanities Research Council of Canada. Ottawa, Canada: McGill University.

Astin, A. W. (1993). An empirical typology of college students. *Journal of College Student Development, 34*, 36–46.

Astin, A. W. (1998). The changing American college student: Thirty-year trends, 1966–1996. *Review of Higher Education, 21*(2), 115–135.

Atwood, M. (1976). *Lady oracle.* Toronto: McClelland & Stewart.

Ausubel, D. P. (1968). *Educational psychology: A cognitive view.* Austin, TX: Holt, Rinehart and Winston.

Barden, L. M., & Pugh, M. (1993, April). *Strategies and skills exhibited by college students during laboratories in first year physics.* Paper presented at the annual meeting of the American Educational Research Association, Atlanta.

Barker, D. (1989). Personality profiles and selection for courses. *Assessment and Evaluation in Higher Education, 14*(2), 87–94.

Barouch, D. H. (1997). *Voyages in conceptual chemistry.* Boston: Jones & Bartlett.

Barrett, G. C. (1992). Chemistry. In B. R. Clark & G. R. Neave (Eds.), *Encyclopedia of higher education* (pp. 2342–2350). New York: Pergamon Press.

Bartlett, F. C. (1932). *Remembering.* Cambridge, UK: Cambridge University Press.

Bateman, D., & Donald, J. G. (1987). Measuring the intellectual development of college students: Testing a theoretical framework. *Canadian Journal of Higher Education, 17*, 27–45.

Baxter Magolda, M. (1992). *Knowing and reasoning in college: Gender-related patterns in students' intellectual development.* San Francisco: Jossey-Bass.

Baxter Magolda, M., & Terenzini, P. (1999). Learning and teaching in the 21st century: Trends and implications for practice. [www.acpa.nche.edu/srsch]

Bazerman, C. (1992). Linguistics and rhetorical studies. In B. R. Clark & G. R. Neave (Eds.), *Encyclopedia of higher education* (pp. 1847–1852). New York: Pergamon Press.

Beasley, D. E., Huey, C. O., Wilkes, J. M., & McCormick, K. (1995). Cognitive styles and implications for the engineering curriculum. *Proceedings of the Frontiers in Education Conference of the American Society for Engineering Education.* Washington, DC.

Becher, R. A. (1981). Towards a definition of disciplinary cultures. *Studies in Higher Education, 6*(2), 109–122.

Becher, R. A. (1989). *Academic tribes and territories.* Bristol, PA: Open University Press.

Berliner, D.C. (1991). Educational psychology and pedagogical expertise: New findings and new opportunities for thinking about training. *Educational Psychologist, 26*(2), 145–155.

Berlyne, D. E. (1965). *Structure and direction in thinking.* New York: Wiley.

Bess, J. (Ed.). (2000). *Teaching alone, teaching together: Transforming the structure of teams for teaching.* San Francisco: Jossey-Bass.

Biggs, J. B. (1988). *The study process questionnaire (SPQ): User's manual.* Hawthorn, Victoria: Australian Council for Educational Research.

Biggs, J. B. (1993). What do inventories of students' learning processes really measure? A theoretical review and clarification. *British Journal of Educational Psychology, 63*, 3–19.

Biglan, A. (1973). The characteristics of subject matter in different academic areas. *Journal of Applied Psychology, 57*(3), 195–203.

Bloom, B. S. (Ed.). (1956). *Taxonomy of educational objectives: Handbook I—Cognitive domain.* New York: David McKay.

Bloom, B. S., Hastings, J. T., & Madaus, G. F. (1971). *Handbook on formative and summative evaluation of student learning.* New York: McGraw-Hill.

Bloom, J. W. (1988, April). *A case study of evolutionary biologists: Implications for secondary biology curriculum and teacher training.* Paper presented at the annual meeting of the American Educational Research Association, New Orleans.

Bogdan, C.A. (1977). *The use of concept mapping as a possible strategy for instructional design and evaluation in college genetics.* Unpublished master's thesis, Cornell University, Ithaca, NY.

Bonwell, C. C., & Eison, J. A. (1991). *Active learning: Creating excitement in the classroom* (ASHE-ERIC Higher Education Report No. 1). Washington, DC: The George Washington University, School of Education and Human Development.

Boud, D., Churches, A. E., & Smith, E. M. (1986). Student self-assessment in an engineering design course: An evaluation. *International Journal of Applied Engineering Education, 2*(2), 83–90.

Bourdieu, P. (1988). *Homo academicus* (P. Collier, Trans.). Stanford, CA: Stanford University Press.

Brandwein, P. F. (1962). *Teacher's notebook in science.* Orlando: Harcourt, Brace.

Braxton, J. M. (1993). Selectivity and rigor in research universities. *Journal of Higher Education, 64*(6), 657–675.

Braxton, J. M., & Hargens, L. L. (1996). Variation among academic disciplines: Analytical frameworks and research. In J. C. Smart (Ed.), *Higher education: Handbook of theory and research* (Vol. 2, pp. 1–46). New York: Agathon.

Brems, C. (1994). Taking the fear out of research: A gentle approach to teaching an appreciation for research. *Teaching of Psychology, 21,* 241–243.

Broudy, H. S. (1977). Types of knowledge and purposes of education. In R. C. Anderson, R. J. Spiro, & W. E. Montagne (Eds.), *Schooling and the acquisition of knowledge* (pp. 1–17). Hillsdale, NJ: Erlbaum.

Brown, D. E. (1992). Using examples and analogies to remediate misconceptions in physics: Factors influencing conceptual change. *Journal of Research in Science Teaching, 29*(1), 17–34.

Brown, J. S., Collins, A., & Duguid, P. (1989). Situated cognition and the culture of learning. *Educational Researcher, 18*(1), 32–42.

Brown, L. T. (1983). Some more misconceptions about psychology among introductory psychology students. *Teaching of Psychology, 10,* 207–210.

Brown, L. T. (1984). Misconceptions about psychology aren't always what they seem. *Teaching of Psychology, 11*(2), 75–78.

Bruner, J. (1960). *The process of education.* Cambridge, MA: Harvard University Press.

Bruner, J. (1966). *Toward a theory of instruction.* Cambridge, MA: Harvard University Press.

Bruner, J. (1996). *The culture of education.* Cambridge, MA: Harvard University Press.

Bruner, J. S., Goodnow, J. J., & Austin, G. A. (1956). *A study of thinking.* New York: Wiley.

Bryden, D. P. (1984). What do law students learn? A pilot study. *Journal of Legal Education, 34,* 479–506.

Buskist, W., & Wylie, D. (1998). A method for enhancing student interest in large introductory classes. *Teaching of Psychology, 25,* 203–205.

Calhoun, E. (1984). Thinking like a lawyer. *Journal of Legal Education, 34,* 507–514.

Callaghan, M. (1936, September). Watching and waiting. *Redbook,* 48–49, 80.

Cardemone, P. F. (1975). *Concept mapping: A technique of analyzing a discipline and its use in the curriculum and instruction in a portion of a college level mathematics skills course.* Unpublished master's thesis, Cornell University, Ithaca, NY.

Carter, R. (1989). Directions in the teaching and study of English stylistics. In M. Short (Ed.), *Reading, analyzing, and teaching literature* (pp. 10–21). White Plains, NY: Longman.

Cashin, W. E., & Downey, R. G. (1995). Disciplinary differences in what is taught and in students' perceptions of what they learn and how they are taught. In N. Hativa & M. Marincovich (Eds.), *Disciplinary differences in teaching and learning* (pp. 81–92). New Directions for Teaching and Learning, no. 64. San Francisco: Jossey-Bass.

Chandler, A. (1977). *The visible hand: The managerial revolution in American business.* Cambridge, MA: Harvard University Press.

Chase, W. G., & Chi, M.T.H. (1980). Cognitive skill: Implications for spatial skill in large-scale environments. In J. Harvey (Ed.), *Cognition, social behavior, and the environment* (pp. 111–136). Hillsdale, NJ: Erlbaum.

Chi, M.T.H., & Bassok, M. (1988). *Learning from examples via self-explanations* (Tech. Rep. No. 11). Pittsburgh: University of Pittsburgh.

Chi, M.T.H., Feltovich, P. J., & Glaser, R. (1981). Categorization and representation of physics problems by experts and novices. *Cognitive Science, 5,* 121–152.

Clark, B. R. (1987). *The academic life: Small worlds, different worlds.* Princeton, NJ: Carnegie Foundation for the Advancement of Teaching.

Clark, B. R., & Neave, G. R. (Eds.). (1992). *Encyclopedia of higher education.* New York: Pergamon Press.

Clark, C. M., & Peterson, P. L. (1986). Teachers' thought processes. In M. C. Wittrock (Ed.), *Handbook of research on teaching* (3rd ed., pp. 255–296). Old Tappan, NJ: Macmillan.

Clement, J. (1982, April). *Spontaneous analogies in problem solving: The progressive construction of mental models.* Paper presented at the annual meeting of the American Educational Research Association, New York.

Coppola, B. P., Ege, S. N., & Lawton, R. G. (1997). The University of Michigan undergraduate chemistry curriculum: 2. Instructional strategies and assessment. *Journal of Chemical Education, 74*(1), 84–94.

Cowles, D. (Ed.). (1994a). *The critical experience* (2nd ed.). Dubuque, IA: Kendall/Hunt.

Cowles, D. (1994b). Formalism. In D. Cowles (Ed.), *The critical experience* (2nd ed., pp. 7–21). Dubuque, IA: Kendall/Hunt.

Cowles, D. (1994c). Structuralism. In D. Cowles (Ed.), *The critical experience* (2nd ed., pp. 86–105). Dubuque, IA: Kendall/Hunt.

Cox, B. D. (1997). Students' basic philosophical assumptions in history of psychology: A measure and teaching tool. *Teaching of Psychology, 24,* 39–41.

Czuchry, M., & Dansereau, D. F. (1996). Node-link mapping as an alternative to traditional writing assignments in undergraduate psychology courses. *Teaching of Psychology, 23,* 91–96.

Danziger, K. (1990). *Constructing the subject: Historical origins of psychological research.* Cambridge: Cambridge University Press.

Darwin, C. R. (1859). *On the origin of species by means of natural selection or the preservation of favored races in the struggle for life.* London: John Murray.

Dasenbrock, R. W. (1992). English department geography: Interpreting the MLA bibliography. In M.-R. Kecht (Ed.), *Pedagogy is politics: Literary theory and critical teaching* (pp. 193–214). Urbana: University of Illinois Press.

Davies, J.M.Q. (Ed.). (1994). *Bridging the gap: Literary theory in the classroom*. West Cornwall, CT: Locust Hill Press.

Davis, T. M., & Murrell, P. H. (1993). *Turning teaching into learning: The role of student responsibility in the collegiate experience*. (ASHE-ERIC Higher Education Rep. No. 8). Washington, DC: The George Washington University, School of Education and Human Development.

Dee-Lucas, D., & Larkin, J. H. (1983, April). *Expert-novice differences in processing scientific texts*. Paper presented at the annual meeting of the American Educational Research Association, Montreal, Canada.

Dee-Lucas, D., & Larkin, J. H. (1984, April). *Novice strategies for processing scientific texts*. Paper presented at the annual meeting of the American Educational Research Association, New Orleans.

Deese, J. (1965). *The structure of associations in language and thought*. Baltimore: Johns Hopkins Press.

Dickie, L. (1994). *Approach to learning and assessment in physics*. Montreal, Canada: John Abbott College. (ERIC Document Reproduction Service No. ED 386 372)

Dillon, J. T. (1980). Paper chase and the Socratic method of teaching law. *Journal of Legal Education, 30*, 529–545.

diSessa, A. A. (1993). Toward an epistemology of physics. *Cognition and Instruction, 10*, 105–225.

Dobzhansky, T. (1973). Nothing in biology makes sense except in light of evolution. *American Biology Teacher, 35*, 125–129.

Donald, J. G. (1983). Knowledge structures: Methods for exploring course content. *Journal of Higher Education, 54*(1), 31–41.

Donald, J. G. (1985). Intellectual skills in higher education. *Canadian Journal of Higher Education, 1*(1), 53–68.

Donald, J. G. (1986). Knowledge and the university curriculum. *Higher Education, 15*(3), 267–282.

Donald, J. G. (1987). Learning schemata: Methods of representing cognitive, content, and curriculum structures in higher education. *Instructional Science, 16*, 187–211.

Donald, J. G. (1988). Professors' expectations of students' ability to think. *Higher Education Research and Development, 17*(1), 19–35.

Donald, J. G. (1990). University professors' views of knowledge and validation processes. *Journal of Educational Psychology, 82*(2), 242–249.

Donald, J. G. (1991). The learning task in engineering courses: A study of professors' perceptions of the learning process in six selected courses. *European Journal of Engineering Education, 16*(2), 181–192.

Donald, J. G. (1992a). The development of thinking processes in postsecondary education: Application of a working model. *Higher Education, 24*(4), 413–430.

Donald, J. G. (1992b). Professors' and students' conceptualizations of the learning task in engineering courses. *European Journal of Engineering Education, 17*(3), 229–245.

Donald, J. G. (1993). Professors' and students' conceptualizations of the learning task in physics courses. *Journal of Research on Science Teaching, 30*, 905–918.

Donald, J. G. (1995a). Disciplinary differences in knowledge validation. In N. Hativa & M. Marincovich (Eds.), *Disciplinary differences in teaching and learning* (pp. 7–17). New Directions for Teaching and Learning, no. 64. San Francisco: Jossey-Bass.

Donald, J. G. (1995b, June). Understanding the task of teaching and learning: Postsecondary students' orientation to learning. Paper presented at the annual meeting of the Canadian Society for the Study of Higher Education, Montreal, Canada.

Donald, J. G. (1997). *Improving the environment for learning: Academic leaders talk about what works.* San Francisco: Jossey-Bass.

Donald, J. G. (1999). The link between knowledge and learning. In J. Brennan, J. Fedrowitz, M. Huber, & T. Shah (Eds.), *What kind of university? International perspectives on knowledge, participation and governance* (pp. 36–55). Buckingham, UK: Open University Press, Society for Research into Higher Education.

Donald, J. G. (2000). The pedagogue: Creating designs for teaching. In J. Bess (Ed.), *Teaching alone, teaching together: Transforming the structure of teams for teaching* (pp. 35–61). San Francisco: Jossey-Bass.

Donald, J. G., & Denison, D. B. (1996). Evaluating undergraduate education: The use of broad indicators. *Assessment and Evaluation in Higher Education, 21*(1), 23–39.

Donald, J. G., & Denison, D. B. (2001). Quality assessment of university students: Student perceptions of quality criteria. *Journal of Higher Education, 72,* 478–501.

Donald, J. G., & Dubuc, P. (1999). *Report on students' conceptualizations of learning, 1994–1995.* Montreal, Canada: McGill University, Centre for University Teaching and Learning.

Donald, J. G., & McMillan-Davey, E. (1998, June). *Transforming learning: Students' and professors' perceptions of the learning interface in first year seminars.* Paper presented at the annual meeting of the Canadian Society for the Study of Higher Education, Ottawa, Canada.

Donald, J. G., McMillan-Davey, E., & Denison, D. B. (1999, June). *Postsecondary institutions of the year 2000: The effect of the learning climate on higher order learning.* Paper presented at the annual meeting of the Canadian Society for the Study of Higher Education, Sherbrooke, Canada.

Donald, J. G., & Nagy, P. (1985). *The portrayal of knowledge structures: A synthesis of methods.* Research report to the Social Science and Humanities Research Council of Canada. Montreal, Canada: McGill University, Centre for University Teaching and Learning.

Donoghue, D. (1998). *The practice of reading.* New Haven, CT: Yale University Press.

Dougherty, R. C., Bowen, C. W., Berger, T., Rees, W., Mellon, E. K., & Pulliam, E. (1995). Cooperative learning and enhanced communication. *Journal of Chemical Education, 72*(9), 793–797.

Dressel, P., & Mayhew, L. (1974). *Higher education as a field of study.* San Francisco: Jossey-Bass.

Dreyfus, H. L., & Dreyfus, S. E. (1986). *Mind over machine.* New York: Free Press.

Duckworth, E. (1987). *The having of wonderful ideas.* New York: Teachers' College Press.

Duemler, D., & Mayer, R. E. (1988). Hidden costs of reflectiveness: Aspects of successful scientific reasoning. *Journal of Educational Psychology, 8*(4), 419–423.

Duerden, R. (1994). Pluralism: The joys of text. In D. Cowles (Ed.), *The critical experience* (2nd ed., pp. 286–304). Dubuque, IA: Kendall/Hunt.

Dym, C. L. (1999). Learning engineering: Design, languages, and experiences. *Journal of Engineering Education, 88*(2), 145–148.

Eaton, M., & Pougiales, R. (1993). Work, reflection, and community: Conditions that support self-evaluations. In J. MacGregor (Ed.), *Student self-evaluation: Fostering reflective learning* (pp. 5–14). New Directions for Teaching and Learning, no. 56. San Francisco: Jossey-Bass.

Engell, J., & Perkins, D. (Eds.). (1988). *Teaching literature: What is needed now.* Cambridge, MA: Harvard University Press.

English, H. B., & English, A. C. (1958). *A comprehensive dictionary of psychological and psychoanalytic terms: A guide to usage.* New York: David McKay.

Entwistle, N. J., & Ramsden, P. (1983). *Understanding student learning.* London: Croom Helm.

Entwistle, N. J., & Tait, H. (1990). Approaches to learning, evaluations of teaching, and preferences for contrasting academic environments. *Higher Education, 19,* 169–194.

Enyeart, M. A., Baker, D., & Vanharlingen, D. (1980). Correlation of inductive and deductive logical reasoning to college physics achievement. *Journal of Research in Science Teaching, 17*(3), 263–267.

Ericksen, A., & Smith, J. (Eds.). (1991). *Study of expertise: Prospects and limits.* Cambridge: Cambridge University Press.

Ericsson, K. A., & Simon, H. A. (1984). *Protocol analysis: Verbal reports as data.* Cambridge, MA: MIT Press.

Evans, C. (1988). *Language people: The experience of teaching and learning modern languages in British Universities.* Bristol, PA: Open University Press.

Ewell, P. (2001). Statewide testing in higher education. *Change, 33,* 21–27.

Eyler, J., & Giles, D. E. (1999). *Where's the learning in service learning?* San Francisco: Jossey-Bass.

Fairweather, J. S. (1989). Academic research and instruction: The industrial connection. *Journal of Higher Education, 60*(4), 388–407.

Feldman, K. A. (1989). Instructional effectiveness of college teachers judged by teachers themselves, current and former students, colleagues, administrators, and external (neutral) observers. *Research in Higher Education, 30,* 137–194.

Feldman, K. A. (1996). Identifying exemplary teaching: Using data from course and teacher evaluations. In M. D. Svinicki & R. J. Menges (Eds.), *Honoring exemplary teaching* (pp. 41–50). New Directions for Teaching and Learning, no. 65. San Francisco: Jossey-Bass.

Ferguson, M., & de Jong, T. (1991, April). *A model of the cognitive aspects of physics instruction.* Paper presented at the annual meeting of the American Educational Research Association, Chicago.

Fish, S. (1995). *Professional correctness: Literary studies and political change.* Oxford: Clarendon Press.

Fisher, K. M. (1988a, April). *Relations used in student-generated knowledge representations.* Paper presented at the annual meeting of the American Educational Research Association, New Orleans.

Fisher, K. M. (1988b, April). *SemNet: Software for student or faculty construction of large relational networks of concepts.* Paper presented at the annual meeting of the American Educational Research Association, New Orleans.

Fleming, J. G. (1983). *The law of torts* (6th ed.). Sydney, Australia: Law Book.

Foley, B. J. (1999, April). *How visualizations alter the conceptual ecology.* Paper presented at the annual meeting of the American Educational Research Association, Montreal, Canada.

Franklin, J., & Theall, M. (1995). The relationship of disciplinary differences and the value of class preparation time to student ratings of teaching. In N. Hativa & M. Marincovich (Eds.), *Disciplinary differences in teaching and learning* (pp. 41–48). New Directions for Teaching and Learning, no. 64. San Francisco: Jossey-Bass.

Fransson, A. (1977). On qualitative differences in learning. IV: Effects of motivation and test anxiety on process and outcome. *British Journal of Educational Psychology, 47,* 244–257.

Frederiksen, N. (1984). Implications of cognitive theory for instruction in problem solving. *Review of Educational Research, 54*(3), 363–407.

Frye, N. (1957). *Anatomy of criticism.* Princeton, NJ: University Press.

Fuchs, S. (1992). *The professional quest for truth: A social theory of science and knowledge.* Albany: State University of New York Press.

Garcia, T., & Pintrich, P. (1992, August). Critical thinking and its relationship to motivation, learning strategies, and classroom experience. Paper presented at the annual meeting of the American Psychological Association, Washington, DC.

Gleitman, H. (1984). Introducing psychology. *American Psychologist, 39*(4), 421–427.

Goldman, R. M., Schoner, P. G., & Pentony, D. E. (1980). *The vocabulary of a discipline: The political science concept inventory.* Santa Barbara, CA: ABC-Clio.

Goldman, S. L. (1992). Engineering education and institutes of technology: United States. In B. R. Clark & G. R. Neave (Eds.), *Encyclopedia of higher education* (pp. 1107–1117). New York: Pergamon Press.

Goldsmith, T. E., Johnson, P. J., & Acton, W. H. (1991). Assessing structural knowledge. *Journal of Educational Psychology, 83,* 88–96.

Graff, G. (1987). *Professing literature: An institutional history.* Chicago: University of Chicago Press.

Graff, G. (1994). Other voices, other rooms: Organizing and teaching the humanities conflict. In J.M.Q. Davies (Ed.), *Bridging the gap: Literary theory in the classroom* (pp. 15–39). West Cornwall, CT: Locust Hill Press.

Gray, T., & Mill, D. (1990). Critical abilities, graduate education (biology vs. English), and belief in unsubstantiated phenomena. *Canadian Journal of Behavioral Science, 22*(2), 162–172.

Griggs, R. A., & Jackson, S. L. (1988). A reexamination of the relationship of high school psychology and natural science courses to performance in a college introductory psychology class. *Teaching of Psychology, 15,* 142–144.

Gruber, G. R., & Gruber, E. C. (1982). *Law school admission test.* New York: Monarch Press.

Hake, R. R. (1998). Interactive-engagement vs. traditional methods: A six-thousand student survey of mechanics test data for introductory physics courses. *American Journal of Physics, 66*(1), 64–74.

Halliday, A., & Resnick, R. (1988). *Fundamentals of physics.* New York: Wiley.

Halloun, I. A., & Hestenes, D. (1985). The initial knowledge state of college physics students. *American Journal of Physics, 53*(11), 1043–1065.

Hammer, D. (1994). Epistemological beliefs in introductory physics. *Cognition and Instruction, 12*(2), 151–183.

Hammer, D. (1995). Epistemological considerations in teaching introductory physics. *Science Education, 79*(4), 393–413.

Hammer, D. (1996). More than misconceptions: Multiple perspectives on student knowledge and reasoning, and an appropriate role for education research. *American Journal of Physics, 64,* 1316–1325.

Hartwell, S., & Hartwell, S. L. (1990). Teaching law: Some things Socrates did not try. *Journal of Legal Education, 40,* 509–523.

Hativa, N. (2000a). Teaching large law classes well—A view of an outsider. *Journal of Legal Education, 50*(1), 95–111.

Hativa, N. (2000b, April). *The tension between perceptions and beliefs of professors and students regarding the academic environment.* Paper presented at the annual meeting of the American Educational Research Association, New Orleans.

Hauff, H. M., & Fogarty, G. J. (1996). Analyzing problem solving behavior of successful and unsuccessful statistics students. *Instructional Science, 24,* 397–409.

Hawkey, C. L. (2000). *Patterns of participation, modes of exclusion: Undergraduate students' experience of community at a research-intensive university.* Unpublished doctoral thesis, University of British Columbia: Vancouver, Canada.

Hawking, S. W. (1988). *A brief history of time: From the Big Bang to black holes.* New York: Bantam Books.

Hazel, E., & Prosser, M. (1994). First year university students' understanding of photosynthesis, their study strategies and learning context. *American Biology Teacher, 56*(5) 274–279.

Hebb, D. O., & Donderi, D. C. (1987). *Textbook of Psychology.* (4th ed.) Hillsdale, NJ: Erlbaum.

Hedges, B. W., & Thomas, J. H. (1980). The effect of high school psychology on precourse knowledge, midterm grades, and final grades in introductory psychology. *Teaching of Psychology, 7*, 221–223.

Hegarty-Hazel, E., & Prosser, M. (1991). Relationship between students' conceptual knowledge and study strategies. Part 1: Student learning in physics. *International Journal of Science Education, 13*(3), 303–312.

Heller, J. I., & Reif, F. (1982, March). *Prescribing effective human problem solving processes: Problem description in physics.* Paper presented at the annual meeting of the American Educational Research Association, New York.

Hestenes, D., Wells, M., & Swackhammer, G. (1992). Force concept inventory. *Physics Teacher, 30*(3), 141–158.

Hewitt, P. G. (1983). Millikan lecture 1982: The missing essential—A conceptual understanding of physics. *American Journal of Physics, 51*(4), 305–331.

Hirsch, E. D. (1967). *Validity in interpretation.* New Haven, CT: Yale University Press.

Hirst, P. (1974). *Knowledge and the curriculum: A collection of philosophical papers.* New York: Routledge.

Hoffman, R. (1988). Marginalia: Nearly circular reasoning. *American Scientist, 76*, 182–185.

Holmes Group. (1986). *Tomorrow's teachers.* East Lansing, MI: Holmes Group.

Houston, G. T. (1994). Feminist criticism. In D. Cowles (Ed.), *The critical experience* (2nd ed., pp. 214–234). Dubuque, IA: Kendall/Hunt.

Huber, L. (1990). Disciplinary cultures and social reproduction. *European Journal of Education, 25*(3), 241–261.

Humphrey, G. (1951). *Thinking: An introduction to its experimental psychology.* London: Methuen.

Indiana University Center for Postsecondary Research and Planning. (2000). *National survey of student engagement: The college student report.* Bloomington: Author.

Johnson, P. E. (1967). Some psychological aspects of subject matter structure. *Journal of Educational Psychology, 58*, 75–83.

Johnston, R. (1998). The university of the future: Boyer revisited. *Higher Education, 36*, 253–272.

Joram, E., & Gabriele, A. J. (1998). Preservice teachers' prior beliefs: Transforming obstacles into opportunities. *Teaching and Teacher Education, 14*(2), 175–191.

Judge, H. (1992). Teacher education. In B. R. Clark & G. R. Neave (Eds.), *Encyclopedia of higher education* (pp. 1229–1240). New York: Pergamon Press.

Kagan, D. M. (1992). Implications of research on teacher belief. *Educational Psychologist, 27*, 65–90.

Kahn, P. (1999). *The cultural study of law: Reconstructing legal scholarship.* Chicago: University of Chicago Press.

Karplus, R. (1981). Educational aspects of the structure of physics. *American Journal of Physics, 49*(3), 238–241.

Kash, D. E. (1987). *The engineering research centers: Leaders in change.* Washington, DC: National Academy of Engineering.

Kecht, M.-R. (Ed.). (1992). *Pedagogy is politics: Literary theory and critical teaching.* Urbana: University of Illinois Press.

King, P. M., & Kitchener, K. S. (1994). *Developing reflective judgment.* San Francisco: Jossey-Bass.

Kirkwood, V., & Symington, D. (1996). Lecturer perceptions of student difficulties in a first year chemistry course. *Journal of Chemical Education, 73*(4), 339–343.

Kleppner, D. (1985). Research in small groups. *Physics Today, 38*(3), 79–85.

Kogut, L. S. (1996). Critical thinking in general chemistry. *Journal of Chemical Education, 73*(3), 218–221.

Kramers-Pals, H., Lambrechts, J., & Wolff, P. J. (1982). Recurrent difficulties: Solving quantitative problems. *Journal of Chemical Education, 59*(6), 509–513.

Krathwohl, D. K. (1985). *Social and behavioral science research.* San Francisco: Jossey-Bass.

Krathwohl, D. K., Bloom, B. S., & Masia, B. B. (1964). *Taxonomy of educational objectives. Handbook II: Affective domain.* New York: David McKay.

Krieger, M. (1994). *The institution of theory.* Baltimore: Johns Hopkins University Press.

Kuh, G. D. (2001). Assessing what really matters to student learning. *Change, 33*(3), 10–17, 66.

Kuh, G. D., & Hu, S. (2001). Learning productivity at research universities. *Journal of Higher Education, 72*(1), 1–28.

Kuhn, T. S. (1970). *The structure of scientific revolutions.* Chicago: University of Chicago Press.

Kusniac, E., & Finley, M. L. (1993). Student self-evaluation: An introduction and rationale. In J. MacGregor (Ed.), *Student self-evaluation: Fostering reflective learning* (pp. 5–14). New Directions for Teaching and Learning, no. 56. San Francisco: Jossey-Bass.

Larkin, J. H., McDermott, J., Simon, D. P., & Simon, H. A. (1980). Expert and novice performance in solving physics problems. *Science, 208,* 1335–1342.

Larkin, J. H., & Reif, F. (1976). Analysis and teaching of general skill for studying scientific text. *Journal of Educational Psychology, 68*(4), 431–440.

Lattuca, L. R., & Stark, J. S. (1993, November). *Modifying the major: Extemporaneous thoughts from ten disciplines.* Paper presented at the annual meeting of the Association for the Study of Higher Education, Pittsburgh, PA.

Leamnson, R. (1999). *Thinking about teaching and learning: Developing habits of learning with first year college and university students.* Sterling, VA: Stylus.

Leary, D. E. (1992). Psychology. In B. R. Clark & G. R. Neave (Eds.), *Encyclopedia of higher education* (pp. 2136–2150). New York: Pergamon Press.

Lehman, D. R., Lempert, R. O., & Nisbett, R. E. (1988). The effects of graduate training on reasoning. *American Psychologist, 43*(6), 431–442.

Lenze, L. F., & Dinham, S. M. (1999). Learning what students understand. In R. J. Menges & Associates (Eds.), *Faculty in new jobs* (pp. 147–165). San Francisco: Jossey-Bass.

Leonard, W. J., Dufresne, R. J., & Mestre, J. P. (1996). Using qualitative problem solving strategies to highlight the role of conceptual knowledge in solving problems. *American Journal of Physics, 64*(12), 1495–1503.

Lewis, P.S.C. (1992). Legal education. In B. R. Clark & G. R. Neave (Eds.), *Encyclopedia of higher education* (pp. 1132–1146). New York: Pergamon Press.

Light, R. J. (2001). *Making the most of college: Students speak their mind.* Cambridge, MA: Harvard University Press.

LoDico, M. F. (2000, April 20). Learning while helping others. *McGill Reporter,* p. 12.

LoPresti, V., & Garafalo, F. (1994). Global organizing themes for biology students. *American Biology Teacher, 56*(6) 342–347.

Lumsdaine, M., & Lumsdaine, E. (1995). Thinking preferences of engineering students: Implications for curriculum restructuring. *Journal of Engineering Education, 84*(2), 193–203.

MacCrate, R. (1994). Preparing lawyers to participate effectively in the legal profession. *Journal of Legal Education, 44*(1), 89–95.

Macgregor, H. C. (1992). Biological sciences: Introduction. In B. R. Clark & G. R. Neave (Eds.), *Encyclopedia of higher education* (pp. 2181–2183). New York: Pergamon Press.

Makosky, V. P. (1985). Teaching psychology in the information age. *Teaching of Psychology, 12,* 23–26.

Manlove, C. (1989). *Critical thinking: A guide to interpreting literary texts.* Old Tappan, NJ: Macmillan.

Marius, R. (1988). Reflections on the freshman English course. In J. Engell & D. Perkins (Eds.), *Teaching literature: What is needed now* (pp. 169–190). Cambridge, MA: Harvard University Press.

Marton, F., & Saljo, R. (1976). On qualitative differences in learning. I: Outcome and process. *British Journal of Educational Psychology, 46,* 4–11.

Marx, M. H. (1963). *Theories in contemporary psychology.* Old Tappan, NJ: Macmillan.

Maurer, N. M., & Mischler, L. F. (1994). Introduction to lawyering: Teaching first-year students to think like professionals. *Journal of Legal Education, 44*(1), 96–115.

Mazur, E. (1997). *Peer instruction: A user's manual.* Englewood Cliffs, NJ: Prentice Hall.

McBurney, D. H. (1995). The problem method of teaching research methods. *Teaching of Psychology, 22,* 36–38.

McDermott, J., & Larkin, J. H. (1978). Re-representing textbook physics problems. In *Proceedings of the Second National Conference of the Canadian Society for Computational Studies of Intelligence.* Toronto, Canada: University of Toronto Press.

Meeker, F., Fox, D., & Whitley, B. E. (1994). Predictors of academic success in the undergraduate psychology major. *Teaching of Psychology, 21,* 238–241.

Meldman, J. A. (1977). A structural model for computer-aided legal analysis. *Rutgers Journal of Computers and the Law, 6*(1), 27–71.

Mettes, C.T.C.W., Pilot, A., Roosink, H. J., & Kramers-Pals, H. (1980). Teaching and learning problem solving in science. Part 1: A general strategy. *Journal of Chemical Education, 57*(12), 882–885.

Mettes, C.T.C.W., Pilot, A., Roosink, H. J., & Kramers-Pals, H. (1981). Teaching and learning problem solving in science. Part 2: Learning problem solving in a thermodynamics course. *Journal of Chemical Education, 58*(1), 51–55.

Meyer, J.H.F., Parsons, P., & Dunne, T. T. (1990). Individual study orchestrations and their association with learning outcome. *Higher Education, 20,* 67–89.

Meyers, C. (1986). *Teaching students to think critically: A guide for faculty in all disciplines.* San Francisco: Jossey-Bass.

Milem, J. F., & Astin, H. S. (1994, April). *Scientists as teachers: A look at their culture, their roles, and their pedagogy.* Paper presented at the annual meeting of the American Educational Research Association, New Orleans.

Millar, S. B., & Regan, T. M. (1993). The process model of teaching/learning for designing first-year engineering design courses. In *Proceedings of the ASEE Annual Conference* (Session 2653). Washington, DC: American Society for Engineering Education.

Miller, G. A. (1956). The magical number seven, plus or minus two: Some limits on our capacity for processing information. *Psychological Review, 63*(2), 81–97.

Miller, J. H. (1988). The function of rhetorical study at the present time. In J. Engell & D. Perkins (Eds.), *Teaching literature: What is needed now* (pp. 87–109). Cambridge, MA: Harvard University Press.

Miller, M. (2001). How are we doing? *Change, 33,* 4.

Moog, R., & Farrell, J. (1999). *Chemistry: A guided inquiry.* New York: Wiley.

Morissette, Y.-M. (1988a). The evaluation of bar admission candidates in Quebec: Testing knowledge and testing skills. *Journal of Professional Legal Education, 6,* 1–21.

Morissette, Y.-M. (1988b, August). Testing professional skills in the Quebec bar admission programme. *Bar Examiner,* 13–25.

Mudd, J. O. (1983). Thinking critically about "thinking like a lawyer." *Journal of Legal Education, 33,* 704–711.

Munro, A. (1974). Something I've been meaning to tell you. In *Three short stories*. New York: McGraw-Hill.

Myers, D. G. (1994). On the teaching of literary theory. In J.M.Q. Davies (Ed.), *Bridging the gap: Literary theory in the classroom* (pp. 3–13). West Cornwall, CT: Locust Hill Press.

Nakhleh, M. B. (1994). Chemical education research in the laboratory environment. *Journal of Chemical Education, 71*(3), 201–205.

Nakhleh, M. B., Lowrey, K. A., & Mitchell, R. C. (1996). Narrowing the gap between concepts and algorithms in freshman chemistry. *Journal of Chemical Education, 73*(8), 758–762.

Nathanson, S. (1994). Developing legal problem solving skills. *Journal of Legal Education, 44*(2), 215–231.

National Academy of Education. (1991). *Research and the renewal of education*. Palo Alto, CA: Stanford University.

National Science Foundation. (1986). *Federal scientists and engineers: Detailed statistical tables, 1985*. Washington, DC: National Science Foundation.

Nelken, M. L. (1995). Negotiation and psychoanalysis: If I'd wanted to learn about feelings, I wouldn't have gone to law school. *Journal of Legal Education, 45*, 420–429.

Nespor, J. (1994). *Knowledge in motion*. Bristol, PA: Falmer Press.

Neumann, Y., & Finaly-Neumann, E. (1989). Examination of alternative models of students' assessment of their college: Differences between hard and soft sciences. *Assessment and Evaluation in Higher Education, 14*(1), 11–19.

Newell, A., & Simon, H. A. (1972). *Human problem solving*. Englewood Cliffs, NJ: Prentice Hall.

Nisbett, R. E., Fong, G. T., Lehman, D. R., & Cheng, P. W. (1987). Teaching reasoning. *Science, 238*, 625–631.

Noble, D. (1977). *America by design: Science, technology, and the rise of corporate capitalism*. New York: Knopf.

Norton, L. S., & Crowley, C. M. (1995). Can students be helped to learn how to learn? An evaluation of an approaches-to-learning programme for first-year degree students. *Higher Education, 29*, 307–328.

Novak, J. D. (1984). Applications of advances in learning theory and philosophy of science to the improvement of chemistry teaching. *Journal of Chemical Education, 61*(7), 607–612.

Novak, J. D. (1985). Metalearning and metaknowledge strategies to help students learn how to learn. In L.H.T. West & A. L. Pines (Eds.), *Cognitive structure and conceptual change* (pp. 189–209). Orlando: Academic Press.

Novak, J. D. (1990). Concept maps and Vee diagrams: Two metacognitive tools to facilitate meaningful learning. *Instructional Science, 19*, 29–52.

Novak, J. D., & Gowin, D. B. (1984). *Learning how to learn*. New York: Cambridge University Press.

Ogden, G. L. (1984). The problem method in legal education. *Journal of Legal Education, 34*, 654–673.

Pace, C. R. (1982). *Achievement and the quality of student effort*. Washington, DC: National Commission on Excellence in Education.

Parry, S. (1998). Disciplinary discourse in doctoral theses. *Higher Education, 36*, 273–299.

Pascarella, E. T., & Terenzini, P. T. (1991). *How college affects students: Findings and insights from twenty years of research*. San Francisco: Jossey-Bass.

Pascarella, E. T., & Terenzini, P. T. (1998). Studying college students in the 21st century: Meeting new challenges. *Review of Higher Education, 21*(2), 151–165.

Pask, G. (1976). Conversational techniques in the study and practice of education. *British Journal of Educational Psychology, 46*(1), 12–25.

Pelikan, J. (1992). *The idea of the university: A reexamination.* New Haven, CT: Yale University Press.

Peltzer, A. (1988). The intellectual factors believed by physicists to be most important to physics students. *Journal of Research in Science Teaching, 25*(9), 721–731.

Pendley, B. D., Bretz, R. L., & Novak, J. D. (1994). Concept maps as a tool to assess learning in chemistry. *Journal of Chemical Education, 71*(1), 9–15.

Perry, W. G. (1970). *Forms of intellectual and ethical development in the college years: A scheme.* Austin, TX: Holt, Rinehart and Winston.

Perry, W. G. (1981). Intellectual and ethical development. In A. W. Chickering & Associates (Eds.), *The modern American college: Responding to the new realities of diverse students and a changing society* (pp. 76–116). San Francisco: Jossey-Bass.

Phenix, P. H. (1964). *Realms of meaning.* New York: McGraw-Hill.

Pike, G. (1991). The effects of background, coursework, and involvement on students' grades and satisfaction. *Research in Higher Education, 32*(1), 15–30.

Pines, A. L., & West, L.H.T. (1986). Conceptual understanding and science learning: An interpretation of research within a sources-of-knowledge framework. *Science Education, 70*(5), 583–604.

Pintrich, P. R. (Ed.). (1995). *Understanding self-regulated learning.* New Directions for Teaching and Learning, no. 63. San Francisco: Jossey-Bass.

Pintrich, P. R., Brown, D., & Weinstein, C. (Eds.). (1994). *Student motivation, cognition, and learning.* Hillsdale, NJ: Erlbaum.

Pintrich, P. R., Marx, R. W. & Boyle, R. A. (1993). Beyond cold conceptual change: The role of motivational beliefs and classroom contextual factors in the process of conceptual change. *Review of Educational Research, 63*(2), 167–199.

Popper, K. R. (1959). *The logic of scientific discovery.* London: Hutchinson.

Popper, K. R. (1963). *Conjectures and refutations: The growth of scientific knowledge.* New York: Routledge.

Powers, D., & Enright, M. (1987). Analytical reasoning skills in graduate study: Perceptions of faculty in six fields. *Journal of Higher Education, 58*(6), 658–682.

Prosser, M. (1979). Cognitive analysis of physics textbooks at the tertiary or college level. *Science Education, 63*(5), 677–683.

Prosser, M. (1983). Relationship between the cognitive abilities of a group of tertiary physics students and the cognitive requirements of their textbook. *Science Education, 67*(1), 75–83.

Prosser, M., Walker, P., & Millar, R. (1996). Differences in students' perceptions of learning physics. *Physics Education, 31*, 43–48.

Rabinowitz, P. J. (1992). Against close reading. In M.-R. Kecht (Ed.), *Pedagogy is politics: Literary theory and critical teaching* (pp. 230–243). Urbana: University of Illinois Press.

Ramsden, P. (1992). *Learning to teach in higher education.* New York: Routledge.

Ratcliff, J. (1992). Reconceptualizing the college curriculum. *Perspectives: Journal of the Association for General and Liberal Studies, 22*, 122–137.

Redish, E. F. (1994). The implications of cognitive studies for teaching physics. *American Journal of Physics, 62*(6), 796–803.

Redish, E. F., Saul, J. M., & Steinberg, R. N. (1998). Student expectations in introductory physics. *American Journal of Physics, 66*(3), 212–224.

Regis, A., Albertazzi, P. G., & Roletto, E. (1996). Concept maps in chemistry education. *Journal of Chemical Education, 73*(11), 1084–1088.

Reif, F. (1983, April). *Acquiring an effective understanding of scientific concepts.* Paper presented at the annual meeting of the American Educational Research Association, Montreal, Canada.

Reif, F., Larkin, J. H., & Brackett, G. C. (1976). Teaching general learning and problem-solving skills. *American Journal of Physics, 44*(3), 212–217.

Resnick, L. (1987). *Education and learning to think.* Washington, DC: National Academy Press.

Ricoeur, P. (1976). *Interpretation theory: Discourse and the surplus of meaning.* Fort Worth: Texas Christian University Press.

Ring, D. G., & Novak, J. D. (1971). The effects of cognitive structure variables on achievement in college chemistry. *Journal of Research in Science Teaching, 8*(4), 325–333.

Ropohl, G. (1997). Knowledge types in technology. *International Journal of Technology and Design Education, 7,* 65–72.

Rosenberg, C. (1979). Towards an ecology of knowledge: On discipline, context, and history. In A. Oleson & J. Voss (Eds.), *The organization of knowledge in modern America, 1860–1920* (pp. 440–455). Baltimore: Johns Hopkins University Press.

Ross, D. (1979). The development of the social sciences. In A. Oleson & J. Voss (Eds.), *The organization of knowledge in modern America, 1860–1920* (pp. 51–106). Baltimore: Johns Hopkins University Press.

Ross, M. R., & Fulton, R. B. (1994). Active learning strategies in the analytical chemistry classroom. *Journal of Chemical Education, 71*(2), 141–143.

Rothman, M. A. (1992). Physics. In B. R. Clark & G. R. Neave (Eds.), *Encyclopedia of higher education* (pp. 2388–2398). New York: Pergamon Press.

Rumelhart, D. E. (1977). *Introduction to human information processing.* New York: Wiley.

Rumelhart, D. E., Lindsay, P. H., & Norman, D. O. (1972). A process model for long-term memory. In E. Tulving & W. Donaldson (Eds.), *Organization of memory* (pp. 197–246). Orlando: Academic Press.

Rumelhart, D. E., & Ortony, A. (1977). The representation of knowledge in memory. In R. C. Anderson, R. J. Spiro, & W. E. Montague (Eds.), *Schooling and the acquisition of knowledge* (pp. 99–135). Hillsdale, NJ: Erlbaum.

Russell, D. (1982). The causal dimension scale: A measure of how individuals perceive causes. *Journal of Personality and Social Psychology, 42*(6), 1137–1145.

Ryan, J. (1988). Study skills for the sciences: A bridge over troubled waters. *Journal of College Science Teaching, 18,* 373–377.

Ryan, M. P. (1984a). Monitoring text comprehension: Individual differences in epistemological standards. *Journal of Educational Psychology, 76,* 248–258.

Ryan, M. P. (1984b). Conceptions of prose coherence: Individual differences in epistemological standards. *Journal of Educational Psychology, 76,* 1226–1238.

Ryle, G. (1949). *The concept of mind.* London: Hutchinson.

Santhanam, E., Leach, C., & Dawson, C. (1998). Concept mapping: How should it be introduced, and is there evidence for long-term benefit? *Higher Education, 35,* 317–328.

Scheffler, J. (1965). *Conditions of knowledge.* Glenview, IL: Scott, Foresman.

Schilb, J. (1992). Poststructuralism, politics, and the subject of pedagogy. In M.-R. Kecht (Ed.), *Pedagogy is politics: Literary theory and critical teaching* (pp. 48–69). Urbana: University of Illinois Press.

Scholes, R. (1998). *The rise and fall of English.* New Haven, CT: Yale University Press.

Schommer, M., & Walker, K. (1995). Are epistemological beliefs similar across domains? *Journal of Educational Psychology, 87,* 424–432.

Schwab, J. J. (1962). The concept of the structure of a discipline. *Educational Record, 43,* 197–205.

Schwab, J. J. (1978). *Science, curriculum, and liberal education.* Chicago: University of Chicago Press.

Scott, R. A. (1992). Social sciences: Introduction. In B. R. Clark & G. R. Neave (Eds.), *Encyclopedia of higher education* (pp. 2071–2080). New York: Pergamon Press.

Shannon, C. E., & Weaver, W. (1949). *Mathematical theory of communication.* Urbana: University of Illinois Press.

Shapiro, S. J. (1996). The use and effectiveness of various learning materials in an evidence class. *Journal of Legal Education, 46*(1), 101–109.

Shavelson, R. J. (1974, April). *Some methods for examining content structure in instruction.* Paper presented at the annual meeting of the American Educational Research Association, Chicago.

Shepard, R. (1978). Externalization of mental images and the act of creation. In B. S. Rhandawa & W. E. Coffman (Eds.), *Visual learning, thinking, and communication* (pp. 133–189). Orlando: Academic Press.

Short, M., & Candlin, C. (1989). Teaching study skills for English literature. In M. Short (Ed.), *Reading, analyzing, and teaching literature* (pp. 178–203). White Plains, NY: Longman.

Shuh, K. L. (1999, April). *Beyond domains: Knowledge structures and constructivism.* Paper presented at the annual meeting of the American Educational Research Association, Montreal, Canada.

Shulman, L. (1986). Those who understand: Knowledge growth in teaching. *Educational Researcher, 15*(2), 4–14.

Shulman, L. (1987). Knowledge and teaching: Foundations of the new reform. *Harvard Educational Review, 57*(1), 1–22.

Silberman, M. (1996). *Active learning: 101 strategies to teach any subject.* Needham Heights, MA: Allyn & Bacon.

Skinner, Q. (Ed.). (1985). *The return of grand theory in the human sciences.* Cambridge: University Press.

Smith, K. A., Mahler, M., Szafranski, J., & Werner, D. (1997). Problem-based freshman engineering course. In *Proceedings of the ASEE Annual Conference* (Session 2530). Washington, DC: American Society for Engineering Education.

Smith, K. J., & Metz, P. A. (1996). Evaluating student understanding of solution chemistry through microscopic representations. *Journal of Chemical Education, 73*(3), 233–235.

Somerville, M. A. (1978). A diagrammatic approach to causation. *McGill Law Journal, 24*(30), 442–458.

Sorenson, P. J. (1994). Historical criticism. In D. Cowles (Ed.), *The critical experience* (2nd ed., pp. 48–59). Dubuque, IA: Kendall/Hunt.

Sparkes, J. J. (1989, July). Quality in engineering education. Engineering Professors' Conference, Occasional papers, No. 1, pp. 11.

Sperna Weiland, J. (1992). Humanities. In B. R. Clark & G. R. Neave (Eds.), *Encyclopedia of higher education* (pp. 1981–1989). New York: Pergamon Press.

Stage, F. K., & Williams, P. D. (1990). Students' motivations and changes in motivation during the first year of college. *Journal of College Student Development, 31*, 516–522.

Sternberg, R.J., & Horvath, J. (1995). A prototype view of expert teaching. *Educational Researcher, 24*(6), 9–17.

Sternberg, R. J. (1981). Intelligence and nonentrenchment. *Journal of Educational Psychology, 73*, 1–16.

Sternberg, R. J. (1985a). *Beyond IQ: A triarchic theory of human intelligence.* New York: Cambridge University Press.

Sternberg, R. J. (1985b, November). Teaching critical thinking. Part 1: Are we making critical mistakes? *Phi Delta Kappan*, pp. 194–198.

Sternberg, R. J. (1987). The triarchic theory of human intelligence. In J.T.E. Richardson (Ed.), *Student learning: Research in education and cognitive psychology* (pp. 66–72). Bristol, PA: Open University Press, Society for Research into Higher Education.

Sternberg, R. J. (1998). Abilities are forms of developing expertise. *Educational Researcher, 27*(3), 11–20.

Sutton, F. X. (1994). The distinction and durability of American research universities. In J. R. Cole, E. G. Barber, & S. R. Graubard (Eds.), *The research university in a time of discontent* (pp. 309–332). Baltimore: Johns Hopkins University Press.

Thompson, J. D., Hawkes, R. W., & Avery, R. W. (1969). Truth strategies and university organization. *Educational Administration Quarterly, 5,* 4–25.

Thorndike, E. L. (1914). *Educational psychology* (Vol. 3). New York: Columbia University, Teacher's College.

Tinto, V. (1998). Colleges as communities: Taking research on student persistence seriously. *Review of Higher Education, 21*(2), 151–165.

Tobias, S. (1988, February). Peer perspectives on physics. *Physics Teacher,* 77–80.

Tolman, E. C. (1949). *Purposive behavior in animals and men.* Englewood Cliffs, NJ: Appleton-Century-Crofts. (Original work published 1932)

Toma, J. D. (1997). Alternative inquiry paradigms, faculty cultures, and the definition of academic lives. *Journal of Higher Education, 68*(6), 679–705.

Tompkins, J. (1996). *A life in school: What the teacher learned.* Reading, MA: Addison-Wesley.

Toulmin, S. (1972). *Human understanding* (Vol. 1). Oxford: Clarendon Press.

Trigwell, K., Prosser, M., Ramsden, P., & Martin, E. (1998). Improving student learning through a focus on the teaching context. In G. Gibbs (Ed.), *Improving student learning.* Oxford: Oxford Centre for Staff Development.

Van Driel, J. H., Verloop, N., Van Werven, H. I., & Dekkers, H. (1997). Teachers' craft knowledge and curriculum innovation in higher engineering education. *Higher Education, 34,* 105–122.

Van Patten, J. V., Chao, C-I, & Reigeluth, C. M. (1986). A review of strategies for sequencing and synthesizing instruction. *Review of Educational Research, 56*(4), 437–471.

Van Peer, W. (1989). How to do things with texts: Towards a pragmatic foundation for the teaching of texts. In M. Short (Ed.), *Reading, analyzing, and teaching literature* (pp. 1267–1297). White Plains, NY: Longman.

van Weeren, J.H.P., de Mul, F.F.M., Peters, M. J., Kramers-Pals, H., & Roosink, H. J. (1982). Teaching problem-solving in physics: A course in electromagnetism. *American Journal of Physics, 50*(8), 725–732.

Varnhagen, C. K., Drake, S. M., & Finley, G. (1997). Teaching statistics with the Internet. *Teaching of Psychology, 24,* 275–278.

Vaughan, E. D. (1977). Misconceptions about psychology among introductory psychology students. *Teaching of Psychology, 4,* 138–141.

Vendler, H. (1988). What we have loved. In J. Engell & D. Perkins (Eds.), *Teaching literature: What is needed now* (pp. 13–25). Cambridge, MA: Harvard University Press.

Verdaasdonk, H. (1992). Literature and literary criticism. In B. R. Clark & G. R. Neave (Eds.), *Encyclopedia of higher education* (pp. 2031–2039). New York: Pergamon Press.

Vermetten, V. J., Lodewijks, H. G., & Vermunt, J. D. (1999). Consistency and variability of learning strategies in different university courses. *Higher Education, 37,* 1–21.

Vosniadou, S., & Brewer, W. F. (1987). Theories of knowledge restructuring in development. *Review of Educational Research, 57*(1), 51–67.

Vygotsky, L. S. (1962). *Thought and language.* New York: Wiley.

Waern, Y. (1972). Structure in similarity matrices. *Scandinavian Journal of Psychology, 13,* 5–16.

Watson, A. (1996). Introduction to law for second-year law students? *Journal of Legal Education, 46*(3), 430–444.

Weidner, D. J. (1997). The crises of legal education: A wake-up call for faculty. *Journal of Legal Education, 47*(1), 92–103.

Wesp, R. (1992). Conducting introductory psychology activity modules as a requirement in advanced undergraduate courses. *Teaching of Psychology, 19,* 219–220.

White, K. M., & Ferstenberg, A. (1978). Professional specialization and formal operations: The balance task. *Journal of Genetic Psychology, 133,* 97–104.

White, R., Gunstone, R., Elterman, E., Macdonald, I., McKittrick, B., Mills, D., & Mulhal, P. (1995). Students' perceptions of teaching and learning in first year university physics. *Research in Science Education, 25*(4), 465–478.

Wigfield, A., Eccles, J. S., & Rodriguez, D. (1998). The development of children's motivation in school contexts. *Review of Research in Education, 23,* 73–118.

Willingham, W. W. (1985). *Success in college: The role of personal qualities and academic ability.* New York: College Entrance Examination Board.

Wilson, E. O. (1998). *Consilience: The unity of knowledge.* New York: Knopf.

Wilson, T. L., & Hershey, D. A. (1996). The research methods script. *Teaching of Psychology, 23,* 97–99.

Winograd, T. (1975). Frame representations and the declarative procedural controversy. In D. G. Bobrow & A. Collins (Eds.), *Representation and understanding: Studies in cognitive science* (pp. 35–82). Orlando: Academic Press.

Woods, D. R., Hrymak, A. N., Marshall, R. R., Wood, P. E., Crowe, C. C., Hoffman, T. W., Wright, J. D., Taylor, P. A., Woodhouse, K. A., & Bouchard, C.G.K. (1997). Developing problem solving skills: The McMaster problem solving program. *Journal of Engineering Education, 86*(2), 75–91.

Woodworth, R. S., & Schlosberg, H. (1954). *Experimental psychology.* Austin, TX: Holt, Rinehart and Winston.

Woolnough, B. E., with Yuying Guo, Leite, M. S., deAlmeida, M. J., Tae Ryu, Zhen Wang, & Young, D. (1997). Factors affecting student choice of career in science and engineering: Parallel studies in Australia, Canada, China, England, Japan and Portugal. *Research in Science and Technological Education, 15*(1) 105–121.

Yokomoto, C. F., & Ware, R. (1997). Coaching students toward better learning: A workshop approach. In *Proceedings of ASEE Annual Conference* (Session 3230). Washington, DC: American Society for Engineering Education.

Young, B. (1994). Moral and philosophical criticism. In D. Cowles (Ed.), *The critical experience* (2nd ed., pp. 22–47). Dubuque, IA: Kendall/Hunt.

Zajchowski, R. (1991). *Differences in the problem solving of stronger and weaker novices in physics: Knowledge, strategies, or knowledge structure?* Unpublished master's thesis, University of Western Ontario, London, Canada.

Zhang, Z., & Richarde, R. S. (1999, March). *Learning-thinking Style Inventory: LISREL and multivariate analyses.* Paper presented at the annual meeting of the American Educational Research Association, Chicago.

Zuckerman, H. (1988). The sociology of science. In N. Smelser (Ed.), *Handbook of sociology* (pp. 511–574). Thousand Oaks, CA: Sage.

Zukav, G. (1979). *The dancing Wu Li masters: An overview of the new physics.* New York: Bantam Books.

NAME INDEX

A

Acton, W. H., 142
Adams, J. L., 73
Adler, M., 7, 52
Albertazzi, P. G., 99, 104
Alexander, P. A., 165, 208, 217
Allen, D. E., 57, 124
American Psychological Association, 134, 165, 294
Anderson, J. R., 71
Anderson, R. C., 15
Angelo, T. A., 295
Arnold, M., 235, 248, 251
Arthurs, H., 176
Astin, A. W., 6, 38
Astin, H. S., 58, 64, 85, 86, 114, 229, 264, 295, 296, 297
Atwood, M., 239
Austin, G. A., 154
Ausubel, D. P., 17, 103
Avery, R. W., 18, 19, 51

B

Baker, D., 48
Barden, L. M., 60

Barker, D., 69
Barouch, D. H., 107
Barrett, G. C., 97
Bartlett, F. C., 15, 137
Bassok, M., 55
Bateman, D., 4
Baxter Magolda, M., 2, 3, 37, 294
Bazerman, C., 235
Beasley, D. E., 87
Becher, R. A., 7, 10, 33, 63, 64, 97, 98, 111, 112, 113, 114, 134, 169, 171, 172, 173, 199, 237, 276–277
Berliner, D. C., 214, 215, 227, 229
Berlyne, D. E., 136
Bess, J., 293
Biggs, J. B., 5
Biglan, A., 7, 10, 19, 29, 97, 111, 198
Bloom, B. S., 7, 8, 10, 46, 50, 151, 206
Bloom, J. W., 112, 113, 114
Bogdan, C. A., 16
Bonwell, C. C., 294
Boud, D., 93
Bourdieu, P., 235–236, 275–276
Boyle, R. A., 3, 5

Brackett, G. C., 24, 44, 45, 46, 47, 51, 54, 57
Brandwein, P. F., 33
Braxton, J. M., 114, 279
Brems, C., 163
Bretz, R. L., 104, 108
Brewer, W. F., 39
Broudy, H. S., 19, 23
Brown, D., 5
Brown, D. E., 54
Brown, J. S., 295
Brown, L. T., 141
Bruner, J., 13, 197, 200, 201, 213, 218, 228
Bruner, J. S., 154
Bryden, D. P., 187
Buskist, W., 160

C

Calhoun, E., 174, 185
Callaghan, M., 238
Candlin, C., 243, 267
Cardemone, P. F., 16
Carter, R., 267
Cashin, W. E., 3, 6, 113, 137, 141, 205, 233

INDEX